Between Popes, Inquisitors and Princes

St Andrews Studies
in Reformation History

Lead Editor

Bridget Heal (*University of St Andrews*)

Editorial Board

Amy Burnett (*University of Nebraska – Lincoln*)
Euan Cameron (*Columbia University*)
Bruce Gordon (*Yale University*)
Kaspar von Greyerz (*Universität Basel*)
Felicity Heal (*Jesus College, Oxford*)
Karin Maag (*Calvin College, Grand Rapids*)
Roger Mason (*University of St Andrews*)
Andrew Pettegree (*University of St Andrews*)
Alec Ryrie (*Durham University*)
Jonathan Willis (*University* of Birmingham)

The titles published in this series are listed at *brill.com/sasrh*

Between Popes, Inquisitors and Princes

How the First Jesuits Negotiated Religious Crisis in Early Modern Italy

By

Jessica M. Dalton

BRILL

LEIDEN | BOSTON

Cover illustration: Karel van Mallery after Juan de Mesa, Plate 11 of Vita beati patris Ignatii Loyolae (Antwerp, 1610). ©The Trustees of the British Museum.

Library of Congress Cataloging-in-Publication Data

Names: Dalton, Jessica M., author.
Title: Between popes, inquisitors and princes : how the first Jesuits negotiated religious crisis in early modern italy / by Jessica M. Dalton.
Description: Leiden ; Boston : Brill, 2020. | Series: St Andrews studies in Reformation history, 2468-4317 | Includes bibliographical references and index. | Summary: "In Venice in the last months of 1556, Jesuit priest Cesare Helmi faced a quandary about a grave matter: should he absolve a potentially dangerous heretic in the secret sacrament of confession? That week, a man had confessed to Helmi that he had 'erred in many matters' fundamental to the Catholic faith.1 He had been part of a sect of 'Anabaptists' and people who espoused 'other various heresies'. He had believed serious errors about 'sacramental matters', 'indulgences' and 'the authority of the pope'. He had even recruited others to join him in the sect. These were serious sins. This man was a heretic"– Provided by publisher.
Identifiers: LCCN 2020011425 | ISBN 9789004413825 (hardback) | ISBN 9789004413832 (ebook)
Subjects: LCSH: Jesuits–Italy–History.
Classification: LCC BX3737 .D35 2020 | DDC 271/.53045–dc23
LC record available at https://lccn.loc.gov/2020011425

Typeface for the Latin, Greek, and Cyrillic scripts: "Brill". See and download: brill.com/brill-typeface.

ISSN 2468-4317
ISBN 978-90-04-41382-5 (hardback)
ISBN 978-90-04-41383-2 (e-book)

Copyright 2020 by Koninklijke Brill NV, Leiden, The Netherlands.
Koninklijke Brill NV incorporates the imprints Brill, Brill Hes & De Graaf, Brill Nijhoff, Brill Rodopi, Brill Sense, Hotei Publishing, mentis Verlag, Verlag Ferdinand Schöningh and Wilhelm Fink Verlag.
All rights reserved. No part of this publication may be reproduced, translated, stored in a retrieval system, or transmitted in any form or by any means, electronic, mechanical, photocopying, recording or otherwise, without prior written permission from the publisher.
Authorization to photocopy items for internal or personal use is granted by Koninklijke Brill NV provided that the appropriate fees are paid directly to The Copyright Clearance Center, 222 Rosewood Drive, Suite 910, Danvers, MA 01923, USA. Fees are subject to change.

This book is printed on acid-free paper and produced in a sustainable manner.

For Holly

Contents

Acknowledgements   IX
Conventions   XI

Introduction   1
 1   Historiography: the Story So Far   11
 2   Sources   24
 3   Overview   30

1   **The Confident Society: Mission Building 1540–1555**   35
 1   Finding Supporters in Tridentine Italy   37
 2   The Council of Bologna, 1547   41
 3   Beyond Papal Obedience   47
 4   Privileges and Pragmatism in the Mission Field   51
 5   Conclusion   58

2   **Collaboration, Competition and Conflict: the Jesuits and the Roman Inquisition**   62
 1   Competitors and Collaborators with the Holy Office   66
 2   Popes, Empires and the Politics of Conversion   72
 3   Good Cop/Bad Cop: Conversion Strategies in the 1560s   80
 4   Conclusion   88

3   **Between the Prince and the Pope: Pius V and the Rise of the Roman Inquisition**   93
 1   Pius V and the Rise of the Roman Inquisition   97
 2   A Jesuit Spy in the Papal States   103
 3   'A Firm Garrison to Resist Heresy' in Savoy-Piedmont   108
 4   Conclusion   122

4   **Bargaining for Autonomy: Challenges and Change at the Close of the Sixteenth Century**   124
 1   Internal Conflicts and External Controversies   127
 2   Troubles Abroad: Controversies in France and Spain   137
 3   Defending the Privilege in the Late 1580s   145
 4   Conclusion   151

VIII

5 **All Roads Lead to Rome: Jesuit Agents and Rebels at the Close of the Sixteenth Century (1587–1605)**   155
   1   The Politics of Conversion at the Turn of the Seventeenth Century   160
   2   Jesuit Disobedience   170
   3   Conclusion   174

Conclusion   178

Bibliography   187
Index   215

Acknowledgements

I could not have produced this book without the help of numerous institutions and individuals, only some of whom I shall name here.

First and foremost, I acknowledge the scrupulous guidance and unstinting support of Dr Emily Michelson and Professor Andrew Pettegree, who supervised the doctoral research that is presented in this book. I also owe heartfelt gratitude to Professor Simon Ditchfield, who has offered me counsel and encouragement with uncommon generosity.

I am grateful to the many eminent scholars who have welcomed me into an international academic community of which I had assumed I would always remain an admiring bystander, particularly, Professor Christopher F. Black, Professor Irene Fosi, Professor Vincenzo Lavenia, Professor Adriano Prosperi and Dr Camilla Russell, who have taken the time to listen to, test and refine my ideas with intellectual generosity and unfailing patience. I also thank them and Dr Matteo Al Kalak, Father Paolo Fontana, Dr Philippa Jackson, Dr Dennj Solera and Dr Carlo Taviani for their invaluable advice on the use, contents, and sometimes even existence of archives for my research. My work has also benefitted from numerous counsels from the talented scholars at the Reformation Studies Institute at the University of St Andrews, particularly Dr John Condren, Dr Nina Lamal and Dr Drew Thomas who have provided both stimulating conversation and sage advice, and Dr Jan Hillgaertner who has helped me to tackle German texts with great patience.

For generously funding my research, in the UK and across Italy, I thank the Alfred Dunhill Links Foundation, the University of St Andrews, the Russell Trust and the Society for Renaissance Studies. I am particularly grateful for the year-long residential scholarship that I received from the British School at Rome, which provided me with both material support and a transformative intellectual environment in which to work.

The success of my research trips has relied upon the advice and courtesy of the staff of many institutions. At the Archivum Romanum Societatis Iesu I thank all of the staff, particularly Father Brian MacCuarta, Dr Carlo Luongo and Hélène Reychler, who first welcomed me to the archive when I was a nervous master's student. I also thank the staff of the Archivio della Congregazione per la Dottrina della Fede, especially Dr Daniel Ponziani, and all those who have helped me at the Archiginnasio, Archivio Segreto Vaticano, Biblioteca Apostolica Vaticana, Archivio della Penitenzieria Apostolica and the state archives of Bologna, Genoa, Modena, Rome and Turin.

ACKNOWLEDGEMENTS

Many personal friends have encouraged and supported my work and intellectual development, directly and indirectly, over decades. I owe particular thanks to Edward Collet, for his patient and thoughtful proof-reading of the final draft of this book, as well as to James Cossey, Dr Teresa Kittler, Christopher Mason, Father Rupert McHardy, Rev. Dr Athanasius McVay and Yvonne Richmond.

My husband, Patrick, has supported this research project with unquestioning patience, despite it putting hundreds of miles between us; I am eternally indebted to him. I am thankful to my father for his help throughout my studies. Finally, I express my heartfelt gratitude for my sister, Holly, who summoned enthusiasm for my work even as she fought for her life. This book is dedicated to her memory and to the friendship that we shared with our brother, Tony, which has sustained me through the final stages of this project.

Conventions

1. Italian place names are anglicised (e.g. Genoa not Genova).
2. Names of people are written in their own original language, rather than italicised as they often are in original sources (e.g. Cristóbal Rodriguez not Cristoforo Rodriguez), except those that are well-known in their anglicised form (e.g. Ignatius Loyola).
3. All original sources are translated or paraphrased in the body text. All translations are the author's unless otherwise indicated.

Introduction

In Venice in the last months of 1556, Jesuit priest Cesare Helmi faced a quandary about a grave matter: should he absolve a potentially dangerous heretic in the secret sacrament of confession?

That week, a man had confessed to Helmi that he had 'erred in many matters' fundamental to the Catholic faith.[1] He had been part of a sect of 'Anabaptists' and people who espoused 'other various heresies'. He had believed serious errors about 'sacramental matters', 'indulgences' and 'the authority of the pope'. He had even recruited others to join him in the sect. These were serious sins. This man was a heretic.

In the mid-sixteenth century, the Catholic Church hierarchy was on high alert for heresy on the Italian peninsula. In the German lands, Martin Luther had boldly challenged the doctrines and authority of the Church; Luther's criticisms had sparked a fierce debate and religious revolutions across northern Europe. Individuals and entire states threw off papal authority, adopting new Protestant confessions as their official religion. And it was not long before Protestant ideas arrived on the Italian peninsula.[2] Whether they came on the pages of books or the tongues of merchants, sailors and scholars, Protestant beliefs found sympathy amongst curious and dissatisfied Catholics as well as non-Catholic Christians like the Waldensians, a group that originated in twelfth-century France.[3] By the mid-sixteenth century, suspicions and accusations of heresy were raised against those at the height of Italy's ecclesiastical and social

---

1   Helmi's letter explaining the dilemma is held in Archivum Romanum Societatis Iesu (hereafter, ARSI), *Epistolae Italiae 107*, f.3r.

2   On heresy in sixteenth-century Italy see Delio Cantimori and Adriano Prosperi (ed.), *Eretici italiani del Cinquecento e altre scritti* (Turin: Einaudi, 1992); Frederic Church, *The Italian reformers, 1534–1564* (New York: Columbia University Press, 1932); Ronald K. Delph, Michelle Fontaine and John Jeffries Martin, *Heresy, Culture, and Religion in Early Modern Italy. Contexts and Contestations* (Kirksville: Truman State University Press, 2006); Adriano Prosperi, *Eresie e devozioni. La religione italiana in età moderna. I. Eresie* (Rome: Edizioni di Storia e Letteratura, 2010) and Antonio Rotondò, *Studi e ricerche di storia ereticale italiana del Cinquecento* (Turin: Giappichelli, 1974).

3   On the Waldensians see Euan Cameron, *The Reformation of the heretics: the Waldenses of the Alps* (Oxford: Oxford University Press, 1984); Vincenzo Tedesco, *Storia dei Valdesi in Calabria. Tra basso medioevo e prima età moderna* (Soveria Mannelli: Rubbettino, 2015) and Pierroberto Scaramella, *L'Inquisizione romana e i Valdesi di Calabria* (Naples: Editoriale Scientifica, 1999).

© KONINKLIJKE BRILL NV, LEIDEN, 2020 | DOI:10.1163/9789004413832_002

2   INTRODUCTION

hierarchies.[4] For successive popes, the vast majority of the curia and clergy and many Italian princes Protestant sympathisers were dangerous heretics. If heresy spread in Italy, it could destroy the Catholic Church, undermine the authority of Catholic princes and consign the souls of the peninsula to an eternity in hell.

Perceiving a grave threat, Rome closed ranks. In 1545 Pope Paul III (pope 1534–49) convoked the Council of Trent to address the claims of the reformers. In 1542 he had begun to address their successes by founding the Holy Office of the Roman Inquisition to find and, if necessary, punish heretics. A congregation of cardinals in Rome ran the inquisition, supervising tribunals, old and new, all over the peninsula. The inquisitors tried thousands of cases during the sixteenth century, investigating, converting and sometimes even executing heretics.[5] Their targets were diverse, from young scholars such as Pomponio Algieri to high-ranking noblemen like Pietro Carnesecchi.[6] As the sixteenth century wore on, the threat of heresy would wane and the inquisition would target a broader range of moral misdemeanours such as sodomy and superstition.[7] At that time, the Church adapted her approach to heretics in Italy, focusing on converting foreigners using softer, more conciliatory methods.[8] But when Helmi heard the confession of the penitent-heretic in 1556, ecclesiastical and temporal authorities were anxious to do whatever it took to eradicate heresy from the Italian peninsula.[9]

---

4   See, for example, the cases of Pietro Carnesecchi and Cardinal Giovanni Morone. Massimo Firpo and Dario Marcatto (eds), *I processi inquisitoriali di Pietro Carnesecchi (1557–1567)* (Vatican City: Archivio Segreto Vaticano, 1998–2000), 2 vols in 4 and *Il processo inquisitoriale del cardinal Giovanni Morone. Edizione critica* (Rome: Istituto storico italiano per l'età moderna e contemporanea, 1981–95), 6 vols in 7.

5   For statistics on trials and executions see Del Col, *L'inquisizione in Italia*, pp.772–82 and John Tedeschi and William Monter, 'Toward a Statistical Profile of the Italian Inquisitions, Sixteenth to Eighteenth Centuries' in Tedeschi (ed.), *The Prosecution of Heresy, Collected Studies on the Inquisition in Early Modern Italy* (Binghampton: Medieval and Renaissance Texts and Studies, 1991), pp.90–102.

6   On Pomponio Algeri, see Daniele Santarelli, 'Morte di un eretico impenitente. Alcune note e documenti su Pomponio Algeri di Nola', *Medioevo Adriatico*, 1 (2007), pp.117–134.

7   Black, *The Italian Inquisition*, pp.131–57.

8   Irene Fosi, *Convertire lo straniero. Forestieri e Inquisizione e Roma in età moderna* (Rome: Viella, 2011) and Peter Mazur, *Conversion to Catholicism in early modern Italy* (New York: Routledge, Taylor and Francis Group, 2016).

9   Venice was seen as particularly vulnerable to the spread of heresy. See Paul Grendler, *The Roman Inquisition and the Venetian Press, 1540–1605* (Princeton: Princeton University Press, 1977); John Martin, *Venice's Hidden Enemies. Italian Heretics in a Renaissance City* (London: University of California Press, 1993); Santarelli, 'Eresia, Riforma e Inquisizione nella Repubblica di Venezia del Cinquecento', *Studi Storici Luigi Simeoni*, LVII (2007), pp.73–105; Anne Jacobson Schutte, *Aspiring saints: pretense of Holiness, Inquisition, and*

INTRODUCTION

The circumstances and admission of the penitent were serious. Nonetheless, Helmi thought that he could help. He could make use of the sacrament of confession. Even before the official foundation of Helmi's order, the Society of Jesus, in 1540, its founder, Ignatius Loyola, had used confession to elicit profound spiritual conversions, both within himself and amongst wayward Catholics.[10] When the Jesuits began their official ministry to believers, infidels and heretics, confession would be central to their work.[11]

More than this, Helmi knew that the Society's confessors had an extraordinary advantage in cases of heresy that distinguished them from other priests. For, in 1551, Pope Julius III (pope 1550–5) had given the Jesuits an unprecedented papal privilege, allowing them to absolve the sin of heresy in *foro conscientiae* and to lift the automatic excommunication that heresy incurred.[12] This meant that Jesuits could reconcile heretics to the Church entirely independently of ecclesiastical superiors such as bishops and inquisitors. And the Jesuits could do all of this in the absolute secrecy of sacramental confession.[13]

In Italy, the use of the Jesuit privilege had a substantial impact on the Catholic Church and wider society. For this reason, Helmi expressed serious concerns about whether he should use the mechanism in this case. Helmi's penitent had made his heresies a 'public matter', imperilling the souls of others as well as his own.[14] His heresy was also a political threat. Venice was exceptionally

---

      Gender in the Republic of Venice, 1618–1750 (London: Johns Hopkins University Press, 2001) and Aldo Stella, *Dall'anabattismo al socinianesimo nel Cinquecento veneto: Richerche storiche* (Padua: Liviana, 1967).

10   O'Malley, *The First Jesuits* (London: Harvard University Press, 1993), pp.32–6.

11   On the Jesuits, confession and conversion see ibid., pp. 136–151; Sabina Pavone, *I gesuiti dalle origini alla soppressione, 1540–1773* (Rome: Laterza, 2004), pp.27–32 and Prosperi, *Tribunali della coscienza*, pp. 485–507. The significance and effects of confession in the Jesuits' public ministry are emphasised in their first official history, Juan Alfonso Polanco's *Chronicon*. See, for example, Juan de Polanco, *Vita Ignatii Loiolae et rerum Societatis Jesu Historia* (Madrid: Typographorum Societas, 1894; Augustinus Avrial, 1894–8), vol. 3, p.149. On the Jesuits' approach to confession see Chapter 2 of Robert Maryks, *Saint Cicero and the Jesuits. The Influence of the Liberal Arts on the Adoption of Moral Probabilism* (Aldershot: Ashgate, 2008).

12   For the bull see A. Tomassetti (ed.), *Bullarum diplomatum et privilegiorum sanctorum romanorum pontificum taurinensis editio* (Turin: Seb. Franco, H. Fory et Henrico Dalmazzo editoribus, 1857–67), 25 vols, vol.6, p.464.

13   On the differences between the different *fora* in which various individuals could absolve heresy and lift the excommunication that it incurred see Juan Valero, *Differentiae inter vtrumque forum, iudiciale videlicet et conscientiae: nondum hac noua luce donatae et magna cum cura studioque iucubratae et concinnatae* (Valldemossa: Emmanuelis Rodriguez, 1616).

14   ARSI, *Epistolae Italiae 107*, f.3r.

4 INTRODUCTION

independent from Rome but, like other Italian states, it was governed by temporal authorities that were inextricably entwined with ecclesiastical powers.[15] Public religious rebellion was an affront to these temporal leaders and, therefore, a danger to social stability.[16] What is more, Helmi's penitent had also confessed that he had incurred 'many debts' and been 'outlawed'.[17] Both ecclesiastical and temporal authorities would be eager to know of these crimes and if Helmi exonerated his penitent in confession they may never find out. Whilst some canon lawyers argued that the secrecy of confession could be broken to reveal dangerous heretics, the Jesuits disagreed.[18] If Helmi absolved this heretic, he might be the only man to ever hear of these grave offences against God, Church and state.

Helmi had a further concern. There was one type of heretic whom the Jesuits could not absolve: heretics already known to inquisitors. These heretics could be relapsed, that is recidivist heretics. As Helmi's penitent had made his heresy a 'public matter' he might have fallen into this category. According to Canon Law, somebody commits the sin of heresy when they obstinately err from Catholic teaching.[19] This sin incurs excommunication from the Church automatically, or *latae sententiae*.[20] If discovered by inquisitors, a heretic could also be excommunicated judicially, or *de iure*. To reconcile a known heretic, therefore, one needed the jurisdiction to absolve the sin of heresy and to lift judicial excommunication. The Jesuits did not have this. There were three types

---

15   The *Tre savi all'eresia*, for example, comprised Venetian noblemen, the patriarch, an inquisitor and the papal legate. Martin, *Venice's Hidden Enemies*, p.51.

16   On heretics as traitors in Venice see Martin, *Venice's Hidden Enemies*, p.51. On the links between Church, society and heresy more broadly see Harro Höpfl, *Jesuit Political Thought. The Society of Jesus and the State, c.1540–1630* (Cambridge: Cambridge University Press, 2004), pp.66–72.

17   ARSI, *Epistolae Italiae 107*, f.3r.

18   On heresy and the seal of confession see Vincenzo Lavenia, *L'infamia e il perdono. Tributi, pene e confessione nella teologia morale della prima età moderna* (Bologna: Il Mulino, 2004), pp.101–30. On private 'fraternal correction' before denunciation to the inquisition see Stefania Pastore, 'A proposito di Matteo 18.15. *Correctio fraterna* e Inquisitione nella Spagna del Cinquecento', *Rivista Storica Italiana*, 113 (2001), pp.352–63 and Stefania Tutino, *Shadows of Doubt: Language and Truth in Post-Reformation Catholic Culture* (New York: Oxford University Press, 2014), pp.13–5.

19   Ambrosium De Vignate, *Elegans ac utilis tractatus de haeresi editus per praeclarum et famosissimum iur. utr.* (Rome: Ex typographia Georgii Ferrarii, 1581), p.11.

20   John P. Beal, James A. Coriden and Thomas J. Green (eds), *New Commentary on the Code of Canon Law* (New York: Paulis Press: 2000), p.1575 (canon 1364); R.H. Helmolz, *The Spirit of Classical Canon Law* (London: University of Georgia Press, 2010), p.384; Lavenia, *L'infamia e il perdono*, p.105.

INTRODUCTION

of jurisdiction over heresy known as *fora*: the *foro externo, foro conscientiae* and *foro interno*. Only jurisdiction in the *foro externo* lifted judicial excommunication.[21] And only inquisitors had this authority.

Still, the Jesuits' jurisdiction over heresy was far greater than that of ordinary priests. For normal clergy had jurisdiction over heresy in the *foro interno*, which pertained only to the sacrament of confession. During this sacrament penitents confess their sins to a priest and ask for God's forgiveness. If the penitent demonstrates contrition, the priest absolves him, assigning small penances such as prayers. If a heretic went to a priest with jurisdiction in the *foro interno* the priest could absolve the heretic of the sin of heresy, repairing his relationship with God.[22] Nonetheless, the priest could not lift the automatic excommunication *latae sententiae* incurred by the sin of heresy.[23] So, the priest would have to send the penitent-heretic to somebody else (usually an inquisitor) with jurisdiction to lift this excommunication – jurisdiction in *foro conscientiae*. Before Pius V (pope 1566–72) revoked it, bishops enjoyed jurisdiction in *foro conscientiae* over heresy within their own dioceses.[24] Through their papal privilege, the Jesuits had an even greater authority – jurisdiction over heresy in *foro conscientiae* anywhere in the world. With this, Jesuits in Italy could absolve unknown heretics and lift their *latae sententiae* excommunication without ever notifying an inquisitor or bishop.[25] For penitent-heretics unknown to the inquisitors, the Jesuits offered a one-stop shop where they could be both absolved and reconciled to the Church. And all of this could be done in the absolute secrecy of confession.

---

21 Polanco, *Breve directorium ad confessarii ac confitentis munus recte obeundum* (Antwerp: Joannes Bellerum, 1575), p.21r. On the jurisdiction of bishops and ordinaries over heresy see Del Col, 'Strutture e attività dell'Inquisizione Romana, pp.361–3 and Fosi, *Papal Justice: Subjects and Courts in the Papal State, 1500–1750* (Washington D.C.: Catholic University of America Press, 2011), pp.105–125. On the changing role of episcopal tribunals in Italy see Thomas Brian Deutscher, *Punishment and Penance: Two Phases in the Hisory of the Bishop's Tribunal of Novara* (Toronto: University of Toronto Press, 2013).

22 Francesco Suarez, *Opera Omnia editio nova, a Carolo Berton, Cathedralis Ecclesiae Ambianensis vicario, iuxta editionem ventiam XXIII tomos in-f[oli]o continentem, accurate recognita, reverendissimo ill[ustrissimo] Domino Sergent, Episcopo Corsopitensi, ab editore dicata* (Paris: Ludovicum Vives, 1861), p.996.

23 Thomas Delbene, *Clerici Regularis Theologiae Professoris, Examinatoris, S. Rom. Universalis Inquisitionis Qualificatoris, aliarumque S.S. Congreg. in Urbe Consultoris. De officio S. Inquisitionis circa haresim* (Lyon: Joannes-Anthony Huguetan, 1666), p.215.

24 Brambilla, *Alle origini del Sant'Uffizio*, p.487.

25 Valero, *Differentiae inter vtrumque forum*, pp.1–2. On the *foro conscientiae*, see Elena Brambilla, 'Il <<foro della coscienza>>. La confessione come strumento di delazione', *Società e Storia*, 81 (1998), pp.591–608.

Helmi's wrote to his superiors in Rome asking 'how much he could do for that heretical person'.[26] Evidently, he was nervous about how his jurisdiction over heresy might clash with the authority and aims of other institutions. Still, Helmi thought that, in the end, a private absolution might achieve the greater good. Helmi claimed that his penitent had promised to 'make every satisfaction' that it 'would be judged he ought to make' for his errors.[27] Moreover, Helmi believed that a private absolution might have benefits beyond just one soul as the penitent had promised that he would 'bring his wife' who was 'in the same error' to be reconciled too.[28] Helmi's doubts about what to do stemmed from a conflict between his desire to save souls and his jurisdictional concerns. Helmi faced a clash between his institutional and pastoral priorities.

Helmi's inner conflict was a microcosm of a broader problem faced by the Catholic Church in sixteenth-century Italy. To fulfil their pastoral mission, popes wanted to convert and save the souls of all those who had rejected Catholic teaching. Nonetheless, successive pontiffs sought to fulfil this mission principally through judicial institutions that allowed them to control jurisdiction over heresy. This approach was often counter-productive. The judicial systems instituted by popes, such as the processes of the Roman Inquisition, often repelled penitents who feared that they would be exposed and punished if they admitted their heresy.[29] Moreover, inquisitors faced political resistance from the many independent and foreign authorities who ruled the patchwork states of the Italian peninsula. Rulers often wanted to control matters of religion and social discipline themselves. Whilst some temporal leaders compromised with Rome others blocked the papal tribunal until the end of the century.[30] At the

---

26 ARSI, *Epistolae Italiae 107*, f.3r.

27 Ibid.

28 Ibid.

29 On hostility towards the Roman Inquisition see Del Col, *L'Inquisizione in Italia*, p.819; Lavenia, 'Il tribunale innominato. Appunti sull'immaginario dell'Inquisizione romana' in Giuliana Ancona and Dario Visintin (eds), *Religione, scritture e storiografia: omaggio ad Andrea Del Col* (Montereale Valcellina: Circolo Culturale Menocchio, 2013), pp.295–6 and Silvana Seidel Menchi, 'The Inquisitor as Mediator' in Delph, Fontaine and Martin, *Heresy, Culture, and Religion in Early Modern Italy*, pp.173–4.

30 For examples see Simonetta Adorni-Bracessi, 'La Repubblica di Lucca e l'<<aborrita>> Inquisizione: istituzione e società' in Andrea del Col and Giovanna Paolin (eds), *L'Inquisizione Romana in Italia nell'età moderna. Archivi, problemi di metodo e nuove ricerche. Atti del seminario internazionale Trieste, 18–20 maggio 1988* (Rome: Ministero per i beni culturali e ambientali ufficio centrale per i beni archivistici, 1991), pp.333–62; Charmarie Jenkins Blaisdell, 'Politics and Heresy in Ferrara, 1534–1559', *The Sixteenth Century Journal*, 6 no.1 (April, 1975), pp.67–93 and Lavenia, 'L'Inquisizione del duca. I domenicani e il Sant'Uffizio in Piemonte nella prima età moderna' in Carlo Longo

INTRODUCTION

height of the post-Reformation crisis, the Catholic Church's central pastoral mission to convert errant souls was often undermined by the very institutions with which she sought to fulfil it.

The Jesuits' privilege to absolve heresy is proof that Jesuits and successive popes were willing to compromise institutional priorities to fulfil pastoral goals in the aftermath of the Reformation. By soliciting the privilege to absolve heretics in confession, the Jesuits prioritised their mission to save the souls of heretics over the maintenance of the usual judicial processes for reconciling religious dissenters. By conceding the privilege, successive popes took the same position, demonstrating their readiness and need to prioritise conversions over their desire to do so through a centrally-controlled judicial system. This decision was particularly remarkable on the Italian peninsula. In areas of northern Europe, the successes of the Protestant Reformation had demolished Catholic ecclesiastical infrastructure. There, Jesuits empowered to reconcile heretics replaced absent episcopal and inquisitorial tribunals. But Italy had both old and new inquisitorial and episcopal systems to find and convert heretics. Despite this, popes still asked Jesuits on the Italian peninsula to reconcile heretics with a power that conflicted with, and sometimes even exceeded, existing jurisdictions.

So far, the Jesuits' privilege to absolve heresy has presented an awkward anomaly to scholars; it simply does not fit into established narratives of the Counter-Reformation. By giving the Jesuits the power to absolve heretics in the absolute secrecy of sacramental confession, successive popes from Julius III to Gregory XIII (pope 1572–85) allowed a new religious order to reconcile potentially dangerous religious rebels without involving the bishops and inquisitors whom they had personally charged to fight heresy. This significant clash between the Jesuits' power and inquisitorial jurisdiction could not be ignored by scholars of the Holy Office. Nonetheless, they have so far only offered partial explanations of the power that are shaped by their focus on inquisitorial matters. Some have suggested that the privilege transformed the Society into obedient agents of the cardinal-inquisitors or a subordinate supplement to the Roman Inquisition.[31] Others have implied that popes granted the privilege so that they might have Jesuit agents who would do their bidding far more loyally than

---

(ed.), *I Domenicani e l'Inquisizione romana* (Rome: Istituto Storico Domenicano, 2008), pp.415–476.

31 Stefania Pastore, *Il Vangelo e la Spada. l'Inquisizione di Castiglia e i suoi critici* (Rome: Edizioni di Storia e Letteratura, 2003), pp.338–40; Prosperi, *Tribunali della coscienza*, pp.236–7 and 492 and Giovanni Romeo, *Ricerche su confessione dei peccati e inquisizione nell'Italia del cinquecento* (Naples: Città del Sole, 1997), pp.63–75.

8   INTRODUCTION

their own Holy Office.[32] All of these explanations suggest that the Jesuits used the privilege as steadfast agents of Rome, chiming with traditional characterisations of the obedient early Society working within a centralised, controlling Tridentine Church. None of these explanations fully incorporate the motives and actions of the Jesuits who solicited and used the privilege, sometimes in the service of other authorities like secular princes and sometimes in complete defiance of papal and inquisitorial demands.

This book will provide the first history of this remarkable papal privilege, assessing its impact in Italy from the Society's first requests for the privilege in the 1540s to some Jesuits' continued use of the power in the seventeenth century – decades after Pope Sixtus v had revoked it. By telling this history, the book will revise our understanding of the Society's role in the fight against heresy, an aspect of Jesuit history that has defined the order since its first decades. The implications of this new narrative are broad. For it indicates that we should modify the established chronology of a period that was formative for the Society and transformative for the Catholic Church. Moreover, it forces us to reassess the relationship between the three most important protagonists in the history of early modern Italy: the Society of Jesus, the papacy and the Roman Inquisition.

Using letters, treatises and institutional documents held at the archives of the Society, Roman Inquisition, Vatican and numerous Italian states, this book will show that, in Italy, the Jesuits used the privilege to absolve heresy to work independently from Roman authorities, not in devoted obedience to them. This conclusion radically undermines traditional accounts of the early Society and the sixteenth-century Church, showing us that autonomy was central to the early Jesuits' contribution to the fight against heresy and that, in the midst of the sixteenth-century religious crisis, the Holy Office and the Holy See valued this Jesuit independence. This research also challenges existing interpretations of the privilege, which suggest that it was only ever a tool of the inquisitors or popes who subordinated the Society. In reality, the key characteristic of the privilege was that it freed the Jesuits from the usual ecclesiastical hierarchy, allowing them to convert heretics independently where papal forces were absent or faced hostility from local princes. Absolving heretics independently and extra-judicially, the Jesuits overcame pastoral and political obstacles that prevented inquisitors from securing converts in sixteenth-century Italy. By doing this, the Jesuits fulfilled their own mission to save souls and helped popes

---

32   Massimo Firpo, *La presa di potere dell'inquisizione Romana*, (Rome: Laterza, 2014), pp.65–6.

INTRODUCTION 9

and inquisitors to fulfil their aims in the post-Reformation crisis. Overall, the description of the anti-heretical role of the Jesuits presented in this book corroborates new histories of the early Society that emphasise its flexibility, diversity and ambivalence, rather than its obedience to Rome.

This book will also show that the Jesuits and successive popes disagreed about how heretics should be dealt with in the long term. By tracing the history of the privilege into the seventeenth century we shall see that, despite superficial agreement in the immediate aftermath of the Reformation, the Jesuits' position on extra-judicial reconciliations actually contrasted with that of successive popes and inquisitors, a conclusion that shatters the traditional image of Jesuits fighting heresy in lock-step with Rome. The Society prioritised pastoral aims over institutional ones as a matter of principle and so wanted to retain the privilege long after the sense of emergency had passed. By contrast, popes and inquisitors were only willing to compromise control over religious and social discipline during the period of emergency that followed the Reformation. When the threat of spreading heresy declined in Italy, so did Rome's willingness to grant the Jesuits a jurisdictional autonomy that undermined Roman power. This change in circumstance exposed a fundamental contrast between the conditional stance of successive popes and inquisitors and the principled position of the Jesuits. Indeed, even when the pope had revoked the privilege, Jesuits continued to use it, showing us that the reliationship between the Society and the papacy could be one contrast and defiance as well as loyalty and obedience.[33] Overall, the research in this volume indicates that, on the crucial question of dealing with religious dissent, the positions of the Jesuits and successive popes were only pushed into harmony briefly as Protestantism began to spread on the Italian peninsula.

The repeated concession of the privilege during the mid-sixteenth century also illustrates polycentrism and pragmatism of the Catholic Church in this period. Indeed, it reveals that, until the turn of the seventeenth century, no single authority or institution was able to assert full control over the means of fighting religious dissent – not even the pope. This was because inquisitorial and episcopal systems could not work successfully alone, facing pastoral and political challenges across the states of Italy. To address this problem, inquisitors and successive sixteenth-century pontiffs relinquished control over heresy, the gravest matter of the day, allowing the Jesuits to reconcile dissenters as and when they saw fit. This arrangement challenges the long-accepted image of an

---

33   On the Jesuits and the papacy see O'Malley, *The Jesuits and the popes: a historical sketch of their relationship* (Philadelphia: Saint Joseph's University Press, 2016). O'Malley also treated the topic more briefly in his *The First Jesuits*, pp.296–310.

10 INTRODUCTION

organised, militant and increasingly centralised Tridentine Church, showing us that many Counter-Reformation popes and inquisitors were forced to adopt a pragmatic and flexible approach to both heretics and the means of addressing heresy. By underlining the Church's reactive approach, the history of the privilege supports recent research that emphasises the pragmatism of the early modern Church and the influence of local agents and issues on the course of early modern Catholicism.[34]

So far, the importance of extra-judicial routes of reconciliation in the mid-sixteenth century religious crisis has not been sufficiently underlined. Their necessity in the aftermath of the Reformation is highlighted by the fact that the Church provided them over decades even though they clashed with its own judicial systems. Generally, inquisitorial and episcopal tribunals dominate scholarship on heresy in sixteenth-century Italy, even when they include discussions of pastoral figures. Even work that considers the anti-heretical role of religious orders focuses on how their work supported that of bishops or judicial bodies like the Roman Inquisition.[35] Redressing this imbalance, the history presented in this book shows that extra-judicial methods were also parallel, autonomous routes to reconciliation. This conclusion underlines the importance of recent scholarship on Catholic institutions that converted heretics extra-judicially in late sixteenth-century and seventeenth-century Italy.[36] It also suggests that the chronology of such discussions should begin earlier, tracing the roots of this approach in the anti-heretical work of the early Jesuits.

---

34 Key works include Simon Ditchfield, 'Decentering the Catholic Reformation. Papacy and Peoples in the Early Modern World', *Archive for Reformation History*, 101 (2010), pp.186–208; 'In search of local knowledge: rewriting early modern Italian religious history', *Cristianesimo nella storia*, 19 (1998), pp.255–296; *Liturgy, Sanctity and History in Tridentine Italy: Pietro Maria Campi and the Preservation of the Particular* (Cambridge: Cambridge University Press, 1995); Fosi, *Papal Justice*; Mary Laven, 'Encountering the Counter-Reformation', *Renaissance Quarterly*, 59 (2006), pp.706–720; 'Introduction' in Alexandra Bamji, Geert H. Janssen and Laven (eds) *Ashgate Companion to the Counter-Reformation* (Farnham: Ashgate, 2013), pp.1–14 and Keith P. Luria, ' "Popular Catholicism" and the Catholic Reformation' in Comerford and Pabel (eds), *Early Modern Catholicism: essays in honour of John W. O'Malley S.J.* (Toronto: University of Toronto, 2001), pp.116–7.

35 Matteo Al Kalak, *Il riformatore dimenticato. Egidio Foscarari tra inquisizione, concilio e governo pastorale (1512–1564)* (Bologna: Il Mulino, 2016); Pastore, *Il Vangelo e la Spada*; Giovanna Paolin, 'Gli ordini religiosi e l'Inquisizione: analisi di un rapporto' in Del Col, Andrea and Giovanna Paolin (eds), *L'Inquisizione romana: metodologia delle fonti e storia istituzionale: atti del seminario internazionale, Montereale Valcellina, 23 e 24 settembre 1999* (Trieste: Edizioni Università di Trieste, 2000), pp.169–185; Prosperi, *Tribunali della coscienza* and Pierroberto Scaramella, 'I primi gesuiti e l'Inquisizione Romana 1547–1562', *Rivista Storica Italiana*, 117 (2005), pp. 135–157.

36 Fosi, *Convertire lo straniero* and Mazur, *Conversion to Catholicism*.

INTRODUCTION

1   Historiography: the Story So Far

The Jesuits' privilege to absolve heresy disrupts both traditional narratives of a centralised Counter-Reformation Church focused on social discipline and the age-old characterisation of a Jesuit order dutifully serving the pope and his inquisitors. It is, therefore, unsurprising that critical scholarly analysis of the privilege has only emerged in the last few decades alongside a radical shift in scholarship on the Society and the sixteenth-century Church. Early Jesuit historians legitimised the privilege, portraying it as perfectly harmonious with inquisitorial activities and eliding any controversy regarding members who were accused of heresy in Spain, France and Italy.[37] This approach cast a long shadow on Jesuit historiography with apology for the Society, if not for the Roman Inquisition, persisting in twentieth-century discussions of the Jesuits' anti-heretical activities. We even see the influence of traditional Jesuit mythologies in late twentieth century inquisitorial histories in which secular historians offered the first discussions of the privilege's broader impact. These texts described the privilege as a political tool of the pope or a mechanism to lure men to a Jesuit confessor who would then shuffle them off to the courts of the Roman Inquisition. Here, Jesuits are painted as loyal collaborators of the Holy Office and the papacy, just as in earlier Jesuit texts. Like contemporary Jesuit scholarship, these inquisitorial histories pulled the Society out of the vacuum in which it had been previously studied, incorporating the Jesuits' work into the broader history of the Church. Nonetheless, they portrayed sixteenth-century ecclesiastical systems as centralised, overbearing and efficient, jarring with newer revised histories of the Society, conversion and early modern Catholicism in general, which have emphasised compromise, contradiction, conflict and failure. Within these revised histories, the Jesuits' anti-heretical activities and relationship with the Church appear ever less uniform. They make it clear that the privilege to absolve heresy, which affected the Jesuits' role and

---

37   On accusations of heresy and the early Jesuits see Pierre-Antoine Fabre, 'Ignace de Loyola en procès d'orthodoxie (1525–1622)' in Susanna Elm, Eric Rebillard and Antonella Romano (eds), *Orthodoxie, christianisme, histoire* (Rome: École française de Rome, 2000), pp.101–24; Pavone, 'A Saint under Trial. Ignatius of Loyola between Alcalá and Rome' in Robert Maryks (ed.), *A Companion to Ignatius of Loyola* (Leiden: Brill, 2014), p.45. On its effect on Jesuit historiography see O'Malley, 'The Historiography of the Society of Jesus: Where does it stand today?' in O'Malley (ed.), O'Malley, *Saints or Devils Incarnate? Studies in Jesuit History* (Leiden: Brill, 2013) pp.1–35 and Guido Mongini, <<*Ad Christi similtudinem*>> *Ignazio di Loyola e i primi gesuiti tra eresia e ortodossia* (Alessandria: Edizioni dell'Orso, 2011), pp.23–44.

12   INTRODUCTION

their links with both the Church and state, must be reconsidered with fuller attention.

Confession, heresy and the Jesuits' service to the Church were enshrined in Jesuit history in the first decades of the Society's existence. The order's first official history, the *Chronicon* of Juan Alfonso Polanco (1517–76), secretary to the first three Superior Generals of the Society, was written as a source book for Jesuit historians.[38] As such it established the legend of Jesuit history for centuries to come. The *Chronicon* is, therefore, a vital key for understanding the early Jesuits' priorities, both in their ministry and their record making. The *Chronicon* portrays Jesuit confession as a central and effective means of reconciling heretics. The Jesuits are painted as a useful pastoral force for combating the threat of religious dissent in sixteenth-century Italy – a pastoral force that worked with total legitimacy and wanted to cooperate harmoniously with other institutions and individuals engaged in the fight against heresy. Polanco underlines the legitimacy of the privilege to absolve heresy, describing its concession 'through apostolic letters in the form of Brief'.[39] The Jesuits' use of the privilege is only alluded to with no mention of queries, controversy or jurisdictional conflict, only missionary success.[40] Describing a bitter clash over the privilege between inquisitors and Jesuits in Spain, for example, Polanco does not call the episode a conflict but an occasion when the Jesuits decided to use their privilege 'most moderately' as the inquisitors only very 'scarcely' ordered 'that faculty to be conceded to others'.[41] Polanco portrayed the Jesuits as important protagonists in the fight against heresy in Italy and elsewhere but he did not reveal the complex and often controversial impact of the privilege that facilitated this role.

Polanco's successors also sought to portray the Jesuits' anti-heretical efforts as effective and uncontroversial; perfectly harmonious with the work of the Roman Inquisition. Pedro de Ribadeneira (1527–1611) underlined the Jesuits'

---

38   Juan   de   Polanco,   *Vita   Ignatii   Loiolae   et   rerum   Societatis   Jesu   historia* (Madrid: Typographorum Societas, 1894; Augustinus Avrial, 1894–8), 6 vols. On Polanco and Jesuit correspondence see Markus Friedrich, 'Government and information management in Early Modern Europe. The Case of the Society of Jesus (1540–1773)', *Journal of Early Modern History*, 12 (2008), pp.539–563 and Mario Scaduto, 'Un scritto ignaziano inedito: Il 'Del offiçio secretario' del 1547', *Archivum Historicum Societatis Iesu*, 29 (1960), pp.305–328. On the intended use of the Chronicon see John Patrick Donnelly (trans.), *Year by year with the early Jesuits (1537–1556): selections from the "Chronicon" of Juan de Polanco, S.J.* (St. Louis: Institute of Jesuit Sources, 2004), p.xiv.

39   Polanco, *Vita Ignatii Loiolae*, vol.2, p.426.

40   See, for example, ibid., pp.481–2.

41   Ibid., p.354.

INTRODUCTION

cooperation with the inquisitors and even claimed that 'Ignatius fought vigilantly' for the institution of an inquisition in Rome.[42] Later, Giampietro Maffei (1533–1603) wrote that Loyola personally led many Lutheran heretics to the Holy Office.[43] Jerónimo Nadal (1507–1580) went even further, proposing that Loyola founded the Society so that its members could combat heresy.[44] This narrative was perpetuated by seventeenth-century Jesuit historians Niccolò Orlandini (1554–1606) and Francesco Sacchini (1570–1625).[45] Indeed, the influence of Polanco has rippled through the centuries. Even in the late twentieth century, André Ravier used the *Chronicon* as the key source for his history of the Society.[46] Moreover, the effects of this early mythologising were not confined to Jesuit scholars nor to positive myths about the Society. Negative readings of Ribadeneira and Maffei soon emerged in Protestant narratives in which Jesuit papal agents fought a heroic Martin Luther.[47]

In the modern period, the Society's scholarly projects continued to neutralise controversy in accounts of the anti-heretical activities of the early Jesuits. Just as in Polanco's history, this involved a careful curation of the Society's correspondence, which was often laced with stories of confusion and conflict over their efforts to fight religious dissent. In the late nineteenth century, Jesuit scholars began publishing selected letters and documents from the Society's central and local archives as the *Monumenta Historica Societatis Iesu*. Stating that they 'separated the useful from the useless', the editors favoured accounts of Jesuits acting as protagonists at major moments of the Counter-Reformation narrative.[48] Discussions of the problems that the Jesuits encountered whilst fighting heresy and using their privilege are under-represented. The omission of questions and queries about jurisdictional clashes and confusing cases

---

42   Pedro de Ribadeneira, *Vita Ignatii Loiolae, Qui Religionem Clericorum Societatis Iesu Instituit.* (Cologne: Birckmannica sumptibus Arnoldi Mylii, 1602), p.262.

43   Giovanni Pietro Maffei, *Vita Ignatii Loiolae Qui Societatem Iesu Fundavit Postremo Recognita.* (Bordeaux: S. Millangius,1589), p.81.

44   Nadal, *Epistolae P. Hieronymi Nadal*, vol.5, pp.315–6.

45   Niccolò Orlandini and Francesco Sacchini, *Historia Societatis Iesu* (Rome; Cologne; Antwerp, 1615–1710), 5 vols.

46   André Ravier, *La Compagnie de Jésus sous le gouvernement d'Ignace de Loyola (1541–1556) d'après les Chroniques de Juan-Alphonso Polanco* (Paris: Desclée de Brouwer, 1991).

47   O'Malley, *The Historiography of the Society of Jesus*, p.11. See, for example, Veit Ludwig von Seckendorff, *Commentarius historicus et apologeticus de Lutheranismo sive de reformatione religionis ductu D. Martini Lutheri in magna Germaniae parte aliisque regionibus* (Frankfurt: J.F. Gleditsch, 1692).

48   Diego Laínez, *Lainii Monumenta: epistolae et acta patris Jacobi Lainii, secundi praepositi generalis Societatis Jesu* (Madrid: Typis G. Lopez del Horno, 1912–8), 8 vols, vol. 1, pp. xiii–xiv.

14   INTRODUCTION

is particularly notable in the collections of letters as the Society used correspondence as a means of problem-solving, as we have already seen in the case
of Cesare Helmi.

Jesuit authors of the modern period also tried to elide controversy surrounding the early Society's role. In the early twentieth century, the Society's
official historian, Pietro Tacchi-Venturi (1861–1956), claimed that his history of
the Jesuits in Italy would buck this trend, providing neither apology nor dia-
tribe.[49] But Tacchi-Venturi still whitewashed the Jesuits' position.[50] Unlike earlier authors, he decided to distance the Society from inquisitorial activities, a
stance that reflected personal and contemporary distaste for policing belief.[51]
To maintain a distance between the Jesuits' activities and inquisitorial matters, Tacchi-Venturi omitted mention of the privilege altogether from his history. Describing the bull that granted the privilege to absolve heresy, he merely
states that it 'conceded some notable privileges' and only cites the privilege 'of
promoting [the Society's] students or scholastics to a doctorate' specifically.[52]

The Society's next official historian, Mario Scaduto (1907–95), continued
this trend. Scaduto's history of the Society and, even more so, articles presented evidence of the Jesuits' most intimate collaborations with the Roman Inquisition.[53] Nonetheless, they insisted that the Jesuits were reluctant supporters
of the Holy Office, stating that the Jesuits' efforts to convert heretics with gen-
tle means were hampered by churchmen who enacted 'ecclesiastical legislation' that 'was not at all indulgent' and 'imposed public abjuration' of heresy 'at
the hands of the inquisitors'.[54] By admitting that Jesuits and inquisitors were

---

49   Pietro Tacchi-Venturi, *Storia della Compagnia di Gesù in Italia, narrata col sussidio di fonti
      inedite dal P. Tacchi Venturi* (Rome: 1910–51), 2 vols, pp.x–xiii. See also Tacchi-Venturi's com-
      ments on Ribadeneira's history in 'Della prima edizione della vita del N.S.P. Ignazio scritta
      dal P. Pietro Ribadeneira. Note storiche e bibliographiche del P. Pietro Tacchi Venturi,
      S.I.', *Lettere Edificanti della Provincia Napoletana*, 9 (1901). On Tacchi Venturi and apolo-
      getics see Alessandro Saggioro, 'Storico, testimonio e parte. Pietro Tacchi Venturi: storia,
      storiografia e storia delle religioni' in *Atti della Accademia Nazionale dei Lincei, storiche e
      filologiche, Rendiconti* 13 (2002), pp.451–489. On the preface to *Storia della Compagnia* and
      Ribadeneira's *Vita* see particularly, pp.463–8.
50   Pavone, 'A Saint under Trial: Ignatius Loyola between Alcalà and Rome', p.45.
51   Prosperi, *L'Inquisizione Romana. Letture e ricerche* (Roma: Edizioni di Storia e Letteratura,
      2003), p.xi. See Robert Maryks, *"Pouring Jewish Water into Fascist Wine": Untold Stories of
      (Catholic) Jews from the Archive of Mussolini's Jesuit Pietro Tacchi Venturi* (Leiden: Brill, 2012).
52   Tacchi-Venturi, *Storia della Compagnia*, vol. 2, part 2, p.540.
53   Scaduto, *Storia della Compagnia di Gesù in Italia. L'Epoca di Giacomo Lainez: l'azione,
      1556–1565* (Rome: La Civiltà Cattolica, 1950). For a typical article see Scaduto, 'Tra inquisi-
      tori e riformati. Le missioni dei gesuiti tra Valdesi della Calabria e delle Puglia', *Archivum
      Historicum Societatis Iesu*, 15 (1946), pp.1–76.
54   Scaduto, *Storia della Compagnia di Gesù in Italia*, p.709.

INTRODUCTION

in conflict over whether heretics should be dealt with 'indulgently' or in public or private, Scaduto went beyond the rose-tinted accounts of his predecessors. That said Scaduto failed to explain why a Society in conflict with the papal inquisition was able to secure and regain their privilege to absolve heresy on multiple occasions, often with inquisitorial support. Scaduto offered details about how the Jesuits used the privilege. But his desire to distance the Jesuits from the Holy Office skewed his explanations of the privilege's role in the relationship between the Society and the inquisitors.

In the last decade of the twentieth century a shift in Jesuit historiography prepared the ground for less apologetic scholarship on the privilege. This development in research on the Society has seen Jesuit and lay scholars collaborate to integrate the Jesuits' history into the broader cultural, intellectual and political history of the early modern period. This methodology was fundamental to *The Jesuits*, a volume that considered the Society's contribution to European history through a range of disciplines; it has found its full fruition in the *Jesuit Historiography Online* which offers historiographical essays to scholars of Jesuit history and 'the many disciplines with which it intersects'.[55] As part of this shift, scholars such as Silvia Mostaccio have called for the extraction of the Jesuits from their own mythologies and traditional narratives of the Counter-Reformation Church; as Luce Giard called it, a '*désenclavement*' of Jesuit history.[56] Much work that uses this approach is comparative, studying

---

55   Gauvin Alexander Bailey and O'Malley (eds), *The Jesuits: cultures, sciences and the arts, 1540–1773* (London: University of Toronto Press, 1999) and *The Jesuits II: Cultures, Sciences, and the Arts, 1540–1773* (Toronto: University of Toronto Press, 2006). For an account of this shift see Emanuele Colombo 'Gesuitomania. Studi recenti sulle missioni gesuitiche (1540–1773)' in Catto, Mongini and Mostaccio (eds), *Evangelizzazione e globalizzazione. Le missioni gesuitiche nell'età moderna tra storia e storiografia*, (Rome: Dante Alighieri, 2010), pp. 31–59, particularly pp.33–5. See also, Ditchfield, 'Of Missions and Models: the Jesuit enterprise (1540–1773) reassessed in recent literature', *Catholic Historical Review*, 93 (2007), p.343 and Fabre and Romano 'Les jésuites dans le monde moderne. Nouvelles approches', *Revue de synthèse*, 120 (1999). *Jesuit Historiography Online* is edited by Robert Maryks. See also, Maryks (ed.), *A Companion to Ignatius of Loyola; Jesuit survival and restoration: a global history, 1773–1900* (Leiden: Brill, 2015); "*Pouring Jewish Water into Fascist Wine*"; *Saint Cicero and the Jesuits*; with James Bernauer, "*The tragic couple": encounters between Jews and Jesuits* (Leiden: Brill, 2014).

56   Luce Giard used this term in her concluding comments in Bailey and O'Malley (eds), *The Jesuits*, pp.707–12. See also Giard, 'Le devoir d'intelligence ou l'insertion des jésuites dans le monde du savoir' in Giard, *Les jésuites à la Renaissance. Système éducatif et production du savoir* (Paris: Presses universitaires de France, 1995), pp.xi–lxxix; Silvia Mostaccio, 'A Conscious Ambiguity: The Jesuits Viewed in Comparative Perspective in Light of Some Recent Italian Literature', *Journal of Early Modern History*, 12 (2008), pp.410–41 and Franco Motta, *Annali di Storia dell'Esegesi*, 19 (2002).

16   INTRODUCTION

the Jesuits' European and extra-European missions and the Jesuits and other religious orders, though some articles and books have focused on one aspect of the Society's character or ministry, such as obedience or confession, or on a particular period.[57] The scholars working with this new approach aim to consider the early Society within the diverse cultural, political and social contexts in which it worked.

This shift in Jesuit scholarship is crucial for understanding the significance of the history of the privilege to absolve heresy, which facilitated the Jesuits' interaction with groups and individuals outside of the Society, from heretics, to inquisitors, to the popes themselves.

It is no coincidence that the first account of the privilege admitting controversy, conflict and confusion was by John O'Malley, a Jesuit scholar who helped to lead the *désenclavement* of Jesuit scholarship. O'Malley's *The First Jesuits*, published in 1993, was the first history to study Jesuit institutional documents in the context of their pastoral ministry and to consider both within the broader history of the Church and European society. In the book, O'Malley mentioned the privilege as part of a discussion of the Society's ministry of confession. O'Malley admitted that the privilege allowed the Jesuits to bypass the tribunals of the Roman Inquisition, that the Jesuits were confused about how it was best used and that other institutions were jealous of the Society's privilege.[58] Though O'Malley only mentioned the privilege briefly, by considering how the power fit into the Society's work as confessors and how others reacted to it O'Malley established a foundation for scholars to examine the role and impact of the privilege within the Jesuits' ministry and in their relationship with other individuals and institutions in the early modern Church.

---

57   Paolo Broggio, *Evangelizzare il mondo: le missioni della Compagnia di Gesù tra Europa e America (secoli XVI–XVII)* (Rome: Carocci, 2005); Marina Caffiero, Franco Motta and Pavone (eds), 'Identità religiose e identità nazionali in età moderna', *Dimensioni e problemi della ricerca storica*, 1 (2005), pp.7–93; E. Corsi (ed), *Órdenes religiosas entre América y Asia. Idea para una historia misionera de los espacios coloniales* (Mexico: El Colegio de Mexico, Centro de Estudios de Asia y Árica, 2008); Y. El Alaoui, *Jésuites, morisques et indiens. Étude comparative des méthodes d'évangélisation de la Compagnie de Jésus d'après les traités de José de Acosta (1588) et d'Ignacio de las Casas (1605–1607)* (Paris: Honoré Champion, 2006); Maryks, *Saint Cicero and the Jesuits. The Influence of the Liberal Arts on the Adoption of Moral Probabilism* (Aldershot: Ashgate, 2008); Mostaccio, *Early modern Jesuits between obedience and conscience during the Generalate of Claudio Acquaviva* (Farnham: Ashgate, 2014) and *Rivista storica italiana* special issue 'Alle origini della Compagnia di Gesù', 117 (2005), pp.5–178.

58   O'Malley, *The First Jesuits*, p.144.

INTRODUCTION

17

In the same period, historians of the Holy Office offered the first critical analysis of the privilege's impact, supporting the *désenclavement* of the Society's history by integrating the work of the Jesuits into the history of religious discipline in Europe. They also underlined the importance of extra-judicial methods of conversion and reconciliation. Nonetheless, their explanations of the privilege itself were limited. Although they described how the privilege might have supported the practical and political aims of the inquisitors or popes at a particular time, they did not fully integrate the aims of the Jesuits who solicited and used the privilege, nor explain how the aims of the Jesuits and their collaborators were negotiated and compromised when they clashed, nor define the role of the privilege in the pastoral and institutional life of the Jesuits, the Church and Italian society.

The most influential existing explanation of the Jesuits' role in the fight against heresy is that of Adriano Prosperi whose *Tribunali della coscienza* (1996) and 'Anima in Trappola' (1999) suggested that inquisitors used adept and appealing Jesuit confessors to attract penitent-heretics who would then be lured to an inquisitorial tribunal.[59] According to Prosperi, the inquisitors did this by obliging confessors to withhold absolution from penitent-heretics until they had made a 'spontaneous appearance' at an inquisitorial tribunal. Although Prosperi admitted that the privilege exempted the Jesuits from the control of the inquisitors at times, he focused on moments when inquisitors overcame this by negating the privilege.[60] Prosperi described some possible motivations of the Jesuits who solicited the power but his understandable focus on the Holy Office subordinated these to the aims of the inquisitors. Moreover, as it focuses on how the privilege was negated to be more useful to the inquisition, Prosperi's book does not explain why popes and inquisitors supported the privilege in its original, unlimited form between, at least, 1551 and 1567, and 1572 and 1587. The answer to this question has been partially addressed by Vincenzo Lavenia, a student of Prosperi, who has incorporated the role of the Jesuits and their privilege into detailed, localised accounts of the inquisition's activities in early modern Italy and the Society's role in inquisitorial missions. Still, Lavenia's scholarly focus on the aims and actions of the inquisition means

---

59   Prosperi, *Tribunali della coscienza*, pp.215–8 and 492 and 'Anime in trappola. Confessione e censura ecclesiastica all'Università di Pisa tra '500 e ' '600', *Belfagor*, 54 (May 1999), pp.265–7. On spontaneous appearances see also Black, *The Italian Inquisition*, pp.61–2; Brambilla, 'Il <<foro della coscienza>>' and Fosi, 'Conversion and Autobiography: Telling Tales before the Roman Inquisition', *Journal of Early Modern History*, 17 (2013), pp.444–5.

60   Prosperi, *Tribunali della coscienza*, p.492.

18   INTRODUCTION

that his texts do not explore in depth the nature, significance and impact of the privilege for the Jesuits who solicited and used the power.[61]

Explanations such as Prosperi's reinforce the notion that sacramental confession was used to control the laity, an idea that is long-established in both Anglophone and Italian scholarship. The roots of this idea can be seen in the work of English historian John Bossy. In the 1970s and 1980s Bossy argued that during the sixteenth century the sacrament of confession transformed from a semi-public act of conflict resolution into an individual encounter during which the confessor acted as a private, moral judge.[62] For Bossy and Italian scholars like Prosperi and Paolo Prodi, the Council of Trent renewed the use of the sacrament as a means of policing the faithful when it reiterated the rule that the laity had to go to confession at least annually and confirmed the role of the confessor as a judge.[63] Recent scholarship has gone some way to reinforcing this interpretation. Wietse de Boer and Patrick O'Banion have shown how the curia in Milan and Spain used annual confession to distinguish believers from heretics.[64] Whilst Jane Wickersham's study of inquisitorial manuals underlined the use of annual confession as a barometer of orthodoxy well into the late sixteenth century.[65]

However, research on the relationship between curia and lay people in early modern Europe suggests that the laity often frustrated such efforts at social control. Marc Foster's study of Catholic reform in Speyer (1992) and several of the essays in *Penitence in the Age of Reformations* (2000) disrupt the image of a submissive laity, showing that people frequently refused to perform public penances and in some areas successfully thwarted the imposition of the

---

61   See, for example, Lavenia, 'Giudici, eretici, infedeli. Per una storia dell'inquisizione nella Marca nella prima età moderna', *Giornale di Storia*, 6 (2011), pp.1–38 and 'L'Inquisizione del duca'.

62   John Bossy, 'The Social History of Confession in the Age of the Reformation', *Transactions of the Royal Historical Society*, 25 (1975), pp. 21–38.

63   Prosperi, *Tribunali della coscienza*, p.469 and Paolo Prodi, 'Il sacramento della penitenza e la *restitutio*' in Prosperi (ed.), *Per Adriano Prosperi* (Pisa: Edizioni della Normale, 2011), p.119; *Una storia della giustizia. Dal pluralismo dei fori al moderno dualismo tra coscienza e diritto* (Bologna: Il Mulino, 2000), p.286.

64   Wietse de Boer, *The Conquest of the Soul: confession, discipline, and public order in Counter-Reformation Milan* (Leiden: Brill, 2001), pp.169–76; Patrick O'Banion, *The Sacrament of Penance and Religious Life in Golden Age Spain* (Pennsylvania: Pennsylvania State University Press, 2012), p.15.

65   Jane Wickersham, *Rituals of Prosecution. The Roman Inquisition and the Prosecution of Philo-Protestants in Sixteenth-Century Italy* (Toronto: University of Toronto Press, 2012), p.85.

INTRODUCTION

decrees of Trent.[66] Ronald Rittger's research on penance in Lutheran Germany and O'Banion's discussion of confession in Catholic Spain have also underlined the centrality of compromise in relationships between laymen and priests.[67] Such conclusions are bolstered by Angelo del Torre's investigation of episcopal visitation records in early modern Piedmont, which shows that sacraments often facilitated a relationship of mutual benefit and responsibility between the laity and clergy not the oppression of laymen by priests.[68] *The Ashgate Companion to the Counter-Reformation* cemented the importance of considering negotiation between Catholic institutions and the laity in any study of religion and religious change in the early modern period.[69] Indeed, Heinrich Schilling and Wietse de Boer have criticised historians who fail to distinguish between rules on confession and the effects of their application.[70]

Moreover, it was not only penitents who resisted the imposition of norms by Rome but confessors themselves, particularly Jesuit confessors. As Giovanni Romeo has argued, Jesuits ignored inquisitorial decrees that ordered them to withhold absolutions pending their penitent's visit to the inquisition and very few Jesuit confessors are named in records of 'spontaneous appearances' at inquisitorial tribunals.[71] Elena Bonora has argued that Barnabite priests behaved similarly.[72] What is more, Romeo has shown that the Jesuits were often exempt

---

66   Marc R. Forster, *The Counter-Reformation in the villages. Religion and reform in the bishopric of Speyer, 1560–1720* (London: Cornell University Press, 1992) and Katharine Jackson Lualdi and Anne T. Thayer (eds), *Penitence in the Age of Reformations* (Aldershot: Ashgate, 2000).

67   O'Banion, *The Sacrament of Penance and Religious Life in Golden Age Spain*, pp.5–6 and Ronald Rittgers, *The Reformation of the Keys: confession, conscience and authority in sixteenth-century Germany* (London: Harvard University Press, 2004).

68   Angelo Torre, *Il consumo di devozioni: religione e comunità nelle campagne dell'ancien régime* (Venice: Marsilio, 1995) and 'Politics cloaked in worship. State, Church and local power in Piedmont 1570–1770', *Past and Present*, 134 (February 1992), pp.42–92.

69   See Laven's introductory overview and remarks in Bamji, Janssen and Laven (eds), *Ashgate Research Companion to the Counter-Reformation*, pp.8–11 and contributions by Clare Copeland, 'Sanctity', pp.225–242 and Nicholas S. Davidson, 'The Inquisition', pp.91–108.

70   De Boer applied this critique to W. David Myers' *"Poor Sinning Folk": Confession and Conscience in Counter-Reformation Germany* in the *Sixteenth Century Journal*, 28 (1997), pp.897–8. For Schilling's observations see, for example, 'Die Kirchenzucht im frühneuzeitlichen Europa in interkonfessionell vergleichender und interdisziplinärer Perspektive – eine Zswishenbilanz' in Schilling, *Kirchenzucht und Sozialdisziplinierung im frühneuzeitlichen Europa: mit einer Ausahlbibliographie* (Berlin: Duncker and Humblot, 1994), p.38.

71   Romeo, *Ricerche su confessione dei peccati*, p.73.

72   Elena Bonora, 'I barnabiti tra storia dell'ordine e storia della Chiesa' in Firpo (ed.), *Nunc alia tempora alii mores. Storici e storia in età postridentina, Atti del convegno internazionale, Torino, 24–27 settembre 2003* (Florence: Olshki, 2005), pp.111–40.

from the obligation to send their penitents to a tribunal before absolving them, even during the pontificate of the arch-inquisitor Paul IV.[73] If the Jesuits were exempt or opted out of the system of spontaneous appearances and other obligations to the Roman Inquisition we must look beyond this system to the Jesuits' actual use of the privilege to explain its role in the fight against heresy and the life of the Society.

Rather than characterising the Jesuits as a tool of the Holy Office, Romeo and others have argued that it is more fruitful to see the Society and its colleges as a crucial supplement to the inquisition, whose presence on the Italian peninsula was fragmentary, problematic and often weak[74] Massimo Firpo has also suggested that the Society were a distinct adjunct to the Roman Inquisition, claiming that Julius III empowered the Jesuits with the privilege to absolve heresy in order to create a distinct, loyal force to fight religious dissent alongside cardinal-inquistors who had become too powerful and disobedient.[75] Recent research on the Holy Office certainly bolsters the notion that the inquisitorial system needed supplementary support, as evidence of the tribunal's inefficiency emerges from the archive of the Roman Inquisition, the Archivio della Congregazione per la Dottrina della Fede (ACDF).[76] Even before the official opening of the archive in 1998, Gigliola Fragnito, a scholar granted early access, soon discovered that the Congregation of the Index, the inquisitorial organ responsible for censorship, was plagued by a lack of expertise, cooperation and personnel at both a central and local level.[77] Even works that illustrate the increasing efficiency of the Holy Office highlight the continued obstacles faced by inquisitors in Italy. The work of Thomas Mayer, a later user of the ACDF, showed how the inquisition became an increasingly bureaucratic and well-controlled tool for the papacy in the late sixteenth and seventeenth centuries but also demonstrated the limits

---

73 Romeo, *L'inquisizione nell'Italia moderna*, p.27 and *Ricerche su confessione dei peccati*, p.43.

74 Romeo, 'Note sull'Inquisizione Romana tra il 1557 e il 1561', *Rivista di Storia e Letteratura Religiosa*, 36 (2000), p.136–40; *Ricerche su confessione*, pp.43–6.

75 Firpo, *La presa di potere*, p.65.

76 For inquisitorial documents held outside of the ACDF and the historical losses to the records of the Roman Inquisition see Tedeschi, 'The Dispersed Archives of the Roman Inquisition' in his *The Prosecution of Heresy*, pp.23–45. On the opening of the ACDF see Anne Jacobson Schutte, 'Palazzo del Sant'Uffizio: the Opening of the Roman Inquisition's Central Archive', *Perspectives on History*, 37 (May 1999), pp.25–8.

77 Gigliola Fragnito, *Bibbia al rogo: la censura ecclesiastica e i volgarizzamenti della Scrittura (1471–1605)* (Bologna: Il Mulino, 1997). See also Fragnito (ed.), *Church, Censorship and Culture in Early Modern Italy* (Cambridge: Cambridge University Press, 2001).

INTRODUCTION   21

of this tool and the persistent political resistance to Roman inquisitors in certain Italian states.[78]

The significant obstacles posed by local context and individual agents are evident in the content and organisation of the *Dizionario Storico dell'Inquisizione* of 2010, one of the most important publications to emerge from the period of fervent research that followed the opening of the ACDF.[79] The Society of Jesus has not one but three entries in the *Dizionario* and there are individual entries for each inquisitorial tribunal, underlining the fact that the type and extent of the activities of both the Jesuits and the inquisitors depended on the demands of the particlar religious, ecclesiastical and political contexts in which they worked, even within Italy.[80]

The Jesuits' privileges often allowed them to respond flexibly to the particular demands of the various locales in which the they worked, a key aspect of the Society underlined by recent scholarship. Studies focused on America and Asia have shown that papal privileges allowed the Jesuits to respond to the particular needs of converts without the ecclesiastical infrastructure found in Europe, highlighting the purpose of papal privileges not as personal gifts but as pragmatic exceptions to overcome obstacles to effective ministry.[81] Other research on the Jesuits' foreign missions has shown that the roots of policies that have been described as innovative and 'Jesuit' are found in the particular settings in which the Jesuits worked.[82] The work of Luke Clossey, Paolo Broggio and many others has demonstrated that Jesuits in Europe, Asia and the Americas were not motivated by the pope's desire to roll back the successes of the Reformation but rather developed strategies to fulfil the Society's key objective to save the souls of their own missionaries and those whom they

---

78   Thomas Mayer, *The Roman Inquisition: a papal bureaucracy and its laws in the Age of Galileo* (Philadelphia: University of Pennsylvania Press, 2013) and *The Roman Inquisition on the Stage of Italy, c.1590–1640* (Philadelphia: University of Pennsylvania Press, 2014).

79   Prosperi, Lavenia and Tedeschi, *Dizionario storico dell'inquisizione*. (Pisa: Edizioni della Normale, 2010), 4 vols.

80   Ibid., vol. 2, pp.665–77.

81   Broggio, 'Le congregazioni romane e la confessione dei neofiti del Nuovo Mondo tra *facultates* e *dubia*: reflessioni e spunti di indagine', *Mélanges de l'École française de Rome – Italie et Méditerranée*, 121 (2009), pp.173–197 and Giovanni Pizzorusso, 'Le Monde et/ou l'Europe: la Congrégation de Propaganda Fide et la politique missionaire du Saint-Siège (XVIIe siècle)', *Institut d'Histoire de la Réformation. Bulletin Annuel*, 35 (2013–2014), pp.40–7.

82   Thomas Banchoff and José Casanova (eds), *The Jesuits and Globalization: Historical Legacies and Contemporary Challenges* (Washington D.C.: Georgetown University Press, 2016), pp.28–9.

INTRODUCTION

encountered in their ministry.[83] Both Sabina Pavone's *I gesuiti* (2004) and Silvia Mostaccio's review article 'A Conscious Ambiguity' (2008) argued that the early Society was characterised by a deliberate inconsistency that allowed the Jesuits to work effectively with the individuals and contexts that they encountered in the mission field.[84] Such interpretations build upon the conclusions of studies on obedience within the Society by Claudia Alfieri, Michela Catto and Antonella Romano, which illustrated the importance of ambivalence in the praxis and development of the early Society.[85]

The notion of Jesuit flexibility and agility is key to scholars who claim that we should not characterise the Jesuits as a supplement to the inquisition, subordinating the Society within an interpretative framework dominated by the Holy Office, but see their role as ever-changing.[86] Pierroberto Scaramella, for example, has argued that the Jesuits worked to convert, absolve and reconcile heretics independently, collaboratively, secretly and openly, sometimes centre-stage of the Counter-Reformation drama and at others well outside of its grand narrative.[87] Corroborating the interpretation of privileges offered above, Scaramella interprets the Jesuits' privilege to absolve heretics as a crucial mechanism for a flexibility that allowed the Society to work outside of traditional hierarchies and to traverse boundaries of jurisdiction.[88] This conclusion is partially bolstered by Stefania Pastore's study of the inquisition in Castile between 1460 and 1598. Pastore concurs with her advisor Prosperi, arguing that the Jesuits worked as agents of the inquisition and supports Prosperi's suggestion that the Jesuits' privilege to absolve heretics facilitated their collaboration with the

---

83   Broggio, *Evangelizzare il mondo*; Luke Clossey, *Salvation and Globalization in the early Jesuit missions* (New York: Cambridge University Press, 2008); Trent Pomplun, *Jesuit on the Roof of the World. Ippolito Desideri's Mission to Tibet* (Oxford: Oxford University Press, 2010); Laven, *Mission to China: Matteo Ricci and the Jesuit encounter with the East* (London: Faber, 2012) and Po-Chia Hsia, *A Jesuit in the Forbidden City: Matteo Ricci 1552–1610* (Oxford: Oxford University Press, 2012).

84   Mostaccio, 'A Conscious Ambiguity' and *Early modern Jesuits between obedience and conscience*.

85   Fernanda Alfieri and Claudio Ferlan (eds), *Avventure dell'obbedienza nella Compagnia di Gesù. teorie e prassi fra XVI e XIX secolo* (Bologna: Il Mulino, 2012). For a reference to Romano's comments, spoken at the conference that instigated this publication see Pavone, 'Dissentire per sopravvivere. La Compagnia di Gesù in Russia alla fine del Settecento' in Alfieri and Ferlan, *Avventure dell'obbedienza nella Compagnia di Gesù*, p.197. See also Michela Catto, *La Compagnia divisa: il dissenso nell'ordine gesuitico tra '500 e '600* (Brescia: Morcelliana, 2009).

86   Scaramella, 'I primi gesuiti e l'Inquisizione romana', p.154.

87   Ibid., pp.138–41.

88   Ibid., p.149.

INTRODUCTION

inquisitors.[89] All the same, Pastore shows that the Jesuits in Castille used accommodating pastoral strategies in these collaborations, despite the severity of local inquisitors. This interpretation indicates that the Jesuits worked with the inquisitors in a relationship of mutual influence and compromise and not one of subordination.

In recent years, many scholars have emphasised the role of negotiation, plurality and compromise in Catholicism in Italy at large, dispelling the notion that the sixteenth-century Church was centralised, oppressive and unreactive.[90] Elena Brambilla has demonstrated that the Church's approach to religious dissent was as pragmatic as the Jesuits' and she and other scholars have argued that judicial and pastoral means of reconciling religious dissenters had coexisted for many centuries and become increasingly important in the late sixteenth and early seventeenth centuries.[91]

The recent reassessment of the Society and the institutional Church calls for and facilitates a reassessment of the Jesuits' privilege to absolve heresy. Moreover, a reassessment of the Jesuits' privilege to absolve heresy casts further light onto our new understanding of post-Reformation Catholicism. Interpretations that present the Jesuits as mere servants of the pope or inquisitors no longer stack up. The Jesuits exercised the privilege with no limitations for long periods of its lifespan. Moreover, the Church tolerated conflicting systems for reconciling heretics. It is clear that, in the religious emergency of the mid-sixteenth century, both the Jesuits and the Church at large tolerated plurality, compromise and even conflict, even at the expense of centralisation, traditional hierarchy and corporate unity. Studying the history of the privilege from the point of view of the Jesuits and those whom it affected, this book will show that the privilege was a mechanism for a jurisdictional autonomy and flexibility that the Jesuits used to overcome obstacles to finding heretics and securing conversions, and to further their own institutional mission. Moreover, this book will continue the story of the privilege beyond the narrative of many existing explanations to show that the Jesuits' ability to be flexible in matters of heresy came to an end when the threat of heresy

---

89   Prosperi, *Tribunali della coscienza*, pp.338–40.

90   Aron-Beller and Black, *The Roman Inquisition: Centre versus Peripheries*; Mary Laven, 'Encountering the Counter-Reformation' and 'Introduction' in *Ashgate Companion to the Counter-Reformation*; Keith P. Luria, ' '"Popular Catholicism" and the Catholic Reformation" in Comerford and Pabel (eds), *Early Modern Catholicism.* p.116–7.

91   Brambilla, *Alle origini del Sant'Uffizio*, pp.492–4; Fosi, *Convertire lo straniero* and Mazur, *Conversion to Catholicism in Early Modern Italy* and Romeo, 'Tribunali della coscienza: inquisitore, confessori e missionari', *Quaderni storici*, 102 (1999), pp.796–800.

24   INTRODUCTION

subsided and the Church's pragmatism led popes to prioritise institutional
concerns over pastoral aims.

2   Sources

This study employs a variety of sources to reconstruct the events and motivations that led to the concession of the privilege and to trace its role and impact
in Italy. Official documents that conceded, negated and revoked the privilege
provide a basic framework for tracing its history. Nonetheless, they do not explain the reasons behind the Jesuits' requests or the popes' decisions. Personal
and diplomatic correspondence, as well as further bulls, briefs and apostolic
letters contextualise the broad strategies and specific concerns of popes. The
Society's abundant correspondence reveals the Jesuits' motivations, even if it
requires careful and critical reading. Letters also help us to piece together the
negotiations and relationships that supported the Jesuits' requests for privileges and record the impact of the privilege, institutionally and pastorally.
Moreover, the Society's correspondence shows us how the Jesuits negotiated
conflicts and collaborations with popes, inquisitors, bishops, princes and their
penitents. Records of the decisions of the Holy Office, such as *decreta* and inquisitorial correspondence, also shed light on these negotiations, as well as
telling us of the privilege's impact on the inquisitors whom the Society worked
with and alongside. None of these sources offer us the view of the penitents
for whom the Jesuits requested the privilege. They do, however, allow us to
understand how and why the Jesuits assumed such a crucial role in the religious, social and political life of Italy, taking shape as a religious order during a
transformative period of early modern history.

   As heads of the Catholic Church and princes of the Papal States, the popes
who conceded the privilege had various and often conflicting motives; the
sources that they have left us reveal little about their reasons for making particular decisions and concessions.[92] Bulls and briefs regarding the privilege
give us some information about the nature of the power. For example, *Sacrae
religionis*, which officialised the concession of the privilege on 22 October
1552, outlined its basic limits. Nonetheless, such documents offer no information on how the Jesuits used the privilege and give no particular reason for its
concession to the Society, beyond general praise for the Jesuits' virtues and

---

92   On this dual role of the pope see Paolo Prodi, *Il sovrano pontefice. Un corpo e due anime: la
        monarchia papale* (Bologna: Il Mulino, 1982).

INTRODUCTION

activities.[93] Later manuscript and printed documents held at the Archivum Romanum Societatis Iesu (ARSI), ACDF, Biblioteca Apostolica Vaticana (BAV) and various regional archives such as the Archiginnasio in Bologna help us to trace the fate of the privilege, recording its re-concession, negation, revocation and subsequent illicit use. Sometimes, manuscript and print copies of bulls and briefs made and stored by the Jesuits and inquisitors offer extra information. They can, for example, include the names of supporters present at the solicitation of the privilege or the printing of a bull.[94] Nonetheless, they too reveal little about the motivations behind decisions, merely providing the basic skeleton of the privilege's history.

Popes did not grant the privilege to absolve heresy on a whim, but were solicited for it specifically by the Jesuits. Jesuit correspondence, therefore, must be our starting point for understanding the intended purpose and actual use of the privilege. The abundance of Jesuit correspondence held at the ARSI comes in three forms: reports, ad hoc queries from Jesuits and the responses of the Superior General and his advisors. These are rich sources yet must be read with some caution. Letter writing was the Jesuits' chief means of governance but also served to record and share important and edifying information within the Society. As a result, letters were often used to minimise controversy and legitimise the Jesuits' position.[95] As we have already seen, the early Society was keen to gloss over conflicts that arose from use of the privilege. This problem is evident not only in the content but also in the selection of letters edited in the Society's *Monumenta Historica Societatis Iesu* (MHSI) (1894–2009).[96] For this reason, this book uses the MHSI as a useful support for extensive original archival research, both at the Jesuit archives and other ecclesiastical and state archives across Italy.

Letters from Jesuits demanding the privilege or asking questions about its use are crucial for understanding its role in the Jesuits' ministry and the Church's fight against heresy. The details of Helmi's case, for example, show

---

93   A. Tomassetti (ed.), *Bullarum diplomatum et privilegiorum*, vol.6, p.464.

94   See, for example, the copy of *Sacrae religionis* in ARSI, *Instutum* 222, f.263r.

95   Friedrich, 'Circulating and Compiling the Litterae Annuae: Towards a History of the Jesuit System of Communication', *Archivum Historicum Societatis Iesu*, 76 (2008), pp.1–39 and 'Government and Information-Management' and 'Ignatius's Governing and Administrating the Society of Jesus' in Maryks (ed.), *A Companion to Ignatius of Loyola. Life, Writings, Spirituality, Influence* (Leiden: Brill, 2014), pp.123–140; Joseph A. Munitiz, 'Communicating Channels: Letters to Reveal and to Govern', *The Way Supplement*, 70 (1991), pp.64–75.

96   On the MHSI see Robert Danieluk, 'Monumenta Historica Societatis Iesu – uno sguardo di insieme sulla collana', *Archivum Historicum Societatis Iesu*, 81 (2012), pp.249–89.

26   INTRODUCTION

his concerns and thus reveal the stakes of the privilege and its effects on the Jesuits' ministry. Responses to queries like Helmi's show us what the Superior Generals would and could compromise in the pursuit of their pastoral and institutional goals, allowing us to discern the order's changing status in the Church and society, over time and across the Italian states. Correspondence also indicates that Jesuits absolved heretics in Italy both before the concession of the privilege and after its revocation, making it clear that we must look beyond normative documents such as bulls of concession and revocation to understand the history of the privilege.[97]

This book also uses inquisitorial letters and *decreta*, which reveal the positive and negative impact of the privilege on the work of the Roman Inquisition. For cardinal-inquisitors and local inquisitors, correspondence was a means of supervision and problem-solving, just as it was for the Jesuits. A vital source for scholars of the inquisition and all of the institutions and individuals with which it interacted, the surviving papers of the inquisitors are now held at regional Italian state archives and the ACDF, and partially published by scholars such as Pierroberto Scaramella.[98] Such letters highlight the successes and failures of the inquisitorial system and the obstacles that it faced, suggesting why the inquisitors might have required or requested the help of the Jesuits in certain areas.[99] The *decreta* record the decisions of the cardinal-inquisitors regarding general inquisitorial policy, often in response to particular cases in tribunals across the peninsula.[100] Though they offer scant information, along

---

97   On absolutions of heresy before the privilege see Caravale, 'Ambrogio Catarino Politi e i primi gesuiti', *Rivista storica italiana*, 117 (2005), p.80–109.

98   Scaramella, *Le lettere della Congregazione del Sant'Ufficio ai Tribunali di Fede di Napoli*. On the history and contents of the ACDF, see Daniel Ponziani, *L'Archivio della Congregazione per la Dottrina della Fede. Profilo storico e descrizione dei fondi documentari*, in Alejandro Cifres (ed.), *Memoria Fidei. Archivi ecclesiastici e nuova evangelizzazione* (Rome, Gangemi, 2016), pp. 85–96. On other inquisitorial sources see Patricia H. Jobe, 'Inquisitorial Manuscripts in the Biblioteca Apostolica Vaticana: A Preliminary Handlist' Charles Amiel, Gustav Henningsen and John Tedeschi (eds), *The Inquisition in Early Modern Europe: studies on sources and methods* (DeKalb: Northern Illinois University Press, 1986), pp.33–53; Tedeschi, 'The Dispersed Archives of the Roman Inquisition' in Amiel, Henningsen and Tedeschi (eds), *The Inquisition in Early Modern Europe*, pp.13–32.

99   Black, 'Relations between Inquisitors in Modena and the Roman Congregation in the seventeenth century' in Black and Aron-Beller (eds), *The Roman Inquisition: centre versus periphery*, pp.91–117; Giuliana Ancona and Dario Visintin, 'Centre and Periphery: The Correspondence between the Congregation of the Holy Office and the Inquisition in Fruili between 1578 and 1653' in Black and Aron-Beller (eds), *The Roman Inquisition: centre versus periphery*, pp.118–38.

100   Aron-Beller and Black in Aron-Beller and Black (eds), *The Roman Inquisition: centre versus peripheries*, pp.11–2; Jonathan Seitz, 'Interconnected Inquisitors. Circulation and

INTRODUCTION 27

with inquisitorial correspondence, the *decreta* record moments when the Jesuits' privilege either complemented or clashed with the work of the Holy Office. A *decretum* of 20 October 1553, for example, tells us of a close collaboration, when a Jesuit confessor 'absolved in the *foro conscientiae*' a Jewish convert whom inquisitors had accused of practicing his old religion, before the man was 'consigned to Lord Ignatius [Loyola] for the effect of instructing' him.[101] On the other hand, a *decretum* from a meeting of 1592 records a clash, stating that cardinal-inquisitors 'read the memorial' prohibiting Superior General Claudio Acquaviva from conceding 'faculties of receiving and absolving any heretics' to the Jesuits.[102] As well as recording the effects of the privilege on the inquisition, inquisitorial letters and *decreta* illustrate how conflicts were resolved. In doing this, they reflect the status and priorities of the inquisitors and Jesuits, and the stakes of the situation at hand.

Treatises written by Jesuits to defend the privilege and now held at the ARSI and ACDF are also central to this study. Until now, these documents have not been used by scholars to understand the history and significance of the privilege, although they offer the most detailed explanation and defence of the privilege ever written by the Jesuits. As such they provide a vital and illuminating supplement to Jesuit letters, which treat the privilege reticently. Such treatises indicate how the Jesuits used the privilege and what they believed its value was. Moreover, the ways in which their authors selected particular examples for their written defences and amended various drafts of these documents reveal what the Society perceived to be the inquisitors' main concerns about the Jesuits' anti-heretical work. The documents that the Jesuits sent to the inquisitors are thus a crucial means of understanding the role of the privilege in both the pastoral and institutional history of the Society and the Church at large.

It must be stated here that these documents do not allow us to reconstruct the experience of the privilege from the penitent's point of view. That said, Jesuit reports and inquisitorial *decreta* do offer us some information on their penitents' backgrounds. Although the specific information learnt in confession was protected by the sacred and absolute seal of secrecy, Jesuits requesting help and reporting success in their efforts to convert heretics offered some general information on their penitents to their correspondents. Queries from the mission field often reveal whom the Jesuits sought to absolve in particular

---

Networks Among Outer Peripheral Tribunals' in Aron-Beller and Black (eds), *The Roman Inquisition: centre versus peripheries*, p.158.

101 ACDF, *Decreta 1548–58*, p.230 / f.119v and p.241/ f.125r.
102 ACDF, *Decreta 1592–3*, f.420v.

28 INTRODUCTION

contexts. For example, requests for the privilege in Turin specify that the Jesuits needed it for the 'French' there.[103] Whilst an inquisitorial decree mentions that the Jewish convert whom the Jesuits absolved was 'Portuguese' and a letter sent to the tribunal in Bologna tells us that a soldier reconciled by a member of the Society was 'German'.[104] Such information was increasingly important from the late sixteenth century as nationality became a key factor in deciding whether an extra-judicial reconciliation could be granted.

Jesuit letters also offer us some information about the social status of penitents and the social dynamics of conversion. This information corroborates our existing understanding of the social dynamics of heresy and conversion in sixteenth-century Italy, indicating that those considered to be heretics existed at all levels of society and illustrating that conversions were often a pragmatic response to the demands of a particular social situation.[105] This is clear from a report from Vulturara in the Kingdom of Naples, which notes that a Jesuit converted the 'most rich' and 'most trusted' man in the community and then charged him to convince the town's obstinate Waldensians to become Catholic too.[106] Similarly, Helmi's query to Rome revealed that his penitent was an outlaw and tells us that his wife who had followed him in heresy was also assumed to join him in conversion.[107] These cases do not appear suspect but we should consider such details critically as some Jesuits emphasised social distinctions to assure inquisitors that the privilege was not used to exonerate dangerous heretics. One request for the privilege, for example, insisted that the Jesuits reconciled only those who were perceived to be the weakest and least threatening figures in society: women, rustics, old people, youths and the infirm, who would 'quake in front of Bishop'.[108]

Generally, the information on penitents given in Jesuit records tends to corroborate the traditional chronology and geography of heresy in sixteenth-century Italy.[109] From the 1530s, Jesuits absolved those who had heard new

---

103 ARSI, *Epistolae Italiae 136*, f.169r.

104 ACDF, *Decreta 1548–58*, p.241/ f.125r and Archiginnasio, *B1866*, f.143r.

105 See Ditchfield and Helen Smith, *Conversions: Gender and Religious Change in Early Modern Europe* (Manchester: Manchester University Press, 2017), p.5; Mazur's *Conversion to Catholicism*, pp.98–115 and Natalie Rothman's *Brokering empire: trans-imperial subjects between Venice and Istanbul* (Ithaca: Cornell University Press, 2011), pp.97–9.

106 ASR, *Miscellanea Famiglie Gesuiti*, B180, fasc.14, f.15.

107 ARSI, *Epistolae Italiae 107*, f.3r.

108 ARSI, *Institutum 187-I*, f.330v.

109 This narrative is clear in Salvatore Caponetto, *La Riforma protestante nell'Italia del Cinquecento* (Turin: Claudiana, 1997) and Cantimori, *Eretici Italiani del Cinquecento* and is also seen in recent texts such as Black, *The Italian Inquisition*.

INTRODUCTION   29

Protestant heresies in learned cities and trading centres such as Bologna, Modena and Venice.[110] In the mid-sixteenth century they catechised and absolved errant Catholics all over the peninsula, particularly in rural, remote and, consequently, neglected places, such as Corsica.[111] From the late 1560s, Jesuits reported that they converted Waldensian groups in the far north and deep south, after other heretical sects had been suppressed.[112] And like Roman authorities, the Society focused on the absolution of foreign heretics in the later sixteenth century.[113] The correlation between the Jesuits' narrative of their own absolutions and the history of religious dissent should be treated with some suspicion. The history of religious dissent in Italy has frequently been told through inquisitorial documents. As the Jesuits were keen to portray their work as harmonious with that of the Holy Office it is likely that they highlighted cases that matched the aims of the inquisitors. Comparison of Jesuit accounts with inquisitorial censures can expose fallacy. For example, Jesuit correspondence after the revocation of the privilege indicates that their focus was the conversion of the same foreigners whom the inquisitors sought to reconcile. Nonetheless, inquisitorial records reveal that Jesuits continued to reconcile Italian heretics whom the inquisitors would never have treated with such mercy.

It is difficult to deduce information from surviving sources about the number of penitents affected by the Jesuits' privilege, let alone the numbers from each particular sect. Jesuits sent varying amounts of information to Rome with some reporting that they had converted eight or ten Lutherans 'who came to confess themselves' and others merely alluding to good numbers of confessants and converts.[114] Moreover, such claims, whether specific or vague, were

---

110   See, for example, ARSI, *Epistolae Italiae 107*, f.3r and Salmerón, *Epistolae P. Alphonsi Salmeronis, Societatis Jesu: ex autographis vel originalibus exemplis potissimum depromptae a patribus ejusdem societatis nunc primum editae* (Madrid: Typis Gabrielis Lopez del Horno, 1906–7), 2 vols, vol. 1, p.63.

111   Juan Alfonso de Polanco, *Epistolae et commentaria P. Joannis Alphonsi de Polanco e Societate Jesu; addenda caeteris ejusdem scriptis dispersis in his monumentis* (Madrid: Typis Gabrielis Lopez, 1916–7), 2 vols, vol. 2, p.455.

112   Scaduto, 'Tra Inquisitori e Riformati'.

113   This is described in ARSI, *Institutum 185-I*, f.314r. On the inquisition, other congregations and foreigners see Fosi, *Convertire lo straniero* and Mazur, *Conversion to Catholicism*.

114   See, for examples, ARSI, *Epistolae Italiae 108*, f.217r; Paschase Broët, *Epistolae PP. Paschasii Broëti, Claudii Jaji, Joannis Codurii et Simonis Rodericii Societatis Jesu ex autographis vel originalibus exemplis potissimum depromptae* (Madrid: Typis Gabrielis Lopez del Horno, 1903), p.44 and Emmanuel Gomez, *Epistolae mixtae ex variis Europae locis ab anno 1537 ad 1556 scriptae nunc primum a patribus Societatis Jesu in lucem editae* (Madrid: Augustinus Avrial, 1898–1901), 5 vols, vol. 3, pp.91–2.

shaped by the Jesuits' aim to edify and encourage their confrères, which could encourage exaggeration. Jesuits' reports to cardinal-inquisitors are similarly suspect. These reports often supported requests for further privileges of absolution and so aimed to emphasise the efficacy of the Jesuits' work. The specific aims of the popes and inquisitors could also affect qualitative information in such documents, as Jesuits described reconciliations that correlated with inquisitorial aims and papal policy, as detailed above. Furthermore, the description of heretics in all such documents may not have reflected their true beliefs. Jesuit accounts, like contemporary inquisitorial documents, deploy narratives and categories that anathematised those who deviated from Catholic orthodoxy, frequently referring to the errant as Lutherans and Anabaptists when they may have been nothing of the sort.[115]

Using abundant Jesuit and inquisitorial correspondence available in archives and, to some extent, publications, as well as papal and institutional documents available in Rome and local Italian archives, this book will reconstruct the history of the privilege. Moreover, it will use this history to illuminate the relationship between the Society, Roman Inquisition and the papacy, during formative years for the Jesuits and the Holy Office and a transformative period for the Holy See. Though the limitations of the sources and the secrecy of sacramental confession prevent us from drawing firm conclusions about the number and type of penitents whom the Jesuits absolved, the history of the privilege to absolve heresy presented here does provide a unique vantage point to consider how popes, inquisitors and Jesuits negotiated their pastoral and institutional priorities whilst responding to the greatest crisis that the Catholic Church had faced in a millennium.

3   Overview

With a generally chronological framework, this book will consider the concession, use, negation and revocation of the privilege to absolve heresy. It will assess the role and impact of the privilege in the fight against heresy through normative institutional documents, manuscript treatises that explain and defend the privilege and geographical case studies based on numerous unpublished archival documents. Tracing the history of the privilege from its precursors, throughout its lifespan and beyond its revocation, the book will deduce patterns of use across

---

115   Lucio Biasori, 'Before the Inquisitor: A Thousand Ways of Being Lutheran' in A. Melloni (ed.), *Martin Luther: A Christian between Reforms and Modernity (1517–2017)* (Berlin: De Gruyter, 2017), pp.509–26.

INTRODUCTION 31

varied contexts, revealing how the privilege affected the secular and ecclesiastical institutions with which the Jesuits interacted. This broader approach will address flaws in explanations that define the privilege according to its outcomes in one particular context, or for one particular institution. Examining how the Jesuits used the privilege independently and in collaborations in different religious, ecclesiastical and political contexts, the book will establish the broader strategies of the Jesuits, the papacy and Roman Inquisition during this period of religious and institutional crisis. These strategies highlight the obstacles that the Catholic Church faced in its efforts to shore up religious orthodoxy in sixteenth-century Italy and how the Church tried to overcome them. By analysing how Jesuits, popes and inquisitors negotiated in conflicts and collaborations, the book will illuminate the priorities, actions and interactions of three of the most important protagonists in the history of the early modern Church and Italian society: the papacy, the Roman Inquisition and the Jesuits.

Chapter 1 will offer the first full history of the solicitation and concession of the privilege, from its limited precursors in the 1540s to its official concession in Julius III's *Sacrae religionis* of 1552. Through rich case studies of the Society's work in contexts as varied as Bologna and Corsica, the chapter will also examine how the Jesuits used the privilege on the ground. With this approach, the chapter will bridge the fundamental gap in existing explanations of the privilege by showing not only how the Jesuits used it to help prominent churchmen during the tumultuous period of the Councils of Trent and Bologna but also how the power fulfilled the Jesuits' pastoral and institutional objectives. By reconstructing the historical context of its solicitation, the chapter will show how the concession was largely the outcome of individual relationships between Jesuits and popes, inquisitors and bishops, driven by a common desire to stem heresy through pragmatic means.

Overall, the chapter will propose two key conclusions about the significance of the privilege's concession and use. Firstly, that the fundamental benefit of the privilege was jurisdictional autonomy. This independence allowed the Jesuits to absolve and reconcile heretics without involving inquisitors or bishops who were often absent or who deterred penitent-heretics otherwise willing to reconcile with the Church. Secondly, we shall see that this autonomy had institutional benefits for the Society as well as pastoral ones, allowing the Jesuits to fight heresy not only on behalf of popes and inquisitors but also for temporal princes who could support the Society's growing ministry. This conclusion undermines existing explanations of the privilege, which consider the power only as an aid to the Roman Inquisition and the papacy. Instead, the chapter will corroborate recent scholarship that emphasises the ambivalence of the early Society and demonstrate the broad benefits of the Jesuits' flexibility.

Chapter 2 will consider the impact of the privilege on the work of the Roman Inquisition: the principal institution for combating heresy in post-Reformation Italy. The chapter will examine collaborations between the Jesuits and the inquisition from the official concession of the privilege in 1552, through the papacy of Paul IV (1555–9), to the pontificate of Pius IV (1559–65). During this period, the Jesuits worked with the inquisition across the peninsula, from Valtellina and Piacenza in the North to Vulturara in the southern stretches of the Kingdom of Naples. Considering collaborations across the Italian states, this chapter will show that, paradoxically, Jesuit autonomy – not subservience – was key to the success of the Society's joint ventures with the inquisition. Despite the fact that the Jesuits were acting as inquisitor-missionaries and papal spies, by appearing to work as a distinct, independent force they were able to distance themselves from the Holy Office and convert and reconcile heretics in places where inquisitors and inquisitorial commissaries faced popular hostility and resistance from local leaders. Building on the conclusions of chapter 1, the case studies in chapter 2 underline the significance of individual relationships for the use of the privilege and emphasise the importance of studying the varied motives of individuals who supported the anti-heretical work of the Jesuits. Overall, chapter 2 will show that, in the emergency of the post-Reformation period, even the most zealous cardinal-inquisitors were pragmatic enough to compromise judicial processes to fight heresy effectively, and that the Jesuits had a similarly practical approach towards their patrons at the Roman Inquisition.

Chapter 3 will trace the history of the privilege and the Society during the pontificate of the inquisitor-pope Pius V (1566–72), a period of subtle yet profound transformation for the Jesuits' role in the fight against heresy. During this pontificate, the pope's view on the privilege diverged increasingly from that of the Jesuits. By studying this growing gulf in approach we see that Rome had only been willing to compromise its own jurisdiction over heresy to tackle the immediate crisis of the Reformation and did not believe that heretics should have a permanent extra-judicial route to reconcile with the Catholic Church. As religious dissent waned and the efficiency of the inquisition increased, Pius V marginalised the Jesuits in the fight against heresy and left the status of their privilege in serious doubt. Until now, Pius's exact position on the privilege has been difficult to discern as he did not explicitly revoke or negate the power, but rather failed to confirm its re-concession. This chapter will establish Pius V's stance by reconstructing what appear to be the only two recorded occasions on which he permitted Jesuits to absolve heretics. The cases are exceptions that prove the rule, showing that Pius was only willing to compromise judicial approaches to religious dissent when it suited his needs: in Savoy-Piedmont

INTRODUCTION 33

where the inquisition faced continued political resistance from Duke Emanuele Filiberto and in the Papal States, where popular fear inhibited the work of explicitly papal agents. Remarkably, we shall see that, despite Pius v's resistance, the Jesuits continued to solicit the privilege to absolve heresy. Their persistence in this matter underlines the fact that when it came to matters of religious disobedience there was a fundamental contrast between the beliefs and actions of the papacy and those of the Society. In doing so, the conclusions of this chapter challenge the centuries-old image of Jesuits fighting heresy in lock-step with Rome.

Chapter 4 will use the history of the privilege during the pontificate of Sixtus v (1585–90) to illuminate how the pastoral and institutional mission of the Society was shaped by influences both within and without the order on a global scale. Taking us from the papal court in Rome to the royal courts of France and Spain, this chapter will illustrate how international politics and the priorities of the pope influenced the fate of the privilege and the Society's role in the fight against heresy more broadly. We shall see that princes, churchmen and even Jesuits had grievances regarding the Society's independence. When these grievances merged with the pope's own concerns he sacrificed the pastoral benefits of the Jesuits' work to reconcile heretics so that he could preserve and strengthen his own authority.

The chapter will also illustrate how the Jesuits' priorities contrasted with those of Rome, analysing previously unpublished defenses of the privilege that Jesuits sent to the pope and the Roman Inquisition during this turbulent period. These remarkable and rich appeals offer detailed descriptions of the privilege, its use and its impact from the Jesuits' point of view. Examining these defenses in detail, the chapter will reveal that, unlike the pope and the powerful princes of Europe, the Jesuits saw the privilege as an ongoing necessity to overcome the failures of bishops and inquisitors, and the fears of penitent-heretics. Ultimately, the Jesuits' protestations did not satisfy Sixtus v, who was keen to centralise authority in the Church. In 1587 he categorically revoked the privilege. Overall, chapter 4 will demonstrate that the Jesuits lost their singular role in the fight against religious dissent because the Church began to prioritise institutional aims over the pastoral benefits of the Jesuits' help. This shift represents a radical change in priorities from the mid to the late sixteenth century. Sixtus v's decision revoke the privilege directly inverted the dynamic that had led its concession in 1551 when Julius III had compromised the Church's judicial systems to prioritise his pastoral mission to bring penitent heretics back into the Catholic fold.

The final chapter of the book will trace the after-life of the privilege in the pontificates of Sixtus v and his successor Clement viii (1592–1605). During this period the Jesuits were finally transformed into agents of the pope, but even then they fought back against Roman control. The chapter will show that popes continued to value the extra-judicial reconciliation of heretics, but only in extremely limited circumstances that suited their particular aims and when they could decide who was to be absolved. Considering amnesties for foreigners and Antonio Possevino's conversion of the family of the French ambassador to Venice, the chapter will show that popes considered both pastoral and political benefits when deciding to grant jurisdiction to the Jesuits. The chapter will also illustrate that merciful approaches towards foreign heretics that are usually attributed to the early to mid-seventeenth century had much earlier precedents in the Jesuits' ministry. Fundamentally, the case studies in this chapter underline the circumstantial nature of the popes' willingness to compromise judicial methods of reconciling heretics during the sixteenth century. In the immediate aftermath of the Reformation popes had granted the Jesuits a broad jurisdiction but as the threat of spreading Protestantism diminished they only conceded such powers on a case-by-case basis.

Forced to seek the approval of the papacy and inquisition for every single reconciliation that they wanted to conduct, by the turn of the century the Jesuits were effectively agents of the pope. Although the Society had little choice but to accept this new state of affairs, many Jesuits continued to absolve heretics independently, repeatedly violating the revocation of their privilege. By showing how papal control of the Jesuits' anti-heretical activity came only after the Reformation crisis had passed, the chapter has significant implications for the established chronology of the Counter-Reformation, showing that centralised, organised and tightly controlled means of fighting heresy developed only in the very late sixteenth century. Far from emerging as agents of Rome on their arrival in Italy, the Jesuits were only forced into this role at the turn of the seventeenth century, and then with considerable reluctance.

Tracing the history of the privilege from the 1540s to the early seventeenth century, this book will consider the factors and events that changed the priorities of the Society, Roman Inquisition and papacy, shaping their roles and relationships during a transformative period for the Catholic Church. Specifically, it will offer an account of the Jesuits' ministerial and institutional development, as the early Society negotiated its pastoral aims with the often conflicting demands of the institutional structure that facilitated its ministry. More broadly, it will offer a study of the grave and complex conflict that faced the Catholic Church and Catholic organisations, like the Society of Jesus, in sixteenth-century Italy: the need to survive as both a body of believers and an ecclesiastical and political organisation.

CHAPTER 1

The Confident Society: Mission Building 1540–1555

'He is a member of a Society founded chiefly for this purpose: to strive especially for the defence and propagation of the faith'.[1] – *Formula of the Institute*, 1550

In 1550, the Society of Jesus made a striking change to its *Formula of the Institute*, the statement that defined its rule and mission. For the first time ever, the 'defence of the faith' became the Society's principal purpose. In the first decade of the the Jesuits' apostolate, their pastoral ministry had emerged as an effective means of addressing one of the fundamental aims of the sixteenth-century Church: defending Catholic orthodoxy.[2] By the end of that decade, this aim was enshrined in the Jesuit mission.

In May 1551, the Jesuits would be empowered for this mission within an eye-wateringly generous gift from Pope Julius III.[3] Calling on the pope after dinner, Jesuit father Alfonso Salmerón knelt at the pontiff's feet and asked him to grant Jesuit confessors the power to absolve heretics anywhere in the world.[4] Julius consented immediately. In so doing, he gave a religious order that was just ten years old a power that put them on par with inquisitors and bishops across the Italian peninsula.[5]

Current explanations of the privilege to absolve heresy focus on the relationships and power dynamics between the Jesuits, Julius III and the Roman Inquisition.[6] Such explanations tell part us of the privilege's history but fail

---

1   Antonio M. de. Aldama, *The Constitutions of the Society of Jesus: the formula of the Institute* (Rome: Centrum Ignatianum Spiritualitatis, 1990), p.3.

2   For various arguments on the chronology of the Counter-Reformation see Firpo, *La presa di potere* and Gleason, 'Who was the First Counter-Reformation Pope?', *Catholic Historical Review*, 81 (1995), pp.179–184. On the correlation of the mission of the Jesuits and the Church seee McCoog, *The Society of Jesus in Ireland, Scotland, and England, 1589–1597: Building the Kingdom of Saint Peter upon the King of Spain's Monarchy* (London: Routledge, 2016), pp.1–3; Mostaccio, 'A Conscious Ambiguity', pp.418–9; O'Malley, 'Introduction' in O'Malley, Bailey, Harris and Kennedy (eds), *The Jesuits II: Cultures, Sciences, and the Arts, 1540–1773*, pp.xxiii-xxvii; Ulderico Parente, 'Note sull'attività missionaria di Nicolás Bobadilla nel mezzogiorno d'Italia prima del Concilio di Trento (1540–1541)', *Rivista Storica Italiana*, 117 (2005), pp.64–79.

3   For the papal bull see A. Tomassetti (ed.), *Bullarum diplomatum et privilegiorum*, vol. 6, pp.422–6.

4   For an account of the meeting see ARSI, *Institutum 222*, f.297.

5   Ibid.

6   Firpo, *La presa di potere*, pp.65–6 and Prosperi, *Tribunali della coscienza*, pp.xv-xvii, 236–7 and pp.496–7.

© KONINKLIJKE BRILL NV, LEIDEN, 2020 | DOI:10.1163/9789004413832_003

to explain the motivations and actions of the Jesuits who solicited the power. Moreover, they do not explain the impact of the privilege when the Jesuits used it to work entirely autonomously or under the orders of powerful secular leaders in Italy.

This chapter will propose an alternative interpretation of the privilege, which addresses the Jesuits' own motivations for soliciting the power and the benefits of using the privilege in the service of secular princes as well as the pope. In this chapter we shall see that the power was solicited by the Jesuits and conceded by Julius III for pragmatic rather than political reasons. Using the privilege to absolve heresy, the Jesuits could win over and reconcile heretics whom they converted but who could or would not approach a bishop or inquisitor because ecclesiastical authorities were absent in their region or simply because they were too afraid to confess to them. Through case studies of the Society's role at the Councils of Trent and Bologna and their mission to Corsica, we shall see that the experiences of the early Jesuits and of Julius III were key to their shared belief in the practical necessity of the privilege. Jesuits soliciting the privilege based their arguments on their personal experience of frightened or neglected penitent-heretics in the mission field. Julius III personally knew of the benefits of private absolutions from his time as a cardinal when he had organised similar temporary powers of absolution to allow Jesuits to reconcile penitents who were too terrified to approach the Holy Office. Presenting the exact context of the privilege's solicitation, concession and earliest use, this chapter will demonstrate that it was the pastoral pragmatism of the Society, Julius III and their mutual allies, that motivated the solicitation, concession and use of the privilege to absolve heresy, not politics or cynical manipulation.

Moreover, the ability to work outside of the normal ecclesiastical hierarchy had political and institutional advantages for the Jesuits, not just pastoral benefits. As their authority was granted by the pope rather than delegated by the local bishop, the Jesuits could work independently or collaborate with secular and ecclesiastical authorities of their choice. This included the very cardinal-inquisitors whom Firpo claims that Julius III sought to undermine, as well as Italian and foreign princes. The Jesuits' freedom to serve any patron or to work alone facilitated what Silvia Mostaccio has termed the 'conscious ambiguity' of the early Society, allowing the Jesuits to respond deftly to calls to obedience from their Superior General, the pope and local temporal and ecclesiastical leaders – even when these calls conflicted. With this political agility, the Jesuits ensured that the alliances that they made through their pastoral service to Church and state were advantageous for both their pastoral ministry and their broad institutional ambitions. If we consider the benefits of the privilege for

THE CONFIDENT SOCIETY: MISSION BUILDING 1540–1555   37

the Jesuits who solicited it, the pope who conceded it and the ecclesiastical and temporal authorities who benefitted from it, we see that the power was a mechanism for radical pastoral and institutional flexibility; a vital tool for a new religious order carving out its role on the peninsula and for ecclesiastical and temporal authorities facing an unprecedented religious crisis.

1   Finding Supporters in Tridentine Italy

The Jesuits' long-standing personal relationships with Julius III and his circle are key to understanding how and why the Society secured the privilege to absolve heresy. These were relationships of mutual benefit. The early Jesuits' ministry served the most fundamental needs of a Church blighted by poorly-trained, negligent clergy and threatened by religious dissent spreading from the Protestant north. In return for the Jesuits' help, powerful ecclesiastical authorities protected and promoted the nascent Society and gave it the powers it needed to fulfil its mission to save souls. And it was not only religious leaders who established mutually beneficial relationships with the Jesuits but also temporal powers. When it came to the battle against religious rebellion, they too had a dog in the fight. For many Italian princes, as well as the Jesuits and the Church at large, the true danger of religious heterodoxy and inobservance lay not in doctrinal error but in the rebellion of those who defied the authority of the pope or their Christian ruler.[7] The sin of heresy could, therefore, also be considered a treacherous crime, in Catholic states both *laesae maiestatis* and *laesae maiestatis divinae*.[8] The Jesuits' pastoral ministry provided a sound orthodox formation to future generations as well as converted heretics and unruly Catholics who threatened the religious, social and political order.[9] Fundamentally, the privilege to absolve heresy made this ministry more effective and so earnt them powerful allies both within and without the Church.

From the time of their arrival on the Italian peninsula in the late 1530s the Jesuits used strategic alliances to establish and advance their Society. These were

---

7 Höpfl, *Jesuit Political Thought*, p.65.
8 Girolamo Giganti, *Tractatus de crimine laesae maiestatis insignis* (Lyon: Jacopo Giunta, 1552), p.445 and Prosperi, *Misericordie: conversioni sotto il patibolo tra Medioevo ed età moderna* (Pisa: Edizioni della Normale, 2006), p.36.
9 Sabina Pavone, 'I gesuiti in Italia (1548–1773)' in G. Pedullà, S. Luzzatto, E. Irace (eds), *Atlante della letteratura italiana. Dalla Controriforma alla Restaurazione. Volume 2: Dalla controriforma alla ristaurazione* (Turin: Einaudi, 2011), p.371 and Prosperi, *La vocazione. Storie di gesuiti tra Cinquecento e Seicento* (Turin: Einaudi, 2016), pp.82–5.

always relationships of mutual benefit. Cardinal Gasparo Contarini admired the Jesuits' spirituality and may even have undergone their main spiritual programme, the *Spiritual Exercises*, guided by Loyola.[10] Contarini also happened to be one of Pope Paul III's closest advisors. After his experience with the Society, Contarini gladly petitioned the pope to accept the Jesuits' loose religious rule.[11] The Jesuits also won over potent Italian princes by serving as teachers, preachers and confessors to their subjects. In return, patrons like Duke Ercole d'Este of Ferrara recommended the early Society at the papal court.[12] The arrangement could also work in reverse, when powerful churchmen lauded the Jesuits to their princely relatives. Cardinal Juan Alvarez de Toledo, for example, commended the Society to his niece, Elenore, Duchess of Florence, who then helped the Jesuits to establish colleges in Tuscany.[13] In the first decade of their ministry, the Jesuits won supporters across the most important dynastic and ecclesiastical networks in Italy and asked for their help to secure the position and privileges that they needed to advance their order and its work.

Early in 1550 one of their supporters became very powerful indeed. For, on the 7 February 1550, Cardinal Giovanni Maria Ciocchi Del Monte became Pope Julius III. There is little evidence that the Jesuits were especially delighted at his unanticipated elevation.[14] But the events following Del Monte's election suggest that the Society's leaders were confident that they could rely on his support. This confidence was inspired by close collaboration with Del Monte throughout the late 1540s. And, as the concession of the privilege to absolve heresy in May 1551 proves, it was a confidence that was soon richly rewarded.

When Del Monte became pope he had already worked in close quarters with Jesuits for years, as papal legate and president of the first session of the Council of Trent (1545–7). At the council's inception Pope Paul III had employed two of the Society's founding members, Diego Laínez and Alfonso Salmerón, as his personal theologians.[15] Del Monte may have also known the French Jesuit Claude Le Jay and the Dutchman Peter Canisius. Both were employed at the

---

10 Gleason, *Gasparo Contarini: Venice, Rome and Reform* (Berkeley: University of California Press, 1993), p.273, fn.62.

11 Ibid., pp.92 and 141.

12 See, for example, Ercole d'Este in *Bobadillae Monumenta*, pp.6–7.

13 Loyola, *Sancti Ignatii de Loyola Societatis Jesu fundatoris epistolae et instructiones*, vol.3, pp.718–9.

14 The *Monumenta* record that Loyola sent letters to various Jesuits about Julius's elevation but nothing that compared to his exuberant response to the accession of Marcellus II. See Loyola, *Sancti Ignatii de Loyola Societatis Jesu fundatoris epistolae et instructiones*, vol.9, pp.13–7.

15 O'Malley, *Trent. What Happened at the Council*, p.118.

THE CONFIDENT SOCIETY: MISSION BUILDING 1540–1555   39

council by Cardinal Otto Truchsess von Walburg, the Prince Bishop of Augsburg who had charged the Jesuits to thwart Lutheranism in his diocese by running a seminary and university.[16] Though Del Monte retired from his position as president in 1547 he continued to play a decisive role in the conciliar debates that the Jesuits attended.[17] Both before and after his retirement, the Council offered the future Julius III the opportunity to interact with some of the most erudite and active early Jesuits.

The future pope would have seen the Society put its best foot forward. At Trent, Laínez and Salmerón cultivated an impression of perfect orthodoxy and obedience. As papal theologians, they were expected to utter the first words on the controversial points of theology and ecclesiology up for discussion.[18] Loyola was sensitive to the importance and prominence of this role. In 1546, he instructed Laínez and Salmerón to steer a safe, moderate course in contentious debates, avoiding polemic, considering both sides of each argument and deferring to wiser, more experienced delegates when necessary.[19] If Loyola saw the council as a means of building a good reputation for the Society, as has been suggested, he wished to cultivate an image of trustworthy and wise servants, undertaking serious tasks in a discerning manner and working as mediators rather than agents eager to deliver specific reforms.[20]

According to the Jesuits, their efforts paid off. Members of the Society claimed that their conduct at the council had kindled Julius III's desire to grant them papal privileges. In a letter to Laínez, Polanco, Loyola's secretary, described the meeting during which Salmerón solicited Julius III for the privilege to absolve heresy, claiming that the pope had a 'very high opinion' of Laínez and Salmerón that was 'not informed by others, but by his own experience'.[21] Trent was central to this experience. There the pope had seen the Jesuits seek 'the service' of God and 'the help of souls' 'without [personal] interest or ambition'.[22] Polanco's claims were borne out by Julius III's actions. Like his

---

16   Allyson Creasman, *Censorship and Civic Order in Reformation Germany, 1517–1648* (Farnham: Ashgate, 2012), p.125 and O'Malley, *The First Jesuits*, p. 324. See also, Jedin and Graf (trans.), *A History of the Council of Trent*, vol.1, p.529, fn.2. and vol. 2, p.20.

17   O'Malley, *The First Jesuits*, pp.87–8.

18   Pavone, 'Preti riformati e riforma della Chiesa: i gesuiti al Concilio di Trento', *Rivista Storica Italiana*, 117 (2005), p.118.

19   Loyola, *Sancti Ignatii de Loyola Societatis Jesu fundatoris epistolae et instructiones*, vol.1, p.386.

20   Pavone, *I gesuiti*, pp.22–3.
        Pavone, 'Preti riformati e riforma della Chiesa', p.115. O'Malley, *The First Jesuits*, p.324–5.

21   Polanco in Loyola, *Sancti Ignatii de Loyola Societatis Jesu fundatoris epistolae et instructiones*, vol.3, p.457.

22   Ibid.

predecessor, Julius sent Salmerón and Laínez to the council as his representatives on the understanding that they would to respond to the leaders of the
Lutherans who were supposed to be on their way.[23] Polanco's emphasis on Julius's trust in the Jesuits' ability to address religious rebels is significant. With
major churchmen suspected of heresy and lively memories of Loyola's own
brushes with the inquisitors, confidence in the Jesuits' religious orthodoxy was
not to be taken for granted.[24] According to Polanco, Julius III's experience of
the Jesuits at Trent had won his confidence and it was for this reason that he,
'very graciously', conceded them the power to absolve heresy.[25]

The details included in Polanco's account are significant. His letter was
much more than a personal communication to Laínez. Although the text was
written on behalf of the Superior General in the format of a missive, the document reads more like a memorial than an informative letter. Such records were
crucial. Until the privilege was ratified by papal bull in October 1552, it was
conceded only *viva vocis oraculo*, face-to-face, and thus had limited legitimacy.
In order to have validity, the privileges conceded and the details of the concession had to be written down.[26] Polanco's account was, therefore, a record not
only of the Jesuits' worthiness to receive the privilege but also of the legitimacy
of the concession itself.

The Jesuits' claim that they won the privilege because of their personal experiences with Julius III corresponds with what we know of the early Society's modus operandi. For the Jesuits had often used individual relationships
to advance their young religious order. The Jesuits' relationship with Julius
III gave them the reputation, status and opportunity to solicit the privilege
to absolve heresy. The notion that Julius empowered the Jesuits because of a
personal trust supports Firpo's suggestion that the pope gave the Society the
privilege in order to make them a loyal papal task force that could counter-
balance an overly dominant Roman Inquisition. However, it was not only
trust that spurred Julius to facilitate the Jesuits' anti-heretical activities. And it
was not only Julius who sought to facilitate the Jesuits' private absolutions of

---

23   Polanco in Loyola, *Sancti Ignatii de Loyola Societatis Jesu fundatoris epistolae et instructiones*, vol.3, p.457.

24   Black, *The Italian Inquisition*, pp.22–3 and Mostaccio, 'A Conscious Ambiguity', p.415. See
also Mongini, <<*Ad Christi similtudinem*>>.

25   Polanco in Loyola, *Sancti Ignatii de Loyola Societatis Jesu fundatoris epistolae et instructiones*, vol.3, p.458.

26   Anacleto Reiffenstuel, *Jus canonicum universum, clara methodo juxta titulos quinque
librorum decretalium. In quaestiones distributum, solidisque responsionibus, and objectionum solutionibus dilucidatum* (Antwerp: Sumptibus Societatis, 1755), vol. 4, p.355. See also
pp.356–7.

THE CONFIDENT SOCIETY: MISSION BUILDING 1540–1555   41

heretics. When a series of events moved the Council south to Bologna in 1547, both the future Julius III and others – including cardinal-inquisitors – gained first-hand experience of the Society's ability to convert heretics one-on-one. The figures who surrounded the Jesuits at this crucial time for the Society and for the Church would come to play a vital role in the Jesuits' work to reconcile religious dissenters, both before and after the concession of the privilege. Their involvement shows us that, whilst the Jesuits' relationship with pope is an essential part of the history of their anti-heretical activities, we must look well beyond the pontiff to understand the significance and impact of the Society's role in the religious crisis of the sixteenth century.

2   The Council of Bologna, 1547

When the sudden death of the twenty-six-year-old bishop of Carpaccio sparked fears of plague at Trent, cardinal-president Giovanni Del Monte called for the immediate transfer of the council.[27] In spite of major objections from the Emperor Charles V, in March 1547 the council moved 228 kilometres south to Bologna, a city in the heart of the Papal States.[28] The move had profound consequences for the relationship between the Jesuits and the future Julius III. For it was in Bologna that the they would first collaborate to reconcile heretics extra-judicially. Del Monte had been governor of Bologna for two years before becoming a cardinal in 1536, so would have known that suspicions of heresy in the city were rife.[29] What is more, he would have known that its inquisition was disfunctional and often failed to pursue heretics in the city.[30] In Bologna, Laínez and Salmerón could follow Loyola's advice to avoid contention at the Council. But they would be hard pushed to escape religious controversy on the streets. There the Jesuits would collaborate with Del Monte and other men such as Ambrogio Catarino Politi, tackling the city's religious rebels without involving the local inquisitors.

It seems that Loyola wanted Laínez and Salmerón to exploit every opportunity to convert the errant in Bologna. Elaborating his instructions on conduct at the council, Loyola told the two fathers that, whenever they were

---

27   O'Malley, *Trent. What happened at the Council*, p.122.
28   Ibid., pp.127–8 and *Jedin, A History of the Council of Trent*, vol. 2, p.313.
29   Umberto Mazzone, *Governare lo Stato e curare le anime: la Chiesa e Bologna dal Quattrocento alla Rivoluzione francese* (Limena: Libreria Universitaria, 2012), p.58. On heresy in Bologna see dall'Olio, *Eretici e inquisitori nella Bologna del Cinquecento*, pp.51–158.
30   Romeo, 'Note sull'Inquisizione Romana', p.129.

unoccupied with conciliar work, they should pursue the pastoral activities central to their ministry as Jesuits: 'to preach, hear confessions and read, teaching youth, giving [good] example, visiting the poor in hospitals, and encouraging neighbours' 'for the greater glory of God'.[31] Obediently, Salmerón kept the Society's future and ministry at the front of his mind. Writing to Loyola in December 1547, Salmerón explained that he had been looking around the city for a good location for a Jesuit college.[32] Salmerón was also pursuing the Jesuits' key mission to help souls and claimed to have found many confessants and people who wanted to go through Loyola's *Exercises*.[33] Through both institutional planning and pastoral ministry, Salmerón was promoting Catholic orthodoxy in the city of Bologna.

What is more, Salmerón told Loyola that he had converted some 'who were in heresy or had read Lutheran books', whom he had then absolved and reconciled to the Church.[34] This was a significant admission. In Bologna in 1547 – four years before receiving the papal privilege to do so – Salmerón was already absolving and reconciling heretics in the secrecy of sacramental confession and without involving the local inquisitors who had jurisdiction over the misdemeanour.

Moreover, Salmerón was not alone in his actions. Another Jesuit in Bologna, Paschase Broët, wrote to Rome to reveal that he had also absolved heretics in the city. Broët had come to Bologna from the nearby city of Faenza, where temporal authorities had requested help to improve morality in the diocese.[35] But once in Bologna Broët had angered local leaders. His letter, which appears to be for Loyola's attention, explained that the vice-inquisitor of the Bolognese monastery of San Domenico was irate that both he and Salmerón had absolved heretics in the city.[36] In his letter, Broët justified his actions, stating that the eight or ten Lutherans who had come to him to confess themselves were truly converted.[37] Crucially, the heretics had not already been tried, 'not by the ordinary, nor by the inquisitor', which would have meant that only the bishop or inquisitor could have absolved them.[38] Despite the fact that the Lutherans converted by Broët and Salmerón were unknown first-time offenders,

---

31   Loyola, *Sancti Ignatii de Loyola Societatis Jesu fundatoris epistolae et instructiones*, vol.1, pp.387–8.
32   Salmerón, *Epistolae P. Alphonsi Salmeronis*, vol.1, p.63.
33   Ibid.
34   Ibid.
35   Polanco, *Vita Ignatii Loiolae et rerum Societatis Jesu historia*, vol.1, pp.176–7 and p.217.
36   Broët, *Epistolae PP. Paschasii Broëti*, pp.43–4.
37   Ibid.
38   Ibid.

THE CONFIDENT SOCIETY: MISSION BUILDING 1540–1555

the inquisitor of San Domenico was furious with the Jesuits for dealing with a matter that he saw as strictly inquisitorial. As a result, the bishop 'had made a complaint about it with the episcopal vicar of Bologna', saying that Broët 'wanted to make a new tribunal' in the city.[39]

Broët's letter raises a serious question: if the Jesuits had not yet received the papal privilege to absolve heresy, who had given them the authority to absolve heretics autonomously in Bologna? Broët's letter suggests that prominent conciliar delegates were involved. Broët states that he went to the episcopal vicar to answer the vice-inquisitor's allegations and to explain that the absolutions were legitimate. According to Broët, the Jesuits had been given the authority to absolve heretics who wished to convert to the obedience of the Holy Church by the Most Reverend Monsignor Santa Croce, otherwise known as Cardinal Marcello Cervini: a cardinal-inquisitor, the future Pope Marcellus II, and Del Monte's right-hand-man at the Council.[40]

Bröet was confident of the support of Santa Croce and the rest of Del Monte's circle; he remained adamant of the legitimacy of his actions. Indeed, when Broët promised the episcopal vicar that the Jesuits would not absolve any more Lutherans in Bologna his reason was not a lack of authority. On the contrary, Broët reiterated that he and Salmerón had been given 'delegated apostolic authority' to absolve heretics 'for the salvation of the souls of these poor creatures'.[41] Even so, Broët suggested that 'for the future' they 'would not absolve similar Lutherans anymore' as he saw 'that [the inquisitors] were not happy about it' and the Jesuits wanted 'to have peace with everybody'.[42] To prove the validity of the Jesuits' actions in the city, Broët enclosed with his letter to Rome a copy of Cardinal Santa Croce's brief granting the fathers the authority to absolve heresy in Bologna.[43] In future conflicts, other Jesuits would act similarly. When their privilege to absolve heresy irked local authorities they asserted its validity even if they relinquished its use for the sake of good relations and institutional stability.[44]

The future Julius III and his friends were also key for the Jesuits' work with heretics elsewhere. The name of Ambrogio Catarino Politi recurs both in

---

39   Ibid.

40   Broët, *Epistolae PP. Paschasii Broëti*, pp.43–4.

41   Ibid.

42   Ibid.

43   No brief is edited with the letter.

44   See, for example, Polanco's exchange with Bishop Egidio Foscarari of Modena: Polanco in Loyola, *Sancti Ignatii de Loyola Societatis Jesu fundatoris epistolae et instructiones*, vol. 5, p. 702. This is discussed in Al Kalak, *Il riformatore dimenticato*, p.160, as are Foscarari's own powers on p.104.

accounts of the Jesuits' anti-heretical activities in Bologna and in records of the concession of the privilege in 1551. Politi had first encountered the Jesuits when their order was in its earliest state in Paris. In 1538 he defended Loyola when he was challenged by the inquisition, testifying of the Jesuits' orthodoxy and zeal against all heretics, whether from old or recent sects.[45] In Bologna, he would facilitate the Society's absolution of religious rebels who had changed their ways. A Dominican theologian, polemicist and canon lawyer, Politi was present at the Council of Bologna in his capacity as bishop of Minori.[46] When Politi's old acquaintance, Giovanni Battista Scotti, arrived in the city seeking forgiveness from the Catholic Church, Politi led Scotti to Cardinal Santa Croce and, eventually, to a private reconciliation with Salmerón.[47] Scotti was a re-lapsed heretic and so, according to Canon Law, he should have been execut-ed.[48] Nonetheless, as Scotti stated at a later inquisitorial trial, 'with Cardinals Del Monte and Santa Croce mediating' and with 'the authority that they had in that [matter] through an apostolic brief from Paul III', he was reconciled in Bologna through 'the absolution and the making of an abjuration to Reverend Father Alfonso Salmerón of the Society of Jesus'.[49] Like the Lutherans absolved by Salmerón and Broët, Scotti was reconciled extra-judicially by a Jesuit em-powered by prominent prelates and without involving the local inquisitors.

All of the heretics absolved extra-judicially in Bologna shared one charac-teristic: fear of the Roman Inquisition. In his letter to Loyola, Salmerón had claimed that the heretics whom he had reconciled came to him because they knew 'how some suspected of heresy are punished in Rome'.[50] Scotti had the same apprehension. On his arrival in Bologna, he carried a letter of recommen-dation from Giovanni della Casa, papal nuncio to Venice with a special charge to represent the Holy Office in that state.[51] The letter said that Scotti had come

---

45 Archivio di Stato di Roma (hereafter, ASR), *Tribunale del Governatore, Investigazioni dal 5 luglio 1538 al 1°gennaio 1539*, busta-registro 12, f.161v. Edited in Marcello del Piazzo and Càndido de Dalmases, 'Il processo sull'ortodossia di S.Ignazio e dei suoi compagni svoltosi a Roma nel 1538. Nuovi documenti', *Archivum Historicum Societatis Iesu*, 89 (1966), p.443.

46 On Politi see Giorgio Caravale, *Sulle tracce dell'eresia. Ambrogio Catarino Politi (1484–1553)* (Florence: Olshki, 2007). On Politi's polemic and scholarly work see also Emily Michelson, *The Pulpit and the Press in Reformation Italy* (London: Harvard University Press, 2013), p.114.

47 Firpo and Marcatto (eds), *Il processo inquisitoriale del Cardinale Giovanni Morone*, vol. 6, p.145.

48 Wickersham, *Rituals of Prosecution*, p.239.

49 Firpo and Marcatto (eds), *Il processo inquisitoriale del Cardinale Giovanni Morone*, vol.2, part 1, p.366.

50 Salmerón, *Epistolae P. Alphonsi Salmeronis*, vol.1, p.63.

51 Martin, *Venice's Hidden Enemies*, p.53.

THE CONFIDENT SOCIETY: MISSION BUILDING 1540–1555

to Bologna rather than Rome for fair treatment 'because his troubles began with the Most Reverend Inquisitors in Rome' and they were not 'well informed of his good works'.[52] It was for this reason that Politi had advised Scotti to go to the cardinals in Bologna, who then referred him to Salmerón.[53] In the cases of the anonymous Lutheran converts and Scotti, a notorious heretic, Cardinals Santa Croce and Del Monte and Archbishop Politi thought that fear of the inquisition was sufficient reason to grant Salmerón the power to absolve and reconcile heretics.

These tales from Bologna demonstrate that the Jesuits were granted faculties to absolve heresy during the first decade of their ministry, before the concession of the papal privilege in 1551. Other records confirm that such faculties were not limited to the city of Bologna. In 1541, just a year after the Society was officially established, Paul III had given Broët and Salmerón the power to absolve heretics, schismatics, and other excommunicates during a mission to Ireland.[54] The same pope conceded similar faculties for use on the Jesuits' missions to non-Christian territories.[55] Later in 1550, papal nuncio Luigi Lippomano – who had also worked alongside the Jesuits at Trent and Bologna – granted the Society the faculty to absolve heretics in the German lands.[56] The privilege of 1551, saw these earlier, individual concessions transformed into a permanent papal privilege, granting the Society the power to absolve heresy without geographical or temporal restriction and giving the Jesuits an autonomous jurisdiction over the sin of heresy and the automatic censures that it incurred.[57]

That said, there were important differences between the ecclesiastical situations in Bologna and Ireland. Broët and Salmerón had been sent to Ireland to reconcile the chieftains of the country and organise resistance against the English king, Henry VIII.[58] Like the non-Christian territories of the New World

---

52 Biblioteca Apostolica Vaticana (hereafter, BAV), *Vat. lat. 14830*, f.20v. Edited in Firpo and Marcatto, *Il processo inquisitoriale del Cardinal Giovanni Morone*, vol.2, part 1, p.366, fn.62.

53 Caravale, *Sulle tracce dell'eresia*, p.248 and Firpo and Marcatto, *Il processo inquisitoriale del Cardinale Giovanni Morone*, vol.1, p.291.

54 The brief granting the faculties for the mission to Ireland is held in ARSI, *Institutum 194*, ff.21r-23v.

55 For the concession of the privilege to absolve heresy in *pars infidelium*, see Francesco Suarez, *Opera Omnia*, p.991.

56 A summary of and patent for the graces that Lippomano conceded to Salmerón, Jay and Canisius in 1550 is held in ARSI, *Institutum 194*, f.69r. On Lippomano see Michelson, 'Luigi Lippomano, His Vicars, and the Reform of Verona from the Pulpit', *Church History*, 78 (September 2009), p.584–605.

57 Caravale, *Sulle tracce dell'eresia*, p.281.

58 McCoog, *The Society of Jesus in Ireland, Scotland, and England 1541–1588. 'Our Way of Proceeding?'* (Leiden: E.J. Brill, 1996), pp.21–2.

46 CHAPTER 1

and the German lands, there was no inquisition in Ireland and, theoretically, the bishops answered to the English king, who had been excommunicated.[59] In other words, this was mission territory. When the Jesuits reconciled penitent dissenters in countries like Ireland they filled a gap in the existing ecclesiastical infrastructure without undermining other authorities with jurisdiction over heresy. Bologna, on the other hand, had both a resident bishop and a long-established inquisition. Salmerón himself stated that heretics came to him for a private absolution precisely to avoid the inquisitors. In Bologna, the cardinal-legates, two of them future popes, empowered the Jesuits in a way that clashed with the jurisdiction of long-established and legitimate ecclesiastical authorities. What is more, the Jesuits do not seem to have been afraid of admitting this clear conflict of interest.

The Bologna cases show that Julius III, Santa Croce and Archbishop Politi believed that institutional norms could be undermined if it meant that they would win converts. Politi's involvement in the solicitation of the privilege to absolve heresy from Julius III in 1551 suggests that, like the faculties in Bologna, the privilege to absolve heresy was a pragmatic compromise. In addition to Polanco's letter to Laínez, two manuscript descriptions of Salmerón's meeting with Julius III are now held at ARSI in larger collections of documents on privileges granted to the Society.[60] Both documents note Politi's presence at the meeting.[61] The details of the account, written by Salmerón, are identical in both documents, matching those given in Polanco's letter. A third record held at the ACDF replicates the details and appears to have been copied from one of the documents at the Jesuit archive.[62] This version was sent to the cardinal-inquisitors during debates on the validity of the privileges in the 1580s and also includes a section of the papal bull, *Sacrae religionis*, which gave the privilege its full validity.[63] The ACDF document also mentions that Politi attended the meeting, underlining his support for the concession and his witness to its legitimacy.[64]

The emphasis on the Jesuits' work at Trent in accounts of the concession and the noted presence of Politi, their ally in Bologna, underline the importance

---

59 W.T.G. Kirby, *Essays on Religion, Politics, and the Public Sphere in Early Modern England* (Leiden: Brill, 2011), p.72.

60 ARSI, *Institutum 190*, f.4r and ARSI, *Institutum 222*, f.297.

61 The account in *Institutum 190* appears to be a copy of the account in *Institutum 222* with the signatures of Salmeron and Politi transcribed.

62 ACDF, *Stanza Storica D-4-A*, ff. 12r-v.

63 A. Tomassetti (ed.), *Bullarum diplomatum et privilegiorum*, vol. 6, p.465.

64 Otto von Truchsess acted similarly, witnessing of the papal bull that granted the faculty officially on 22 October 1552. See ARSI, *Institutum 222*, f.263r.

THE CONFIDENT SOCIETY: MISSION BUILDING 1540–1555 47

of the Society's previous experience with Julius III and his circle for the concession of the privilege to absolve heresy. These details support Giorgio Caravale's suggestion that the official concession of the privilege in 1551 put into law actions that had become commonplace during Julius III's cardinalate.[65] But despite the importance of Julius III and his circle in the Jesuits' early use of such powers, the Jesuits also used the privilege outside of their collaborations with the pope and his friends. In fact, far from making them servants of the pope, the independent jurisdiction that the privilege afforded the Society allowed Jesuits to reconcile heretics autonomously in collaboration with a range of ecclesiastical and temporal authorities. The Jesuits' relationship with the pope may seem to have been one of great intimacy and loyalty, as suggested by Firpo's explanation of the privilege. Yet in practice this did not mean that they worked for the pope alone. Paradoxically, papal support and powers were vital for the Jesuits precisely because they allowed them to work independently in the mission field.

3 Beyond Papal Obedience

One of the key benefits of papal privileges was that they granted the Jesuits the autonomy to work outside of the usual ecclesiastical hierarchies.[66] This is evident in the early Jesuits' use of the privilege to absolve heresy in the service of temporal as well as ecclesiastical powers. This view of the privilege and its use concurs with recent research that has shattered the traditional image of a Society working in perfect alignment with Rome.[67] Reviewing recent shifts to scholarship on the Society, Silvia Mostaccio has identified a 'conscious ambiguity' in the approach of the early Jesuits as they adapted to the situations and stakes of the various contexts in which they worked.[68] The privilege to absolve heresy was a mechanism that granted the Jesuits the ability to be flexible, the autonomy to pursue their mission to save souls alone and to develop working relationships with a variety of authorities as and when it suited

65   Caravale, *Sulle tracce dell'eresia*, p.281.
66   Mongini, <<*Ad Christi similtudinem*>>, p.44.
67   See Mostaccio's historiographical review 'A Conscious Ambiguity' and the articles it discusses, especially Pierroberto Scaramella, 'I primi Gesuiti e l'Inquisizione Romana' and Pastore, 'I Primi Gesuiti e la Spagna: Strategie, compromessi, ambiguità', *Rivista Storica Italiana*, 117 (2005), pp.158–178. See also Mongini,<<*Ad Christi similtudinem*>> and Mostaccio, *Early modern Jesuits between obedience and conscience*.
68   Mostaccio, 'A Conscious Ambiguity', pp.440–1.

them. Interpretations of the Jesuits' privilege to absolve heresy that examine the power's impact on only one of the Society's collaborators, such as the pope or the Roman Inquisition, fall short because the most important gift afforded by the privilege was jurisdictional and operational independence.

There is some evidence to suggest that Julius III favoured the pastoral strategies that the Jesuits used to convert heretics. In his first year as pope, as he inaugurated a year of jubilee, Julius III granted extraordinary measures to penitent-heretics. Indeed, Julius was the first pope to promulgate edicts of grace to encourage heretics to come back to the fold.[69] The first, *Cum meditatio cordis nostri*, declared that all who owned heretical books could choose a confessor to absolve them and lift the automatic excommunication that their crime had incurred as long as they consigned the books to the inquisition within two months.[70] The second, *Illius qui misericors*, offered heretics a private absolution and abjuration if they denounced themselves to local inquisitors.[71] The commonalities between Julius III's edicts of grace and the private reconciliations facilitated by the Jesuits' privilege are clear. Like the Jesuit privilege, the jubilee edicts aimed to encourage those who 'delay returning to the flock of Christ' out of fear, 'abhorring public penance'.[72] Julius III's predilection for compromising, pastoral methods of reconciliation supports Firpo's conjecture that the Jesuits were empowered to further the pope's own agenda to fight heresy, undermining the harsh and sometimes political inquisitorial strategies of which he disapproved.[73] With the concession of the privilege to absolve heresy, the pope empowered able, itinerant Jesuits to undertake a pastoral approach to religious dissent that complemented his own.

The notion that Julius empowered the Jesuits to bolster his personal anti-heretical agenda is also supported by traditional explanations of the Society's obedience to the Holy See. The early Jesuits' first journey to Rome is the nucleus of traditional interpretations of the Jesuits' subservience to the pope, as Loyola and his earliest companions put themselves in the service of Pope Paul III.[74] The first Jesuits' promise to Paul III found its full expression in the

---

69   Brambilla, 'Giulio III' in Prosperi, Lavenia and Tedeschi (eds), *Dizionario storico dell'inquisizione*, vol.2, p.712.

70   Bartolomeo Fontana, *Documenti vaticani contro l'eresia Luterana in Italia* (Rome: Società Romana di storia patria, 1892), pp.412–4.

71   Tomassetti (ed.), *Bullarium diplomatum et privilegiorum*, vol. 6, pp.414–5.

72   Ibid., p.414.

73   Firpo, *La presa di potere*, p.66. Girolamo Muzzarelli said that the pope was 'continually irritated with the office of the Inquisition'. See Firpo and Marcatto, *Il processo inquisitoriale del Cardinal Giovanni Morone*, vol.2, part 2, p.804.

74   Fabre, 'The Writings of Ignaius of Loyola as a Seminal Text' in Maryks (ed.), *A Companion to Ignatius of Loyola*, p.111.

THE CONFIDENT SOCIETY: MISSION BUILDING 1540–1555   49

Society's vow to obey the pontiff regarding missions, which Loyola drafted into the Society's *Constitutions*.[75] When Loyola outlined his ideal of obedience for the Society he called for the total submission of judgment and will: obedience *perinde ac cadaver* or in the manner of a corpse.[76] According to Prosperi, the Jesuits made a vow of obedience to the papacy just as popes began to get involved in the organisation of missions, transforming their Society into 'the instrument of the papacy'.[77]

However, recent research on the Society has suggested that, in practice, papal obedience was not so clear cut. As soon as the Jesuits went out into the mission field, Loyola's ideal of obedience was compromised by a host of social, economic and political demands that dictated the success of the Society's missions.[78] Despite the ostensibly strict implications of the Society's vow to obey 'the supreme pontiff regarding missions', in reality, the principle of papal obedience was applied flexibly and often used by the Society as a shield or court of appeal rather than an uncompromising standard.[79] The Society's *Constitutions* even gave the Superior General parity with the pope when dictating where members should be sent on missions and whom should be sent.[80] In practice, the Jesuits' vow of obedience to the papacy was limited and applied flexibly, according to the Society's needs.

This flexible attitude to papal obedience is evident in the Jesuits' shrewd negotiations over the transfer of missionaries. When Nicolás Bobadilla left the service of Duke Ercole d'Este in July 1539, he shielded himself from charges of disloyalty by telling the duke that, although the Society wished to serve in his territories more than any other in the world, the will of the pope compelled him to leave.[81] Here, papal obedience allowed Bobadilla to avoid responsibility

---

75 O'Malley, 'Mission and the Early Jesuits', p.7.

76 Loyola's most widely-read letter on obedience is edited in *Sancti Ignatii de Loyola Societatis Jesu fundatoris epistolae et instructione*, vol.4, pp.669–681. See also 'Rules for Thinking with the Church', Loyola's supplement to the Spiritual Exercises, edited in Loyola, *Monumenta Ignatiana. Series secunda: Exercitia spiritualia Sancti Ignatii de Loyola et eorum directoria* (Rome: Institutum Historicum Societatis Iesu, 1955), pp.326–8.

77 Prosperi, *Tribunali della coscienza.*, pp.567–9.

78 Flavio Rurale in introduction to Mostaccio, *Early modern Jesuits between obedience and conscience*, p.xiii.

79 For the vow see the Society's bull of foundation, *Regimini militantis Ecclesiae* in Tomassetti (ed.), *Bullarum diplomatum et privilegiorum*, vol. 6, p.304.

80 *Constitutions (Part VII, Chapter 2, par. 618)* in George E. Ganss (trans.), *The Constitutions of the Society of Jesus* (St. Louis: The Institute of Jesuit Sources, 1970), p.271. See also O'Malley, *The Jesuits and the Popes: A Historical Sketch of Their Relationship* (Philadelphia: Saint Josephs University Press, 2016), pp.16–21.

81 Bobadilla, *Bobadillae monumenta*, p.16.

50   CHAPTER 1

for upsetting the duke. In 1550, Loyola applied the principle differently, compromising the vow of obedience for that very same duke. Discussing the potential transfer of Jesuit missionary Silvestro Landini, Loyola told the duke that 'the commandment of the said [Holy] See' was that Landini go to Corsica but that this '[did] not force' the Jesuits to take the missionary out of the duke's service, and so Loyola had commanded Landini to continue working in his duchy.[82] In practice, the vow of papal obedience was applied strategically, invoked to free the Society from obligations or ignored as a barrier to continuing a particular mission.

The Jesuits also appealed to their close ties with the papacy when they faced opposition from local ecclesiastical authorities. This is evident in a letter from Francesco Stefano, a Jesuit working at the Society's college in Messina in the late 1550s.[83] When a cardinal wanted to prohibit the Jesuits in the city from administering the sacraments to a local convent, Stefano referred to the papal privileges that allowed them to do so. In addition to indicating their delegated apostolic authority, which trumped the power of the cardinal, Stefano suggested that he could call upon allies at the top of the ecclesiastical and secular hierarchies to fight his corner. Writing to the Superior General, Stefano asked if he should appeal to the pope or to the Spanish monarchy (who ruled Sicily) to reverse the cardinal's order. Stefano demonstrated his certainty of the pontiff's support suggesting a third option: that Julius III write to the cardinal himself to tell him 'that he cannot proceed like this with us'.[84]

The Jesuits' pragmatic and bold application of the principle of papal obedience undermines the notion that their vow regarding missions made them instruments of papal will. Quite the opposite. The Jesuits often used their relationship with the pope to act independently, invoking their vow as a means of remaining independent from local ties and even as a trump card in ecclesiastical and jurisdictional squabbles.

The Society used the privilege to absolve heresy in the same way, working confidently alone, and with a range of ecclesiastical and temporal leaders. This included dukes, bankers and the zealous agents of inquisitorial rigour whom Firpo claims Julius III sought to undercut. Pierroberto Scaramella has highlighted the need to consider the variety of anti-heretical work that the Jesuits undertook, underlining their shifting relationships with the institutions and

---

82   Loyola, *Sancti Ignatii de Loyola Societatis Jesu fundatoris epistolae et instructiones*, vol.3, p.56.
83   ARSI, *Epistolae Italiae* 107, f.312r.
84   Ibid.

THE CONFIDENT SOCIETY: MISSION BUILDING 1540–1555   51

individuals with whom they collaborated.[85] In the Jesuits' discussion and solicitation of the privilege to absolve heresy it was this flexibility to adapt their
mission, negating canonical norms and operating with jurisdictional and institutional autonomy, that emerges as the privilege's key asset. Far from considering the privilege in relation to the mission of the papacy or, worse still, one
pope, we must ground our understanding of the privilege in the missionary experiences of the Jesuits who sought and used it across sixteenth-century Italy.

4   Privileges and Pragmatism in the Mission Field

The Jesuits' privilege to absolve heresy can only be explained within the context of the Society's pastoral ministry. This is the context in which the Jesuits
solicited and used the privilege and spoke of its purpose. In Salmerón's letter
from Bologna in 1547, he discussed the private reconciliation of heretics as a
mechanism that transformed sacramental confession and the ministration of
the *Spiritual Exercises* into a means of reconciling Lutherans to the Catholic
Church; a pastoral means of addressing the religious crisis faced by the Church
in Italy. The Lutherans whom Broët wrote about had also come to him as a
confessor, looking for an alternative, extra-judicial route back into the Church.
It is clear from the Jesuits' own correspondence that, for them, the significance
of the privilege to absolve heresy was its role in their pastoral activities. When
we examine how the Jesuits used their privilege in their pastoral ministry it
becomes clear that the power was a pragmatic measure to overcome the obstacles that they faced on the ground, not a mechanism to tie them to one party at
the papal court or a cunning inquisitorial lure.

Polanco's very description of the concession of the privilege suggests that it
solved a practical problem in the Jesuits' ministry. Polanco stated that the authority 'to absolve from cases appertaining to heresy' had been 'lacking in ...
the graces already conceded by the Apostolic See' and was granted 'to console
many souls', that is for pastoral purposes.[86] Moreover, the privilege to absolve
heresy was just one of several privileges requested at the meeting of 1551. All
of these privileges were pragmatic, helping the Society to overcome practical
and pastoral obstacles that inhibited the success of their ministry. Amongst
these concessions was the authority to exempt Jesuits from obligatory fasts
that could weaken a confessor or preacher burdened with a heavy workload

---

85   Scaramella, 'I primi Gesuiti e l'Inquisizione Romana', p.154.
86   Polanco in Loyola, *Sancti Ignatii de Loyola Societatis Jesu fundatoris epistolae et instruc-
        tiones*, vol. 3, p.457.

in an area with few local pastors.[87] Seen in similarly pragmatic terms, the privilege to absolve heresy gave Jesuit missionaries the means to overcome the fear and canonical rules that could impede their efforts to save the souls of penitent-heretics who would otherwise languish outside of the Catholic Church.

The Jesuits had requested dispensations and privileges to overcome practical problems from the very earliest days of their ministry.[88] Such concessions were central to the form of the Society approved by Paul III in 1540. The Society's religious rule freed Jesuits from obligations to pray and fast regularly like other orders so that they might work more intensely and freely in the mission field.[89] This early approach was borne out by later missionary experience. Speaking of his work on the island of Corsica, Jesuit father Emmanuel Gomez claimed that he did not have time to pray the liturgy of the hours at all, let alone in choir, never having a moment 'to take bodily refreshment [and] never to say my [divine] office'.[90] Gomez claimed that he could pray the office at night, but prioritised his duties to give spiritual counsel and absolutions, exclaiming 'how many nights I stay here in [my] room until midnight to hear confessions!'[91] For the Jesuits, the ministration of the sacraments and its effect on the laity was always a far more vital part of their mission than the observance of institutional norms. As the Jesuits' missionary experience grew, so did their knowledge of potential obstacles to their task and so, therefore, their requests for privileges multiplied. This was the process through which the Jesuits carved out their role and praxis in the religious and ecclesiastical fabric of sixteenth-century Italy. And it is within this process that we should define the privilege to absolve heresy.

The pragmatic pastoral concerns that drove the Society to request the privilege to absolve heresy are evident in entreaties for the privilege from individual Jesuit missionaries. Two years before Salmerón's solicitation of the privilege from Julius III, it was requested by Silvestro Landini, a Jesuit missionary working in Correggio, a small town on the outskirts of Ferrara. In July 1549, Landini sent Loyola a list of powers and dispensations that he required to make the

---

87   Ibid.

88   On the pragmatic motivations for soliciting faculties for foreign missions see Paolo Broggio, 'Le congregazioni romane e la confessione dei neofiti del Nuovo Mondo tra *facultates* e *dubia* riflessioni e spunti di indagine', *Mélanges de l'École Françiase de Rome – Italie et Méditerranée*, 121 (2009), *pp.173–197*.

89   David Crook, 'Music at the Jesuit College in Paris, 1575–1590' in O'Malley, Bailey, Harris, and Kennedy (eds), *The Jesuits II*, p.465.

90   Emmanuel Gomez in *Epistolae mixtae*, vol.3, p.93.

91   Ibid.

THE CONFIDENT SOCIETY: MISSION BUILDING 1540–1555

most of his efforts to save souls in Correggio.[92] Landini claimed to enjoy great success converting people through the sacraments, claiming that many 'come every day to confession and communion' and that some 'kneel on the uneven ground in the middle of the street to implore me that I want to confess them'.[93] Many who had previously failed to fulfil their annual obligation to go to Mass now went daily. Every day, Landini claimed, was like a jubilee.[94] Landini was pleased with his work so far, but in order to make the most of his mission he needed some papal dispensations. Amongst those requested was the power to give absolution from heresy.[95] Just like Salmerón's request to Julius III, Landini's appeal for the authority to absolve heresy was couched in a longer entreaty for faculties to aid his missionary work, underlining the pragmatic motivations behind the privilege.

Scrutiny of the other powers and dispensations requested by Landini supports this conclusion. In the very same letter, Landini requested permission to be able to read heretical books and to absolve people who had contracted incestuous or otherwise prohibited marriages.[96] Although Landini does not specify his exact reason for needing the faculty to absolve heresy, his explanation for requesting the power to absolve irregular marriages suggests pragmatic motives. Landini requests this second power of absolution 'because the majority of such people, in every region, are already married in this way with children, and they do not confess or receive communion'.[97] As many people in Correggio had already had children within a marriage that was prohibited by Canon Law, Landini thought that it better to absolve them of the misdemeanour than to let husband and wife languish outside of the Church in mortal sin and excommunication *latae sententiae*.[98] By absolving these people, who had not intended any harm, Landini would save them from social exclusion and, more importantly, the fires of hell. Landini's reason for his need for a licence to read heretical books was similarly pragmatic, stating that 'there are many of them in these parts ... and they do a great damage, and mainly because there

---

92 Landini in *Litterae quadrimestres: ex universis praeter Indiam et Brasiliam locis in quibus aliqui de Societate Jesu versabantur Romam missae* (Madrid: Augustinus Avrial, 1894–1932), 7 vols, vol.1, pp.161–3.

93 Ibid., p.162.

94 Ibid.

95 Landini, *Litterae quadrimestres*, vol.1, p.164.

96 Ibid., p.163.

97 Ibid.

98 Carolo Antonio Tesauro, *De poenis ecclesiasticis, seu canonicis. Latae sententiae à Iure communi, and Constitutionibus Apostolicis, Decretisq[ue]; sacrarum Congregationum* (Rome: Hermann Scheus, 1640), p.14.

is not anybody there who answers against [them]'.[99] If Landini had a licence to read such texts, he could know their arguments and refute them. Landini requested privileges that would allow him to achieve positive outcomes from the imperfect situations that he had discovered in Correggio, even if it meant bending Canon Law.

This pragmatic principle can be applied to Landini's request for the power to absolve heretics. If somebody in Correggio had fallen into heresy but was now penitent, Landini need not put him off with the prospect of an unnecessary or impossible inquisitorial process. With the power to absolve heresy, Landini could reconcile him to the Christian community and save his soul immediately. Later in the century, when the Jesuits' privilege to absolve heresy was under threat, they would defend it in similarly pragmatic terms. A treatise given to the head of the Roman Inquisition in 1586, for example, states that the Jesuits needed the authority to absolve heretics independently of the inquisition 'because, as experience has taught, [heretics] never convert' as they feared the inquisition would deny them absolution and there will be fear for the salvation of that soul.[100] If Landini did not absolve the penitent-heretics of Correggio, no one would.

Other requests for the privilege had similarly pragmatic emphases. Just a couple of years after his mission to Correggio, Landini found himself working on the island of Corsica. There the absence of ecclesiastical authority had led to ignorance and corruption amongst the clergy and left many islanders in a state of serious sin, with numerous excommunicates. With the privilege to absolve heresy, Jesuits on Corsica replaced absent bishops and inquisitors, reconciling anyone whom they could convert. Moreover, freed from the need to cooperate with local ecclesiastical authorities in order to fulfil their mission, the privilege to absolve heresy allowed the Jesuits to work in the direct service of the island's temporal powers who were keen to combat religious dissent amongst the clergy, religious and lay-people that they ruled.

Just like the list of faculties for Correggio, the other powers listed in the concession to Landini and Gomez for their mission to Corsica indicate that the Jesuits saw the privilege to absolve heresy as a pragmatic measure. Although the privilege to absolve heresy had been granted by papal bull when the Jesuits arrived in Corsica in 1552 it was delegated selectively by the Superior General.[101] A papal brief dated August 1552 states that on Corsica Landini and Gomez

---

99   Landini, *Epistolae quadrimestres*, vol.1, p.163.

100   ARSI, *Institutum 185-I*, f. 314r.

101   For examples of letters patent in which it was delegated see *Sancti Ignatii de Loyola Societatis Jesu fundatoris epistolae et instructiones*, vol.3, p.487; p.488; p.489; p.537; p.538; p.540 and p.551.

THE CONFIDENT SOCIETY: MISSION BUILDING 1540–1555   55

could 'totally liberate' heretics if they humbly sought reconciliation and vowed not to commit heresies thereafter.[102] This brief is of the type that missionaries often requested and carried to prove their powers to authorities in the mission field.[103] The brief also cites the Jesuits' powers to absolve anybody on the island of sins and crimes ordinarily reserved to the Holy See, and to visit, investigate, punish and reform universities, colleges and the heads and members of churches and religious communities.[104] All of these powers were pragmatic, transforming the Jesuits' pastoral ministry into a means of converting sinners and reforming the Church without relying upon ecclesiastical powers who were absent or whose conduct and reputation deterred penitents from converting.

Another document, published in the Jesuits' *Monumenta*, indicates that the Jesuits' knowledge of the problems on Corsica instigated their request to use the privilege. Listing graces that could be useful for the help of souls in Corsica, the document notes that the Jesuits would like the power to reconcile heretics, especially those who were neither relapsed nor leaders.[105] Although the editors of the Society's *Monumenta* have dated this document to 10 September 1552, a month after brief listing the privileges was granted, this attribution is based on a date written on a letter in the same collection rather than the content of the document itself.[106] The attribution appears to be incorrect. The author of the list of 'graces' frequently uses the future tense, indicating that these were concessions to be requested for the mission rather than privileges that had been granted a month before. Just as in Bologna and Correggio, it seems that the power to absolve heretics on Corsica was requested by Jesuits because of the practical and pastoral demands of the mission.

The rich correspondence that Landini and Gomez wrote during their mission to Corsica illustrates the remarkably problematic situation that they found on the island and underlines their need to address it independently. The letters that Landini and Gomez wrote to each other when they worked on different parts of the island, as well as their correspondence with the temporal rulers of Corsica is now held at the state archive of Genoa. We also have some of their letters to Jesuit superiors in Rome published in the Society's *Monumenta*. Altogether their correspondence indicates that, on Corsica, Landini and Gomez

---

102   ARSI, *Institutum 194*, f.65r.
103   Examples are held in ARSI, *Institutum 194*.
104   ARSI, *Institutum 194*, ff.65r-66v.
105   Loyola, *Sancti Ignatii de Loyola Societatis Jesu fundatoris epistolae et instructiones*, vol.4, pp.415–6.
106   Ibid., p.407, fn.1.

filled gaps in the ecclesiastical hierarchy that had been left by bishops and priests who had abandoned or neglected their flocks.[107] 'The Church of this land is totally lost', Gomez lamented, 'there are no priests here, no vestments, no chalices, nothing at all for divine worship'.[108] Even though there were six hundred families in the capital of Bastia, the Jesuits told their colleagues in Rome that they had only 'one priest: old, ignorant and of little talent', who had to spread his limited gifts across three or four further benefices on the island.[109] Letters from the missionaries to the *Compere di San Giorgio*, who governed the island from Genoa, revealed that where priests were present they were corrupt, that 'there is no pastor here except to drink the milk and steal the wool from the poor sheep'.[110] With no functioning ecclesiastical hierarchy, without even reliable parish priests, the Jesuits had no choice but to address the situation alone.

According to Landini and Gomez, their help was sorely needed. They claimed that the lack of pastoral care had left the people in a state of sin and excommunication with no means of reforming their lives. In a report to Rome, the two Jesuits claimed that the people of Corsica were 'tainted by every stain of sin', 'by heresy, blasphemy and wicked vice'.[111] Many had broken Canon Law in acts of heresy, in prohibited marriages and in other misdemeanours that incurred *ipso facto* excommunication. This was a censure that could be lifted by an inquisitor, bishop, or somebody with a special delegated privilege to do so.[112] But on Corsica there appear to have been neither bishops nor inquisitors. Polanco's *Chronicon*, which was based on the letters of the early Jesuits, claimed that when Landini and Gomez arrived on Corsica there had been no bishop resident for 60 or 70 years, even though there were seven dioceses on the island.[113] Moreover, whilst scholars note an inquisitorial presence on the island in the fourteenth century, the Jesuits' desire to learn from the inquisitor at Genoa if there was any inquisitor on the island indicates that, by the

---

107 The Constitutions declare that when choosing mission territory the Superior General should consider areas of 'greater need, because of the lack of other workers'. *Constitutions* (Part VII, chapter 2, paragraph 622a).

108 Archivio di Stato di Genova (hereafter, ASG), *Banco di San Giorgio – Cancellieri – Sala 35/233*.

109 ARSI, *Mediolanensis Historia 79*, f.7v.

110 ASG, *Banco di San Giorgio – Cancellieri – Sala 35/233*.

111 ARSI, *Mediolanensis Historia 79*, f.1r.

112 Tentler, *Sin and Confession on the Eve of the Reformation*, pp.303–4.

113 Polanco, *Vita Ignatii Loiolae et rerum Societatis Jesu historia*, vol. 2, p.455. Balduino de Barga, the bishop of Mariana, for example, was resident in Rome. Carlo Luongo, *Silvestro Landini e le "nostre indie"* (Florence: Firenze Atheneum, 2008), p.251.

THE CONFIDENT SOCIETY: MISSION BUILDING 1540–1555

mid-sixteenth century, Roman authorities were unaware of a tribunal there.[114] The Jesuit missionaries claimed that they attempted to remedy the situation by nourishing the neglected laity with the 'food of the word of God' and healing their souls with 'the medicine of the Most Holy Sacraments'.[115] Their privileges of absolution became a vital life-line to the excommunicates of Corsica. According to the missionaries, some came 'from 60 or 100 miles away in order to be absolved from excommunication', and others complained 'that we can't delegate [the power] to other confessors to absolve their wives, who cannot come here'.[116] Empowered by the privilege to absolve heresy and other grave sins and to lift the excommunication that they incurred, the Jesuits claimed that they reconciled many willing souls on the island.

The Jesuits' jurisdictional autonomy over heresy gave them institutional as well as pastoral flexibility, allowing them to work independently and for temporal leaders. On Corsica, Landini and Gomez used the powers delegated to them by the pope in the service of the *Compere di San Giorgio*, the administrative arm of the Genoese bank that governed the island.[117] Throughout the year 1550, the protectors of the *Compere* corresponded with Stefano Usodimare, a Genoese Dominican working at the heart of the papal court in Rome, begging him to send men to reform 'the little regulated life of the priests' of the island.[118] The *Compere* discussed the grave situation with the governor of Corsica, Lamba Doria, who told them of the heretical, alchemist monks and armed, unruly priests on the island.[119] On 27 October 1552, after months of requests, Landini and Gomez arrived at the *Compere*'s headquarters, the grand Palazzo di San Giorgio in Genoa. The two Jesuits carried with them a letter of recommendation from Usodimare praising them as men 'of good letters, utmost zeal for salvation of souls ... [and with] ... the greatest faculties from His Holiness'.[120] On top of their papal brief, the protectors of the *Compere* gave the Jesuits their

---

114 Henry Charles Lea, *A History of the Inquisition of the Middle Ages. Volume three* (New York: Cosimo Classics, 2005), p.254 and Loyola, *Sancti Ignatii de Loyola Societatis Jesu fundatoris epistolae et instructiones*, vol.4, p.416.
115 ASG, *Banco di San Giorgio – Cancellieri – Sala 35 /233*.
116 ARSI, *Mediolanensis Historia 79*, 7v.
117 Antoine-Marie Graziani, 'Ruptures et continuites dans la politique de Saint-Georges en Corse (1453–1562)' in Giuseppe Felloni (ed.), *La Casa di San Giorgio: il potere del credito. Atti del convegno, Genova, 11 e 12 novembre 2004* (Genoa: Società Ligure di Storia Patria, 2006) and Felloni, *1407. La fondazione del Banco di San Giorgio* (Rome: Laterza, 2010).
118 ASG, *Banco di San Giorgio – Cancellieri – Corsica litterarum – Sala 34 – 607/2401*, f.88v.
119 See descriptions by Doria in ASG, *Banco di San Giorgio – Cancellieri – Sala 35 – 232* and the Jesuits in ARSI, *Mediolanensis Historia 79*, f.7v.
120 ASG, *Banco di San Giorgio – Cancellieri – Corsica litterarum – Sala 34 – 232*.

own patent, charging all Corsicans to allow the Jesuits 'to execute all the things that are committed to them, declared in the said [papal] brief and pertinent to the Christian Religion', particularly regarding 'the little regulated life of priests of this island and things pertinent to the divine worship and the salvation of souls'.[121] Records of decisions taken by the *Compere* indicate that the bank also provided financial support for the mission, noting 'expenses made for the reverend Don Silvestro Landini of Sarzana and Don Emanuele of Monte Maior, priests of the Society of Jesus in the city of Rome, sent to the island of Corsica' on 21 November 1552.[122] On Corsica, the Jesuits may have used papal powers, but they were employed and protected by temporal leaders.

The privilege to absolve heresy allowed the Jesuits to work independently of ecclesiastical authorities who could be unreliable, and with a range of individuals and institutions concerned with the fight against religious dissent. On Corsica, papal powers gave the Jesuits the authority that they needed to convert and reconcile the people of the island, in spite of the absence and inadequacies of the local clergy and prelates. The Jesuits were driven by the pursuit of what their own *Constitutions* defined as the 'universal good', not the service of those who sought help 'to fulfil their own spiritual obligations to their flocks'.[123] Nonetheless, the Jesuits' mission did complement the aims of others. On Corsica, the Jesuits work broadly served Julius III's objective to ensure that the Italian states remained Catholic. But it also served the particular aims of the temporal *Compere di San Giorgio*. In this mission we see that, far from binding the Society to serve as agents of the Holy See, papal privileges gave the Jesuits the freedom to collaborate with temporal powers to remedy the neglect of corrupt ecclesiastical authorities. In doing this, the Society furthered its pastoral mission and won new institutional allies.

5 Conclusion

The institutional and pastoral freedom afforded to the Jesuits by their papal privileges offered the Society occasions to cast its net a little further, to establish new missions and colleges to help souls. Papal privileges furthered the Jesuits' pastoral mission and when executed in the service of certain authorities this also helped the Jesuits to expand their Society, the institution that

---

121   ARSI, *Institutum 194*, ff.66r-v.

122   ASG, *Banco di San Giorgio – Cancellieri – Corsica litterarum – Sala 34 – 593/1382*, f.56v.

123   *Constitutions* (Part VII, chapter 2, paragraphs 618 and 622) in Ganss (trans.), *The Constitutions of the Society of Jesus*, p.271 and p.274.

THE CONFIDENT SOCIETY: MISSION BUILDING 1540–1555   59

supported their growing pastoral ministry. On their way to Genoa, Landini and Gomez were ordered by Loyola to stop in Bologna to visit the Genoese Archbishop, Gerolamo Sauli, who was living in the city as papal pro-legate.[124] Sauli was clearly impressed by the two men. He approved the mission to Corsica on the condition that the Jesuits perform a full visitation of his Genoese archdiocese first.[125] Loyola charged Landini and Gomez to undertake Sauli's task in Genoa and, in doing so, to give a good impression of the Society.[126] It seems that they succeeded. In 1554, the governors of the republic formally requested a Jesuit college for Genoa. In the request, they cited the praise of Genoese lords and citizens who had seen the good work of Landini and Gomez before they departed for Corsica.[127] That the pastoral and institutional progress of the Society were intrinsically linked is clear in Sauli's strong support for the project and in the appointment of Tomasso de Spinola, procurator of Corsica, to oversee the establishment of the college in Genoa.[128] In Corsica and Genoa the Jesuits used delegated apostolic authority to serve an authority completely distinct from the papacy and in doing so they won themselves a base in an important Italian state.

The Jesuits relied upon the institutions and individuals with whom they collaborated to carry out and expand their ministry. This is evident in the concession of powers of absolution through the Society's relationship with Julius III and his circle. It is also clear in the relationship between Landini and Gomez and the *Compere*, to which they wrote daily detailing their requirements so that it could send help as best as it could.[129] The much broader institutional benefits of these collaborative missions are evident in the establishment of the Jesuit college in Genoa.

Whether the Jesuits worked in Bologna, Correggio or Corsica, they used flexibility to fulfil their institutional aims as well as their pastoral mission. No matter how far the Jesuits' ministry appealed to the objectives of others and

---

124   Loyola, *Sancti Ignatii de Loyola Societatis Jesu fundatoris epistolae et instructiones*, vol.4, p.416.

125   The patent for this extra mission was given by cardinals Bernardino Maffei and Giovanni Ricci and is published in ibid., pp.422–3.

126   Ibid., p.416.

127   *Epistolae mixtae*, vol.4, pp.142–3. On the Jesuits in Genoa see Davide Ferraris, 'I rapporti della Compagnia di Gesù, <<incarnazione della riforma>>, con il potere religioso e temporale a Genova' in *Atti della Società Ligure si Storia Patria Nuova Serie LV CXXIX fasc II* (Genova: Nella sede della Società Ligure di Storia Patria Palazzo Ducale, 2015), pp.75–106.

128   *Epistolae mixtae*, vol.4, pp.142–3.

129   Loyola, *Sancti Ignatii de Loyola Societatis Jesu fundatoris epistolae et instructiones*, vol.4, p.416.

relied upon their support their main objective was the salvation of souls not the service of men. Ultimately, the Jesuits did not care particularly whom they collaborated with as long as it helped them to fulfil their mission. The Society's connections with external authorities – from the pope, to the Duke of Ferrara, to the *Compere di San Giorgio* – sustained their work but they did not define it.

When the island of Corsica was stormed by French soldiers in August 1553, the Jesuits demonstrated remarkable political agility, adapting working relationships so that they could continue their mission to the Corsicans. Situated on the sea route between Italy and Spain, Corsica was a highly sought-after prize in the Italian wars between the French kings and the Holy Roman Emperors.[130] On 22 August 1552 a company of French and Turkish soldiers, along with a number of Corsican exiles, took Bastia, declaring the liberation of Corsica from Genoese tyranny.[131] The Jesuits reacted rapidly to the changing political dynamics. By 7 September Polanco was able to tell Landini that he had written to French Cardinal Eustache du Bellay and secured the favour of the French authorities for the Jesuit mission on the island.[132] Polanco ordered Landini to take this notice by hand to Antoine Escalin des Aimars, the general in command of the galleys of the French king.[133] Whilst Corsica's fate hung in the balance, Loyola told the Jesuit missionaries to continue converting the islanders but to remain silent on matters of state.[134] Working with delegated apostolic authority, the powers that the Jesuits needed to fulfil their mission were independent of the territorial authorities who had requested and funded their presence on the island. For the Jesuits, allegiances were only relevant as far as they helped the Society to pursue its pastoral mission. And in the summer of 1553 the *Compere di San Giorgio* no longer fit the bill.

Members of the Society requested special privileges not to serve one individual or institution but so that they might reconcile their converts, in spite of the obstacles presented by the varied contexts in which they worked. In cities and villages across sixteenth-century Italy, the Jesuits preached, taught and heard confessions to correct those who had erred from Catholic orthodoxy. Empowered with the authority to absolve heresy, they transformed this pastoral ministry into an effective means of addressing the problem of religious dissent that plagued the Catholic Church in the sixteenth century. In doing

---

130   Ilario Rinieri, *I vescovi della Corsica* (Milan: Istituto per gli studi di politica internazionale, 1934), p.70.
131   Ibid., pp.70–1.
132   ARSI, *Epistolae nostrorum 50*, f.25r.
133   Ibid.
134   Ibid.

THE CONFIDENT SOCIETY: MISSION BUILDING 1540–1555

this the Society fulfilled its fundamental mission to help souls and, at the same time, satisfied the pressing concerns of princes and popes. By the first years of the 1550s, the Jesuits' extensive missionary experience had allowed them to discern what powers were necessary for their ministry. In turn, the valuable service that the Jesuits had offered others put them in the position to secure such privileges. Like the addition of the 'defence of the faith' to the *Formula* in 1550, the solicitation of the authority to absolve heresy is evidence of the Jesuits' growing awareness of their role in efforts to address the religious crisis in sixteenth-century Europe. It is also a testament to their confidence to request the necessary, but often controversial, powers that they needed to fulfil this duty.

CHAPTER 2

Collaboration, Competition and Conflict: the Jesuits and the Roman Inquisition

On 2 October 1567, Cardinal Michele Bonelli instructed the Portuguese Jesuit Cristóbal Rodriguez for an investigative mission to Le Marche in the Papal States.[1] Bonelli gave Rodriguez orders on behalf of his great-uncle Pope Pius V, the former cardinal-inquisitor who continued his efforts to eradicate heresy when he was elected to the papacy in January 1566.[2] Through Bonelli, Pius charged Rodriguez to investigate disobedience in Le Marche, 'secretly finding out how the clergy, religious, bishops, governors and other public persons do their duty, about the divine cult, about the residence of rectors and bishops, about the observance of the Council of Trent and of the orders of His Holiness, and also if there are any abuses, disorders and public sins, like concubinage, usury, simony, blasphemy, suspicions of heresy etc'.[3] In other words, Rodriguez was to spy on all those under the obedience of the Roman Church and report what he discovered to the pope.

Rodriguez's investigations were to be clandestine and his image as a Jesuit pastor would be vital to the deception.[4] 'Firstly', Bonelli instructed, 'go with a companion, teaching Christian Doctrine and hearing confessions etc, according to the usual [manner] of the Society'.[5] If Rodriguez carried out the pastoral duties that were ordinary for the Jesuits, Bonelli believed that heretics and lax ecclesiastics would 'not become aware of what is intended'.[6] In short, Rodriguez was to act like a Jesuit so that he would not be suspected as a Roman spy. Indeed, the instructions to Rodriguez contrasted starkly with the usual procedure for the arrival of an inquisitor. Ordinarily an inquisitor was announced with a sermon in the local church and an edict of grace displayed publicly.[7] In Le Marche, Rodriguez's pastoral activity would act as a disguise

---

1   The instructions are held in ARSI, *Institutum 187*, f.87r.
2   On the life and career of Michele Bonelli see Prosperi, 'Michele Bonelli' in *Dizionario Biografico degli Italiani. Vol. 11* (Rome: Istituto della Enciclopedia italiana, 1969), pp.766–774.
3   ARSI, *Institutum 187*, f.87r.
4   Ibid.
5   Ibid.
6   Ibid.
7   Romeo, *L'Inquisizione nell'età moderna*, p.20.

© KONINKLIJKE BRILL NV, LEIDEN, 2020 | DOI:10.1163/9789004413832_004

COLLABORATION, COMPETITION AND CONFLICT

that would would allow him to win the trust of potential informants, mining them for information but claiming that 'under pain of excommunication ... [he would] keep their secret'.[8] Given this promise, Bonelli assured Rodriguez that any informant would say 'what he knows about that monastery etc and about anything that you ask him' – information that was then to be sent to Rome.[9] 'Remember well that which they will tell you', Bonelli instructed Rodriguez, 'and afterwards, in your room, write it down'.[10] In Le Marche, Rodriguez could work successfully as a papal and inquisitorial spy, just as long as he did not appear to be one.

This chapter will argue that the jurisdictional and institutional autonomy that allowed the Society to work independently, and sometimes in competition with the Roman Inquisition, was also an asset in its collaborations with the Holy Office. As well as working alone and for temporal patrons, the Jesuits tackled religious disobedience on missions for the pope and Roman Inquisition. On these missions, their strategies often relied on their ability to disassociate themselves from their Roman patrons. This was especially true of the Society's collaborations with the Holy Office, whose links to the papacy and reputation for cruelty often impeded its work on the Italian peninsula. As we shall see, Rodriguez and Pius v had developed the strategy used in Le Marche during earlier collaborations when Pius ran the Roman Inquisition as Cardinal Michele Ghislieri. As ostensibly independent agents, absolving heretics without involving inquisitors or bishops, the Jesuits could convert and reconcile heretics where inquisitorial commissaries faced insurmountable pastoral and political obstacles, even as they worked hand-in-glove with the inquisition, sending vital information on religious rebels directly to Rome.

The leaders of the Society had always negotiated their relationship to the Roman Inquisition with great care, cultivating a useful working dynamic whilst keeping a safe distance. The early Jesuits neutralised suspicions about their own orthodoxy by declaring their absolute support for the work of the cardinal-inquisitors.[11] Moreover, inquisitorial *decreta*, histories of the Society and mission reports describe the Jesuits collaborating with cardinal-inquisitors from the early 1550s. At the same time, however, Jesuit sources indicate that the Society wanted to maintain a clear autonomy from the Holy Office. Institutional independence meant that Jesuit Superior Generals could deploy their

---

8   ARSI, *Institutum 187*, f.87r.
9   Ibid.
10 Ibid.
11 See, for examples, Jerónimo Nadal, *Epistolae P. Hieronumi Nadal Societatis Jesu*, vol. 5, pp.314–5 and Ribadeneira, *Vita Ignatii Loiolae*, p.262.

64   CHAPTER 2

personnel in a manner that suited the Society's mission, rather than being dictated by a cardinal-inquisitor. It also allowed the Society to distance itself from the fear of the Roman Inquisition that was widespread amongst the laity. Working autonomously, the Jesuits could forge a range of alliances within the Church – as well as without – hedging their bets with the most advantageous associations. This agility was vital during our period, in which ecclesiastical power dynamics were often in a state of flux. Whilst the Jesuits sought all of the opportunities and protection that inquisitorial collaboration offered, they did not want hostility to the tribunal or the fate of any of its individual members to harm their pastoral or institutional progress.

The Roman Inquisition were also wise to the benefits of Jesuit autonomy. Records indicate that both the Jesuits and cardinal-inquisitors believed that their collaborations were more successful if the Jesuits worked independently. For the Holy Office, the Society provided orthodox agents from a range of European backgrounds who were not yet tied to the papacy in the popular imagination.[12] In sixteenth-century Italy, the Holy Office could not undertake its mission to combat religious dissent alone because of weak and inefficient local tribunals, lay resistance to judicial methods and political hostility.[13] Across Italy, lay confraternities bolstered the work of local tribunals and inquisitorial commissaries.[14] Jesuits fulfilled many of the same roles and more, but they had the added value of a distinct and novel institutional identity that distanced them from the inquisition. Thus, in Piacenza, a city with Spanish governors, an independent Spanish Jesuit agent could act as an inquisitor without representing the intervention of foreign, papal power. Moreover, in a diocese such as Vulturara, where earlier inquisitorial violence prevented commissaries of the Holy Office from securing conversions, a member of the Society with a benign reputation could endear himself to the local populace before executing inquisitorial orders. On a peninsula where inquisitors faced barriers of political diplomacy and public image, the privilege to absolve heresy that empowered the Society to work in competition with the Holy Office also made Jesuits some its most valuable collaborators.

Whilst recent scholarship has incorporated the work of the Jesuits into accounts of the Roman Inquisition's use of pastoral means to control religion and morality, it has often presented the Society as a mere tool of the Holy Office.[15] The Jesuits' use of the privilege to absolve heresy as a mechanism of

---

12   Romeo, 'Note sull'Inquisizione Romana'.
13   Black, *The Italian Inquisition*, pp.27–9.
14   Ibid, p.28.
15   Prosperi, *Tribunali della coscienza*, pp.xiv-xvii.

COLLABORATION, COMPETITION AND CONFLICT 65

autonomy in their inquisitorial collaborations proves that their role was much more independent. The Jesuits had to work autonomously for many of their inquisitorial missions to succeed. This conclusion fits into new interpretations of social discipline in the sixteenth-century Church, which have revised traditional portrayals of a rigid and centralised Tridentine system by highlighting the significance of local resistance to Roman schemes.[16] Scholarship on the Society has also challenged the notion that the Jesuits were subordinated to central agendas, underlining the variety of roles that the Society assumed as well as its flexible approach to obedience.[17] By studying the role of the privilege to absolve heresy in inquisitorial collaborations we shall see that the Jesuits' flexibility and autonomy not only served the Society but also the Roman Inquisition, allowing us to reconcile the picture of a fragmented and imperfect inquisitorial system with new interpretations of the Society of Jesus.

It was also institutionally beneficial for the Jesuits to appear distinct from the Holy Office. These benefits intensified as the Jesuits' relationship with the inquisition became more intimate and sophisticated. In the first half of the 1550s, Loyola resisted the election of fathers to permanent inquisitorial positions. For Loyola Jesuit inquisitors would be impractical for the Society, taking fathers out of his obedience and hampering his ability to send Jesuits where the most spiritual fruit could be harvested. In the 1560s, the Jesuits explicitly asserted their autonomy from the inquisition to protect the Society from the poor reputation of the tribunal. In 1564, Rodriguez even memorialised his refusal to work as an inquisitorial judge in an official report from a mission in the Kingdom of Naples, distancing himself from the Holy Office in a land where it was hated. In the same year, the Jesuits asked Pope Pius IV for a bull that would prevent the meddling of inquisitors in cases of heresy related to the Society.[18] Moreover, when soliciting this privilege under Pius IV the Jesuits did not call

---

16   This approach is typified in the work of scholars such as Simon Ditchfield and Mary Laven. For a list of works see footnote 34 of the introduction to this book.

17   The concept of 'negotiated obedience', through which Jesuits reconciled norms of obedience with the demands of their own conscience, was proposed by Antonella Romano. For a reference to Romano's verbal comments see Alfieri and Ferlan (eds), *Avventure dell'obbedienza nella Compagnia di Gesù*, p.197. See also *Early modern Jesuits between obedience and conscience* and "Perinde ac si cadaver essent'. Les jésuites dans une perspective comparative: la tension constitutive entre l'obéissance et le 'representar' dans les sources normatives des réguliers', *Revue d'Histoire Ecclésiastique*, 105 (2010), pp.44–73. For more traditional interpretations see Benedetto Croce *Storia della età barocca in Italia. Pensiero, poesia e letteratura.Vita morale* (Bari: Gius. Laterza and Figli, 1929), p.19. See also, Catto, *La Compagnia divisa*. On the Jesuits' flexible relationship with the Roman Inquisition see Scaramella, 'I primi gesuiti e l'inquisizione Romana'.

18   For the request see ASR, *Miscellanea Famiglie Gesuiti*, B180, filza 14, f.48r.

for support from their usual ally in such matters, cardinal-inquisitor Michele Ghislieri. Instead they sought the help of another member of the Holy Office who was in better standing with the pope and not directly involved in the Society's anti-heretical missions. As the pastoral and political problems faced by the inquisition and its members worsened in the second half of the sixteenth century, the Society's autonomy became all the more valuable to the Jesuits – for missionary success and for their future as an institution.

1   Competitors and Collaborators with the Holy Office

The Jesuits' solicitation and early use of the privilege to reconcile heretics is emblematic of their relationship with the Roman Inquisition. By requesting and using a power analogous to that of the inquisitors the Jesuits confirmed their mission's reach into the realm of inquisitorial jurisdiction whilst ensuring that they could work independently of the Holy Office. Similar strategies can be seen in the interactions between the two institutions in the early 1550s. In these years we find the earliest records of Jesuits working directly with the Holy Office, even as they undertook independent missions to convert and reconcile heretics. It was also in this period that Loyola confirmed that members of the Society would not assume permanent or long-standing inquisitorial posts. Loyola's aims were more strategic than they were substantial. It was not that the Jesuits explicitly objected to inquisitorial work. Indeed, Jesuits collaborated with inquisitors so that they might increase their opportunities to save souls. Nevertheless, by establishing the Society's institutional autonomy from the Holy Office Loyola could maintain control over the Jesuits' ministry and reputation during a crucial period for the Society's formation.

In order to understand the Society's relationship to the Roman Inquisition, we must consider when and why Jesuits asserted their autonomy from the Holy Office. Such incidents allow us to see the limits of the Society's relationship with the inquisitors and where Jesuit superiors wanted to draw red lines. From the early 1550s to the mid-1560s, the Jesuits themselves explained why they needed to distinguish themselves from the early modern inquisitions. Despite the value of this written reasoning it must be compared critically with the decisions taken by the Society on a case-by-case basis as the Jesuits' statements and actions were not always consistent. Emerging in the stormy religious, ecclesiastical and political climate of sixteenth-century Europe, members of the Society soon revealed themselves as consummate diplomats. As Rodriguez's instructions for Le Marche prove, even outright deception was on the cards if it was done in pursuit of the greater good. By looking critically at the Jesuits'

COLLABORATION, COMPETITION AND CONFLICT 67

words and actions we can assess the priorities of the Society in its dealings with the Holy Office, clarifying the motivations for decisions that might at first appear ambivalent.[19]

In the mid-sixteenth century, Jesuits certainly worked in direct competition with the inquisitors as well as in collaboration with them. As we have seen, the privilege to absolve heretics in *foro conscientiae* gave the Society a power analogous to that of the Holy Office, allowing Jesuits to use a distinct, secret process to reconcile heretics whom the inquisitors had not yet detected. In Siena, Father Jerónimo Rubiols absolved and reconciled heretics autonomously, telling Duchess Elenore de Toledo that the Jesuit college was working to purge the city of its Lutherans.[20] Rubiols and his confreres worked independently until they were noticed by Paul IV's inquisitors and asked to cooperate with the inquisitorial commissary in Siena, a collaboration that they abandoned as soon as the pope died.[21] At the Jesuit college in Turin the rector, Achille Gagliardi, also took the matter of reconciling heretics into his own hands. Sidelining the Holy Office, the rector claimed that 'it was not necessary to speak of inquisitors, nor of abjuration, which is a most hateful thing' to the penitent Huguenots who sought his help.[22] When using their privilege, Jesuits like Rubiols and Gagliardi replaced and competed with the inquisitors in the cities where they worked, offering an appealing alternative to judicial reconciliation.

The Society's privilege to absolve heresy was so close to the authority of the Holy Office that some people conflated the work of the Jesuits with that of inquisitors – despite the Jesuits' efforts to distance themselves from the tribunal. As we saw in the last chapter, the angry inquisitor in Bologna accused Salmerón and Broët of trying to establish 'a new tribunal' when they absolved heretics. A manuscript biography of Silvestro Landini, now held at the ARSI, indicates that sixteenth-century Corsicans mistook the Jesuits for inquisitors simply because they had the authority to absolve heresy. The author writes that 'those first fathers [on Corsica] had some extraordinary authority, even [an] exterior [authority], so that they were commonly called the inquisitors'.[23] Although this biography was produced after the mission, first-hand reports

---

19   Mostaccio, 'A Conscious Ambiguity', pp.440–1 and Scaramella, 'I primi Gesuiti e l'Inquisizione Romana', p.148.

20   Rubiols in Diego Laínez, *Lainii Monumenta*, vol. 3, pp. 548–9.

21   Valerio Marchetti. *Gruppi ereticali senesi del cinquecento* (Florence: La Nuova Italia, 1975), pp.172–6.

22   ARSI, *Epistolae Italiae 136*, f.169r.

23   ARSI, *Mediolanensis historia 98*, f.5v.

68 CHAPTER 2

corroborate this statement.[24] When scandalous rumours about Landini and Gomez reached the papal court in Rome, Loyola sent Sebastiano Romei, a man from outside of the Society, as an incognito investigator to interview Corsicans about the Jesuits' conduct.[25] In his report to Polanco, Romei noted that the Corsicans habitually referred to the Jesuit missionaries as the *inquisitori*.[26] Both consciously and by mistake, it seems that Jesuits in Italy were identified with the inquisition because of their ability to reconcile heretics.

The Society may have competed with the inquisitors but they also collaborated with the Holy Office from early on in their ministry. In Rome, Jesuit theologians catechised and absolved men in the jails of the inquisition.[27] Other Jesuits helped to compile the Index of Prohibited Books.[28] In Modena, Siena, Florence and Naples, members of the Society informed the Holy Office of local dissenters, bringing inquisitors news of suspect parishioners and dangerous preachers working in their area.[29] Some fathers even took on official inquisitorial roles on a temporary basis, working as delegates or commissaries of the Holy Office in a particular locale.[30] On 6 October 1553, for example, inquisitorial *decreta* note that 'Doctor Bobadilla of the Society of Jesus shall be made commissary in the province of the Marches of Ancona'.[31] Just a few weeks later, a *decretum* tells us that 'an Anconian apostate shall be reconciled by the Reverend Commissary', indicating that Bobadilla had told them of plans to absolve a penitent-heretic.[32] Such records make it clear that members of the Society used their privilege in direct collaboration with the cardinal-inquisitors.

---

24 The document is undated, but was clearly written sometime after Landini's death in 1554, possibly in preparation for a failed canonisation attempt in 1612. Luongo, *Silvestro Landini e le "nostre Indie"*, p.15.

25 See note in Loyola, *Sancti Ignatii de Loyola. Epistolae et instructiones*, vol.2, p.657, fn.2.

26 Romei, *Epistolae Mixtae*, vol.3, p.128.

27 See the case of Diego Perez, a Portuguese Jew jailed by the Roman Inquisition after being accused of practicing Judaism after Catholic baptism. Perez was absolved by the Jesuits and sent to them for catechesis: ACDF, *Decreta 1548–58 copia*, p.230 and p.241.

28 Pavone, *I gesuiti*, p.24.

29 See the case of Bobadilla and Father Andrea de Oviedo informing on Franciscan preacher Sisto di Siena in Naples in 1552. For Oviedo's denunciation see ACDF, *Stanza Storica R-4-E*, ff.329r-331r. On the case see, Scaramella, *L'inquisizioni, eresie, etnie: dissenso religioso e giustizia ecclesiastica in Italia (secc. XVI–XVIII)* (Bari: Carucci, 2005), pp.98–100.

30 On inquisitorial commissaries see Andrea Del Col, 'Commissario del Sant'Uffizio, Italia' in Prosperi (ed.), *Dizionario storico dell'Inquisizione*, vol.1, p.352. On the lay police or *familiares* of the Holy Office see Dennj Solera, 'I familiares del Sant'Uffizio romano. Un profilo istituzionale e sociale dei servitori dell'Inquisizione papale', *Riforma e movimenti religiosi: rivista della Società di studi valdesi* (Turin: Claudiana, 2017), pp.277–286.

31 ACDF, *Decreta 1548–58 copia*, p.228.

32 Ibid., p.230.

COLLABORATION, COMPETITION AND CONFLICT

The Jesuits' desire and need to collaborate with the Holy Office is more than understandable. By the early 1550s, the Roman Inquisition was the most powerful body of cardinals in the Catholic Church. Making enemies amongst the cardinal-inquisitors was ill-advised. Prominent inquisitors such as Gian Pietro Carafa – later Pope Paul IV – had a clear agenda for post-Reformation Catholicism and used the inquisition to punish those who obstructed their goals.[33] Alliances with cardinal-inquisitors, on the other hand, were deeply valuable indeed. In exchange for help hunting heretics members of the congregation offered the Jesuits support through their inquisitorial roles and dynastic influence. Silvestro Landini responded to cardinal-inquisitor Juan Alvarez Toledo's call to address heresy in 'the environs of Florence, Ferrara and Lucca and others nearby' whilst other Jesuits informed Toledo about individual heretics whom they had discovered.[34] In return, the Jesuits claimed that the cardinal-inquisitor was an exceptional patron of the Society: a 'defender of us in all our affairs'.[35] This claim was borne out by the Jesuits' experiences in Tuscany. When Loyola sent fathers to establish a college in the duchy they went armed with letters of recommendation from Toledo and gave them not to Duke Cosimo I de' Medici, but to his wife, Duchess Elenore, who happened to be Toledo's niece.[36] Toledo also supported the establishment of Jesuit colleges in Pisa and Spain, making it clear that collaborations with the Roman Inquisition not only gave the Jesuits security and occasions to save more souls but also opportunities for institutional expansion.

Such collaborations were not accepted by the Jesuits unconditionally. Sometimes Jesuits refused or even terminated work for the Holy Office. Such incidences were infrequent. Nonetheless, the scarcity of these refusals makes them all the more valuable as they offer an insight into the freedoms that the Society fought to retain even in negotiations with their most important allies.

Some refusals were motivated by reasons of government. Loyola and Laínez, the first Superior Generals of the Society, worried that placing Jesuits in official, permanent inquisitorial offices would disturb the internal hierarchy of the order. This was evident in their discussion of the request of King John III of Portugal who asked that the Society staff his inquisition in Lisbon in 1556. Loyola and Laínez had serious misgivings about the project. Loyola was concerned

---

33   Firpo, *La presa di potere*, p.ix.
34   Polanco, *Vita ignatii Loiolae*, vol.2, p.23.
35   Luis Gonçalves da Câmara in Alexander Eaglestone and Joseph A. Munitz (eds.), *Remembering Iñigo: glimpses of the life of Saint Ignatius of Loyola: the Memoriale of Luis Gonçalves da Câmara* (Leominster: Gracewing, 2005), p.225.
36   Loyola, *Sancti Ignatii de Loyola. Epistolae et instructiones*, vol.3, pp.718–9.

70   CHAPTER 2

with the authority that an inquisitorial position would confer, worrying 'about
the honour of the occupation' of 'taking and condemning' heretics.[37] Likewise,
Laínez objected because of the 'great deal of authority that the inquisitors have
in Spain', which could undermine the Society's aim 'to help souls with the spirit
of humility'.[38] These concerns show that the Jesuits thought that the status
of the inquisitor was contrary to the Jesuits' mission rather than the aims or
methods of the Holy Office. Indeed, on a committee of prominent Jesuits, half
of whom had already undertaken inquisitorial duties, the Superior General
and his successor were outnumbered by fathers who saw no problem with inquisitorial work and wished to accept the task, despite the potential problems
of governance.[39] The plan fell through for other reasons, but during the debate
it was clear that Superior General Loyola and his successor did not object to
fathers working for the Holy Office per se they just wanted as much authority
as possible to dictate, who, when and where.

By the time of this discussion Loyola had already demonstrated his desire to
decide when and where Jesuits should exert their energies in the fight against
religious dissent in Italy. In 1552, on the request of cardinal-inquisitor Toledo,
Loyola had sent Father Andrea Galvanello to act as ordinary in the town of
Morbegno in Valtellina. This Alpine territory was a refuge for heretics from Italy and northern Europe and governed by the Zwinglian Three Grey Leagues.[40]
An inquisitor had been sent to the region but had been unsuccessful in his
mission to convert Protestants and encourage the Catholic community in the
area.[41] The cardinal-inquisitors in Rome charged Galvanello to protect the orthodox from heretical contamination whilst they undertook the difficult task
of finding a permanent ordinary who was not 'a wolf, being a heretic'.[42] However, when this endeavour took longer than the 'five or six months' that Loyola

---

37   Loyola to Jacob Miro in ibid., p.163.
38   Laínez in Candidus de Dalmases and Fernandez Zapico (eds), *Monumenta Ignatiana.*
      Series quarta. Scripta de S. Ignatio. Fontes Narrativi de Sancto Ignatio de Loyola et de
      Societatis Iesu initiis. Narrationes scriptae ante annum 1557 (Rome: Societatis Iesu, 1943),
      pp.732–3.
39   Polanco in Loyola, *Sancti Ignatii de Loyola. Epistolae et instructiones*, vol.9, p.215.
40   On Valtellina see Giancarlo Andenna, 'The Lombard Church in the Late Middle Ages' in
      Gamberini (ed.), *A Companion to Late Medieval and Early Modern Milan. The Distinctive*
      Features of an Italian State, p.101; Antonio Rotondó, 'Esuli italiani in Valtellina nel
      cinquecento', *Rivista storica italiana*, 88 (1976), p.759 and Giampaolo Zucchini, *Riforma*
      e società nei Grigioni (Coira: Archivio di Stato e Biblioteca Cantonale dei Grigioni,
      1978), p.14.
41   Scaduto, *L'Epoca di Giacomo Lainez: l'azione, 1556–1565* (Rome: La Civiltà Cattolica,
      1974), p.660.
42   Polanco in Loyola, *Sancti Ignatii de Loyola. Epistolae et instructiones*, vol.5, p.631.

COLLABORATION, COMPETITION AND CONFLICT

had envisaged the Superior General revoked Galvanello from the inquisitorial mission.[43]

As Loyola would confirm in the *Constitutions*, he did not want Jesuits working in fixed positions for external authorities for longer than three months.[44] This could only be 'longer or shorter in proportion to the greater or lesser spiritual fruit that is seen to be reaped there or is expected elsewhere'.[45] In September 1553, the spiritual harvest in the difficult mission territory of Valtellina could not compare with the 'great need' of Galvanello at the Society's college in Venice.[46] Loyola was willing to help the inquisition but asserted his authority to assign members of the Society to the tasks that he thought most important, even when this took them away from inquisitorial roles.

Loyola was clearly in a position to negotiate the Society's dealings with the Roman Inquisition. The cardinal-inquisitors' assent to Loyola's request is recorded in the *decreta* of 31 August 1553.[47] As the Superior General explained to Galvanello, 'I have informed those Most Reverend Cardinal Inquisitors and they were happy that we get you out of there to help us with your work in our colleges'.[48] Loyola's subsequent instructions to Galvanello underline that he intended to assert his will over the needs of the Roman Inquisition. Although Galvanello would be travelling to the Jesuit college in Venice first, he would soon return to Valtellina. Next time, however, Galvanello would work under Loyola's direction not that of the Roman Inquisition. The Superior General was well aware of the local desire to retain Galvanello in Morbegno and knew that there might be upset about the Superior General's decision to move him to Venice. For this reason, Loyola ordered Galvanello to 'keep all of this secret' 'so that those from Morbegno who want you cannot write to Rome, nor put an obstacle in the way of this revocation'.[49] Despite the wishes of the inquisitors and strong local demand, Loyola wanted his men under his control not locked into long-term posts for the Holy Office.

The Jesuits' own privileges and numerous collaborations with the Roman Inquisition are a testament to their willingness to lend a hand in the battle against heresy, even in explicitly inquisitorial roles. The cardinal-inquisitors

---

43   Polanco in Loyola, *Sancti Ignatii de Loyola. Epistolae et instructiones*, vol.5, p.631. See also Loyola, ibid., p.530.
44   Loyola, Ganss (ed. and trans.), *The Constitutions*, p.270.
45   Ibid.
46   Polanco in Loyola, *Sancti Ignatii de Loyola. Epistolae et instructiones*, vol.5, p.529.
47   ACDF, *Decreta 1548–58 – copia*, p.222 [f.115r].
48   Loyola, *Sancti Ignatii de Loyola. Epistolae et instructiones*, vol.5, p.530.
49   Ibid., p.459.

offered the Jesuits opportunities for ministry and institutional support as a powerful political body in the Catholic Church and through their broader dynastic links. Despite these alliances, in the Society's formative years, Jesuit authorities maintained operational independence from the inquisitions, so that they might control their own pastoral and institutional mission. The cardinal-inquisitors' easy assent to Loyola's inconvenient revocation of Galvanello indicates that they both recognised and respected Jesuit autonomy. As we shall see in the remainder of this chapter, the Holy Office was not acting selflessly in doing so. For, the Jesuits' ability to act independently, or, at least, to appear to act independently, benefitted the inquisition as well as the Society.

2 Popes, Empires and the Politics of Conversion

The papal inquisition faced problematic political hostility in Italy, which the Jesuits could overcome. This hostility stemmed from the dual role of the pope who was both a spiritual and a temporal power: the head of the Roman Catholic Church and the prince of the Papal States, which, by this time, cut a vast swathe across Central Italy. On the Italian peninsula the pope was just one prince amongst many. Depending on the occupant of the See of St Peter, his family ties and his ambitions, the pope of Rome was either an ally or rival to the princes who ruled the other Italian states.[50] To complicate matters further, the patchwork of territories in sixteenth-century Italy was dominated by foreign rule. From the Duchy of Milan to the Kingdom of Naples, some of Italy's largest and most powerful lands fell within the Habsburg sphere of influence.[51] Relations between the papacy and empire could be frosty and sometimes bloody. Although the pope had given the Roman Inquisition jurisdiction over heresy across the peninsula, political hostility between the pope, rulers of Italian states and their foreign allies often impeded the cardinal-inquisitors' ability to assert their influence on or through local inquisitorial tribunals. As members of a new religious order with no formal, public tie to the pope or his inquisition, the early Jesuits did not face the same resistance. When Jesuits worked for the Holy Office in states hostile to Roman interference, both the Society and

---

50 In his *Il sovrano pontefice* Paolo Prodi argued that, from the fifteenth century, the papacy played a decisive role in the development of the modern state.

51 On the Spanish in early modern Italy, see Piers Baker-Bates and Miles Pattenden (eds), *The Spanish Presence in sixteenth-century Italy. Images of Iberia* (Farnham: Ashgate, 2015) and Thomas James Dandelet and John A. Marino (eds), *Spain in Italy. Politics, Society, and Religion 1500–1700* (Leiden: Brill, 2007).

COLLABORATION, COMPETITION AND CONFLICT

the papal inquisition benefitted from the independence established by Loyola in the early 1550s.

The papal inquisition found its jurisdiction blocked by temporal leaders in many states of sixteenth-century Italy. The government of Venice refused to cede complete control over the prosecution of heresy.[52] In Lucca, the papal tribunal was seen as an instrument of foreign power seeking to intervene in state affairs and with no respect for local civic laws.[53] In Florence, ten years after the establishment of the Roman Inquisition, Gian Pietro Carafa had to ask Father Laínez if he would recommend the authority of the Holy Office to the Duke Cosimo I de' Medici, who insisted on electing his own inquisitors and demanded the presence of state representatives at almost every stage of the inquisitorial process.[54] Though Paul III had established the inquisition in 1542 to find, convert or prosecute heretics across the peninsula, secular princes continually frustrated it in this task.

In some lands, state control of anti-heretical measures was a matter of great political and diplomatic sensitivity. This was certainly true in the Duchy of Ferrara and the Duchy and Principality of Savoy-Piedmont.[55] In an attempt to build alliances with France, both Duke Ercole d'Este of Ferrara and Duke Emanuele Filiberto of Savoy had married French princesses. But the standing of both dukes in Italy was damaged by their wives' suspected heresy.[56] What is more, when it came to addressing this problem, their hands were effectively tied. The diplomatic advantages of both men's' marriages would have been entirely compromised if they had angered their French allies with embarrassing investigations into the orthodoxy of the princesses, by local investigators or the papal inquisition. The pope was head of the Catholic Church, but his position as prince of the Papal States and the potential political backlash from

---

52   Del Col, 'Le strutture territoriali e l'attività dell'Inquisizione Romana' in Agostino Borromeo (ed.), *L'Inquisizione. Atti del Simposio internazionale* (Vatican City: Biblioteca Apostolica Vaticana, 2003), pp.356–357. On the inquisition in Venice see Riccardo Calimani, *L'Inquisizione a Venezia: eretici e processi, 1548–1674* (Milan: Mondadori, 2002) and Del Col, 'Organizzazione, composizione e giurisdizione dei tribunali dell'Inquisizione romana nella repubblica di Venezia (1500–1550)', *Critica storica*, 25 (1988), pp. 244–294.

53   Adorni-Bracessi, 'La Repubblica di Lucca e l'<<aborrita>> Inquisizione' in Del Col and Paolin (eds), *L'Inquisizione Romana in Italia nell'età moderna*, p.234.

54   Polanco, *Vita ignatii Loiolae*, vol.2, p.177.

55   On Ferrara see Blaisdell, 'Politics and Heresy in Ferrara'. On Piedmont see Lavenia, 'L'Inquisizione del duca'.

56   Blaisdell, 'Politics and Heresy in Ferrara', p.71 and Lavenia, 'L'Inquisizione del duca', pp.418–9.

inquisitorial investigations meant that there was real resistance to the Roman Inquisition, even amongst Catholic princes in Italy.

Relations between state powers and the delegates of the Roman Inquisition were particularly complex in Piacenza. In 1547, after half a century of jostling between the papacy, France and Habsburg forces, Piacenza was ceded to the governors of Emperor Charles v.[57] Triumph for the imperial side came with a highly personal attack on Pope Paul III – the murder of his most beloved son, Pierluigi Farnese, whom he had made duke of Parma and Piacenza.[58] The murder was thought to have been carried out by allies of the imperial viceroy of Milan, Ferrante Gonzaga.[59] Gonzaga was soon to deal another blow to the pope. When Paul III founded the papal inquisition in 1542, Piacenza's own inquisitorial tribunal became subject to the Holy Office at Rome. However, after taking control of the city in 1547 Gonzaga repudiated the authority of the pope's inquisition, declaring that the new Piacentine state had supreme jurisdiction in all cases of heresy.[60]

Throughout the late 1540s and early 1550s, the governing élite of Piacenza failed to cooperate with the local inquisitors to combat the heresy that was rampant in the city.[61] When the *podestà* of Piacenza, Pietro Antonio Marliano,

---

57   Piero Castignoli, *Eresia e inquisizione a Piacenza nel cinquecento* (Piacenza: Tipleco, 2008), p.81. On political-jurisdictional changes in sixteenth-century Piacenza see Ditchfield, *Liturgy, sanctity and history in Tridentine Italy*, pp.9–10.

58   Hubert Jedin in Erwin Iserloh, Joseph Glazik and Hubert Jedin, Anselm Biggs and Peter W. Becker (trans.), *Reformation and Counter Reformation* (London: Burns and Oates, 1980), p.474. See also, María José Bertomeu Masiá, *La guerra secreta de Carlos V contra el Papa. La cuestión de Parma y Piacenza en la corrispondencia del cardenal Granvela. Edición, estudio y notas* (Valencia: Universitat de València, 2009), pp.28–52. On the relocation of the Council of Trent see O'Malley, *Trent: What happened at the Council*, p.134.

59   O'Malley, *Trent: What happened at the Council*, p.134. On the assassination of Pier Luigi Farnese see also Stefano dall'Aglio & Donald Weinstein (trans.), *The Duke's Assassin: Exile and Death of Lorenzino De'Medici* (New Haven: Yale University Press, 2015), p. 102 and 179.

60   Castignoli, *Eresia e inquisizione a Piacenza*, p.83.

61   Umberto Locati, *Cronica dell'origine di Piacenza già latinamente fatta per il R.P. Omberto Locati, e hora dal medesimo, ridotta fedelmente nella volgare nostra favella* (Cremona: Vincenzo Conti, 1564), p.305. On heresy in Piacenza see, Gianmarco Braghi, *L'accademia degli Ortolani (1543–1545). Eresia, stampa e cultura a Piacenza nel medio Cinquecento* (Piacenza: Edizioni L.I.R., 2011); Castignoli, *Eresia e inquisizione a Piacenza nel cinquecento*; Salvatore Caponetto, Anne C. Tedeschi and John Tedeschi (trans.), *The Protestant Reformation in sixteenth-century Italy* (Kirksville: Thomas Jefferson University Press, 1999), p.226; Federico Chabod, *Per la storia religiosa dello Stato di Milano durante il dominio di Carlo V. Note e documenti* (Rome: Istituto Storico Italiano, 1962), pp.168–70; 191–2 and Franco Molinari, *Il cardinale teatino beato Paolo Buriali e la riforma tridentina a Piacenza (1568–1576)* (Rome: Aedes Universitatis Gregorianae, 1957).

COLLABORATION, COMPETITION AND CONFLICT

asked inquisitor Callisto Fornari for the names of those whom he suspected of heresy and what evidence he had against them Fornari rejected the request outright.[62] Inquisitor Fornari even threatened the governors of the city, telling them that temporal authorities had no right to interfere in his work, lest they incur 'the censures and excommunications provided by His Holiness Julius III for such cases.[63] Hostility towards Fornari was equally vehement. In a letter to Ferrante Gonzaga, Marliano wrote that Fornari was so disliked in Piacenza that an insulting sonnet mocking the inquisitor had been 'found attached to diverse places of the city'.[64] This in-fighting did nothing for efforts to fight heresy. Years of hostility between the inquisitorial tribunal and the city's Spanish governors hampered the ability of both inquisitorial and state authorities to identify and convert the city's heretics.[65]

The acrimony between Piacenza's inquisitors and temporal authorities was further exacerbated when accusations of heresy were directed against the city's élite. In a sermon of 1549, Fornari had claimed that Protestantism was rife amongst the Piacentine nobility.[66] Moreover, the local inquisitor did not see the high social status of his accusants as an obstacle to acting upon his suspicions. According to a letter written in May 1552 by the governor of Piacenza, Garcia Manrique, the officials of the inquisition tried to proceed against many citizens of the city, acting impertinently and 'putting the spirits of many in a mess and a muddle'.[67] Manrique had admonished Fornari, suggesting that, in the future, the inquisitor proceed with the necessary finesse in such matters.[68] But Fornari proved unresponsive and relations between the papal tribunal and the Piacentine élite remained antagonistic.

---

62   ASMil, *Documenti diplomatici post 1535*, 148, ff.514 and 519, edited in Chabod, *Per la storia religiosa dello Stato di Milano durante il dominio di Carlo V. Note e documenti*, p.274 and ASMil, *Documenti diplomatici post 1535*, 148, f.517. Edited in Chabod, *Per la storia religiosa dello Stato di Milano durante il dominio di Carlo V. Note e documenti*, p.273.

63   See letter edited in Chabod, *Per la storia religiosa dello Stato di Milano durante il dominio di Carlo V. Note e documenti*, p.273. Fornari referred to a brief of Pope Julius III of March 1551, which stated that civil authorities could not intervene in inquisitorial business.

64   ASMil, *Documenti diplomatici post 1535*, 149, f.672. Edited in Chabod, *Per la storia religiosa dello Stato di Milano durante il dominio di Carlo V. Note e documenti*, p.275.

65   This persisted even after the Farnese returned to Piacenza, for example in the duke's attempted revocation of local inquisitor Umberto Locati. Ditchfield, 'Umberto Locati O.P. (1503–1587): Inquisitore, Vescovo e Storico – un profilo bio-bibliografico', *Bolletino Storico Piacentino*, 84, (1989), p.212.

66   Molinari, *Il cardinale teatino beato Paolo Buriali*, p.33.

67   ASMil, *Documenti diplomatici post 1535*, 148, f.79. Edited in Chabod, *Per la storia religiosa dello Stato di Milano durante il dominio di Carlo V. Note e documenti*, p.273.

68   Ibid.

76   CHAPTER 2

The cardinal-inquisitors of Rome wanted to resolve this stale-mate so they sent a Spanish Jesuit to reconcile heretics in the city. The mission was instigated by Manrique himself, who had expressed severe concerns about the orthodoxy of his wife, Isabella Bresegna, in a conversation with his nephew Cardinal Francesco Bobadilla y Mendoza.[69] Manrique did not want to humiliate his wife but the accusations of heterodoxy that had followed her since the 1540s were a source of considerable public scandal.[70] Recognising the delicacy of the situation, Cardinal Mendoza contacted Loyola through a secretary who travelled to Rome in person to discuss what was simply too sensitive to be committed to correspondence.[71] Mendoza liaised with Loyola and their mutual ally Cardinal Toledo to find somebody who could undertake the task successfully, seeing to the 'spiritual health of that person who has such necessity of it' whilst 'procuring it without any particular dishonour or hearsay'.[72] Father Martin Olave was selected for the mission and officially charged by cardinal-inquisitor Toledo to visit 'a certain court' at Piacenza, which was 'infected by the fraud of the Demon, by Lutheran heresy, or certainly vehemently suspected' to be.[73] In Piacenza, Toledo ordered Olave to convert and absolve Bresegna and any heretics in her circle, reconciling 'everyone, who is in the said house or family'.[74]

The patent given to Olave by cardinal-inquisitor Toledo granted the Jesuit powers that were even greater than those that the Society had received from the Julius III, extending them so that he could absolve heretics in *utroque foro*, that is in either the internal or external forum.[75] Whilst Olave's papal privileges allowed him to absolve and reconcile heretics in place of an inquisitor, they did not empower him to reverse any existing inquisitorial condemnation or censure. With Toledo's patent, Olave could not only reconcile heretics unknown to the Holy Office but also reverse any sentences that had been executed by

---

69   Polanco, *Vita Ignatii Loiolae*, vol.4, pp.139–40.

70   On Bresegna see Hugo Rahner, *Ignatius von Loyola als Mensch und Theologe* (Freiburg: Herder, 1964), pp. 197–206; Camilla Russell, *Giulia Gonzaga and the religious controversies of sixteenth-century Italy* (Turnhout: Brepols, 2006), pp.80–1 and 87. See also, Caponetto (ed.), *Benedetto da Mantova. Il Beneficio di Cristo. Con le versioni del secolo XVI, documenti e testimonianze* (Chicago: Newberry Library, 1972), pp.449–50, fn.11. Caponetto is incorrect when he states that Isabella fled Piacenza in 1553, a year before Olave's arrival.

71   Polanco, *Vita Ignatii Loiolae*, vol.4, p.139. See also Mendoza to Loyola, *Sancti Ignatii de Loyola epistolae et instructiones*, vol.6, p.704.

72   Mendoza to Loyola, *Sancti Ignatii de Loyola epistolae et instructiones*, vol.6, p.506.

73   See his instructions and patent in ARSI, *Institutum 194*, f.73r.

74   Ibid.

75   Ibid.

COLLABORATION, COMPETITION AND CONFLICT

Fornari. The instructions from Toledo make the intention of Olave's powers clear, stating that he 'should restore [members of the court] to integrity of reputation' and make 'them and their descendants suitable for each and every position, dignity, honour, office and benefice'.[76] In his official instructions for the mission, Loyola told Olave that all were to be treated with discretion and that Toledo had ordered the Jesuit to receive 'the abjurations and acts [of faith] from them, [so] that matters that relate to the external forum proceed judicially, but secretly'.[77] In Piacenza, Olave had both the power to replace the failed inquisitors and delicately – and secretly – reverse any damage that they had done.

Just as in Rodriguez's mission to Le Marche, the Jesuits' distinct identity was key to the mission strategy. As a Jesuit rather than an inquisitor Olave had a distinct identity that was removed from the notion of papal interference. Olave's Iberian patrimony also distanced him from association with Roman power. In Spanish Italy, there was a belief in the strength of Iberian identity, a *unitas generis* based on language, morality, psychology and thought.[78] During the early 1550s, for example, many wished to see solely Spanish governors in the Duchy of Milan.[79] The Jesuits themselves acknowledged common nationality as a diplomatic tool, sending Spanish fathers to govern Jesuits in Iberian-ruled areas of the peninsula where Italian fathers complained of their characteristically Spanish rigour.[80] Olave's Iberian identity was certainly seen as an asset by those who organised the mission to Piacenza who wrote that Olave had the 'ears and tongue necessary for this matter'.[81] Olave's background also helped him practically. Bresegna herself spoke Italian only with some difficulty.[82] In the wake of conflicts between papal nobility and Spanish Habsburg forces,

---

76 Ibid.

77 Loyola, *Sancti Ignatii de Loyola epistolae et instructiones*, vol.6, p.507.

78 Chabod, *Lo Stato e la vita religiosa a Milano nell'epoca di Carlo V* (Turin: Giulio Einaudi Editore, 1971), pp.215–6. On the importance of Spanish identity in the politics of the Duchy of Milan at the end of the reign of Charles V and the beginning of Philip II, see Chabod, *Lo Stato e la vita religiosa a Milano nell'epoca di Carlo V*, pp.215–225. On the Spanish in Italy see Dandelet and Marino (eds), *Spain in Italy*. On the Jesuits and other religious orders in Spanish Italy see Flavio Rurale, 'Male religious orders in Sixteenth-century Italy' in Dandelet and Marino (eds), ibid., pp. 481–516.

79 Chabod, *Lo Stato e la vita religiosa a Milano nell'epoca di Carlo V*, p.219 and pp.222–3.

80 Esther Jimenez Pablo, 'The Evolution of the Society of Jesus during the Sixteenth and Seventeenth Centuries: an Order that Favoured the Papacy or the Hispanic Monarchy?' in Massimo Carlo Giannini, *Papacy, Religious Orders, and International Politics in the Sixteenth and Seventeenth Centuries* (Rome: Viella, 2013), pp.54–5.

81 Loyola, *Sancti Ignatii de Loyola epistolae et instructiones*, vol.6, p.506.

82 Castignoli, *Eresia e inquisizione a Piacenza*, p.85.

Olave's Jesuit identity and kinship with Manrique's house ingratiated him with his Piacentine hosts whilst alienating him from the local inquisitors and all that they represented.

It was not only on missions to Spanish territories that Jesuits would use their institutional distinctiveness and shared patrimony to try to convert heretics. In the same month as Olave set out for Piacenza, French Jesuit Jean Pelletier went to the court of Ercole d'Este to convert his Protestant wife, Renée of France. In a mission of similarly acute sensitivity, Pelletier assumed a role that could not be undertaken by the duke's local inquisitors or directly by the cardinal-inquisitors of Rome.[83] This was a highly important case. In Ferrara, Renée's heresy was a scandal.[84] She had even invited John Calvin to the ducal court.[85] Despite the apparent depth of Renée's Protestant beliefs and the gravity of her actions political concerns prevented the local inquisitors and the cardinals of the Holy Office from even trying to convert her. This was a political problem. Renée was the daughter of the late King Louis XII of France and cousin to the king regnant, Henry II. In an effort to win French favour, Pope Paul III had banned d'Este's local inquisitors from trying to convert the princess.[86] This put Renée directly under the jurisdiction of the cardinal-inquisitors but, as delegates of the pope, they were unlikely to risk an intervention that could anger or embarrass the king of France.[87] Once again, a Jesuit offered the diplomatic solution. Pelletier was not only a Frenchman, as a Jesuit he was also an ally of Ferrara and Rome. Moreover, with his autonomous identity and jurisdiction, he could act independently of both the duke and the pope. As with Olave in Piacenza, Pelletier distanced himself from the political acrimony excited by the ducal and Roman inquisitions to intervene in the conversion of a member of the foreign élite. In doing so, Pelletier made himself an asset to both the state and to Rome.

Ultimately, both Olave and Pelletier were unsuccessful in their attempts to convert the foreign noblewomen and their circles. Just weeks after Olave's arrival in Piacenza in March 1554, Manrique wrote to Loyola of his great sadness at the Jesuit's imminent departure.[88] The following year Bresegna's

---

83 For Pelletier's plan to convert Renée see his letter to Loyola in *Epistolae mixtae*, vol.4, pp.119–21.

84 On Renée of France see also, Bartolomeo Fontana, *Renata di Francia, duchessa di Ferrara* (Rome: Forzani, 1889–1890).

85 Church, *The Italian Reformers*, p.86.

86 Blaisdell, 'Politics and Heresy in Ferrara', p.81.

87 Ibid., p.82.

88 Manrique in Loyola, *Sancti Ignatii de Loyola epistolae et instructiones*, vol.6, p.498.

COLLABORATION, COMPETITION AND CONFLICT

rejection of Catholic norms was confirmed when Giulio Basalù told the inquisition at Venice that she had an heretical 'opinion of justification' and had denied the value of 'the sacraments and the Mass'.[89] In 1557, Bresegna vindicated her accusers, fleeing Italy for Protestant Tübingen before travelling to Zürich and settling in Calvinist Chiavenna.[90] Renée may have abjured her heresy under Pelletier's influence but she too fled the peninsula for France after her husband's death in 1559.[91] Later, the demise of her powerful Catholic son-in-law, Francois, Duke of Guise, granted Renée the liberty to live openly as a Calvinist in France where she acted as a patroness and protector of Protestants.

Although both missions failed, the examples of Piacenza and Ferrara illuminate the extent to which politics, within and without the peninsula, affected the operations of the Roman Inquisition and its satellite tribunals. The cases also highlight the important role of Jesuits in attempts to overcome these political obstacles. The Society had not yet earned the indelible association with papal Rome that would come to ornament, or, in the work of their detractors, taint the Jesuits' reputation in the future.[92] As a new religious order with an international membership, the Society provided inquisitors with autonomous agents who could execute the will of the Holy Office where politics hampered the success of explicitly inquisitorial delegates. Common heritage with temporal powers further alienated these Jesuits from Italian papal power and ingratiated them with their hosts. On other missions, the Jesuits' distinction from the Roman Inquisition facilitated dialogue with heretics on a personal as well as a political level. As the years wore on and popular hostility to the Holy Office grew, the contrast between the pastoral image of the Jesuits and the more authoritarian character of the inquisitors became starker and so an increasingly important asset for the Society's work for the Roman Inquisition.

---

89   See the denunciation of Giulio Basalù to the Venetian inquisition in Archivio di Stato di Venezia, *Sant'Uffizio*, busta 159, ff.37r-v and 38v. Edited in Caponetto (ed.), *Benedetto da Mantova*, pp.448–9. Russell, *Giulia Gonzaga*, p.166.

90   Russell, *Giulia Gonzaga*, p.166.

91   Blaisdell, 'Politics and Heresy in Ferrara', p.87; Caponetto, *The Protestant Reformation in sixteenth-century Italy*, pp.242–3.

92   On the historiography and mythologies surrounding the history of the Jesuits see, for example, O'Malley, 'The Historiography of the Society of Jesus: Where does it stand today?' and Pavone, *The Wily Jesuits and the Monita secreta: The Forged Secret Instructions of the Jesuits: Myth and Reality* (St Louis: Institute of Jesuit Sources, 2005).

80   CHAPTER 2

3   Good Cop/Bad Cop: Conversion Strategies in the 1560s

Pope Paul IV had sought to undermine the Jesuits' role in the fight against heresy, but events of the 1560s indicate that, ultimately, his harsh anti-heretical initiatives made them a more valuable asset in the fight against heresy, especially
to the Roman Inquisition. During his pontificate as Paul IV former cardinal-
inquisitor Gian Pietro Carafa expanded inquisitorial authority, jealously guard-
ing the tribunal's power and limiting the jurisdiction of others involved in the
fight against heresy.[93] Carafa was a vehement opponent of religious dissenters,
reputedly claiming that 'if my own father were a heretic, I would gather the
wood to burn him'.[94] Carafa firmly believed that his inquisition's jurisdiction
trumped that of secular powers.[95] In the last years of the 1550s, Paul IV ordered
confessors to refuse absolution to penitent dissenters who had not revealed
themselves to his all-powerful inquisitors, effectively undermining the Jesuits' privilege until cardinal-inquisitor Ghislieri won them an exemption.[96] By
his death in 1559, Paul IV's focus on punitive means of combating heresy had
damaged the reputation of the Roman Inquisition, with the general public as
well as political leaders. Inadvertently, therefore, Carafa had made the inquisition's Jesuit collaborators all the more valuable as the Society offered loyal,
ostensibly benign agents who could solicit penitents on behalf of the Holy Office. There are few traces of collaborations between the Society and the Roman
Inquisition during Paul IV's reign. However, after the pope's demise flurries of
letters between the Jesuits and cardinal-inquisitor Ghislieri indicate that the
Society and the Holy Office instrumentalised the contrast between the pastoral character of the Jesuits and public perceptions of a formidable inquisition,
an image that had significantly worsened under the Carafa pope.[97]
      During the sixteenth century, Jesuits across the peninsula reported that
penitent-heretics came to them to avoid a Holy Office that they feared.

---

93   Daniele Santarelli, 'Dinamiche interne della Congregazione del Sant'Uffizio dal 1542 al
      1572', *Nuova Rivista Storica*, 97 (2013), pp.9–10. See also, Firpo, *La presa di potere*.
94   The quote was given by Venetian ambassador, Bernardo Navagero on 23 Oct 1557. See
      Santarelli (ed.), *La correspondenza di Bernardo Navagero, ambasciatore veneziano a Roma
      (1555–1558)* (Rome: Aracne, 2011), p.587–90.
95   Santarelli, *Il papato di Paolo IV nella crisi politico-religiosa del Cinquecento: le relazioni con
      la Repubblica di Venezia e l'atteggiamento nei confronti di Carlo V e Filippo II* (Rome: Aracne,
      2008), pp.170–1.
96   Peter Canisius, *Beati Petri Canisii, Societatis Iesu, epistulae et acta. Collegit et adnotationi-
      bus illustravit Otto Braunsberger* (Freiburg: 1896–1923), 8 vols, vol.2, p.658.
97   See, for example, the collection of letters from Ghislieri to Rodriguez edited in Scaduto,
      'Tra Inquisitori e Riformati'.

COLLABORATION, COMPETITION AND CONFLICT 81

According to the Jesuits, these penitents were terrified that if they handed themselves in the tribunal would prove unmerciful. In Turin, a father reported that going to the Holy Office would be a 'most hateful matter' for penitent-heretics.[98] In Bologna, Salmerón wrote that Lutherans converted but would not approach inquisitors as they 'had heard how in Rome [people] went castigating some suspected heretics'.[99] Working in the Kingdom of Naples, Father Cristóbal Rodriguez said that people were so scared of the inquisitors that they would not even come to church, because 'they were frightened, remembering those who had been taken [by the Holy Office] the previous year'.[100] Later arguments for the Society's privilege to absolve heretics were often framed around their ability to reconcile heretics who dreaded the Holy Office, as we shall in chapter 4. Already during the mid-sixteenth century, from the north to the south of the peninsula, Jesuits in Italy argued that negative perceptions of the inquisitors and their methods stopped penitents from approaching the tribunal.

Inquisitorial documents indicate that the Holy Office and its delegates also acknowledged that fear of the tribunal was a major obstacle to penitents. Moreover, they show that the inquisition attempted to overcome this hurdle. In the 1570s, the inquisitor of Turin argued that more conciliatory techniques and fewer punishments would make the tribunal that was 'hateful to all' more successful, claiming that he had converted many heretics with no threat of penalties.[101] An earlier edict announcing the arrival of an inquisitor in Bergamo tried to soften the reputation of the inquisition, declaring that, in spite of their threats of punishment, they sought 'the salvation of souls and not the death of persons'.[102] A similar edict of the 1560s also attempted to allay fears that the tribunal was unmerciful, encouraging heretics to 'leave the shadows' for the 'living rays of the kindness of Pope Pius V', claiming that the inquisitors' 'ears are always ready to hear you' and 'arms are always ready to welcome you, and you will always find our heart soft ... and our spirit inclined to indulgence'.[103] Vincenzo Lavenia has corroborated the link between the punishments of the Roman Inquisition and its reputation, arguing that the Holy Office of Rome did not earn a Black Legend as terrifying as the Spanish tribunal because it abandoned public punishments after the 1570s.[104] In the period covered in

---

98 ARSI, *Epistolae Italiae 136*, f.169r.
99 Salmerón, *Epistolae Salmeronis*, vol. 1, p.63.
100 See his report in ASR, *Miscellanea Famiglie Gesuiti*, B180, fasc. 14, filza 15.
101 For a discussion of this account see Lavenia, 'L'Inquisizione del duca', p.443.
102 Archivio di Stato di Modena (hereafter, ASM), *Inquisizione*, busta 270, fasc. 1.
103 ASM, *Inquisizione*, busta 270, fasc. 3.
104 Lavenia, 'Il tribunale innominato', pp.295–6.

82   CHAPTER 2

this chapter, these penalties were still used and both Jesuits and inquisitors acknowledged that public fear of the inquisition was a major impediment to securing conversions.

The cruel image of the Holy Office was grounded in tales of the medieval Italian inquisitors and their early modern Spanish counterparts but contemporary accounts indicate that the sixteenth-century tribunal also earnt hostility.[105] One of the inquisition's founding fathers, Gian Pietro Carafa, had a clear influence on negative perceptions of the papal tribunal. As cardinal-inquisitor and, from 1555, as Pope Paul IV, Carafa intensified the scope and severity of the Roman Inquisition. Carafa's influence over the tribunal was so great that he attempted to use it as a tool to define the limits of Catholic orthodoxy on his own terms, condemning all those who did not live up to his ideal, despite the diverse viewpoints present in the papal curia.[106] As Pietro Carnesecchi wrote in a letter of 1557, as pope, Carafa seemed to be 'taking care to fill the prisons with cardinals and bishops on behalf of the inquisition'.[107] Carnesecchi's own release from the jails of the Holy Office on Paul's death in 1559 is a testament to the extent of the pope's influence over the fate of those whom he distrusted. Carnesecchi's eventual condemnation and execution by Carafa's protegée, Michele Ghislieri, has been identified by scholars as the ultimate triumph of the inquisitor-pope's campaign against those who took a compromising stance towards Reformation ideas.[108]

Paul IV's vehemence against heretics was well-known during his lifetime. In his first year on the papal throne, Neapolitan student Pomponio Algeri was condemned as a heretic and boiled in oil in Rome's Piazza Navona.[109] This highly unusual and cruel execution was quickly memorialised in Protestant

---

105   Del Col, *L'Inquisizione in Italia,* p.819.
106   Firpo, *Inquisizione Romana e Controriforma. Studi sul cardinal Giovanni Morone e il suo processo d'eresia* (Bologna: Il Mulino, 1992), p.13.
107   Carnesecchi quoted in Firpo and Marcatto (eds), *I processi inquisitoriali di Pietro Carnesecchi (1557–1567)* (Vatican City: Archivio Segreto Vaticano, 1998–2000), 3 vols, vol. 2, part 1, pp.268–9. On the influence of Carafa's accusations in the failure of Reginald Pole's papal candidature see Dermot Fenlon, *Heresy and Obedience in Tridentine Italy: Cardinal Pole and the Counter-Reformation* (Cambridge: Cambridge University Press, 1972), pp.224–235 and Firpo, *La presa di potere.* On the trial of Giovanni Morone see Firpo and Marcatto, *Il Processo Inquisitoriale del cardinal Giovanni Morone.*
108   See Ditchfield, 'Innovation and its limits. The case of Italy ca.1512-ca.1572' in Philip Benedict, Seidel-Menchi and Alain Tallon (eds), *La Réforme en France et en Italie* (Rome: École Française de Rome, 2007), pp.154–6. See also, 'The Carnesecchi Moment' in Black, *The Italian Inquisition,* pp.123–130.
109   On Algeri's case see Santarelli, 'Morte di un eretico impenitente'.

COLLABORATION, COMPETITION AND CONFLICT

martyrologies.[110] Such accounts further tainted the image painted by books on Carafa's tribunal written by Italian religious exiles such as Girolamo Massari.[111] Sixteenth-century correspondence also illustrates that there was a clear public perception of particular popes' attitudes towards heretics. During the pontificate of Paul's successor, Pius IV, pamphlets stated that Paul IV 'was made hateful and almost dreaded' for his inquisitorial rigour.[112] Conversely, a letter sent to a prisoner of the Roman Inquisition during the pontificate of the more lenient Gregory XIII calls the man to request pardon 'from the present pope, who is a very benign, benevolent prince, and who happily pardons each person who comes penitent and humbled'.[113] Taking charge of the tribunal during its formative years, Carafa's zealotry towards religious dissenters left a black mark on his reputation and that of the Roman Inquisition. This was an ill repute that would survive Carafa's death in 1559.

Supreme Inquisitor Michele Ghislieri was dedicated to continuing Carafa's agenda after his death but well-aware of the obstacles posed by hostility towards the inquisition.[114] To overcome these obstacles he turned to the Jesuits. Ghislieri was familiar with the hostility faced by the Holy Office. In 1551, he had fled Como when popular resistance to his own investigations became violent.[115] Such experience surely contributed to the inquisitor's appreciation of Jesuit agents who could circumvent opposition to the tribunal. As we have seen in his later instructions to Rodriguez in Le Marche – written after he had

---

110 See, for example, Heinrich Pantaleon, *Martyrum historia. Hoc est maximarum per Europam persecutionem ac sanctorum Dei Martyrym, caeterarum que rerum insignium, in Ecclesia Christi postremis and periculosis his temporibus gestarum, atque certo cnsilioper Regna and Nationes distributarum, Commentarii* (Basel: Nicolaus Brylingerus, 1563), p.329.

111 See, for example, Massari's counterfeit inquisitorial manual with a false Roman imprint: [Girolamo Massari] *Modus solennis et autenticus, ad inquirendum and convincendum Luteranos, valde necessarius, ad salutem Sanctae Apostolicae Sedis, and omnium Ecclesiasticorum, anno 1519 compositus, in Martini Luteri perditionem, and eius sequacium* ([Basel: Johannes Oporin], 1553). On historical and literary accounts of the early modern inquisitions see Prosperi, 'L'Inquisizione nella storia: i caratteri originali di una controversia secolare' in Prosperi, *Inquisizione Romana: letture e ricerche*, pp.69–96; Lavenia 'Il Tribunale Innominato' and Michaela Valente, *Contro l'Inquisizione: il dibattito europeo, secc. XVI–XVIII* (Turin: Claudiana, 2009).

112 Eugenio Albèri (ed.), *Relazioni degli ambasciatori veneti al senato* (Florence: Società Editrice Fiorentina, 1839–1863), 15 vols, vol. 10, pp. 29; 46–51. On sixteenth-century descriptions of Paul IV and links to contemporary politics see Alberto Aubert, *Paolo IV. Politica, Inquisizione e storiografia* (Florence: Le Lettere, 1990) particularly pp.109–223.

113 Archiginnasio, *B1860*, CCXLV.

114 Elena Bonora, *Giudicare i vescovi. La definizione dei poteri nella Chiesa postridentina* (Rome: Laterza, 2007), p.xii.

115 Church, *The Italian Reformers*, p.165.

become Pope Pius V – Ghislieri clearly recognised that Jesuits were more readily trusted than papal agents.[116] In the early 1560s, Ghislieri and the Jesuits began to develop these strategies, using the Society's benign reputation to combat heresy in parts of the peninsula where the inquisition had marred its own reputation and so inhibited its chances of securing conversions.

The Jesuits were active collaborators in these inquisitorial strategies. During a mission to the Puglian diocese of Vulturara in the early 1560s, Cristóbal Rodriguez would insist upon his autonomy from the Roman Inquisition even as he worked hand-in-glove with his patron cardinal-inquisitor Ghislieri. The year after the mission in a report to Jesuit father Francesco Borja, Rodriguez stated that he had not worked as an inquisitor in Vulturara, despite the fact that he went to the diocese on the orders of the Roman Inquisition.[117] Rodriguez stated that '... the Society did not want the father sent by the Holy Office to go as a commissary or judge of the Holy Office'.[118] In fact, Rodriguez had asserted this distinction at the time. Rodriguez claimed that when he and his missionary companion had announced their arrival to the local authorities in Vulturara – normal practice for members of the Society – they made it clear that they had not come as inquisitorial judges but only on behalf of the Holy Office to preach the truth of the faith and to comfort souls 'so that those who had incurred excommunication were absolved of it'.[119] Further distancing himself from the Holy Office, Rodriguez asserted that he had not only rejected inquisitorial office in Vulturara but that he had defied the papal tribunal in doing so, refusing to 'go as a commissary or judge of the Holy Office like the cardinals [of the inquisition] had asked'.[120] In Rodriguez's report to Borja and his account of the announcement to the governor in Vulturara he wanted to make it crystal clear that he did not act as an inquisitor.

Yet Rodriguez's claim that he did not work as an inquisitorial commissary or judge contradicts his own descriptions of his actions in Vulturara. In the very report in which he denied acting in an inquisitorial office, Rodriguez wrote that he was given orders on how to impose sentences, abjurations, and penances for those who would confess the truth and 'to pick and imprison the others'.[121] In both the nature of his duties and his obedience to the Holy Office

---

116   Michele Miele, 'Pio V e la presenza dei Domenicani nel corso della sua vita' in Guasco and Angelo Torre (eds), *Pio V nella società e nella politica del suo tempo* (Bologna: Il Mulino, 2005), p.30.

117   On this mission and others in the area see, Scaduto, 'Tra Inquisitori e Riformati'.

118   ASR, *Miscellanea Famiglie Gesuiti*, B180, fasc. 14, filza 15.

119   Ibid.

120   Ibid.

121   Ibid.

COLLABORATION, COMPETITION AND CONFLICT

Rodriguez acted as an inquisitorial commissary. Furthermore, in an earlier, personal letter to Laínez Rodriguez admits to the fact, writing that in Vulturara he was undertaking the same service as 'Reverend Father Valero' Malvicino, the inquisitorial commissary to the region before Rodriguez's arrival.[122] A memorial written in the second half of the 1560s, now held at the ARSI, also reveals that Rodriguez acted as an inquisitorial commissary in Vulturara, stating that, 'In the past years, the said Reverend Father Christophoro Rodriguez, doctor of Holy Theology and commissary of the Holy Office of Rome, was in the diocese of Vulturara'.[123] Despite his protestations, it is clear from evidence produced during and after the mission that Rodriguez's rejection of inquisitorial status in Vulturara was a matter of appearances and not of reality.

Rodriguez alienated himself from the inquisitors for both political and pastoral reasons. His motivations are illuminated by a second report dated to July of 1564, a *littera quadrimestra*, which was a standard four-monthly update written for circulation within the Society.[124] The report clearly states that Rodriguez was sent to Vulturara by the Holy Office, working 'at the insistence of the cardinal inquisitors [for] the conversion and instruction of some lands ... [where] almost everybody is a heretic'.[125] Like Rodriguez's own report to Borja, this report underlines Rodriguez's status as an independent agent, stating that he 'did not do the work as an inquisitor, but as that which was proper to our Society'.[126] A small detail in the report reveals why this distinction was vital. It tells us that Rodriguez's work in Vulturara was almost brought to an abrupt end when 'ministers of the devil' spread rumours that he 'was acting in an office of the Roman Inquisition'.[127] On hearing these accusations, the state authorities arrested Rodriguez as, in Vulturara, the activities of the Roman Inquisition were not only despised but illicit.[128] The reason that Rodriguez was so keen to underline his status as a Jesuit rather than an inquisitor was because, in the territory of Vulturara, the negative repercussions of association with the Holy Office would have robbed him of both his mission and his freedom.

---

122 ARSI, *Epistolae nostrorum 86*, f.182r. On Malvicino see Lavenia, 'Un inquisitore e i valdesi di Calabria. Valerio Malvicini' in Renata Ciaccio and Alfonso Tortora (eds), *Valdismo mediterraneo. Tra centro e periferia. Sulla storia moderna dei valdesi di Calabria* (Salerno: ViValiber, 2013), pp.105–22.

123 ARSI, *Epistolae Italiae 134*, f.412r.

124 Friedrich, 'Ignatius's Governing and Administrating the Society of Jesus', p.138.

125 ASR, *Miscellanea Famiglie Gesuiti*, B180, fasc.14, filza 23, f.10r.

126 Ibid.

127 Ibid., f.10v.

128 Ibid.

The Roman tribunal faced significant political obstacles in the Kingdom of Naples. Since the early 1540s, its Spanish rulers had blocked the establishment of a papal tribunal in the land.[129] In his report, Rodriguez argued that heresies were discovered so late in Vulturara for precisely this reason: because there was not 'an inquisition of the Holy Office in the Kingdom of Naples to use the means that it uses in the lands of His Holiness'.[130] In the absence of a permanent tribunal, the inquisition in Naples was run by bishops. That Rodriguez was well-aware of this important difference is clear from the multiple episcopal patents that he won for the prosecution of heresy in the various dioceses of the Kingdom in 1564.[131] These patents were a legitimate route to securing full jurisdiction over heresy in the diocese.[132] Nonetheless, whether using an episcopal patent or his own papal privileges, Rodriguez still worked as an inquisitor whilst stating that he was merely a pastor.[133]

The cardinal-inquisitors also faced serious pastoral problems in the Kingdom of Naples. Trust between the inquisition and the people of the region was almost non-existent. During the early 1560s, state authorities and delegates of the Roman Inquisition cooperated to convert the region's centuries-old Waldensian communities.[134] During these interventions, in the years immediately preceding Rodriguez's arrival in 1563, the name of the Holy Office had been utterly blackened when the inquisition violently repressed the Waldensian communities in San Sisto and La Guardia.[135] Persistent heretics were executed, villages were razed to the ground, the bones of the deceased were dug up and burnt.[136] Arriving at the close of one of the most bloody chapters in the history of the Italian inquisitions, Rodriguez would have enjoyed little success soliciting conversions as a representative of the Holy Office.

---

129 Henry Charles Lea, *The Inquisition in the Spanish dependencies: Sicily-Naples-Sardinia-Milan-The Canaries-Mexico-Peru-New Granada* (London: Macmillan, 1922), pp. 49–88, especially pp.78–80. Peter Mazur, *The New Christians of Spanish Naples 1528–1671: a fragile elite* (Palgrave Macmillan: Houndsmills, Basingstoke, 2013), p.3.

130 ASR, *Miscellanea Famiglie Gesuiti*, B180, fasc.14, f.15.

131 Multiple examples can be found in ARSI, *Institutum 194*, ff.160r-v; f.165r, f.166r, f.167r. Scaduto, 'Cristoforo Rodriguez tra i valdesi della Capitanata e dell'Irpinia', *Archivum Historicum Societatis Iesu*, 35 (1966), p.21.

132 Brambilla, *Alle origini del Sant'Uffizio*, p.480–1.

133 Prosperi, 'L'inquisitore come confessore' in Prodi (ed.), *Disciplina dell'anima, disciplina del corpo e disciplina della società tra medioevo ed età moderna* (Bologna: Il Mulino, 1993), p.196.

134 On the Waldensians in the Kingdom of Naples see Scaramella, *L'Inquisizione romana e i valdesi*.

135 Prosperi, *Tribunali della coscienza*, pp.5–7.

136 Ibid.

COLLABORATION, COMPETITION AND CONFLICT

Appearing to work autonomously, Rodriguez could convert and reconcile heretics without exciting the fear associated with commissaries who had caused such devastation in the recent past. Rodriguez himself recognised the need to overcome recent inquisitorial history in a territory where he found 'the whole land very terrified and alarmed', frightened that the Jesuit would be another Malvicino, who had 'put many in prison, and from there to the galleys'.[137] Using other means and acting with great gentleness, Rodriguez distinguished himself from the negative memories of the last commissary, working with the Waldensian communities and managing 'slowly to encourage them and to persuade them to confess the truth' of their heresy so that he might give them lighter penances and reconcile them to the Church.[138]

Rodriguez instrumentalised the contrast between his benign reputation and the ferocious record of his inquisitorial predecessors. When some locals remained obstinate in their heresy, the local vicar with whom Rodriguez worked called upon the richest and most trusted man in the community, telling him that if he ordered the people to confess and convert he and Rodriguez would write to the cardinal-inquisitors to ask that mercy be used on his brother who languished 'at the prison of the Holy Office in Rome'.[139] The efficacy of such a deal relied on the man's trust in the pastoral mission led by Rodriguez as well as his belief that the inquisitors in Rome were likely to be treating his brother cruelly. When the Jesuit and his companions exploited the contrast between negative perceptions of the Roman Inquisition and their pastoral character they used a classic strategy of good cop, bad cop.

Rodriguez used a pastoral approach in Vulturara but, like his strategy in Le Marche, its effectiveness relied on his pastoral image as a Jesuit. The methods used on his mission contrasted with the brutality of the inquisitorial commissaries of the recent past. As Rodriguez wrote in his report, at the beginning of his mission he went to the local church where the vicar 'spoke [to the people] with sweetness, assuring them that, if they did their due, not only would they not be molested' as they had in the past, 'but liberated and absolved'.[140] In order to receive this mercy, the people must be prepared to tell the truth when they were called, a deal that echoed inquisitorial edicts that promised mercy for the cooperative.[141] There were certainly clear parallels between the approaches of some inquisitors and the Jesuits. The Society's policy of reconciling those who

---

137 ARSI, *Epistolae nostrorum 86*, f.182r.
138 Ibid.
139 ASR, *Miscellanea Famiglie Gesuiti*, B180, fasc.14, filza 15.
140 ASR, *Miscellanea Famiglie Gesuiti*, B180, fasc.14, filza 15.
141 Ibid.

came and confessed their heresy willingly was similar to policies of more lenient inquisitors, who gave lighter penalties to those who presented themselves to the tribunal. Nonetheless, in an area where popular perceptions of the inquisition had been so tainted by delegates working in the merciless manner of men like Carafa, Ghislieri and Rodriguez believed that promises of mercy would prove unconvincing from the lips of an open inquisitorial commissary.

4   Conclusion

As we saw in chapter 1, the Jesuits believed that privileges would improve the success of their missions by allowing their members to act pragmatically and independently on the ground. The studies presented in this chapter show that the Jesuits' formal independence of the ecclesiastical hierarchy, including the Holy Office, was also valuable for their inquisitorial collaborators. Despite the increasing power of the central tribunal during the 1550s, the Roman Inquisition faced practical, political and pastoral obstacles when it sought to assert its influence across the Italian peninsula. Sometimes, it could not find a suitable, effective and orthodox authority, as in Valtellina. At other times, political and popular hostility made it impossible for open delegates of the tribunal to secure conversions, as we have seen in the cases of Piacenza, Ferrara and Vulturara. As a pastoral religious order with powers analogous to those of the inquisitors, the Jesuits provided the cardinal-inquisitors with an attractive alternative to the usual inquisitorial personnel.

The Society's inquisitorial collaborations were dominated by powerful individuals with whom the Jesuits developed close working relationships. The letters exchanged between Rodriguez and Ghislieri indicate that their alliance was one of mutual respect and, at times, affection. As Pope Pius V, Ghislieri expressed a confidence in Rodriguez's abilities that was based on his long experience of the Jesuit's 'usual diligence and prudence'.[142] The Society's earlier inquisitorial collaborations were dominated by the influence of Juan Alvarez de Toledo, whose patronage of the Jesuits went far beyond his inquisitorial role. Like all client-patron relationships, these were alliances of mutual benefit, granting the Jesuits opportunities and protection in exchange for their services to the Holy Office.[143]

---

142   ARSI, *Epistolae Externorum 7 – I*, f.325r.
143   On patron-client relationships see Daniel H. Nexon, *The Struggle for Power in Early Modern Europe. Religious conflict, dynastic empires and international change* (Oxford: Princeton University Press, 2009), pp.40–2 and Maria Antonietta Visceglia, 'Factions in the Sacred

COLLABORATION, COMPETITION AND CONFLICT 89

Ghislieri was an advocate for the Jesuits at the papal court because the Society's jurisdictional autonomy allowed its members to work as the pastoral face of the Roman Inquisition. In exchange he was a valuable supporter of the Society. In the last year of Paul IV's reign, Ghislieri's petitions for the Jesuits reversed the pope's limitation of the Society's privileges to northern Europe. Although confessors were generally bound to oblige penitents to make a spontaneous appearance at an inquisitorial tribunal before receiving absolution, with help from Ghislieri, the Jesuits won an exemption to this rule. Writing to the rector of Genoa on 20 January 1559, Superior General Laínez confirmed this, stating that 'it is true that we had the faculty for heresy through our privileges and that His Holiness [Paul IV] has confirmed those privileges, in these past days'.[144] The cardinal-inquisitor was also a crucial supporter when the Society was challenged on the ground. When an inquisitor in the town of Recanati looked upon their privilege to read prohibited books 'with discontent', Laínez confidently stated 'if he is not happy ... it is enough for us if the Supreme Inquisitor is happy, from whom [the licence] was procured and obtained'.[145] In the difficult years of Paul IV's papacy, Ghislieri was a crucial ally for the Jesuits at the papal court and elsewhere. But his support for the Jesuits was self-interested. Eager to fight heresy but compromised by the limitations of his own tribunal, Ghislieri's empowerment of the Jesuits ensured that inquisitorial and papal interests were represented across the peninsula.[146]

By the early 1560s the intimacy of the Jesuits' relationship with Ghislieri was beginning to compromise the very independence that they had solicited him to protect. During the pontificates of Paul IV (1555–9) and Pius IV (1559–65), Ghislieri was the Jesuits' main point of contact at the Holy Office.[147] But soon his personal interest in their privileges began to limit the Society. In the first years of the 1560s, Jesuit correspondence indicates that the Superior General consulted the cardinal-inquisitor on when and how the Jesuits could use their privileges. A letter from Laínez to the Jesuit rector in Venice, states that

---

College in the sixteenth and seventeenth centuries' in Gianvittorio Signorotto and Visceglia (eds), *Court and Politics in Papal Rome, 1492–1700* (Cambridge: Cambridge University Press, 2002), p.103.

144 ARSI, *Epistolae Generalium Italiae 61*, 381v.

145 Ibid., 428r.

146 Romeo, 'Note sull'Inquisizione Romana', p.135.

147 In 1561, Ghislieri's name, Cardinal Alessandrino, appears next to that of Otto von Truchsess on a document securing the Society's privilege to absolve heresy see ARSI, *Institutum* 222, f.273r-234r. See Romeo, 'Pio V nelle fonti gesuite: Le *Epistolae Generalium Italiae* e le *Epistolae Italiae*' in Guasco and Torre (eds), *Pio V nella società e nella politica del suo tempo*, pp.85–110.

Ghislieri 'has given the faculty so that [the rector] can give absolution to that young woman who is fallen into a case of heresy', suggesting that they had consulted the cardinal-inquisitor before using the power.[148] In 1561, Laínez complained that Ghislieri had put so many provisos on their use of the papal privilege that to use it was 'nearly as much as to do nothing'.[149] This statement underlines the importance of autonomy to the Jesuits' understanding of the privilege and its impact: if they could not use their power independently then they may as well not have it at all. Father Pedro Ribadeneira agreed with Laínez when he said that the cardinal-inquisitor's advice on how to use the power seemed 'as much as revoking the authority that His Holiness had given to us'.[150] The Jesuits sought papal privileges as a means of having autonomous power, so that they would not need to rely on permissions from the broader ecclesiastical hierarchy. A decade after the Jesuits had first received their privilege to absolve heretics their relationship with Ghislieri had begun to undermine the fundamental advantage that the privilege gave them – autonomy.

The Jesuits soon sought to assert their independence from Ghislieri and to find a less problematic ally. Two documents, now held in the state archive in Rome, indicate that the Jesuits sought to secure papal privileges independently of Ghislieri during the height of their collaborations in the mid-1560s. The first document, dated November 1564, comprises notes for writing a draft bull that would confirm and amplify the privileges and graces previously granted by popes to the Society of Jesus, clarifying points of controversy.[151] In this document, the Jesuits asked Pius IV for affirmation of the faculty conceded by Paul III 'of absolving from each and every sin, crime, excess, misdemeanour, and from those certain sentences, censures and ecclesiastical penances resulting from these cases ... without the pre-judgement of anyone'.[152] Such a concession would have provided papal documentation to answer anybody who questioned the Jesuits' power to absolve censures incurred by serious sins such as heresy. The Society also requested freedom from the obligation to use or delegate the faculty on demand.[153] Another document in the same collection, also dated to 1564, makes a clear request for independence from the Holy

---

148   ARSI, *Epistolae Generalium Italiae 63*, ff.117r-v.
149   Ibid., f.116r.
150   Ribadeneira, *Patris Petri de Ribadeneira Societatis Jesu sacerdotis: confessiones, epistolae, scripta inedita, ex autographis, antiquissimus apographis et regestis deprompta* (Madrid: Ex officina typographis, 1920–3), 2 vols, vol. 1, pp.379–80.
151   The document is held in ASR, *Miscellanea Famiglie Gesuiti*, B180, fasc.14, f.47r.
152   Ibid.
153   Ibid.

COLLABORATION, COMPETITION AND CONFLICT

Office, asking 'that the Superior General himself, or through others, proceeds and punishes those suspected of heresy [in the Society]', stating that 'no other inquisitors are to meddle in this as everybody in the Society is immediately subject to the pope'.[154] When the Society's relationship with Ghislieri was at its most intimate, the Jesuits were taking measures to ensure that they were not reliant on his support.

The Society's assertion of independence from Ghislieri was both practically and politically astute. In June of 1564, Pius IV had imposed radical reforms on the Holy Office, undermining Ghislieri's power as the head of the Roman Inquisition and granting the pope more authority over the tribunal.[155] Ghislieri had begun to anger the pope and looked set to fall from grace at any moment.[156] Conscious to avoid the negative repercussions of these fluctuations in the ecclesiastical hierarchy the Jesuits aligned themselves with the pontiff and his allies. In 1564, it was not to their usual inquisitorial supporter that they handed their papal solicitations but to Cardinal Marcantonio Amulio.[157] Amulio had been appointed to the inquisition by Pius himself and was previously his ambassador to Venice.[158] During Pius IV's pontificate Amulio was certainly a better guarantor of the Jesuits' interests than his boss at the Roman Inquisition. For the Jesuits too, the relationship between the Society and the Roman Inquisition was one of mutual benefit and self-interest. They worked with the inquisitors how and when it suited them best. It is therefore unsurprising that the Jesuits' loyalty to particular cardinal-inquisitors was contingent, just like the Society's alliance with the temporal authorities of Genoa discussed in chapter 1.

In this chapter we have seen how the Society cooperated with the Roman Inquisition to address weaknesses in its tribunal system. We have also seen that this cooperation was facilitated by autonomy and political agility. The picture that emerges from close study of the Jesuits' use of the privilege in collaboration with the Roman Inquisition contrasts with interpretations that subordinate the Society's work to that of the Roman Inquisition. Rather, it fully incorporates the Jesuits' anti-heretical efforts into the picture of a consciously

---

154 Ibid, f.48r.

155 Guasco, *Pio V nella Societa e Politica del suo tempo*, pp.16–18 and Elena Bonora, *Roma 1564: La congiura contro il papa*, (Rome: Laterza, 2011), p.149–50.

156 Pattenden, *Pius IV and the Fall of the Carafa. Nepotism and papal authority in Counter-Reformation Rome* (Oxford: Oxford University Press, 2013), pp.116–7.

157 Amulio's participation is noted in the document: ASR, *Miscellanea Famiglie Gesuiti*, B180, fasc.14., f.47.

158 Pattenden, *Pius IV and the Fall of the Carafa*, p.141.

ambiguous, pragmatic and flexible Society that has emerged in recent scholarship. In the pages to come we shall see that these bold characteristics were also evident when Jesuits fought heresy for temporal leaders – some of whom were openly hostile to the pope and his inquisition.

CHAPTER 3

Between the Prince and the Pope: Pius V and the Rise of the Roman Inquisition

When cardinal-inquisitor Michele Ghislieri became Pope Pius V in January 1566 senior Jesuits predicted that, as pope, he would prioritise the work of the Roman Inquisition. Just days after the conclave closed, Superior General Francesco Borja wrote that 'matters of Reform and the Inquisition [would] come first' under a Ghislieri pope.[1] Others in Rome agreed. In a letter of March 1566, the Venetian ambassador to the Holy See claimed that 'matters of religion would be the most favoured' by Pius, 'and particularly of the Inquisition'.[2] Another Italian writer told the Archbishop of Santa Severina, Giulio Antonio Santoro, that Pius V's pontificate would herald a return to the inquisitorial severity of his mentor, Pope Paul IV (1555–9). 'To Rome, to Rome, what awaits you?' he asked, 'come happily, God has revived Paul IV there'.[3]

Pius V soon corroborated these predictions. As pope, he established the Roman Inquisition as a stable institution, building permanent headquarters for the congregation at a cost of more than 50,000 scudi.[4] In 1568, he publicly executed Paul IV's enemy Pietro Carnesecchi, the Florentine nobleman who had escaped condemnation for heresy at Paul's death in 1559.[5] In 1570, Pius established the Congregation of the Index, re-imposing Paul IV's rigorous censorship of heretical books and reversing the more moderate guidelines set by

---

1 ARSI, *Epistolae Generalium Italiae 66*, f.122r.
2 Paolo Tiepolo in Fabio Mutinelli, *Storia arcana e aneddotica d'Italia, raccontata dai veneti ambasciatori* (Venice: Pietro Naratovich, 1855–6), vol. 1, p.38.
3 Marcantonio Fiorenzo to Giulio Antonio Santoro, 9 January 1566, published in G. Cugnoni (ed.), *Autobiografia di monsignor G. Antonio Santori, cardinale di Santa Severina* in *Archivio della Società romana di storia patria*, 12 (1889), p. 339.
4 David Coffin, *Pirro Ligorio: The Renaissance Artist, Architect, and Antiquarian* (University Park: Pennsylvania State University Press), p.77 and Ludwig von Pastor, Frederick Ignatius Antrobus and Ralph Francis Kerr (eds), *The History of the Popes from the close of the Middle Ages drawn from the secret archives of the Vatican and other original sources; from the German of late Ludwig Pastor* (London: Kegan, Paul, Trench, Trübner and Co., 1874–1928), 40 vols, vol.17, p.288.
5 On the case of Pietro Carnesecchi see, Firpo and Marcatto (eds), *I processi inquisitoriali di Pietro Carnesecchi*.

© KONINKLIJKE BRILL NV, LEIDEN, 2020 | DOI:10.1163/9789004413832_005

94   CHAPTER 3

his own predecessor Pius IV.[6] He also re-appointed Scipione Rebiba, Francisco
Pacheco and Gian Francesco Gambara, cardinal-inquisitors who had been loyal servants of Paul IV and who had been sacked by the more lenient Pius IV.[7]
Some feared that Pius V's inquisition would be even harsher than that of his
mentor. A witness at the trial of Count Niccolò Orsini claimed that 'at the time
of Pope Paul [IV] ... [Orsini] never went to mass'.[8] It seemed that the count
was not so afraid of Carafa. Under Pius V, however, it was said that Orsini was
terrified about the potential consequences of his past transgressions.[9]

If Pius V was to take a similar or even harsher approach to that of Paul IV
it was very bad news for the Society's privilege to absolve heresy. Paul IV had
tried to negate the Jesuits' privilege, issuing a brief that required all confessors,
including Jesuits, to refuse absolutions until penitent-heretics had visited the
Holy Office, though the Jesuits do not appear to have been held to this.[10] Documents produced to defend the privilege in the 1580s suggest that Pius V followed the example of his mentor. The papers list concessions of the privilege
from Julius III's pontificate onwards. Some fall silent after the concession of
Pius V's predecessor, Pius IV, before moving on to the concessions of his successor, Gregory XIII, suggesting that Pius failed to re-concede the power.[11] Another list notes that Pius V did concede the privilege, before stating that Gregory XIII granted the same but 'also in Italy'.[12] This wording implies that Pius V
only confirmed the privilege for northern Europe and that Gregory extended
it to Italy to restore the power to the same level as the Jesuits had previously

---

6   Romeo, *L'Inquisizione nell'Italia moderna*, p.19. On the Index and its congregation see
     Fragnito, *Church, censorship and culture in early modern Italy*; Fragnito, *La Bibbia al rogo*
     and Vittorio Frajese, *Nascita dell'Indice. La censura ecclesiastica dal Rinascimento alla
     Controriforma* (Brescia: Morcelliana, 2006).

7   The decision is recorded at ACDF, *Sant'Uffico Decreta, 1565–7*, f.35r. See also, Bonora, 'L'In-
     quisizione e papato tra Pio IV e Pio V' in Guasco and Torre (eds), *Pio V nella società e nella
     politica del suo tempo*, pp.54–55 and Santarelli, 'Dinamiche interne della Congregazione
     di Sant'Uffizio', p.12.

8   ACDF, *Stanza Storica R-2-m*, f.226v. Fosi, *Papal Justice*. p.96.

9   Fosi, *Papal Justice*. p.96.

10   On Paul's brief in the context of papal edicts on confession and the inquisition see
     Brambilla, *Alle origini del Sant'Uffizio*, pp.406–409. On the brief's effects see Prosperi,
     Tribunali della coscienza, pp.231–3. Romeo argues that there is no evidence that the Jesuits
     were held to this rule in his *Ricerche su confessione*, p.44. A letter by Laínez in January 1559
     confirms this: ARSI, *Epistolae Generalium Italiae 61*, 381v.

11   See, for example, a record from the last years of the sixteenth century: 'Absolvendi ab
     haeresi et lectione librorum prohibitorum ... Idem Pius 4 X. Martii 1561 ... Absolvendi ab
     haeresi. Gregor[io] ult[im]o Martii 1573'.ARSI, *Institutum 185 – I*, f.313v.

12   'Absolvendi ab haeresi andc Pius Quintus die 12 Maii 1568. Absolvendi ab haeresi etiam in
     Italia. Greg[ori]o Ult[im]o Martii 1573'. ACDF, *Stanza Storica I-5-B*, ff.45r-v.

BETWEEN THE PRINCE AND THE POPE

enjoyed. As these documents relayed the history of papal support for the privilege in order to defend it it is likely that the authors did not want to highlight Pius V's effective limitation of the privilege and so only implied the facts in the comment on Gregory XIII's concession. For the same reasons, the authors of the first list would not have omitted a full concession of the privilege by Pius V had he granted one.[13] The caution and silence in these later records reflect the Society's uncertainty about the status of the privilege during the reign of Pius V, an uncertainty that is patent in Jesuit correspondence between the mission field and Rome.

Looking at this correspondence and other institutional documents, we see that the Jesuits' confusion stemmed from a genuine ambiguity. Though Pius V did not explicitly revoke the Jesuits' privilege to absolve heresy he certainly curtailed their jurisdiction. Pius V only allowed Jesuits to reconcile heretics when it served his inquisitorial interests directly. By studying this strategy we can better understand how the Jesuits' role in the fight against heresy changed in the later sixteenth century and how the Church's approach to religious dissent developed in this period. The documents of this period also illustrate the growing contrast between the Jesuits' approach to heresy and the strategy of the Church. Continued requests for the privilege show that the Jesuits still deemed a genuinely autonomous jurisdiction over heresy necessary. Pius V evidently disagreed. When Pius V failed to reconfirm the privilege, Borja advised Jesuits to exercise caution with heretics seeking reconciliation. The Superior General wanted to avoid conflict with a former ally of the Society on whom all of its privileges now relied. Both contemporary and later records show us that, at least twice, Pius V agreed when Jesuits requested the privilege in Italy. But these concessions came with severe jurisdictional and geographical limitations. Whilst at first they seem to represent exceptions to Pius V's broader inquisitorial agenda they actually show that he had no intention of supporting the blanket privilege that had previously provided penitent-heretics with a genuine alternative to inquisitorial process. As Pius V limited the Jesuits' role he exposed the contrast between papal perceptions of extra-judicial reconciliations and those of the Society.

---

13   These records comprise a dossier sent to the Roman Inquisition in response to challenges to the Society's privilege in 1585–6. The lists of privileges to absolve heresy and more limited concessions given to the Society end with concessions granted by Pope Gregory XIII (1572–1585) and do not include any of the privileges and more limited concessions given by Gregory XIV (1590–1) and Clement VIII (1592–1605), suggesting that the records were put together during the pontificate of Pope Sixtus V (1580–1590). ARSI, *Institutum 185-I*, ff.309r-317r.

In our first case study, we shall see how the pope allowed Cristóbal Rodriguez to absolve heretics in Le Marche. Here Pius V used the privilege as a lure, ordering Rodriguez to act as a spy and to gather information from heretics who came to him for pastoral care. Once Pius V had Rodriguez's intelligence, he overturned his reconciliations and imprisoned his penitents. A later Jesuit history claimed that Rodriguez was betrayed by Pius. However, contemporary sources suggest that the Jesuit was complicit in the pope's scheme. On the basis of the extant sources, it is difficult to deduce Rodriguez's strategy. Nonetheless, his successful solicitation and, eventually, use of the privilege demonstrate that the Jesuits insisted that extra-judicial absolutions were still necessary even as the pope sought an inquisitorial monopoly on reconciliations.

The Jesuits' insistence on the necessity of extra-judicial reconciliations is also evident in our second case study. This is quite a different story to Rodriguez's mission in Le Marche. For, in this case, Pius V granted Jesuits in Savoy-Piedmont permission to absolve heresy with absolutely no obligation to involve the inquisition. This concession demonstrates that, despite the pope's evident desire to control the absolution and reconciliation of heretics, there were territories where he had no choice but to support the Jesuits' independent anti-heretical activities. In the mid-sixteenth century Savoy-Piedmont was certainly one of these territories. At the time, this north-easterly Italian state was seen as a gateway for heresies from northern Europe to enter Italy. Worse still, it was also the only Italian state where Pius failed to impose inquisitorial influence which was persistently resisted by the duke. Although it is an exception to Pius's inquisitorial monopoly in Italy, it is an exception that proves the rule. That Savoy-Piedmont was the only Italian territory where the Jesuits appear to have received the privilege without limitations demonstrates that, in this period, Pius successfully marginalised the Jesuits and enforced inquisitorial authority almost every else on the peninsula.

At first, both of these cases support interpretations of the privilege that describe its use within an overbearing inquisitorial system that subordinated the Jesuits.[14] That said, the case studies correct the chronology of these explanations, tracing the roots of this dynamic to the late 1560s, more than ten years after the concession of the privilege. This chronological correction supports my argument that we must look to the earlier history of the privilege to fully explain its role and impact not to these later limitations of the power. What is more, these case studies nuance explanations of the privilege that emphasise the inquisition's oppression of the Jesuits, showing that circumstances forced

---

14   Prosperi, *Tribunali della coscienza*, pp.xv-ii and pp.236–7.

BETWEEN THE PRINCE AND THE POPE

even Pius V to negate his ideal of a dominant, efficient inquisitorial system. Finally, it is important to note that in these exceptions it was Jesuit autonomy, perceived and real, that allowed the Society to work effectively for the pope. This conclusion shows us that Jesuit autonomy was still valued by Pius V in some circumstances, even as he marginalised the Society. Overall, by studying the problems that Pius V faced imposing his inquisitorial ideal in Italy, this chapter underlines the need to investigate the outcomes of papal directives, rather than assuming their success, and to look beyond the official papal agenda to discover other methods through which Rome fulfilled its central aim to save souls.

1   Pius V and the Rise of the Roman Inquisition

Superior General Borja was initially confident of Pius V's approval of the privilege to absolve heresy but the Jesuits soon discovered that Pius's support was far from sure. In letters to colleagues, Borja claimed that Pius had confirmed all of the Society's privileges during their first papal audience. Nonetheless, Pius's responses to entreaties regarding the privilege and his broader limitation of extra-judicial reconciliations soon cast doubt on the status of the Jesuits' jurisdiction. In letters, Jesuits expressed uncertainty, telling the Superior General that they had abandoned plans to absolve heretics to avoid acting illicitly. Eager to retain papal favour, soon even Borja refused to extend the privilege and advised Jesuits to exercise caution with penitent-heretics. During previous pontificates, Superior Generals had advised Jesuits to avoid conflicts of jurisdiction in cases of heresy and, under Paul IV, there had been some doubt about when and where the Society could absolve heretics.[15] During Pius V's papacy these fears returned, intensified and were eventually corroborated.

After Borja's first meeting with Pius V in January 1566, he was fairly confident that the Jesuits' privilege to absolve heresy was secure. Writing to Salmerón and the Society's provincials, Borja said that he had 'supplicated [Pius V] for the confirmation of all the graces of our Society, thus conceded by other popes, as by himself, when he was inquisitor, and he granted them lovingly'.[16] According to Borja, Pius had ordered that Cardinal Marcantonio Amulio 'should act as

---

15   See, for example, Polanco's advice in *De licentia petenda ab ordinariis pro confessionibus* of 1564 in ARSI, *Epistolae Generalium Rom. 1*, f.16r.

    On doubts about the privilege under Paul IV see Bobadilla, *Epistolae Bobadillae*, pp.250–3 and Ribadeneira, *Epistolae Ribadeneira*, vol.1, p.380.

16   Borja, *Sancti Francisci Borgiae Epistolae*, vol. 4, p.170.

witness of [the concession]', a standard means of confirming the concession of privileges granted orally, or *viva vocis oraculo*.[17] Borja told Salmerón that he did not 'request' all of 'the graces that were conceded to Your Reverence through His Holiness when he was a cardinal' 'anew' as Pius 'had confirmed for us all those [privileges] that his predecessors and [he] himself, when he was a cardinal, had conceded to us'.[18] As cardinal-inquisitor Ghislieri, Pius V had confirmed the Jesuits' privilege to absolve heretics in Italy provided the heretics had not already been 'reported to the inquisitors'.[19] For Borja, Pius's blanket confirmation was enough to confirm the privilege to absolve heresy. Borja advised Salmerón that he 'could use [his privileges] as before'.[20]

Still, Borja lacked any evidence that Pius V had confirmed the Society's privileges. In fact, it is unclear whether the Jesuits ever received it. A record written by Polanco before his death in 1576 states that on 29 September 1566 'confirmation and record of every grace of the Society was requested from the pope'.[21] But nine months after Borja's first meeting with Pius, Amulio's testimony of what had transpired had still not arrived.[22] A later Jesuit history of the privilege sent to the Roman Inquisition in the 1580s complicates the picture, stating that on 29 September 1566, the same day as the request recorded by Polanco, Pius V 'confirmed for the Society all the privileges and faculties that had been conceded to it'.[23] This later source suggests that Pius responded to the request of 29 September immediately. Nonetheless, as a defence of the privilege, it may have attempted to extrapolate the request recorded by Polanco into evidence for continued papal support for the privilege. Unlike Bishop Politi's confirmation of Julius III's concession of the privilege, there is no testimony of Pius V's meeting with Borja amongst records of privileges granted *viva vocis oraculo* at the ARSI.[24] It seems most likely that the paperwork never arrived.

A year after Pius V's election, Jesuit authorities remained confused about the privilege. Seeking clarification, they consulted the Superior General, institutional documents and even the pope himself. Although some believed

---

17   Borja in Salmerón, *Epistolae Salmeronis*, vol. 2, p.69.

18   Salmerón, *Epistolae Salmeronis*, vol. 2, pp.88–9.

19   See, for example, Laínez's reference to Ghislieri's confirmation of the privilege from Julius III, allowing them to reconcile all heretics who were not relapsed in ARSI, *Epistolae Generalium Italiae 63*, f.132r.

20   Salmerón, *Epistolae Salmeronis*, vol.2, p.88.

21   ARSI, *Institutum 190*, f.5r.

22   ARSI, *Epistolae Generalium Italiae 66*, ff.249r-v.

23   ACDF, *Stanza Storica D-4-A*, f.10r.

24   See a copy witnessed by Ambrogio Catarino Politi, now held at the Jesuit archive in ARSI, *Institutum 194*, f.2v.

BETWEEN THE PRINCE AND THE POPE

Borja's claim that Pius had confirmed the Society's privileges *viva vocis oraculo*, the pope subsequently provoked doubts about this. Before departing for the German lands, Borja's principal assistant, Jerónimo Nadal, asked Pius about the validity of the privilege. Nadal did not record Pius's response but said that 'certain words that the pope said to him' made him question whether Jesuits could absolve heretics in the forum of the conscience without abjuration, as they had been able to in the past.[25] Discussing the question with Fathers Diego Ledesma and Peter Canisius, Nadal referred to a record of privileges given to the Society by Pius v's predecessor, Pius IV, stating that they 'could absolve in those regions from all cases reserved [to the pope] in Coena Domini'.[26] These cases included heresy.[27] The fathers' willingness to refer to a document produced under the previous pope suggests that, despite being confused by Pius's comments, they ultimately accepted that he had reconfirmed their privileges verbally in his meeting with Borja in January 1566. Indeed, in light of Pius IV's document, Nadal, Ledesma and Canisius resolved that they could absolve heretics as before, even if they had no proof of Pius v's confirmation of their privilege.[28]

But Pius v soon instigated more doubts. According to Nadal, when Canisius asked if the Jesuits could also absolve relapsed heretics in Germany 'the response that His Holiness gave was that all this [was] to proceed in a judicial manner in [cases of] heresy in Germany'.[29] Pius's insistence on a 'judicial manner', that is on inquisitorial reconciliations, made Nadal think that the Jesuits could not act in any cases of heresy as they acted in the *foro conscientiae*, which was a secret, extra-judicial jurisdiction.[30] To Nadal 'it appear[ed] very difficult that a confessor put or make [someone else] put the things that he has heard in sacramental confession in another forum'.[31] For him, the process would compromise the role of a confessor, as the penitent's 'sin would not only be reduced to the external forum, but also to the criminal external forum', taking the penitent from a sacramental confession to a judicial court.[32] If the Jesuits were to do this without breaking the secrecy of confession they would need

---

25   Jerónimo Nadal, *Epistolae P. Hieronymi Nadal Societatis Iesu*, vol. 3, p.316.

26   Nadal, *Epistolae P. Hieronymi Nadal Societatis Iesu*, vol. 3, p.316.

27   Luis de Paramo, *De origine et progressu officii Sanctae Inquisitionis, eiusque dignitate and utilitate, de Romani pontificis potestate and delegata Inquisitorum: Edicto Fidei, and ordine iudiciario Sancti Officii, quaestiones decem* (Madrid: Ex Typographia Regia, 1598), p.786.

28   Nadal, *Epistolae P. Hieronymi Nadal Societatis Iesu*, vol. 3, p.316.

29   Ibid., pp.316–7.

30   Brambilla, *Alle origini del Sant'Uffizio*, p.492.

31   Nadal, *Epistolae P. Hieronymi Nadal Societatis Iesu*, vol. 3, p.317.

32   Ibid.

100   CHAPTER 3

to secure 'the consent of the penitent' every time and they believed that the penitent 'ought not to be forced to this'.[33] For Nadal, Pius v's orders meant that Jesuits could not fulfil their duty as confessors to penitent-heretics and could not fully reconcile heretics to the Church. Later, Nadal reasserted this opinion, telling Borja in December 1566 that 'His Holiness simply gives us the faculty to absolve from every heresy, and schism etc only in the internal forum in confession, reserving to himself and bishops, who by law are inquisitors, all exterior jurisdiction, since they act as commissaries of the inquisition in Rome'.[34] If, as Nadal suggests, Pius v had limited the Jesuits to actions in the internal forum of confession rather than the *foro conscientiae* – with which they could absolve the sin of heresy and the consequent excommunication – the Jesuits' authority had been severely curtailed.

Soon Jesuits across Italy had doubts about the validity of the privilege. In the summer of 1567, a father at the Jesuits' college in Loreto asked Superior General Borja to clarify the status of the power. Twice this father had needed to communicate the authority to lift excommunication for heresy but he was given conflicting advice on the matter. Some fathers told him that the rector still had the privilege to pass on to other Jesuits, whilst others said that the Superior General had revoked the power.[35] To avoid acting illicitly, the father took 'the path that says that they do not have the faculty – as it was safer'.[36] Jesuit authorities were confused about their powers to absolve other grave sins too. In June 1568, Borja wrote to the Jesuit provincial in Lombardy, stating that he should never have been ordered to delegate the power to absolve excommunicates who had 'usurped ecclesiastical jurisdiction' because only provincials in France and Germany could this.[37] Although letters between Rome and Loreto do not mention Pius and the letter to Lombardy concerns another misdemeanour, both documents indicate that, during this pontificate, significant doubts about the validity of the Jesuits' privileges pervaded the Society.

Pius v's broader measures exacerbated reservations about the Jesuits' authority to absolve heresy in Italy. In 1568, he promulgated a new version of *In Coena Domini*, a bull that listed the sins that only the pope could absolve.[38] The bull reserved the sin of heresy to the pope.[39] This was not unusual. However,

---

33   Ibid. On heresy and the seal see Lavenia, *L'infamia e il perdone*, pp.101–30.
34   Nadal, *Epistolae P. Hieronymi Nadal Societatis Iesu*, vol.3, p.349.
35   His letter is in ARSI, *Epistolae Italiae 134*, f.12r.
36   Ibid.
37   ARSI, *Epistolae Generalium Italiae 67*, f.128v.
38   O'Banion, *The Sacrament of Penance and Religious Life in Golden Age Spain*, p.66.
39   See summary and copy of the bull in Mario Canepa, 'La bolla "In Coena Domini" del 1567 in un memoriale del viceré spagnolo di Sardegna', *Archivio Storico Sardo*, 29 (1967), p.125.

BETWEEN THE PRINCE AND THE POPE 101

unlike earlier bulls, Pius v's *In Coena Domini* explicitly nullified all existing privileges that contradicted its aims.[40] The Jesuits' privilege to absolve heretics contradicted Pius v's reservation of heresy to his own jurisdiction, so, technically, it would have been nullified by the bull.[41] In the past, the Jesuits had secured special exemptions from *In Coena Domini*. A record of the Jesuits' 'faculties of absolving from heresy' indicates that the Society requested an exception from Pius but that he granted it only 'in the Transalpine provinces'.[42] In another document of 1570, Pius told members of the Society that they could not use their privileges in ways that affected judicial processes in the Papal States.[43] These mandates confirm that Pius v did not want the Jesuits to impede the work of his inquisition in Italy and that, in some places, through their privileges, he believed that they did this.[44]

By November 1568, the Jesuits recognised that these measures curtailed their jurisdiction over heresy. Advising the rector of the Society's college in Milan, Borja wrote that Jesuits could only absolve heretics in the internal forum and could no longer remove the censures that excommunicated them from the Church. Borja wrote that 'the penitents are to go to the inquisitors ... to reveal

---

40 Canepa, 'La bolla "In Coena Domini" del 1567, p.132. For the controversy regarding the nullification of ancient privileges enjoyed by Spain, for example, see Canepa, 'La bolla "In Coena Domini" del 1567', pp.75–137. For other examples of the bull In Coena Domini, see editions of bulls by one of Pius V's predecessors, Clement VII (9 April 1528), and his immediate successor, Gregory XIII (5 April 1583): [Clement VII], *Bulla Clementis vii In Cena Domini lecta in Urbe veteri anno MDccviii in qua Urbis direptores perhorre[n]do eterne maledictio[n]is anathemate nunc primus da[n]ati sunt* (Rome: 1528) and [Gregory XIII] in *Liste et extraits de divers actes d'appel, au futur concile general, interjettez par les eglises, princes, etats, Communautez Ecclesiastiques and Seculieres des Pays-Bas Autrichiens and François, à laquelle on a ajouté les Bulles Unam Sanctam, and In Coena Domini* (1719), pp.xxi-xxx.

41 Brambilla argues that Pius's bull In Coena Domini effectively nullified privileges to absolve heretics extra-judicially. *Alle origini del Sant'Uffizio*, p.487.

42 Ibid. That the Jesuits saw the exemption from *In Coena Domini* of 12 May 1568 as a licence to absolve heretics in the lands north of the Alps is evident in a document to the Roman Inquisition in which the Jesuits refer to the exemption as a faculty: 'Absolvendi ab haeresi etc. Pius Quintus die 12 Maii 1568' before moving on to refer to 'Absolvendi ab haeresi etiam in Italia. Greg[ori]o Ult[im]o Martii 1573'. ACDF, *Stanza Storica I-5-B*, f.45r. 'Facultates absolvendi ab haeresi re. Societati Jesù concessae ... De facultate absolvendi ab haeresi Societati Jesu à Sum[m]is Pontificibus concessa ... De eadem facultate pro Transalpinis provinciis ... Facultates omnes, de quibus supra, non censeri revocatas per bullam Coenae, concessit Pius 4. X Martii 1561. Et Pius V die 12 Maii 1568'. ARSI, *Institutum 185-I*, f.313r. See another version of this document in ACDF, *Stanza Storica I-5-B*, [f.46v].

43 ARSI, *Epistolae Generalium Italiae 68*, f.143v.

44 Romeo, 'Pio V nelle fonti gesuiti', p.124.

102   CHAPTER 3

their accomplices; and, whether they go or not, [the penitent] ought to understand that he is absolved in the internal forum before God but not in the external [forum]'.[45] In other words, the rector of Milan could only absolve heretics of their sin. He would have to send them to the local inquisition to have their excommunication lifted. By this time, the Milanese inquisition was effectively supervised by Rome. Although imperial governors had tried to establish the Spanish Inquisition in Milan, by the late 1560s inquisitorial activity in the city was directed by Archbishop Carlo Borromeo with support from the cardinal-inquisitors at the Roman tribunal.[46] Borja's statement regarding the situation in Milan indicates that, under Pius V, the Jesuits' jurisdiction over heresy in Italy was restricted in favour of local tribunals overseen by the pope's Holy Office.

Pius V also curtailed the powers of other institutions that reconciled heretics extra-judicially. The bull *In Coena Domini* of 1568 prevented not only the Jesuits but anybody in Italy from absolving heretics, except the pope and the inquisition.[47] This effectively revoked bishops' authority over heresy, reversing a decree of the Council of Trent.[48] In 1569, Pius also restricted the power of the Apostolic Penitentiary – the body traditionally responsible for granting faculties of absolution – so that it could only concede faculties in the *foro conscientiae*, that is for heretics unknown to the inquisitors.[49] The Penitentiary was also banned from absolving or conceding privileges to others to absolve heretics who had spoken of their heresy publicly.[50] It seems that Pius's aim was to limit all jurisdictions that affected the powers and interests of the Roman Inquisition.

---

45   ARSI, *Epistolae Italiae 67*, f.180r.
46   In this period it seems that the local inquisitor and head of the Roman congregation were in close contact. See, for example, correspondence held in ACDF, *Stanza Storica N-3-f*, ff.327v-328r. On conflicts between state, Roman and episcopal authorities over heresy in Milan see, Black, *The Italian Inquisition*, pp.38–40.
47   Brambilla, *Alle origini del Sant'Uffizio*, pp.546–8.
48   The bull is discussed, with edited excerpts, in Ludwig Von Pastor, *Storia dei papi dalla fine del medioevo. Compilata col sussidio dell'Archivio segreto pontificio e di molti altri Archivi. Volume VIII* (Rome: Deslée and C.i, 1964), pp.606–8. For the decree of Trent see the sixth chapter of the twenty-fourth session: Philippus Chiffletius (ed.), *Sacrosancti et oecumenici Concilii Tridentini Paulo III. Julio III. et Pio IV. Pontificibus maximis celebrati canones et decreta* (Brussells: Joannis Van Vlaenderen, 1741), p.221. For numerous references to inquisitorial manuals noting the change to the concession see, Brambilla, *Alle origini del Sant'Uffizio*, p.547, fn.7. See also, Prosperi, 'L'inquisitore come confessore', p.210.
49   Tomassetti (ed.), *Bullarum, diplomatum et privilegiorum*, vol. 7, p.750. Brambilla, *Alle origini del Sant'Uffizio*, p.550.
50   Brambilla, *Alle origini del Sant'Uffizio*, p.550.

BETWEEN THE PRINCE AND THE POPE

Pius V even wanted inquisitorial jurisdiction to be supreme over temporal authority. In the Papal States, he ordered all judges and princes to obey inquisitorial mandates and to send all suspects of the inquisition to Rome, even if they were already imprisoned for a greater crime.[51] In 1569, the bull *Si de protegendiis* reaffirmed the tribunal's supreme and infrangible authority, protecting the inquisitors' freedom to work 'under the shield of the inviolate authority of the faith, outside of any danger in exercising any duty'.[52] From the end of the 1560s, correspondence between the cardinal-inquisitors and the peripheral tribunals grew in frequency and length as Pius V increased the inquisition's efficiency and authority over satellite courts.[53] These changes were significant and enduring. The republication of *Si de protegendiis* well into the seventeenth century demonstrates that inquisitors continued to refer to Pius's reforms when asserting their supreme authority.[54]

Pius V wanted to abolish the extra-judicial reconciliation of heretics in Italy, where he gave the Roman Inquisition supreme jurisdiction. His legal reforms and the acquiescence of doubtful Jesuits, anxious to retain the pope's favour, demonstrate how close he came to achieving this. This situation reflects Pierroberto Scaramella's claim that Ghislieri's ascension to the papal throne saw 'the effervescence of the repressive apparatus' of the Roman Inquisition and, consequently, 'the impossibility, on the part of the Jesuits, to use or to assert their own prerogatives and privileges'.[55] Our first case study bolsters this interpretation, illustrating that, even when Rodriguez won papal permission to reconcile heretics, his actions lacked true autonomy. Nonetheless, as our second case study will show, the 'effervescence' of the Roman Inquisition was still limited in some corners of Italy such as Savoy-Piedmont. There, Pius V was forced to empower Jesuits to carry out the 'personal management of affairs of religion' from which Scaramella claims that they were excluded by the pope.[56]

2   A Jesuit Spy in the Papal States

Pius V allowed Jesuits to absolve heretics privately at least twice. These exceptions indicate that the Jesuits insisted on the continued necessity of

---

51   BAV, *Urb. Lat. 1040*, f.303r.
52   For a copy of the bull see ASM, *Inquisizione*, busta 270, fasc. 3.
53   Romeo, 'Note sull'Inquisizione Romana', p.128 and Scaramella, 'I primi gesuiti e l'inquisizione Romana', p.155.
54   See, for example, a copy published in 1632 in ASM, *Inquisizione*, busta 270, fasc. 3.
55   Scaramella, 'I primi gesuiti', p.155.
56   Ibid.

104   CHAPTER 3

extra-judicial reconciliations and that, in some circumstances, the pope agreed. One such concession was to Cristóbal Rodriguez, the Portuguese Jesuit with whom Pius had collaborated as a cardinal-inquisitor. In 1567, Pius sent Rodriguez to investigate heresy and other forms of disobedience in Le Marche in the Papal States. In return, Pius V gave Rodriguez permission to absolve heretics autonomously. As we saw in chapter 2, the pair had a history of collaboration in inquisitorial matters. Despite broader efforts to limit extra-judicial reconciliations, it seems that Pius was willing to allow his old ally to continue to reconcile penitent-heretics. However, the dynamic between the two men had changed. After the mission, the pope overturned Rodriguez's absolutions and jailed his penitents. Rodriguez demanded that his jurisdiction be respected and his penitents were released. Despite this happy conclusion for Rodriguez, the case exposes a fundamental contrast between the position of the pope and that of the Jesuits. Whilst the Society continued to think that genuinely autonomous extra-judicial reconciliations were essential, Pius V only respected them as far as they supported inquisitorial endeavours, and even then with increasing reluctance.

The change in the relationship between Pius and the Jesuits is undoubtedly due to his elevation to the pontificate. Before becoming Pius V, cardinal-inquisitor Ghislieri had had to compromise with the Jesuits. During the pontificate of Pius IV, Ghislieri's dominance over the Roman Inquisition was severely diminished as the pope transferred executive powers to himself and other members of the congregation. Ghislieri and Pius IV did not see eye to eye on inquisitorial matters. In stark contrast to Ghislieri's hard-line policies, Pius IV promoted compromise solutions, allowing inquisitors to reconcile first-time offenders privately.[57] To execute his wishes, Pius IV filled the Holy Office with more moderate cardinals and ensured that cases were discussed by the whole congregation and not just pronounced upon by Ghislieri.[58] The attack on Ghislieri's authority was obvious. As the Venetian ambassador to Rome wrote, 'the whole of the Inquisition is no longer in the hands of the Most Illustrious [Cardinal] Alessandrino [i.e. Ghislieri] but His Holiness has appointed seven cardinals with equal authority who attend to the affairs of the Inquisition, the cases are divided between them'.[59] In his biography of Pius V, Girolamo Catena also declared that Pius IV's actions severely limited the authority of Supreme

---

57 'See Pius V's 'Pastoralis officii munus' published in *Bullarium diplomatum et privilegiorum*, vol.7, p.238.

58 Bonora, 'L'Inquisizione e papato tra Pio IV e Pio V', p.55.

59 Paolo Tiepolo, ASV, *Capi dei consiglio dei Dieci, Lettere degli ambasciatori, Roma*, b.24. Edited in Bonora, 'L'Inquisizione e papato tra Pio IV e Pio V', p.55.

BETWEEN THE PRINCE AND THE POPE

Inquisitor Ghislieri.[60] With his power restricted and a pope amenable to the Jesuits' approach, Ghislieri had been in no position to undermine the Society's papal privileges or to lose the assistance of Jesuits who could overcome the significant obstacles that his inquisition faced.

As Pius V, Ghislieri did not have to support the Jesuits in the same way but he still had a strong working relationship with Cristóbal Rodriguez, whom he lauded for his zeal and diligence.[61] After a mission to Naples, the pope praised Rodriguez's 'usual goodness and ingenuity' and for having 'spoken the truth to him so sincere[ly] and freely'.[62] During his first papal audience with Superior General Borja, the second item on their agenda, after the confirmation of the Jesuits' privileges, had been 'the matter of D[octor] Rodriguez', who was discussed 'with the enthusiasm of His Holiness'.[63] The new pope demonstrated his continued trust in Rodriguez by putting him in charge of the *'inquisizione del mare'*, which monitored heresy on Spanish galleys fighting the Turks and, later, on the ships sailing into the Battle of Lepanto (a battle in which Pius's Holy League famously triumphed).[64] In return for this service, Pius rewarded Rodriguez with great responsibilities in matters of religion – the inquisitor-pope's central concern.

In fact, Pius V trusted Rodriguez enough to make him a papal spy. As we saw at the beginning of chapter 2, Pius ordered Rodriguez to go to Le Marche to gather information on religious disobedience and then to relay it to the pope. In Le Marche, Rodriguez was not only a papal informer he was also an agent of the Roman Inquisition. A Jesuit account written in 1581 tells us that Rodriguez was tasked by Pius V to quash 'the most pernicious seeds and sprouts of heresy' in San Ginesio.[65] And, when he arrived in the city of Macerata, Rodriguez found a letter instructing him 'to go to San Ginesio to exhort certain men that they should go to present themselves to the Holy Office'.[66] According to this later account, Rodriguez was asked to ensure that 'the public ploughmen and

---

60   Girolamo Catena, *Vita del gloriosissimo Papa Pio Quinto. Con una raccolta di lettere di Pio V à diuersi principi, andle risposte, con altre particolari. Et i nomi delle galee e de' capitani, cosi Christiani, come Turchi, che si trouarano alla battaglia nauale* (Mantua: F. Osanna, 1587).

61   ARSI, *Epistolae Externorum 1*, f.78r. Edited in Scaduto, 'Tra Inquisitori e riformati', p.50.

62   ARSI, *Epistolae Externorum 7-I*, f.315r.

63   Borja in Salmerón, *Epistolae Salmeronis*, vol.2, pp.69–70.

64   G. Civale, *Guerrieri di Cristo. Inquisitori, gesuiti e soldati alla battaglia di Lepanto* (Unicopli: Milano, 2009); E. García Hernán, 'La asistencia religiosa en la Armada de Lepanto', *Anthologica Annua*, 43 (1996), pp. 213–263; Scaduto, 'Tra inquisitori e riformati', pp.17–18.

65   ARSI, *Rom. 185 (Necrologia 1602–1656)*, f.44v.

66   ARSI, *Epistolae Italiae 135*, f.9r.

106   CHAPTER 3

sowers of evil [were] thoroughly investigated' and that he fined and punished them.[67] Contrary to Scaramella's claim that the Jesuits were precluded from judicial roles under Pius V, this Jesuit account suggests that Rodriguez's role in San Ginesio was explicitly inquisitorial.

Rodriguez also reconciled penitent-heretics in San Ginesio. According to the Society's sources this was a result of bargaining by Rodriguez. A later Jesuit account claims that Rodriguez demanded Pius's permission to reconcile heretics privately as a condition of accepting the inquisitorial role. Written in the early seventeenth century, the document states that Rodriguez accepted 'the grave command imposed' regarding San Ginesio 'with a willing spirit but in caution, so that whomever he should have found guilty and also harmless, he should absolve [and] compel to abjure their heresy not in public in the churches but permit it to be fulfilled in private'.[68] Although Pius had failed to approve the Jesuits' privilege in Italy, this account claims that he allowed Rodriguez to reconcile heretics in the Papal States, despite the presence of inquisitors in the region.[69]

Yet this account also claims that Pius V subsequently overturned Rodriguez's absolutions. According to the document, after allowing Rodriguez to absolve penitent-heretics secretly, Pius summoned several of them to Rome where they were 'thrust into the prison, which is vernacularly named the Holy office, just as fugitives or deserters of their ancestral religion'.[70] The account claims that Rodriguez was outraged at this violation of his jurisdiction and dashed immediately Rome, where he admonished Pius that 'he ought to remain [firm] in the promises to him'.[71] Pius apparently acquiesced right away, releasing the men from the jails of the Holy Office and accepting the legitimacy of Rodriguez's absolutions.[72] This account suggests that Pius disregarded the validity of the Jesuits' jurisdiction when he wanted information from Rodriguez's penitents and respected it only after they had been imprisoned and, most likely, questioned, by his Holy Office.

The later Jesuit account claims that Rodriguez was betrayed by the pope but it is possible that Rodriguez and Pius worked together to entrap penitent-heretics who had been lured to Rodriguez by the promise of a private absolution. Indeed, Vincenzo Lavenia has suggested that the Jesuit document

---

67   ARSI, *Rom. 185*, f.44v.
68   Ibid.
69   Lavenia, 'Giudici, eretici, infedeli', pp.20–23.
70   ARSI, *Rom. 185*, f.44v.
71   Ibid., ff.44v-45r.
72   Ibid., f.45r.

probably represents an attempt to conceal Rodriguez's complicity in a trick that violated the seal of secrecy that protected sacramental confession.[73] This interpretation is supported by Pius's instructions to Rodriguez when he set out for Le Marche. In these the pope instructed Rodriguez to act like a Jesuit pastor, rather than a papal agent, so that heretics on whom he spied would 'not become aware of that which is intended'.[74] The fact that Pius was able to identify those whom Rodriguez had absolved from heresy and summon them to the Holy Office suggests that Rodriguez fulfilled the pope's request to relay all that he was told to Rome. If Rodriguez used his Jesuit identity to conceal his role as a papal spy and followed Pius's instructions to send intelligence on heretics back to Rome it is surely possible that he was also willing to deceive those whom he absolved to further inquisitorial investigations. In Le Marche, it is perfectly possible that Rodriguez helped Pius V to facilitate an inquisitorial spy ring.

Whether Pius V betrayed Rodriguez or conspired with him directly, the San Ginesio episode indicates that the pope respected the private reconciliation of heretics only as far as it aided inquisitorial ends. This attitude reflects Pius V's fears about the privilege when he was a cardinal-inquisitor. Writing in September 1563, the then cardinal-inquisitor told Rodriguez not to pardon heretics too quickly as 'it always was and is the characteristic of heretics to go with deception and to swindle Catholics'.[75] Jesuits using the privilege of absolution worked on exactly the opposite premise to Pius's suspicious stance. For the Jesuits, the penitence of heretics seeking reconciliation with the Church was self-evident. If they did not regret their heresy or wish to renounce it they would not have approached their confessor. Ghislieri, on the other hand, believed that only the inquisition could sort the penitent from deceivers, explaining that whilst 'the confessor believes everything that happens [to be] said to him: the judge always doubts the offender of the truth'.[76] As pope, his position had not changed. In February 1568 a Jesuit noted that Pius V 'knows that public heretics sometimes go to the sacrament to confess falsely and to mock it', indicating that his concern about feigned conversions persisted well into his pontificate along with his reticence about extra-judicial reconciliations.[77]

Whilst the concession to Rodriguez in 1567 echoed Ghislieri's use of the Jesuits during his time as a cardinal-inquisitor his subsequent reversal of

---

73 Lavenia, 'Giudici, eretici, infedeli', p.6.

74 ARSI, *Institutum 187*, f.87r.

75 ARSI, *Epistolae Externorum 1*, f.68. Edited in Scaduto, 'Tra inquisitori e riformati', p.44.

76 Ibid.

77 ARSI, *Institutum 190*, f.6r.

Rodriguez's absolutions indicates a shift in dynamic that came with his ascension to the papal throne. During his cardinalate Ghislieri's standing and inquisitorial agenda had been diminished by contrasts with Pius IV, who disliked him and supported the approach and privileges of the Jesuits. But as Pope Pius V Ghislieri could pursue his own agenda, granting Rodriguez the privilege to absolve heresy before undermining him to pursue his own inquisitorial ideal. Of course, Pius V had greater power as pope in the Papal States than he had had as a Roman inquisitor in the various territories of Italy. Nonetheless, it was not only in the Papal States that Pius was emboldened in his tough inquisitorial strategy. Pius V's actions in his own territories were typical of his broader curtailment of the extra-judicial reconciliation of heretics across the Italian peninsula. Ultimately, Pius permitted extra-judicial reconciliations in Italy only as far as they facilitated the triumph of his inquisition. If Rodriguez was complicit in Pius's scheme in San Ginesio, as he was in his role as papal spy, it seems that a Jesuit who had valued the private absolution of heretics as a legitimate, autonomous route to reconciliation, was now forced or willing to use it as a cynical trap for the Roman Inquisition. Whilst at first the case of San Ginesio might appear to be an exception to Pius V's broader agenda, on closer inspection it is an exception that proves the rule.

3   'A Firm Garrison to Resist Heresy' in Savoy-Piedmont

The year after Rodriguez's mission to Le Marche, Pius V made another exception to his inquisitorial agenda, extending the privilege to absolve heresy to Jesuits in Savoy-Piedmont. There, Duke Emanuele Filiberto I had welcomed the Society but frustrated the influence of Pius V and his Roman Inquisition. In the mid-sixteenth century, Savoy-Piedmont was a notable exception to the pope's largely successful mission to monopolise anti-heretical activity across the Italian peninsula. Unfortunately for Pius V, this was the very last place he would want the prosecution of heresy out of his own hands. The Catholic orthodoxy of Savoy-Piedmont was considered crucial for the conservation of Catholicism in Italy. The state was home to communities of Waldensian heretics. Moreover, it bordered France, Switzerland and the German lands, where Protestantism imperilled both Catholic religion and public order. The pope thought that this state needed strict inquisitorial processes supervised from Rome. But the dukes of Savoy-Piedmont consistently resisted both Roman interference and a strict inquisitorial agenda. They did so for both political and pastoral reasons. Relations between the duke, the Roman Inquisition and the Jesuits during this period illustrate that the Society's organisation and approach allowed it to fight heresy hand-in-glove with the duke where Pius and his inquisition could not. When Emanuele Filiberto resisted the pope's tough inquisitorial agenda to follow his own conciliatory policies, Jesuits in Savoy-Piedmont worked as intermediaries, diligently converting heretics to please both the prince and the pope.

Three records indicate that Pius V granted the power to absolve heresy to Jesuits on 22 November 1568. One specifies that the concession was for the city of Turin and two others refer to a concession for northern Europe.[78] The first is a letter written by Borja on 22 November 1568, telling fathers at the Jesuit college in Turin that Pius V had granted them the privilege. The other two records date to the late 1580s and inform the Roman Inquisition that the privilege was granted to Jesuits in the northern or transalpine parts of Europe on that same day. One of these later records tells us that, just like his mentor Paul IV, Pius V granted Superiors of the Society – and others judged suitable by Superiors – faculties so that they would be able to absolve cases of heresy and schismaticism in every part of northern Europe.[79] The second document refers to the concession of the faculty of absolving heresy for the Transalpine provinces.[80] These documents and similar contemporary lists use the term 'northern' or 'septentrionalis' interchangeably with 'transalpinis', indicating that they referred to privileges for areas north of the Alps, beyond the Italian states. These documents seem to refer to two or three separate concessions: one for the Italian city of Turin, south of the Alps, and two beyond the Italian peninsula in northern Europe.

The Turin concession complicates our understanding of Pius V's agenda so far. Read alone, the concessions for the northern territories appear consistent with Pius's willingness to grant the privilege to Jesuits in northern Europe but not in Italy. Although Savoy-Piedmont comprised territories in modern-day France as well as Italy much of the state, including Turin, lay south of the Alps in Italian territory. The city was Italian ecclesiastically as well as geographically. Formally, Emanuele Filiberto had accepted the jurisdiction of the Roman Inquisition, distinguishing himself from neighbouring northern European

---

78 For Turin: ARSI, *Epistolae Italiae 136*, f.232r. For the two records of concessions for northern or transalpine parts: ARSI, *Institutum 185-I*, f.310r and ACDF, *Stanza Storica D – 4 – A*, f.61r.

79 'Paulus Quartus 8 mensis Maii 1557 ... concessit, ut in omnibus partibus Septentrionalibus Superiores Societatis, et alii à Superioribus iudicati idonei, quibus id committeretur absolvere possint à casibus haereseos et schismaticis ... Idem concessit Pius V 22 Novembris 1568 pro eis'. ACDF, *Stanza Storica D-4-A*, f.61r.

80 'De facultate absolvendi ab haeresi Societati Jesu à Sum[m]is Pontificibus concessa ... De eadem facultate pro Transalpinis provinciis'. ARSI, *Institutum 185-I*, f.310r.

110 CHAPTER 3

states like France.[81] Our three records could refer to just one occasion on which Pius conceded the privilege, or to three separate episodes. Either way, the concession to Jesuits in Turin appears to contradict Pius v's broad anti-heretical agenda in Italy. Therefore, the document demands that we reassess the interpretation suggested by documents such as the bull *In Coena Domini* of 1568 and Rodriguez's mission in Le Marche. In Le Marche, Rodriguez's jurisdiction was granted as a lure to further the inquisitorial agenda that is evident in legal documents. But in Savoy-Piedmont Jesuits in an Italian city were given a genuinely autonomous jurisdiction to reconcile heretics.

The concession of the privilege to Jesuits in Turin came after a series of requests from Achille Gagliardi, rector of the Jesuit college in the city. Just like the rector in Loreto, Gagliardi believed that he already had the privilege to absolve heretics. In July 1568, he wrote to Borja to ask for his permission to extend the faculty to absolve heretics to other priests because he 'could not attend to hearing confessions'.[82] Gagliardi reported that even if there were another three or four priests there they would be well occupied with confessions. Moreover, confession was vital to their ministry as Gagliardi said that through confessions some penitents 'were converted from errors to the Catholic faith, and others are [going] to do so'.[83] Gagliardi insisted that his desire to extend the privilege to other Jesuits in Turin was purely practical as there were some French people who came to confession whom he did not understand.[84] Without extending the privilege to others Gagliardi said that there was no other way to help them.[85] For Gagliardi, the extension of the Jesuit privilege was simply a pragmatic necessity.

Furthermore, according to Gagliardi, the Jesuits' work to convert heretics in Turin was vital for the orthodoxy of all of Italy. Gagliardi argued that the city was vitally important to Italian efforts to resist heresy from France.[86] During the Italian Wars, Turin had been occupied by French forces.[87] The French

---

81 On Savoy-Piedmont see Black, *The Italian Inquisition*, p.30; Lavenia, 'L'Inquisizione del Duca' and 'L'Inquisizione negli Stati sabaudi: Roma, Torino e la politica religiosa' in Jean-François Chauvard, Andrea Merlotti and Maria Antonietta Visceglia (eds), *Casa Savoia e Curia romana dal Cinquecento al Risorgimento* (Rome: École Française de Rome, 2015), pp.113–128.

82 ARSI, *Epistolae Italiae 136*, f.132r.

83 Ibid., ff.130–1r.

84 Ibid., f.132r and f.232r.

85 Ibid., f.131r.

86 Ibid., f.131v.

87 Gustavo Mola di Nomaglio, *Feudi e nobiltà negli stati dei Savoia. Materiali, spunti, spigolature bibliografiche per una storia* (Turin: Società storica delle Valli di Lanzo, 2006), p.80.

BETWEEN THE PRINCE AND THE POPE

left in 1560 but remnants of their community and Protestant beliefs remained. This threat was exacerbated by French merchants travelling through the city and official alliances between French Protestants and older Waldensian communities of rural Savoy-Piedmont.[88] Gagliardi told Borja that if nothing was done to stem the spread of religious heterodoxy in Turin heresy would be disseminated through all of Italy.[89] Gagliardi alleged that this had already begun, telling Borja that 'it is known that those of Geneva make every effort to enter through this door into Italy'.[90] If Gagliardi was to be believed, Jesuit confessors in Turin should be empowered to absolve heresy so that they could save the entire Italian peninsula from heretical contamination.

Gagliardi was neither the first person nor the first Jesuit to express fears that Savoy-Piedmont could provide a gateway for dangerous heresies to enter into Italy.[91] In 1560, Antonio Possevino, who established the Jesuits' presence in Savoy-Piedmont, wrote to Superior General Laínez to tell him that Protestants were sending catechists from Geneva into the state.[92] Both political and religious leaders echoed the Jesuits' concerns about the region.[93] The Venetian ambassador to Savoy-Piedmont reported that Huguenots from the valleys had already attempted to occupy certain towns in the Duchy so that they might establish another Geneva in Italy.[94] Pius IV took the threat of heresy in Savoy-Piedmont seriously, electing bishop François Bachaud as the first papal nuncio to the state in 1559 and granting him powers to work on behalf of the Roman Inquisition.[95] Two years later, cardinal-inquisitor Ghislieri himself would visit Savoy-Piedmont with 'the greatest faculty to proceed against heretics'.[96] When

---

88   Scaduto, *Storia della Compagnia di Gesù in Italia: L'Epoca di Giacomo Lainez: l'azione*, pp.673–4.On the Synod of Chanforan where this alliance was made and the Waldensians generally, see Cameron, *The Reformation of the Heretics*, p.133.

89   ARSI, *Epistolae Italiae 136*, ff.71r-72v.

90   Ibid., f.131v.

91   On fears about heresy and Protestant neighbour states see Michelson, *The Pulpit and the Press in Reformation Italy*, p.125.

92   ARSI, *Institutum 187*, ff.126r.

93   Black, *The Italian Inquisition*, p.30 and Caponetto, *The Protestant Reformation in sixteenth-century Italy*, p.135.

94   Edited Giovanni Jalla, *Storia della Riforma in Piemonte fino alla morte di Emanuele Filiberto 1517–1580* (Florence: Claudiana, 1914), p.348.

95   Lavenia, 'L'Inquisizione negli Stati Sabaudi', p.117 and Scaduto, 'Le missioni di A. Possevino in Piemonte', Archivum Historicum Societatis Iesu, 28 (1959), p.71. On the foundation of the nunziature see Fausto Fonzi, *Nunziature di Savoia. Volume primo. (15 ottobre 1560-giugno 1573)* (Rome: Istituto storico italiano per l'età moderna e contemporanea, 1960), pp.ix-xvi.

96   ASV, *Savoia Nunziatura*, 224, ff.18v-20v. Edited in Fonzi, *Nunziature di Savoia. Volume primo*, pp.68–9. See also, Fonzi, *Nunziature di Savoia. Volume primo*, p. xii.

112   CHAPTER 3

Ghislieri became Pius v, he showed similarly serious concern, personally se-
lecting the state's inquisitors to ensure that tribunals were staffed by men who
would execute his anti-heretical agenda.[97] Of course, Gagliardi's claims may
have been exaggerated to support his request for the privilege. However, they
reflected an accepted view that the religious situation in Savoy-Piedmont was
deeply concerning.

Duke Emanuele Filiberto also feared heresy in his state. Moreover, he believed that protecting Catholic orthodoxy was crucial for preserving his sover-
eignty. In 1555, the Peace of Augsburg had declared that the religious confession of a state's subjects would be dictated by their ruler.[98] This decision tied
religion, territory and temporal authority, making religious rebellion an act
of treason.[99] In Savoy-Piedmont, Emanuele Filberto feared that heresy could
stoke political sedition, that 'under the pretext of religion, a popular state
would go taking root little by little'.[100] As the ruler of territories that traversed
the Alps, Emanuele-Filiberto had first-hand experience of the grave political consequences of religious rebellion. The triumph of Calvinism in Geneva
had contributed to his loss of the city in the 1530s whilst the religious wars in
France had offered him a vivid demonstration of the destabilising and bloody
consequences of confessional conflict.[101] Summarising his views on the vital
connection between religion and politics, the duke was alleged to have said
that 'the ruin of every State came from not conserving the Catholic religion
intact'.[102]

Despite widespread concerns about heresy in Savoy-Piedmont, Borja had to
negotiate Gagliardi's request for the privilege to absolve heresy with Pius v. In
a letter to Gagliardi, Borja wrote that he had told the pope that many heretics
were converted by the Jesuits in Turin.[103] In response, the ever sceptical Pius

---

97   Lavenia, 'L'Inquisizione negli Stati Sabaudi', p.120.
98   Nadia Urbinati, 'Concordia and the Limits of Dialogue' in Alfred Stepan and Charles Taylor
      (eds), *Boundaries of Toleration* (New York: Columbia University Press, 2014), pp.132–3.
99   Nexon, *The Struggle for Power in Early Modern Europe*, p.181.
100   Emanuele Filiberto to Alfonso d'Este quoted in Scaduto, *Storia della Compagnia di Gesù in
      Italia: L'Epoca di Giacomo Lainez: l'azione*, p.676.
101   Fonzi (ed.), *Nunziature di Savoia. Volume primo*, p.x and Lavenia, 'L'Inquisizione negli
      Stati Sabaudi', p.114.
102   Jean Dorigny and Niccolo Ghezzi (trans.), *Vita del P. Antonio Possevino della Compagnia
      di Gesu gia' scritta in lingua francese dal padre Giovanni Dorigny, Ora tradotta nella vol-
      gare italiana, Ed illustrata con varie note, e piu lettere inedite, e parecchi Monumenti aggi-
      unti al fine* (Venice: Remondini, 1759), vol. 2, p.55. Quoted in Jalla, *Storia della Riforma in
      Piemonte*, p.138. See also, Höpfl, *Jesuit political thought*, p.72.
103   ARSI, *Epistolae Generalium Italiae 61*, f.145r.

v 'pointed out [that Gagliardi should] maintain that these conversions are not feigned, as they are often in France'.[104] Pius's allusion to France suggests that he knew that Gagliardi sought the extension of the privilege for Frenchmen in Piedmont, that is to stem the migration of heresy into Italy. Despite this, Pius refused the request, stating that 'it would be very expedient [that], wishing to return to the womb of the Church, [the penitent-heretics] make the abjurations in the hands of the inquisitor, if they are not secret heresies'.[105] Even in Savoy-Piedmont where he feared growing religious dissent, Pius was reluctant to use private reconciliations to quell the threat of spreading heresy.

In September 1568, Gagliardi tried to convince Pius, through Borja, that the Jesuits in Turin should and could deal with some cases of heresy alone. According to Gagliardi, in the cases that he heard it was 'not necessary to speak of inquisitors, nor of abjuration' because the 'heretics are secret and seduced through ignorance'.[106] Gagliardi's claim suggests that the heretics who he met were not notorious or known to the inquisitors and could therefore be absolved and reconciled to the Church *in foro conscientiae*. Gagliardi also argued that heretics would not approach the inquisition as they thought it 'a most hateful thing' through which even 'the Catholics are scandalised'.[107] Appealing to the concerns of both Pius and Borja, Gagliardi promised that, if granted, the power to absolve heretics autonomously would be used with every caution.[108]

Two weeks later, on 22 November 1568, Borja told Gagliardi that the pope had acquiesced. 'Our Father gives the faculty to absolve from heresy in the *foro conscientiae*, in the same way that was conceded to Y[our] R[everence], to F[ather] Antonio Genovese, because only he knows the French language. And also to F[ather] Francesco Butiron'.[109] In a territory where the Roman Inquisition had official jurisdiction Pius v made an exception to his agenda, granting the Jesuits there permission to absolve heretics independently.

Pius v's concession is explained by the ecclesiastical and political situation in Savoy-Piedmont. Although Emanuele Filiberto had agreed to cooperate with the Roman Inquisition, he never truly accepted its agenda. Officially things looked clear cut. Whilst ecclesiastics in the territory that had formed the Duchy of Savoy claimed Gallican privileges that gave them autonomy from Rome, in the Principality of Piedmont the Holy Office had established tribunals in four

---

104 Ibid.
105 Ibid.
106 ARSI, *Epistolae Italiae 136*, f.169r.
107 Ibid.
108 Ibid.
109 ARSI, *Epistolae Generalium Italiae 67*, f.169v.

114   CHAPTER 3

key cities, including the capital Turin.[110] Pietro Ferrero, bishop of Vercelli and ducal ambassador to Rome, recorded that the fight against heresy in Savoy-Piedmont was 'principally committed' to 'ordinaries and inquisitors', that is to ecclesiastical authorities elected by the Holy See.[111] All the same, 'His Highness [the duke] might wish to make some of his [own men] intervene'.[112] This last point was crucial. For Emanuele Filiberto never really relinquished control over the anti-heretical agenda in his state. Whilst advisors to his son, Duke Carlo Emmanuele, would characterise his approach as an unsuccessful imitation of Venice – which famously asserted its independence from Rome – his actions exemplify the broader tendency of secular princes to direct religious discipline in their own lands in this period.[113] The duke may have come to a formal agreement with the popes of Rome but in reality he thought that he was the only one who should decide how to confront the heretics in his territories.

Emanuele Filiberto employed the full apparatus of the state to crush heresy in Savoy-Piedmont and the Jesuits soon became part of this system. In the first year of the duke's reign he banned his subjects from educating their children in Protestant countries.[114] He also had buildings constructed for Protestant ministry destroyed and those who constructed them confronted with military force.[115] Moreover, Emanuele Filiberto outlawed attendance at Protestant

---

110   Lavenia, 'L'Inquisizione negli Stati Sabaudi', p.121 and Prosperi, *Tribunali della coscienza*, pp.104–5.
        On the resistance to the inquisition in Savoy see Achille Erba, *La Chiesa sabauda tra Cinque e Seicento. Ortodossia tridentina, gallicanesimo savoiardo e assolutismo ducale (1580–1640)* (Rome: Herder, 1979).
111   Biblioteca Reale di Torino (hereafter, BRTO), *Miscellanea patria 101*, no. 6.
112   Ibid.
113   Edited in Jalla, *Storia della Riforma in Piemonte*, p.109. On the Roman Inquisition in Venice see, for example, Pio Paschini, *Venezia e l'Inquisizione Romana da Giulio III a Pio IV* (Padua: Editrice Atenore, 1959). Emanuele Filiberto's strategies are an example of 'confessionalisation'. Still his failures to convert well-established heretical groups such as the Waldensians support later criticisms of this thesis, which underline the failures of such policies and the resistance of lay people. On the confessionalisation thesis see Wolfgang Reinhard, 'Konfession und Konfessionalisierung in Europa' in Reinhard (ed.), *Bekenntnis und Geschichte. Die Confessio Augustana im historischen Zusammenhang*, (Munich: Vögel, 1981), pp.165–89 and Heinrich Schilling, 'Zwang zur Konfessionalisierung? Prolegomena zu einer Theorie des konfessionellen Zeitalters', *Zeitschrift für historische Forschung*, 10 (1983), pp.257–77. See also, Laven, 'Encountering the Counter-Reformation'; O'Malley, *Trent and All That*, pp.108–17; Ronnie Po-Chia Hsia, *Social Discipline in the Reformation: Central Europe, 1550–1750* (New York: Routledge, 1990) and Reinhard and Schilling, 'Reformation, Counter-Reformation, and the Early Modern State. A Reassessment', *Catholic Historical Review*, 75 (1989), pp.383–494.
114   Scaduto, 'Le missioni di A. Possevino in Piedmonte', p.68.
115   Ibid.

BETWEEN THE PRINCE AND THE POPE

sermons, fining first-time offenders 100 scudi and consigning repeat offenders to a lifetime rowing galleys.[116] The duke also introduced financial incentives for those who denounced heretics, giving judicial officials, community syndicates and subjects a third of any fine paid by a heretic whom they revealed.[117] Emanuele Filiberto elected a committee of loyal state officials to execute these edicts, comprising Don Filippo di Savoia (Signor di Racconiggi), Count Giorgio Costa della Trinità (the Captain of Justice), Senator Corbis and his inquisitor Tomasso Giacomello.[118] As an armed, roving, state inquisition, this group converted or punished those who had deviated from Catholic orthodoxy and, in so doing, rebelled against the duke.[119] In 1560, Jesuit Antonio Possevino would join the group, providing preaching and catechesis to convert and instruct penitent-heretics.[120] Possevino's involvement in these missions established a pattern that was then followed by Jesuits who supported state forces to fight heresy in Savoy-Piedmont.

Emanuele Filiberto had resisted Roman authority since the foundation of Savoy-Piedmont in 1559, despite the efforts of successive popes. When Ghislieri arrived as an inquisitor in 1561, Pius IV had granted him general superintendence over the whole state.[121] Ghislieri ordered the duke to abandon his autonomous actions and cooperate with Rome.[122] It seems that the duke continued to resist. Ghislieri complained that the duke's edicts on heresy encroached on ecclesiastical jurisdiction and so Pius IV ordered Emanuele Filiberto to revoke his anti-heretical laws. According to Ghislieri, the duke merely paid lip-service to this command before continuing to 'observe [his own edicts] more than ever'.[123] In fact, when successive popes enforced their religious authority using political instruments, such as inquisitors and nuncios, Emanuele Filiberto

---

116   Marco Aurelio Rorengo, *Memorie historiche dell'introduttione dell'Heresie nelle Valli di Lucerna, Marchesato di Saluzzo, and altre di Piemonte, Editti, Prouisioni, Diligenze delle Altezze di Sauoia per estirparle* (Turin: Giovanni Domenico Tarino, 1649), pp.39–40.
117   Ibid., p.40.
118   Ibid.
119   Scaduto, *Storia della Compagnia di Gesù in Italia: L'Epoca di Giacomo Lainez: l'azione*, p.677.
120   On Possevino's missions in Savoy-Piedmont see, Camillo Crivelli, 'La disputa di Antonio Possevino con i Valdesi', *Archivum Historicum Societatis Iesu*, 7 (1938), pp.79–91; Raffaele Di Simone, *Tre anni decisivi di storia valdese. Missioni, repressione e tolleranza nelle valli piemontesi dal 1559 al 1561* (Rome: Università Gregoriana, 1958) and Scaduto, 'Le missioni di A. Possevino in Piemonte'.
121   Scaduto, *Storia della Compagnia di Gesù in Italia: L'Epoca di Giacomo Lainez: l'azione*, p.677.
122   Ibid.
123   ASV, *Savoia Nunziatura*, 224, ff.21v-22r. Edited in Fonzi, *Nunziature di Savoia. Volume primo*, p.71.

appeared to see their actions as an illicit interference.[124] Religious rebellion threatened the duke's authority and the safety of his subjects; he thought that he – not the pope – should decide how to confront it.

Emanuele Filiberto resisted Roman authority well into Ghislieri's pontificate as Pius v.[125] In his first year, Pius v nominated the Dominican Francesco Papardo as inquisitor general in Savoy-Piedmont, empowering him with 'every type of faculty and each and every authority that pertains to a duty of this kind, by law and [by] custom'.[126] Despite this sweeping power, Emanuele Filiberto's secular forces refused to hand over wanted heretics to Papardo.[127] Their actions reflected the attitude of the duke himself, who had refused to cooperate with the nuncio who had been elected as an intermediary between Turin and Rome. In November 1568, Pius v ordered his new nuncio, Vincenzo Lauro, 'to persuade and exhort His Highness [the Duke] to provide that heretics do not settle in his state and see to it with every diligence to expunge [his states] of all infected persons'.[128] But Lauro failed to convince the duke to support the Roman Inquisition.[129] When Pius v personally pressed Emanuele Filiberto to allow his Roman Inquisition to work unimpeded, the duke said that he would 'without any exception' but only if Pius lent military support to his efforts to recapture Geneva.[130] Pius had given his inquisition the power to pursue heretics across the Italian peninsula. But Emanuele Filiberto treated Rome as a political power to be bargained with not a universal religious authority to be obeyed.

Emanuele Filiberto also resisted Rome because he believed that his own methods were more effective than those of the popes. Emanuele Filiberto was keen to demonstrate that he took a hard line on heresy, particularly as his French wife, Marguerite of Valois, was rumoured to protect heretics at the ducal court. Nonetheless, he openly disagreed with Pius v's fierce

---

124 Prodi, *The Papal Prince: One Body Two Souls. The Papal Monarchy in Early Modern Europe* (Cambridge: Cambridge University Press, 1987), p.167.

125 Lavenia, 'L'Inquisizione del duca', p.420.

126 Quoted in Romano Canosa, *Storia dell'Inquisizione in Italia dalla metà del cinquecento alla fine del settecento. Torino e Genova. Vol. III* (Bari: Sapere 2000, 1988), p.32.

127 Ibid., p.33.

128 ASV, *Nunziatura di Polonia*, 171, ff.32r-33r. Edited in Fonzi, *Nunziature di Savoia. Volume primo*, p.145.

129 ASV, *Nunziatura di Polonia*, 171, ff.114r-v. Edited in Fonzi, *Nunziature di Savoia. Volume primo*, p.226.

130 This is recorded in a letter to cardinal-nephew Michele Bonelli from nuncio Vincenzo Lauro in ASV, *Savoia Nunziatura*, ff.46v-49r. Edited in Fonzi, *Nunziature di Savoia*, pp.244–5.

BETWEEN THE PRINCE AND THE POPE

approach.[131] For example, Emanuele Filiberto disputed Pius's view that the Waldensians should be exterminated, arguing that it was not always best 'to burn a man, the death of whom will not make [other] men better'.[132] And when Pius V continued his efforts to impose his hard line in Savoy-Piedmont, appointing inquisitors from Rome and ordering them to use violence if necessary, Emanuele Filiberto argued 'that one has to use mediocrity as much as is necessary in these times', working towards 'that which builds and does not destroy'.[133] In some cases, Emanuele Filiberto even tolerated long-established groups like the Waldensians, which bloody interventions had failed to convert.[134] Ecclesiastical and temporal leaders in the Kingdom of Naples had taken a similar stance with their own Waldensian communities, recognising that violence and the evacuation of taxable land were less desirable than the presence of known heretics.[135] For Emanuele Filiberto, peace and stability were paramount: the preservation of the Church 'in general' but above all in his own lands.[136]

The contrast between Emanuele Filiberto's clemency and some of the popes' harsher policies caused tension between Turin and Rome. Popes even blamed the duke for the persistent threat of heresy spreading in and from Savoy-Piedmont. In June 1561, Pius IV's nephew, Carlo Borromeo, wrote to Emanuele Filiberto, telling him that his toleration of the Waldensians infuriated the pope who wanted to see the eradication of heresy and the punishment of obstinate heretics.[137] Emanuele Filiberto was equally critical of Rome. During

---

131 On Marguerite of Valois see, Rosanna Gorris Camos, '«Pia ricevitrice di ogni cristiano »: poésie, exil et religion autour de Marguerite de France, duchesse de Savoie' in Jean Balsamo (ed.), *Chemins de l'exil havres de paix: migrations d'hommes et d'idées au XVIe siècle; actes du colloque de Tours, 8–9 novembre 2007* (Paris: Champion, 2010), pp.177–228; Cesare Cantù, *Gli eretici d'Italia. Discorsi Storici. Vol. 3* (Turin: Unione Tipografico-Editrice, 1866), p.359 and C. Rosso, 'Margherita di Valois e lo Stato sabaudo (1559–1574)' in Firpo, Fragnito and Peyronel Rambaldi (eds), *Atti del convegno Olimpia Morata: cultura umanistica e Riforma protestante tra Ferrara e l'Europa* (Ferrara: Panini, 2007), pp.149–156.

132 Quoted in A. Pascal, 'La lotta contro la Riforma in Piemonte al tempo di Emanuele Filiberto, studiata nelle relazioni diplomatiche tra la corte sabauda e la Santa Sede (1559–1580)', *Bulletin de la Societé d'Histoire Vaudoise*, 53 (1929), p.56. Pius V had suggested that the Waldensians of Naples might be dealt with through 'l'esterminio di quella città et di tutta quella generatione'. ARSI, *Epistolae externorum 1*, f.68r. Edited in Scaduto, 'Tra inquisitori e riformati', p.44.

133 Edited in Pascal, 'La lotta contro la Riforma in Piemonte', p.56.

134 On the duke's efforts to convert the Waldensians see, de Simone, *Tre anni decisivi di storia valdese.*

135 Scaduto, 'Tra Inquisitori e riformati', pp.3–5.

136 Pascal, 'La lotta contro la Riforma in Piemonte', pp.54–5.

137 ASV, *Savoia Nunziatura*, 224, doc. n.19, ff.16r-17r. Edited in de Simone, *Tre anni decisivi di storia valdese*, pp.249–50.

Pius V's pontificate, the duke told his ambassador to the Holy See, Abbot Vincenzo Parpaglia, that he was better able to judge the best way of proceeding based on the nature and circumstances of each case than those in Rome 'a long way from the dangers'.[138] Emanuele Filiberto certainly did not think it compulsory to follow the advice of Rome. Discussing the work of Pius V's inquisitor, Papardo, the duke suggested that the orders of Roman authorities were merely advisory, arguing that it was important to refer 'to another judgement [to consider] if the way of proceeding is apt to destruct or truly to build'.[139] This conflict of approaches reflected a conflict of interests. Whilst Emanuele Filiberto was principally concerned with balancing discipline and tolerance to stabilise his state, successive popes wanted stricter measures to secure the orthodoxy of all of Italy.

In contrast to the inquisition, the Jesuits presented themselves as loyal servants of the duke's plans. The first Jesuit to meet with Emanuele Filiberto was Antonio Possevino who visited the ducal court to commend the Society when he went to Savoy-Piedmont as Commendatore of Fossano.[140] Possevino emphasised the Jesuits' support for the duke's anti-heretical strategy. Rather than focusing on Roman ecclesiastical jurisdiction over heresy, Possevino underlined the duke's own duty to see 'the souls [of his state] restored to God' just as the 'state has been restored to His Highness by divine majesty'.[141] By discussing the problem of heresy in these terms, Possevino complemented the duke's strong belief that he and not the Roman inquisitorial authorities should set the anti-heretical agenda in his state. Possevino also concurred with Emanuele Filiberto's concerns about the political ramifications of religious dissent, claiming that the protection of Catholicism in Savoy-Piedmont would bring about 'the establishment of his states' and prevent another episode like 'the disunion of Geneva and other places because of heretics' as once they leave the Church heretics 'also disengage from temporal power'.[142] Possevino proposed himself as an intermediary between Turin and Rome who could solicit help for ecclesiastical reform in Savoy-Piedmont and remind papal representatives and the Jesuit Superior General of what might be done to end '*rumori*'

---

138   Quoted in Pascal, 'La lotta contro la Riforma in Piemonte', p.55.

139   Ibid., p.54.

140   Alessandro Monti, *La Compagnia di Gesù nel territorio della Provincia Torinese* (Chieri: M. Ghirardi, 1914), 5 vols, vol.1, p.106.

141   ARSI, *Opera Nostrorum 324-I*, ff.8r-13v. Edited in Scaduto, 'Le missioni di A. Possevino in Piedmonte', p.93.

142   ARSI, *Opera Nostrorum 324-I*, f.8r. Edited in Scaduto, 'Le missioni di A. Possevino in Piedmonte', p.93..

BETWEEN THE PRINCE AND THE POPE

in the duchy whilst protecting the dignity of the duke.[143] In Savoy-Piedmont, Possevino proposed the Society of Jesus as a tool of state.

Unlike Roman nuncios and inquisitors, Possevino claimed that the Jesuits would work in perfect harmony with the state authorities. According to Possevino heresy in Savoy-Piedmont could only be fought with 'a great tempering of wise religious [men]' 'who do not damage the temporal with the spiritual but [see to it] that the one is the support of the other'.[144] Such statements suggest that the Jesuits agreed that heavy-handed interventions caused problems rather than resolving them. Jesuits like Loyola had long claimed that, through their pastoral approach to heresy they could 'preserve that which stays healthy' and 'cure that which is already corrupted by the heretical plague'.[145] This method complemented the duke's aim to curb religious rebellion whilst preventing the social unrest that had been exacerbated by more violent attempts to convert heretics.[146]

Possevino made sure that the Jesuits were perfectly placed to fight for Catholic orthodoxy for the duke. Immediately on arriving in Savoy-Piedmont he sought ducal support for the establishment of Jesuit colleges in the duchy. From these bases, Possevino claimed that the Society could deliver education to protect the duke's subjects from the perils of religious error and offer pastoral care to Catholics and heretics who sought reconciliation with the Church.[147] Gagliardi fought for a college in the city of Turin, claiming that, as 'a place that is so close to various lands and of great concourse and passage', it needed a Jesuit college to increase 'the number of people who could resist the heresies' that travelled through the city.[148] According to Gagliardi, a Jesuit college would

---

143   Archivio di Stato di Torino (hereafter, ASTO), *Lettere di particolari – P*, Mazzo 58.

144   ARSI, *Opera Nostrorum 324-I*, f.21r. Edited in Scaduto, 'Le missioni di A. Possevino in Piedmonte', p.102.

145   Loyola, *Sancti Ignatii de Loyola. Epistolae et instructiones*, vol.12, pp.259–60. See also Höpfl, *Jesuit political thought*, p.67.

146   Lavenia, 'L'Inquisizione del Duca', p.437.

147   On Jesuit colleges see, Paul F. Grendler, 'Laínez and the Schools' in Paul Oberholzer (ed.), *Diego Laínez (1512–1565) and his Generalate. Jesuit with Jewish Roots, Close Confidant of Ignatius Loyola, Preeminent Theologian of the Council of Trent* (Rome: Institutum Historicum Societatis Iesu, 2015), pp.649–78; Grendler, *The Jesuits and Italian Universities* (Washington D.C.: The Catholic University of America Press, 2017); O'Malley, *The First Jesuits*, pp.200–39; Ladislaus Lukács, 'De origine collegiorum externorum deque controversiis circa eorum paupertatem obortis 1539–1608', *Archivum Historicum Societatis Iesu*, 29, (1960), pp.189–245; Pavone, 'I gesuiti in Italia' and Aldo Scaglione, *The Liberal Arts and the Jesuit College System* (Amsterdam: John Benjamins, 1986). For an overview of literature on Jesuit colleges see Grendler, 'Jesuit Schools in Europe. A Historiographical Essay', *Journal of Jesuit Studies*, 1 (2014) pp.7–25.

148   ARSI, *Epistolae Italiae 139*, f.219v-220r.

be 'a firm garrison to resist heresy' in Savoy-Piedmont.[149] Possevino was similarly confident in the impact of Jesuit colleges. During his first meeting with Emanuele Filiberto, Possevino had claimed that if there had been a strong Jesuit college in Annecy the nearby city of Geneva may not have been lost to the duke.[150] Years later, Possevino clearly believed that the Jesuits had succeeded in protecting the duke's lands. Writing to the duke of Monferrat in the 1580s, Possevino claimed that it was Jesuit colleges that had solved Emanuele Filiberto's problems with heresy, stating that the duke had found 'all Piedmont with many stains of heresy and ignorance' but had eradicated heresy by founding Jesuit colleges in Mondovì, Turin, Chambery, Vercelli and Annecy.[151]

When Gagliardi requested the extension of the privilege to absolve heresy at the college in Turin in 1568 the Society had already won the duke's support for their plan to fight heresy from colleges across Savoy-Piedmont. Unlike the Roman Inquisition, the Jesuits had been accepted by the duke as a key part of his anti-heretical agenda. Emanuele Filiberto personally funded their establishments, giving an annual endowment of 400 scudi to the colleges at Mondovì and Chambéry and 150 scudi each for Cuneo and Carignano.[152] In Turin, the Society inherited a property and money from a private donor, Aleramo Becutto, but the Jesuits also secured a substantial stipend from the duke.[153] As confessors, preachers and teachers, Jesuits were fully integrated into Emanuele Filiberto's state-run schemes for fighting heresy. From the early 1560s, the Society influenced the duke's anti-heretical agenda in ways that the pope and his inquisition could not.

The concession of 22 November 1568 indicates that, eventually, even Pius V realised that his power was limited in Savoy-Piedmont. One of the three documents that mention concessions on 22 November 1568 confirms that Pius V's willingness to grant the privilege to absolve heresy in Savoy-Piedmont was connected to his frustration with the duke. In the later record of privileges granted for Jesuits in the 'northern parts', the reference to the concession of the 22 November 1568 states that Pius V allowed Jesuits to absolve heresy in areas where

---

149   ARSI, *Epistolae Italiae 136*, f.72r.
150   ARSI, *Opera Nostrorum 324-I*, f.8v. Edited in Scaduto, 'Le missioni di A. Possevino in Piedmonte', p.94.
151   ASTO, *Monteferrato – Feudi per A e B*, Mazzo 1, fasc. 11, f.4r.
152   The *minuta* for the patent for the college at Mondovì is held in ASTO, *Regolari di qua da Monti*, Mazzo 10, Mondovì, [fasc.] no.1.
153   The official record of Beccuto's donation of 300 scudi per year is held in: ASTO, *Materie ecclesiastiche – Regolari diversi – Torino – Gesuiti*, Mazzo 1, fasc. no. 33. On the various colleges in Savoy-Piedmont see Alessandro Monti, *La Compagnia di Gesù nel territorio della Provincia Torinese*, vol.1.

'ecclesiastical liberty [was] violated'.[154] Since the eleventh century, the principle of ecclesiastical liberty held that temporal powers could not impede the Church's authority.[155] Instructing his nuncio in Turin, Vincenzo Lauro, Pius V claimed that ecclesiastical liberty had been violated in Savoy-Piedmont, ordering Lauro to make continual efforts for 'the immunity of ecclesiastical matters and for the conservation of ecclesiastical liberty and jurisdiction'.[156] Pius V had even predicted that the protection of ecclesiastical liberty would be necessary in 'occurrences that could come daily with H[is] H[ighness]', even if the duke was called to the 'obedience and devotion that every Catholic prince owes to this H[oly] See'.[157] When Lauro failed to persuade the duke to submit to the pope, Pius V warned him that he was considering abolishing the nunciature altogether. Angered by Lauro's 'coldness' in seeking 'to give a hand to the Holy Office' and ensure that it had 'every help and favour', Pius contemplated 'getting rid of the nuncio at that court'.[158] This extreme threat reflects the extent of Pius's frustration at the duke's continued violation of ecclesiastical liberty and at his own inability to check it.

The reference to 'violated ecclesiastical liberty' in the later record of privileges suggests that this and the other documents noting a concession for northern or transalpine parts on 22 November 1568 refer to the concession to Gagliardi in Turin on the very same day. Closer analysis of the documents corroborates this interpretation. These references to privileges for northern and transalpine territories appear on lists of concessions written and sent by the Jesuits to the Roman Inquisition in the late 1580s as proof of the continued papal support for the Society's privilege to absolve heresy. Given this aim, it is probable that the Jesuit authors retrospectively extrapolated the Turin concession of 22 November 1568 as a concession for all areas outside of the jurisdiction of the Roman Inquisition. We have already seen an example of this strategic interpretation in their extrapolation of Pius V's exemption to the bull *In Coena Domini* as a concession of the privilege to absolve heresy for all of northern Europe. Although the references in these lists were written by Jesuits and are not, therefore, direct evidence of Pius V's interpretation of the

---

154 ARSI, *Institutum 187*, f.310v.

155 On the principle and its application in the late fifteenth and early sixteenth centuries, see Kenneth Pennington, 'Ecclesiastical Liberty on the Eve of the Reformation', *Bulletin of Medieval Canon Law*, 185 (2016), pp, 185–207.

156 ASV, *Nunziatura di Polonia 171*, ff.32r-33r. Edited in Fonzi, *Nunziature di Savoia. Volume primo*, p.145.

157 Ibid.

158 ASV, *Nunziatura di Savoia 10*, f.341r. Edited in Fonzi, *Nunziature di Savoia. Volume primo*, p.225.

situation, their conflation of Turin and northern Europe would also reflect the pope's broader view that Roman authority was frustrated in Savoy-Piedmont just as it was beyond the Alps.

Gagliardi's request for the privilege in Savoy-Piedmont echoes those from other corners of the peninsula, showing us that the Jesuits still believed that some heretics required a genuinely autonomous route to reconciliation with the Church. Such requests met with caution from Borja who was keen to maintain good relations with Pius V, a pope whose support for the Society's privileges was far from certain. At first, Gagliardi's request was no different. Nonetheless, the fear and frustration caused by the religious and ecclesiastical situation in Savoy-Piedmont led Pius V to make an unusual exception and grant the privilege to Jesuit confessors in Turin. Unlike other Italian states where Pius V had formed working relationships with temporal leaders, in Savoy-Piedmont the Jesuits were in a better position to combat heresy than the papal inquisitors. Working with Emanuele Filiberto from state-sponsored colleges, the Jesuits could make a strong case for their ability to fight heresy where the inquisition continued to be obstructed. It seems that Pius V reluctantly agreed.

4 Conclusion

Pius V's pontificate heralded a transformation in the Jesuits' role in the fight against heresy. This did not come with a bold, explicit revocation of the privilege, but a gradual marginalisation of the Jesuits and their jurisdiction over heresy. Pius V increased the efficiency of his inquisition and extended its power across Italy. He established compromises with secular and ecclesiastical authorities in states that had previously resisted Roman influence, such as Lucca, Naples, Milan and Venice.[159] Pius did not need the Jesuits across the peninsula and so failed to confirm the papal privilege that gave the Jesuits a truly autonomous jurisdiction over heresy. Any concessions on this score were cases when extra-judicial reconciliations could be used as an inquisitorial lure or a desperate replacement for Roman influence in the small corner of Italy where Pius had failed.

---

159   On Lucca see Adorni-Bracessi, 'La Repubblica di Lucca', especially pp.260–1; On Naples, Scaramella, *Le lettere della Congregazione del Sant'Ufficio ai Tribunali di Fede di Napoli 1563–1625* and 'Inquisizione, eresia e potere feudali nel Viceregno napoletana alla metà del cinquecento', in Maurizio Sangalli (ed.), *Per il cinquecento religioso italiano. Clero, cultura, società* (Rome: Edizioni dell'Ateneo, 2003), vol.2, pp.513–21. On Venice see, Black, *The Italian Inquisition*, pp.31–8.

BETWEEN THE PRINCE AND THE POPE

The use of the privilege under Pius V reflects the picture painted by scholars who have suggested that the privilege was conceded to support the work of the inquisitors. Nonetheless, the case studies in this chapter establish that the Jesuits' privilege was only limited to serve the needs of the inquisition in the late 1560s, and not before. It is therefore evident that we cannot define the privilege solely as a papal and inquisitorial tool, as such interpretations represent only a part of the privilege's history. Moreover, it is a part of the privilege's history that stands in stark contrast to the power's intended and actual use during the first fifteen years after its concession. The pontificate of Pius V was a turning point in the history of the privilege and saw permanent changes to the Jesuits' role in the fight against heresy, as argued by Scaramella. Although the Jesuits quickly regained their privilege to absolve heresy at the ascension of Pope Gregory XIII in 1573, the development of the inquisition under Pius V and the waning threat of heresy in Italy meant that the Jesuits' privileges were increasingly seen as excessive, as a power that undermined papal authority rather than supported it. When the throne of Saint Peter passed from Gregory XIII to former inquisitor Sixtus V, the Jesuits' privilege to absolve heresy in Italy would be revoked forever and their autonomy as an institution permanently curbed.

CHAPTER 4

Bargaining for Autonomy: Challenges and Change at the Close of the Sixteenth Century

In a letter written to the cardinals of the Roman Inquisition, Superior General Claudio Acquaviva (Superior General 1581–1615) acknowledged that the Society's privilege to absolve heretics should be completely revoked. The undated letter appears to have been written in the first months of 1587, at the close of an intense dispute over the privilege between the Society and the Roman and Spanish Inquisitions.[1] In numerous documents the Jesuits had presented a detailed case for the value of the privilege but Pope Sixtus V (1585–90) was unconvinced. Resigned to the pope's decision, Acquaviva's letter stated that, 'in the future', Jesuits would 'neither claim, nor ask for' any special right of 'proceeding in cases of heresy'.[2] Acquaviva gave just one justification for his acceptance of the revocation of the privilege: the Jesuits 'saw well' that they were not unique in matters of heresy.[3] In 1571, Pius V had made the Society a mendicant order, putting them in the same category as older religious orders like the Dominicans.[4] In his letter of 1587, Acquaviva fully accepted this change, writing that it 'would be a very hateful matter' if any Jesuits claimed that they could proceed in cases of heresy where other mendicants could not.[5]

With this letter, Acquaviva complied with a judgement on the privilege that directly conflicted with his own. Before the revocation, Jesuit authorities had sent at least three treatises to the Roman Inquisition, arguing that the Society should retain its privilege precisely because it made a unique contribution to the fight against heresy. Although inquisitorial systems were now efficient and far-reaching, the Jesuits claimed that they needed the privilege as fear prevented many penitent-heretics from approaching tribunals. If the privilege was revoked in Italy, the Jesuits claimed that the Church would see many lost sheep err eternally.[6] In treatises and letters sent to the cardinal-inquisitors, the Jesuits

---

1 We know about this discussion through documents held in ARSI, *Institutum 185-I* and ACDF, *Stanza Storica I-5-B*, which will be examined extensively in this chapter.
2 ACDF, *Stanza Storica I-5-B*, f. 75r.
3 Ibid.
4 Tomassetti (ed.), *Bullarum diplomatum*, vol.7, pp.923–6.
5 ACDF, *Stanza Storica I-5-B*, f. 75r.
6 ARSI, *Institutum 185- I*, f.330r.

© KONINKLIJKE BRILL NV, LEIDEN, 2020 | DOI:10.1163/9789004413832_006

reflected on fifty years of ministry and argued that in matters of heresy the Society should enjoy a privilege that was as unique as its contribution.

This chapter will explain why Acquaviva had to shift his position on the Society's role in the fight against heresy. It will illustrate that the Jesuits lost their privilege because claims for the singularity of their ministry aggravated rather than appeased the institutional concerns of Sixtus v. Since 1551, the privilege had given Jesuit Superior Generals jurisdictional autonomy in the grave matter of heresy. Nonetheless, the continued concession and use of that autonomy often depended on the compliance of local leaders and, crucially, the approval of the pope. There had been murmurings against the privilege in the past. But during the pontificate of Sixtus v persistent Jesuit factionalism and complaints from external authorities grew and converged with Sixtus's own concerns about the Jesuits' role. The problem for Sixtus was that the privilege to absolve heresy gave the Jesuits autonomy in cases of religious dissent, an area that he sought to control. Moreover, the privilege encapsulated the pope's broader apprehensions about the Society. When the privilege came under attack, Sixtus asked the Jesuits to answer their critics. However, when the Jesuits' defence focused on pastoral advantages rather than his concerns about the Society's peculiar autonomy and governance Sixtus revoked the Jesuits' jurisdiction over heresy entirely. Without papal support for the privilege and the modus operandi that it facilitated Acquaviva had no choice but to comply.

The generalate of Claudio Acquaviva is often heralded as a long period of internal reform for the Society, sparked by both internal debates and external pressures.[7] We saw early signs of this shift in the pontificate of Pius v, during which the Society's autonomy contrasted increasingly with the agenda of a pope who wanted to control initiatives to fight heresy. That said, the debate that erupted in Sixtus v's pontificate had even earlier origins. For it began when Loyola and his advisors established a uniquely centralised government and acquired papal privileges that allowed Jesuits to work outside of normal ecclesiastical and temporal hierarchies. From the 1550s to the 1590s, men inside and outside of the Society argued that the figure of the Superior General wielded excessive authority and autonomy. During Sixtus's papacy, this long-standing quarrel was intensified by disputes in Spain and France as well as the pope's own concerns. As a unique mechanism of autonomous jurisdiction over the grave matter of heresy, the Jesuits' privilege to absolve heretics soon became central to this broader and much older controversy.

---

7 Mostaccio, *Early modern Jesuits between obedience and conscience*, pp.13–6 and 'Codificare l'obbedienza. Le fonti normative di gesuiti, oratoriani e cappuccini a fine Cinquecento', *Dimensioni e Problemi della Ricerca Storica*, 1 (2005), p.51.

126   CHAPTER 4

In the late 1580s, the Society could not continue to operate as it had in its first forty years. As we saw in chapter 1, the first Jesuits defined their institution according to the demands of ministry, accruing roles from churchmen and princes who faced spreading religious dissent and securing papal privileges that allowed them to fulfil these tasks. But by the pontificate of Sixtus V, the Church's response to heresy had changed radically. The notion that the Roman Inquisition would be a temporary measure was abandoned during the pontificates of Pius IV (pope 1559–65) and Pius V (pope 1566–72).[8] From that period onwards, the Holy Office became a permanent, efficient system, cooperating with the majority of Italian princes and run by popes with an increasingly firm hand. In this situation, the Jesuits' flexible approach to penitents and the papal privilege that facilitated this approach were no longer an asset to the Holy See but rather an obstacle to papal plans.

Pius V's successor, Gregory XIII (pope 1572–85), had been a great supporter of the Society and its privilege but the Jesuits' autonomous reconciliation of heretics jarred with Sixtus V's agenda. Sixtus wanted a centralised ecclesiastical hierarchy governed through congregations of cardinals that answered directly to the pope. Of these congregations, the inquisition would be the most powerful. Sixtus was not the first pope to limit the Jesuits' autonomy. As we have seen, Paul IV and Pius V had sought to restrict their role in the fight against heresy.[9] Nonetheless, these measures were limited because the inquisition still relied on the Society's help to overcome pastoral and political obstacles. Moreover, the Jesuits successfully requested the reversal of such restrictions during the more favourable pontificates of Pius IV and Gregory XIII.[10] During the pontificate of Sixtus V, the Jesuits' privilege still suited their pastoral mission. However, it no longer served the powers whom they worked for and alongside and, in the case of the pope, who were the ultimate source of their authority. In his efforts to impose discipline on religious orders, Sixtus V sought to repeal everything that distinguished the Jesuits from their fellow mendicants. This included their jurisdiction over heresy.

---

8   See *Licet ab initio* which founded the Roman Inquisition: Tomassetti (ed.), *Bullarum diplomatum*, vol. 6, p.344. On its shift from a temporary institution to a permanent one see Maria Anna Noto, *Viva la Chiesa, mora il Tiranno. Il sovrano, la legge, la communità e i ribello (Benevento 1566)* (Naples: Alfredo Guida Editore, 2010), pp.46–8 and Prosperi, *Tribunali della coscienza*, pp.133–4.

9   Paul IV imposed obligation to refuse absolution to penitent heretics until they had visited an inquisitorial tribunal. Pavone, *I gesuiti*, p.27 and O'Malley, *The First Jesuits*, pp.329–335. Pius V demanded that the Society conform to rules imposed on other religious orders. Pastor, *The History of the Popes*, vol. 17, pp.279–84.

10   See ACDF, *Stanza Storica N-3-g*, f.92r and ACDF, *Stanza Storica D-4-a*, f.63r.

BARGAINING FOR AUTONOMY

By considering the fate of the privilege during the pontificate of Sixtus V, this chapter demonstrates that in order to understand the Jesuits' changing status we must look to external and transnational ecclesiastical and political factors, as well as pressures from within and without the Society. This approach is adopted in recent historiography on the Society, particularly during Acquaviva's generalate. Works by Paolo Broggio, Silvia Mostaccio and Giovanni Pizzorusso have considered the Jesuits' changing missionary approach and status in relation to Acquaviva's efforts to reinvigorate the evangelical spirit of the Society and legitimise the Jesuits' position in countries such as Spain and in a Church and world where the pope was increasing his control over missions.[11] This chapter will build upon this work, showing that the profound transformation of the Society during this period was not only the fruit of Acquaviva's impulses, or those of the popes, but rather the result of various pressures from inside and outside the order all over Europe and motivated by both religious and political concerns. During this period, the Society was forced to permanently evolve so that it could survive in an ecclesiastical and political world that increasingly favoured centralised systems for controlling ecclesiastical discipline. Within these systems the Jesuits' privilege to absolve heresy was completely anomalous.

1 Internal Conflicts and External Controversies

Calls for major changes to the Society's form of government emerged throughout the sixteenth century. Generally, these complaints focused on two issues, the authority of the Superior General and the entry of men of Jewish descent in the Society. These matters were both bound up with nationalist concerns. The Jesuits' needed to cooperate with local leaders on their missions. Yet factions emerged within the Society as Jesuits in France and Spain grew closer to local authorities who shared their grievances about Roman interference in

---

11   See Broggio, Francesca Cantù, Pierre-Antoine Fabre and Antonella Romano (eds), *I gesuiti ai tempi di Claudio Acquaviva: strategie politiche e religiose tra Cinque e Seicento* (Brescia: Morcelliana, 2007), particularly, Pizzorusso, 'La Compagnia di Gesù, gli ordini regolari e il processo di affermazione della giurisdizione pontificia sulle missioni tra fine XVI e inizio XVII: tracce di una ricerca' in Broggio, Cantù and Romano, *I gesuiti ai tempi di Claudio Acquaviva*, pp.237–270 and Mostaccio, *Early modern Jesuits between obedience and conscience*, especially pp.83–104. Alessandro Guerra advocated this change in approach in his *Un generale fra le milizie del papa*, pp.15–6, and identified it in Mario Rosa's much earlier account of Acquaviva in the *Dizionario Biografico degli Italiani*, vol.4, pp.168–78.

128   CHAPTER 4

their countries and, frequently, their discriminatory views. Successive Superior Generals knew that factionalism damaged and endangered the Society. Even so, they refused to compromise their traditional government, pastoral approach or privileges in order to quash complaints. From Loyola's formation of the Society to the first years of Acquaviva's generalate, central Jesuit authorities firmly reasserted the Society's traditional way of proceeding.

The Superior General's authority over individual Jesuits and the Society as a whole was much greater than leaders of other religious orders.[12] And Jesuits were called to serve their Superior General with absolute obedience. The principle of obedience was fundamental to the identity, spirit and work of the Society.[13] Like many men of their era, Jesuit authorities saw obedience as a virtue that was part of the natural order.[14] But unlike other religious orders, Jesuit obedience worked through a highly centralised internal hierarchy. The Superior General ruled for life, elected all other authorities within the Society, personally approved all members, and corresponded with Jesuits all over the globe.[15] This system was established by Loyola as he believed that, through centralisation and obedience, it would unite Jesuits dispersed all over the world and ensure that they had a universal sense of purpose.[16] That said, even Loyola accepted that his ideal of blind obedience was often compromised by the realities of mission life. Away from Rome, Jesuits were called to obey local temporal and ecclesiastical powers whose commands might conflict with those of the Superior General. Moreover, Jesuits with strong local alliances and familiarity with particular contexts might be better placed to make decisions than their superiors. Therefore, the Jesuits accepted that sometimes disobedience was necessary, particularly when obedience to Rome could endanger the success of the mission or even the life of the missionaries.[17] Recent scholarship has confirmed that this 'negotiated obedience' was normal in the Society.[18] Even if

---

12   Loyola, *Sancti Ignatii de Loyola Constitutiones Societatis Jesu* (Rome: Societatis Iesu, 1934–8), 3 vols, vol.3, p.201. Generals of the Franciscan and Dominican orders, for example, had short terms and their local authorities were elected locally. William A. Hinnebusch, *The History of the Dominican Order* (New York: Alba House, 1966), 2 vols, vol. 1, p.217 and Höpfl, *Jesuit Political Thought*, p.26.

13   Mostaccio, 'Codificare l'obbedienza', p.50.

14   Höpfl, *Jesuit Political Thought*, p.26.

15   Friedrich, 'Government and Information-Management in Early Modern Europe', pp.541–3; Höpfl, *Jesuit Political Thought*, p.26 and Mostaccio, *Early modern Jesuits between obedience and conscience*, p.84.

16   Loyola, *Constitutiones*, vol.1, pp.6–7 and *Sancti Ignatii de Loyola. Epistolae et instructiones*, vol.1, p.559.

17   Clossey, *Salvation and Globalization*, pp.45–52.

18   This scholarship is discussed in chapter 2 footnote 17.

BARGAINING FOR AUTONOMY

the Jesuits' principles of hierarchical obedience set the Society apart from all other religious institutions.

The organisation of the Society had profound effects on the delegation of the privilege; these effects were felt both within and without the Society. *Sacrae religionis*, the bull that granted the privilege, declared that the Superior General could concede the privilege to whomever he chose.[19] When he delegated the privilege, the Superior General chose from men whom he had admitted to the Society and decided which of these men could reconcile heretics. Moreover, when those members asked for his advice about use of the privilege, the Superior General decided which heretics they could reconcile. Combined, the Jesuits' system of government and privilege meant that cases of heresy discovered by the Society were dealt with in a closed system led by the Superior General. This system extracted the Jesuits from the usual ecclesiastical hierarchy, which demanded that all clergy go to a papal institution, such as the inquisition or the Apostolic Penitentiary, to request faculties of absolution. It also exempted the Jesuits from the rule that ordered ordinary priests to send penitent-heretics to bishops or inquisitors to lift their excommunication.[20] In short, the Jesuits' system circumvented external supervision or intervention. Moreover, when the Jesuits made decisions about reconciling heretics those decisions affected not only the pastoral mission of the Society but also the security of the Church and state and ecclesiastical and temporal efforts to fight heresy.

The role of the Superior General was criticised from the Society's first days. As early as 1556, a founding member of the Society, Nicolás de Bobadilla, decried the figure of the Superior General as tyrannical and contrary to the fraternal spirit in which the first Jesuits had first come together.[21] On Loyola's death, Bobadilla argued that the Society should reform its *Constitutions* to emulate the older rules used by Franciscans and Dominicans, orders that had long worked successfully as global missionaries.[22] In the 1560s and 1570s, Jesuits such as Antonio Araoz and Edmond Auger agreed with Bobadilla, arguing that the Society should localise both authority and resources. In the 1580s, Bobadilla's concerns reverberated in the protest of Father Vincent Julien who criticised the Superior General's authority to dictate on matters of orthodoxy

---

19 Tomassetti (ed.), *Bullarum diplomatum*, vol. 6, p. 464.

20 For an outline of the processes of denunciations, by penitent-heretics and others, see Black, *The Italian Inquisition*, pp.56–7.

21 Nadal, *Epistolae P. Hieronymi Nadal*, vol. 3, pp.50–1.

22 Arthur L. Fisher, 'A Study in Early Jesuit Government: The Nature and Origins of the Dissent of Nicolás Bobadilla', *Viator*, 10 (1979), p.407. On Bobadilla's complaints see also the first chapter of Catto, *La Compagnia Divisa*.

130   CHAPTER 4

and heresy.[23] Throughout the sixteenth century, numerous Jesuits objected vehemently to the Society's traditional form of government.

These Jesuit protestors successfully solicited support from external authorities. Calls to localise authority within the order appealed to kings, bishops and inquisitors who resented Roman interference in ecclesiastical matters in their territories.[24] Even King John III of Portugal, an early Jesuit supporter, sought to release Jesuits from their obedience to the Superior General so that they could run the Portuguese inquisition under his royal authority.[25] The reaction to this request exposed contrasts in the early Society as Loyola and his successor Diego Laínez objected and Bobadilla, Martin Olave and Alfonso Salmerón saw no problem with the proposal.[26] Contrasts between Roman Jesuit authorities supporting centralisation and Jesuit missionaries valuing local alliances would re-emerge throughout the sixteenth century.

Protests from within the Society also echoed grievances that were particular to the territories where the Jesuits worked. Both Antonio Araoz and King Philip II of Spain believed that Iberian authorities should direct Spanish Catholicism.[27] Araoz's calls for the localisation of power and funds within the Society concurred with Spanish law, which banned Spanish students and money from leaving Spain.[28] Araoz's most radical demand of all, that the Society institute an independent Superior General for Spain 'to avoid danger of heresy', mirrored a long tradition of Spanish condescension to Rome.[29] Araoz

---

23   For a discussion of the case of Vincent Julien see Mostaccio, *Early modern Jesuits between obedience and conscience*, pp.86–94.

24   Höpfl, *Jesuit Political Thought*, p.26.

25   Dauril Alden, *The making of an enterprise: the Society of Jesus in Portugal, its empire, and beyond, 1540–1750* (Stanford: Stanford University Press, 1996), p.671 and O'Malley, *The First Jesuits*, p.312.

26   Polanco in Loyola, *Sancti Ignatii de Loyola. Epistolae et instructiones*, vol.9, p.215. See also, Candidus de Dalmases [et al], *Fontes Narrativi de S. Ignatio de Loyola et de Societatis Iesu initiis ... Narrationes scriptae ante annum 1557*, pp.732–3 and O'Malley, *The First Jesuits*, p.312.

27   On power struggles between Philip II's Spain and Rome see Geoffrey Parker, *Imprudent King. A New Life of Philip II* (London: Yale University Press, 2014), pp.89–95; 'Vescovi e Inquisitori nella Spagna Post-Tridentina', chapter seven in Pastore, *Il Vangelo e la Spada*, pp.349–404 and Pattenden, 'Rome as a 'Spanish Avignon'? The Spanish Faction and the Monarchy of Philip II' in Baker-Bates and Pattenden (eds), *The Spanish Presence in sixteenth-century Italy*, pp.65–84.

28   Catto, *La Compagnia Divisa*, pp.42–3.

29   For Araoz's five points see Antonio Astraín, *Historia de la Compañia de Jesús en la asistencia de España* (Madrid: Tipográfico <<Sucesores de Rivadeneyra>>, 1902–25), 7 vols, vol.3, p.105. On the hostility faced by Jesuits in Spain, nationalist suspicions of disloyalty and Ultramontanism see Catto, *La Compagnia divisa*, p.42. J. A. Fernández-Santamaría,

also supported the Spanish crown's attempts to bar foreign ideas and Jewish blood in Spanish institutions. The Society's official stance would shift to match Araoz's anti-Semitic views after the election of Superior General Everard Mercurian in 1573 before being crystalised in Acquaviva's statutes of 1593.[30] Nonetheless, between 1540 and his death in 1573 Araoz's position conflicted with the stance of powerful sections of the Society, including Loyola, Nadal and Ribadeneira, as well as Laínez and Polanco who were both of Jewish descent or *conversos*.[31] Although Jesuits of other nationalities agreed with Araoz, it is notable that Loyola perceived his prejudice as peculiarly Iberian, calling it '*el humor español*' or even the '*humor de la corte y del Rey de España*'.[32]

Jesuit protests also echoed popes' criticisms of the Society's government and way of proceeding. In 1556, Bobadilla made sure that Paul IV heard about his protest, telling the pope that the Society's *Constitutions* contained 'things, which the Holy See would never concede' and 'contrary to the order that the holy Church observes'.[33] According to Bobadilla, these aspects of the *Constitutions* undermined the Jesuits' vow of obedience to Holy See, which should 'act as absolute master of this Society'. Bobadilla's tale-telling worked. Paul IV shortened the Superior General's term from life to three years and ordered the Jesuits to live the disciplined liturgical routine of traditional religious orders, mandates that the Society avoided until they were nullified at Paul's death in 1559.[34] Similarly, in 1587–9, Vincent Julien's protests regarding obedience to the Superior General spurred Sixtus V to order an inquisitorial investigation into the Society's rules and government, areas about which the pope himself had concerns.[35]

     Natural Law, Constitutionalism, Reason of State, and War. Counter-Reformation Spanish Political Thought, Volume II (New York: Peter Lang, 2006), p.34.

30   For a full account of debates on Jewish ancestry in the Society see, Maryks, *The Jesuit Order as a synagogue of Jews: Jesuits of Jewish ancestry and purity-of-blood laws in the early Society of Jesus* (Leiden: Brill, 2009). See also, Emanuele Colombo, 'The Watershed of Conversion: Antonio Possevino, New Christians and Jews' in Bernauer and Markys (eds), *The Tragic Couple*, pp.25–42 and Maryks, 'Ignatius of Loyola and the Converso Question' in Maryks (ed.), *A Companion to Ignatius of Loyola*, pp.84–102.

31   Catto, *La Compagnia divisa*, p.42 and O'Malley, *The First Jesuits*, p.190. On Philip II's ban on all Spaniards going to foreign universities except specific, approved colleges at Bologna, Coimbra, Naples and Rome, see Henry Kamen, *The Spanish Inquisition* (London: Weidenfeld and Nicholson, 1965), p.83.

32   Kamen, *The Spanish Inquisition*, p.129.

33   Bobadilla in Nadal, *Epistolae Hieronymi Nadal*, vol.4, p.101, p.733 and p.735.

34   Kathleen Comerford, *Jesuit Foundations and Medici Power, 1532–1621* (Leiden: Brill, 2017), p.91.

35   Mostaccio, *Early modern Jesuits between obedience and conscience*, p.93.

132   CHAPTER 4

Inadvertently, some Jesuit protests alerted external authorities to the fact that the Society's privilege to absolve heresy undermined their authority. Araoz does not appear to have objected to any of the Society's privileges. Nonetheless, as king of Spain, Philip II's concerns about the influence of the Society's Roman authorities extended to their jurisdiction over heresy. In Spain, heresy had been in royal hands since 1478.[36] A century later, Philip II increased his jurisdiction, using his inquisition to exercise royal authority in Spain and in his overseas territories.[37] For the king, a jurisdiction over heresy delegated by the Jesuit Superior General in Rome undermined his authority. Philip agreed when Araoz argued that authority should be localised within the Society but went further than Araoz, believing that Jesuits in Spain should also abandon any jurisdiction that came from the pope.[38] Similarly, when Edmond Auger supported the bishop of Paris in his protest against Roman interference in France, he unintentionally gave the bishop the means to complain about the Jesuits' privilege to absolve heresy, a power that Auger did not seem to oppose.

In the face of internal conflict and external challenges, the Society's leaders did not bow to pressure. Instead they reasserted their traditional approach and government, elaborating its principles and seeking confirmation of their privileges. This began with Loyola, who first defined his ideal of obedience in response to the rebellion of Father Simão Rodrigues, who encouraged Portuguese Jesuits to defy the Society's rules.[39] Loyola was unflinching in asserting his position. When Father Miguel de Torres went to Portugal to enforce Loyola's authority, he told Jesuits to submit or leave the order. During Torres' visit, more than 30 Jesuits were expelled or voluntarily left the Society.[40] After Loyola's death, Polanco and Nadal would respond similarly to Bobadilla's petitions, re-approving the *Constitutions* and electing Laínez as a Superior General who would uphold the Society's traditional hierarchy.[41] Laínez did not disappoint.

---

36   Kamen, *The Spanish Inquisition*, pp.3–5.

37   Ibid., p.27.

38   For many years, Jesuits seem uncertain about the status of the privilege in Spain. The matter was resolved decisively in the pontificate of Sixtus V. See Pastore, *Il Vangelo e la Spada*, pp.338–40. Laínez corrected Ribadeneira in a letter of 16 May 1564, edited in Laínez, *Lainii Monumenta*, vol.8, p.15.

39   Catto, *La Compagnia divisa*, p.24 and O'Malley, *The First Jesuits*, p.331.

40   Dennis Edmond Pate, 'Jeronimo Nadal and the Early Development of the Society of Jesus, 1545–1573' (PhD Dissertstion, University of California, Los Angeles, 1980), p.143 and p.216 fn. 15.

41   Fisher, 'A Study in Early Jesuit Government', p.397.

BARGAINING FOR AUTONOMY

133

When Araoz accused him of breaking Spanish law by sending money from Spain to Rome, Laínez stood his ground and refused to reform.[42]

This stubborn stance did nothing to quell Jesuit dissent. At the death of Superior General Borja in 1573 nationalist factions lobbied to decide the Society's leadership. Like earlier protests, this factionalism was motivated by an often indistinguishable combination of nationalism, racial prejudice and desire for change. A group of prominent Italian Jesuits went to Gregory XIII arguing that the next Superior General should not be a Spaniard as Spaniards were harsh governors.[43] Moreover, for them Spanish was synonymous with *converso* and attempts to exclude Iberian candidates were also efforts to ensure that the Society's next leader did not have Jewish blood.[44] A Portuguese faction, supported by King Sebastian I and Portuguese cardinal Infante Don Enrique, were bolder, openly protesting that the next Superior General should have neither Jewish nor Moorish roots.[45] These protests also had a more particular aim: preventing the election of Juan de Polanco, the Spanish *converso* who was a key architect of Loyola's hierarchical government.[46]

The Congregation's forty-seven delegates were well aware of this factionalism. They comprised superiors from each province, two representatives elected by each province, the four assistants to the deceased Superior General and the vicar-general, Polanco.[47] Provincial delegates were acutely conscious of and even involved in protests in their own region. The delegate for Portugal, Father Leão Henriques, collaborated directly with the Portuguese king and cardinal to lobby for their nation's interests.[48] Regional delegates and central authorities deliberately engaged with such issues at the Congregation in a special commission to examine 'actual and possible harm to the Society', which was overseen by Polanco and informed by reports from Germany, Italy, France, Spain and Portugal.[49] The seriousness of the situation was underlined by the

---

42 Riccardo G. Villoslada, *Storia del Collegio Romano dal suo inizio (1551) alla soppressione della Compagnia di Gesù (1773)* (Rome: Apud Aedes Universitatis Gregorianae, 1954), p.136.

43 Mario Fois, 'Everard Mercurian' in McCoog (ed.), *The Mercurian project: forming Jesuit culture, 1573–1580*, (Rome: Institutum Historicum Societatis Iesu, 2004), pp.27–8.

44 Maryks, *The Jesuit Order as a Synagogue of Jews*, p.xxvi.

45 John W. Padberg, 'The Third General Congregation – – 1573' in McCoog (ed.), *The Mercurian project*, pp.53–4.

46 Maryks, *The Jesuit Order as a Synagogue of Jews*, p.117.

47 Padberg, 'The Third General Congregation – 1573', p.50.

48 Ibid., p.53.

49 Padberg, Martin D. O'Keefe and John L. McCarthy (eds), *For Matters of Greater Moment: the first thirty Jesuit General Congregations: a brief history and a translation of the decrees* (St Louis: Institute of Jesuit Sources, 1994), pp.135–6.

134   CHAPTER 4

intervention of Pope Gregory XIII himself following a complaint from an influential Italian Jesuit, most probably Benedetto Palmio.[50] Before the Congregation had even convened the pope asked Polanco not to elect a Spaniard.[51] Factionalism would dictate the outcome of the election, even if indirectly, as Gregory encouraged the Jesuits to elect Everard Mercurian, his friend and a Walloon, who was seen as a neutral figure.

Although the reassertion of the Jesuits' traditional way of proceeding had failed to solve problems before, the Society's Roman authorities were adamant that the new Superior General continue to pursue this strategy. The Congregation's twenty-third decree declared that the *Constitutions* 'remain inviolate' to 'be handed on to [their] successors exactly as they were received from our reverend father Ignatius'.[52] To strengthen their position, the Congregation ordered the new Superior General to request papal bulls approving the Society's *Constitutions* and affirming that the Jesuits enjoyed privileges that exceeded those of the other religious orders.[53] Even before the Congregation, Jesuit authorities had successfully solicited the reconcession of their privilege to absolve heresy from Gregory XIII.[54] The Superior General did not disappoint. He protected the Jesuits' privileges by securing an exemption to a recently-promulgated bull that imposed the decrees of the Council of Trent on all priests and religious and revoked all 'the privileges and indults heretofore allowed them'.[55]

Everard Mercurian went to some lengths to fulfil his brief. To ensure that all Jesuits understood Loyola's standards, he published a 'Summary of the Constitutions' as well as some 'Common Rules' and 'Rules for Important Offices', highlighting and explaining significant points.[56] Mercurian also published the Jesuits' first *compendio privilegiorum*, an important, confidential reference work that recorded the many privileges enjoyed by the Society.[57] Mercurian also expanded these privileges. Whilst Pius V had limited the Jesuits' privileges, Gregory gave them the privilege 'of absolving heresy, also in Italy', 'of absolving Ultramontanes who have read or held prohibited books', 'of absolving from the

---

50   This identification is based on an account by Antonio Possevino held in ARSI, *Cong. 20B*, f.206r. See also Astraín, *Historia de la Compañía de Jesús en la asistencia de España* (Madrid: 1912–25), 3 vols, vol.3, pp.7–8, fn.2.
51   Padberg, 'The Third General Congregation', p.52.
52   Quoted and translated by Padberg, *For Matters of Greater Moment*, p.243.
53   Padberg, 'The Third General Congregation', p.59. See the decree in Padberg, *For Matters of Greater Moment*, p.145.
54   'Absolvendi ab haeresi. Gregor[io] ult[im]o Martii 1573'. ARSI, *Institutum 185-I*, f.313v.
55   Padberg, *For Matters of Greater Moment*, p.164.
56   Fois, 'Everard Mercurian', p.26.
57   Padberg, 'The Third General Congregation', p.61.

BARGAINING FOR AUTONOMY

reading of prohibited books where and who we can absolve from heresy' and 'of absolving from apostasy from faith those we can [absolve] from heresy'.[58] In the end, with Gregory's support, Mercurian not only protected what the Jesuits had at his elevation but restored the authority that they had enjoyed under Loyola.

Mercurian's successor, Claudio Acquaviva, took the same approach, explaining the way of proceeding that Loyola had established and never deviating from it. In the first year of his generalate, Acquaviva published the *Ratio Studiorum*, which outlined the Society's teachings and strategy, confirming Loyola's approach to discipline.[59] Aiming to unify the Society in its ministry, Acquaviva published a *Directorium* for Loyola's *Spiritual Exercises* and numerous letters on the Society's missionary activity.[60] Acquaviva recognised that the conflicts within the Society stemmed from a tension between centralised authority and the demands placed upon Jesuits spread across the globe. Like Loyola he suggested that members do their best to reconcile orders from Rome, commands from local authorities and their own consciences, though, fundamentally, he shared Loyola's belief that blind obedience to authority was the ideal.[61] When powerful groups like the Dominicans claimed that the Society was overly autonomous, theologically suspect and determined to undermine other religious orders, Acquaviva could rely upon Gregory's XIII's support for their traditional structure and privileges, just as Loyola had relied on Paul III and Julius III.[62]

Gregory XIII's support for the Society was crucial for the maintenance of their traditional government and privileges. And Pope Gregory supported the Jesuits as he made good use them, charging them to run the newly established English College in Rome and sending them to evangelise China and Japan.[63] In return for this service, the pope funded the Society's Collegio Romano and Collegio Germanico in Rome and confirmed and enlarged their privileges.[64] Gregory's broader backing for the Society's missions and confirmation of its privilege to absolve heresy in Italy indicates that the pope valued the Jesuits' work to support Catholics and convert heretics and was confident that they could work harmoniously with his inquisition. This support allowed the

---

58 ACDF, *Stanza Storica I-5-B*, ff.45r-v.
59 Pastore, *Il vangelo e la spada*, p.440. See also, Guerra, *Un Generale fra le milizie del papa*, p.99.
60 Mostaccio, *Early modern Jesuits between obedience and conscience*, pp.114–5.
61 Ibid.
62 Guerra, *Un Generale fra le milizie del papa*, p.101.
63 Pastor, *The History of the Popes*, vol. 19, pp.234–258; Mostaccio, *Early modern Jesuits between obedience and conscience*, p.83.
64 Pastor, *The History of the Popes*, vol. 19, pp.250–4.

136   CHAPTER 4

Superior Generals to reassert the Jesuits' traditional authority and approach, despite continued controversy within and surrounding the Society.

The Society's troubles persisted throughout Mercurian's generalate as old protests gained new supporters. Araoz died in 1573 but his ideas survived him. Two memorials sent to Philip II in 1577 complained about the centralisation of the Society, claiming that the Superior General's control over who took final vows made the system arbitrary and that Spanish houses and provinces should have more autonomy.[65] Like earlier protests, these complaints mingled nationalism with specific concerns about *conversos* in the Society. Unlike Araoz, the Jesuits behind these memorials were either *conversos* or pro-*converso*; their protest was, partially, a response to the Society's increasingly anti-semitic policies.[66] Things were no quieter on the Italian peninsula. In 1578, three Italian professors of the Collegio Romano visited Gregory XIII and wrote to twelve cardinals to bemoan the state of the Society under Mercurian.[67] Like Spanish dissenters of the 1570s, they wanted to democratize the peripheral structures of the Society.[68] In Spain and Italy, the Society's two major geographical centres, Jesuit authorities faced internal protesters who called upon the highest authorities for support.

Factionalism may have threatened the stability and unity of the Society but it was an almost inevitable consequence of the Jesuits' missionary work. The Society needed to maintain close relationships with the local secular and ecclesiastical authorities who facilitated its missions. Even Nadal, who loathed Araoz, admitted that the Spaniard could not be sacked as the Society needed his court connections to fund and expand their Spanish institutions.[69] The case of Araoz corroborates the conclusions of scholars who have emphasised that Jesuits who criticised central authorities were not dissidents but a crucial element of the Society's modus operandi.[70] During the pontificate of Sixtus, the Jesuits could no longer hold back the broad agenda of the protestors by simply confirming their traditional way of proceeding. When the concerns of the pope himself merged with existing grievances this strategy would prove totally ineffective and, eventually, fatal for the Jesuits' privilege to absolve

---

65   Catto, *La Compagnia Divisa*, pp.44–5.

66   Maryks, *The Jesuit Order as a Synagogue of Jews*, pp.125–6.

67   Fois, 'Everard Mercurian', p.29.

68   Catto, *La Compagnia Divisa*, p.49.

69   Nadal, *Epistolae Hieronymi Nadal*, vol.1, p.252.

70   See Pavone's reference to Romano's spoken comments in 'Dissentire per sopravvivere' in Alfieri and Ferlan (eds), *Avventure nella obbedienza*, p.197 and Alfieri and Ferlan's comments on pp.7–9.

BARGAINING FOR AUTONOMY

137

heresy. Whilst Jesuits did not express any concerns about their privilege, it encapsulated many of the grievances of ecclesiastical and temporal authorities who wanted to control religion locally. It was not long until the pope added his voice to their complaints. The privilege to absolve heresy represented the willingness of Jesuits and popes to compromise institutional norms for pastoral goals. When Sixtus v objected to the privilege, the Society's leaders would have to prioritise their institutional survival over their belief in the continued pastoral benefits of the power.

2   Troubles Abroad: Controversies in France and Spain

When King Philip II of Spain and Bishop Pierre de Gondi of Paris complained about the Jesuits to Sixtus v, the pope would not countenance the reassertion of the Society's traditional way of proceeding. For the grievances of the king and the bishop alerted Sixtus to the contrasts between the Jesuits' government and his own agenda for the Catholic Church. During his pontificate, Sixtus pushed for an ever-more centralised ecclesiastical government within the Church. The authority of the Superior General contrasted with these plans. Moreover, in the hierarchy of specialist congregations that reported to the pope, the Holy Office was meant to rule supreme and the Jesuits' autonomous action to fight heresy undermined its power.[71] Sixtus v also wanted to homogenise and control religious orders. The Society's peculiarities, including its unique privilege to absolve heresy, conflicted with the pope's key aims. When Sixtus's own concerns were compounded by persistent complaints from Jesuit dissenters and their supporters the pope announced major reforms. Whilst Pius v had failed to confirm the privilege, making the Jesuits unsure of its status, Sixtus v revoked the power categorically.

From the beginning of his pontificate, Sixtus v sought to centralise the papacy. In December 1585, he implemented an old yet often ignored rule that all ecclesiastical authorities should receive his blessing and instructions before being consecrated.[72] In January 1588, Sixtus promulgated *Immensa aeterni*

---

71   Brambilla, *Alle origini del Sant'Uffizio*, p.450, fn. 29; Alessandro Hübner, *Sisto Quinto. Dietro la scorta delle corrispondenze diplomatiche inedite tratte dagli archivi di stato del Vaticano, di Simancas, di Venezia di Parigi, di Vienna e di Firenze* (Rome: Tipografia dei Lincei, 1887), 2 vols, vol.1, p.369 and Pietro Palazzini, 'Le Congregazioni Romane da Sisto V a Giovani Paolo II' in Marcello Fagiolo and Maria Luisa Madonna (eds), *Sisto V. I. Roma e il Lazio* (Rome: Libreria dello Stato, 1992), p.23.

72   Silvano Giordano, 'Sisto V' in *Enciclopedia dei papi* (Rome: Istituto della Enciclopedia Italiana, 2000) 3 vols, vol.3, p.206.

Dei, a bull to formalise and increase the number of congregations of cardinals who advised him.[73] In May 1586, Sixtus had established the Congregation for Regulars, uniting his desire to govern through congregations and to control religious orders more closely.[74] Sixtus also sought to control religious by enclosing convents and reinforcing the strict rules already imposed on enclosed sisters.[75] Sixtus also personally intervened in controversies caused by religious orders with multiple papal privileges, charging a special body to resolve such disputes.[76] Whilst research on the various congregations of cardinals has underlined their persistent independence from papal control, Sixtus's legislative measures show his clear desire to establish a strictly centralised ecclesiastical government, even if he was not wholly successful in achieving his aims.[77]

Sixtus soon realised that the Jesuits' loose religious rule and numerous privileges contrasted with his ecclesiastical ideals. In 1588, Sixtus localised the process of admission to the Society, taking away the Superior General's exclusive power and declaring that 'Provincials have the power of admitting, doing it with the advice of their advisors'.[78] He also took Jesuit disputes under his own judgement. When French Jesuit Vincent Julien condemned Loyola's ideal of obedience to the Roman Inquisition in 1588, Sixtus ordered a commission to investigate any errors contained in the Society's *Constitutions*.[79] That same year, Sixtus learned of the theological dispute between Jesuit Lenaert Leys and professors at the University of Louvain and demanded that he receive all

---

73 As scholars such as Agostino Borromeo and Simon Ditchfield have underlined, this reorganisation was not a revolution in Church governance but rather the completion of a process that had begun at least a decade earlier.

 Agostino Borromeo, 'I vescovi italiani e l'applicazione del concilio di Trento' in Cesare Mozzarelli and Danilo Zardin (eds), *I Tempi del Concilio: religione, cultura e società nell'Europa tridentina* (Rome: Bulzoni, 1997), p.32 and Ditchfield, 'In Search of Local Knowledge', pp.268–9. See also, Hübner, *Sisto Quinto.*, p.363–91; Fosi, *Papal Justice*, p.26; Giordano, 'Sisto V, papa (Felice Peretti)' in *Dizionario Storico dell'Inquisizione*, vol. 3, p.1439; Mayer, *The Roman Inquisition: A Papal Bureaucracy*, p.11 and Palazzini, 'Le Congregazioni Romane da Sisto V a Giovani Paolo II', pp.19–38.

74 Giordano, 'Sisto V', p.218.

75 Ibid.

76 Ibid.

77 On Sixtus's attempts at centralisation see Ditchfield, 'In Search of Local Knowledge', p.270; Fragnito, *La Bibbia al rogo*, pp.173–198; Fausto Parente, 'The Index, the Holy Office, the condemnation of the Talmud and publication of Clement VIII's Index' in Fragnito (ed.) and Belton (trans.), *Church, censorship and culture in early modern Italy*, p.190.

78 ARSI, *Epistolae Generalium Rom. 1*, f.103r.

79 ACDF, *Stanza Storica M-3-g*, p.452. See also McCoog, *The Society of Jesus in Ireland, Scotland and England, 1589–1597*, p.229.

BARGAINING FOR AUTONOMY

the details so that he could declare the outcome.[80] Moreover, when Luis de Santander, a Spanish supporter of Vincent Julien, complained about Jesuit government in Spain, Sixtus sent Bishop Jerónimo Manrique as his own investigator, demanding to know how the Jesuits differed from other religious orders in matters such as their vows, liturgical life and habit.[81] In Rome and abroad, Sixtus personally intervened in complaints about the peculiar aspects of the Society that clashed with his own ecclesiastical ideal and that perturbed men within and without the order.

Still, at first, the Jesuits seemed confident in Sixtus's support for their privileges. On 5 March 1586, Jesuit Roman authorities wrote to cardinal-inquisitor Giulio Antonio Santoro, asking the Holy Office to draft a brief confirming the privilege to absolve heresy.[82] This letter stated that the Society required proof of the privilege as the bishop of Paris, Pierre de Gondi, had complained and denied that they held the privilege.[83] The author claimed that Sixtus V had 'explained that it was well that [they] should request [proof of] this faculty, because when it would be worthwhile for prelates, or for others … we can show them our faculty'.[84] So, the Jesuits wanted a document to prove and explain the faculty clearly.[85] Moreover, they assumed that Santoro would comply as he knew how important the privilege was and why it was particularly necessary in northern Europe.[86]

The author of the letter was clearly sensitive to controversy regarding the privilege. In the draft now held at the ARSI, the author has crossed out a reference to absolved heretics and changed it to some who were absolved from heresy instead.[87] This small change is significant as it underplays the figure of the dangerous heretic to focus on the generalised sin of heresy. Thus, the author stressed the act of absolving sins, which was the proper duty of the confessor, rather than the liberation of heretics, which was more controversial and commonly associated with the inquisition rather than ordinary priests and religious. We also see such changes in focus in Jesuit texts produced after Sixtus V's revocation. In a report of 1592, for example, the Jesuit author changed his

---

80   Mostaccio, *Early modern Jesuits between obedience and conscience*, pp.95–6.

81   Padberg, *For Matters of Greater Moment*, p.10.

82   ARSI, *Institutum 185-I*, f.309r.

83   Ibid. On Bishop Pierre de Gondi see Joanna Milstein, *The Gondi: family strategy and survival in early modern France* (Farnham: Ashgate, 2014), pp.137–172.

84   ARSI, *Institutum 185-I*, f.309r.

85   Ibid.

86   Ibid.

87   '… convenisse vedere quanto legittimamente fussero assoluti 'alcuni dalla' gli heretici/ sia'. Ibid.

reference to the 'revocation of the privilege of absolving from heresy' to the 'revocation of the privilege of absolving manifest heretics'.[88] Here, the modified reference minimised Sixtus's revocation by implying that the privilege could still be used in some cases of heresy just not those in which the penitent was a flagrant rebel. In this case, the shift in emphasis seen in the 1586 document is inverted and the act that had been banned is made to appear graver rather than less serious. Both documents reveal the Jesuits' caution about how others perceived their privilege and their efforts to ensure that their writing about the privilege did not spark any controversy.

The letters of 1586 and 1592 stress that the private reconciliation of heretics would not cause scandal at all, a criticism that was levelled against the Jesuits in this period. Indeed, the treatise held with the 1586 letter confirms that the letter to Santoro was a direct response to such criticism from Bishop Gondi in Paris. With this document, entitled a 'Response to questions from France', Jesuit Stefano Tucci disputed the notion that the Jesuits' privilege undermined episcopal processes and scandalised Catholics who saw former heretics who had been secretly reconciled receiving Holy Communion.[89] Tucci argued that public sinners whom the Jesuits absolved secretly could not receive Holy Communion in Church before being absolved by a bishop and before it was publicly known that they had been reconciled.[90] That said, Tucci also argued that the Jesuits should be allowed to act autonomously before episcopal intervention or else there was no point in their privilege. Tucci claimed that 'if, before private absolution and penitence, public abjuration in front of the bishop is to be expected the privilege conceded to some of absolving heretics in *foro conscientiae* would be vain'.[91] Tucci's statement was a clear defence of the validity and value of the Jesuits' autonomous jurisdiction over heresy, which Tucci's treatise and the 1586 letter suggest that Gondi had attacked.

Remarkably, it seems that Gondi's complaints about the privilege were inadvertently instigated by a member of the Society. This is revealed by the bishop's communications with Rome. In January 1586, Gondi complained to Acquaviva, by then Superior General, on behalf of King Henri III of France. He wrote Acquaviva a letter asking him to ban Jesuits in France from interfering with matters of state.[92] This request aimed to stop Jesuit support for the Catholic

---

88   '... fuisset nobis intimata Sixto Papae V revocatio privilegii absolvendi ab haeresi manifestos haereticos ...'.

      Ibid., f.318r.

89   ARSI, *Institutum 185-I*, ff.323r-329r.

90   Ibid., f.323v.

91   Ibid., ff.324v-325r.

92   A. Lynn Martin, *Henry III and the Jesuit Politicians* (Geneva: Librairie Droz, 1973), p.177.

BARGAINING FOR AUTONOMY

League, which had been established by Henri, Duke of Guise, to eradicate Protestantism in France and which was critical of Henri III's attitude towards Calvinists.[93] In his correspondence, Gondi also decried aspects of the Society's governance and authority that were outlined in its *Constitutions* and *compendio privilegiorum*. This included their power to absolve heresy. On hearing Gondi's complaints Acquaviva had been shocked. As he told the Jesuit provincial of France, Odon Pigenat, both the *Constitutions* and *compendio privilegiorum* were strictly confidential and circulated only within the Society.[94] Acquaviva asked Pigenat to work secretly to find out how Gondi had obtained these documents.[95] It was not long before Pigenat discovered that the bishop had been aided by none other than Edmond Auger, a senior member of the Society in France and confessor to King Henri III.[96]

Auger shared Gondi's discontent with papal authority. Like Gondi he wanted to assert the Gallican privileges that gave French ecclesiastical authorities independence from the Holy See. Some Jesuits even claimed that Auger opposed the promulgation of the decrees of the Council of Trent in France.[97] Moreover, Auger's distaste for Roman authority seems to have extended to the orders of the Superior General. Even though the *Constitutions* banned ecclesiastical ambition some said that Auger coveted high office – even a cardinal's hat.[98] The rector of the Jesuit house at Paris, who was not Auger's enemy, claimed that Auger believed that he was exempt from his vows of obedience and poverty, heeding the will of the king above his promises to the Society.[99] Auger's attachment to Henri III certainly defied a Jesuit decree, which stated that 'no one of our religious ought to be assigned to princes or other lords ... to attach themselves to their courts or dwell with them as confessors or theologians'.[100]

---

93   On the Jesuits, the League and French politics see Eric Nelson, *The Jesuits and the Monarchy. Catholic Reform and Political Authority in France (1590–1615)* (Aldershot: Ashgate, 2005) and Martin, *Henry III and the Jesuit Politicians*.

94   ARSI, *Institutum 185-I*, f.259r.

95   ARSI, *Franc. 1 – II*, f.259r.

96   Martin, *Henry III and the Jesuit Politicians*, p.181. Auger mentioned this allegation in a letter to Acquaviva on 13 May 1586, see ARSI, *Gall. 92*, f.129r. Acquaviva spoke of it to Auger again in 15 July 1586, see ARSI, *Franc. 1*, f.248r. Auger denied the allegation in a letter to Acquaviva of 24 June 1586, see ARSI, *Gal. 64*, 13v.

97   Martin, *Henry III and the Jesuit Politicians*, p.180. On the earlier history of the Council of Trent and France, see Alain Tallon, *La France et le Concile de Trente (1518–1563)* (Rome: École Française de Rome, 1997). On Gallicanism and Trent see especially, pp.795–800.

98   Martin, *Henry III and the Jesuit Politicians*, p.183. Saffores made this accusation in a letter to Acquaviva of 28 April 1586, see ARSI, *Gal.92*, f.117r.

99   Ibid, f.101v.

100   Quoted and translated by Padberg, *For Matters of Greater Moment*, p.122.

142 CHAPTER 4

Despite this decree, Auger spent more time at the royal palace than amongst his fellow Jesuits. Auger never publicly opposed the privilege to absolve heresy but his discontent with Roman authority motivated him to collaborate with Gondi who sought to undermine the Society in matters of both state and religion.

The status of the privilege soon became more precarious. In June 1586, the French Provincial Claude Matthieu reported from Loreto that the privilege should be used only for *transalpinos* and that 'it is preferable to abstain' from using it on those from other countries.[101] This statement indicated that the privilege was now effectively invalid for use with Italians in Italy.

Serious complaints about the privilege also came from Spain. Around 1585, Philip II's Spanish inquisitors discovered that the Jesuit Provincial of Castile, Antonio Maracen, had personally punished Father Francesco di Ribera for preaching heresy and Fathers Sebastián de Briviesca and Cristóbal de Trugillo for teaching heresy to female penitents and soliciting the same penitents for sexual favours in 1583–4.[102] In Spain, the king's inquisition had absolute authority over heresy, and the sexual solicitation of penitents by confessors (*sollecitatio ad turpia*) had been under inquisitorial jurisdiction, in both Spain and Italy, since 1559.[103] Nonetheless, Briviesca kept the whole affair secret, dismissing the men privately and sending them away from Spain without consulting with the inquisitors.[104] In doing so, Maracen and his advisors had undermined the jurisdiction of the Spanish Inquisition and, therefore, the authority of the king. It is not known how the Spanish Inquisition discovered the case.[105] But in 1585 the king's inquisitors arrested Maracen and his consultants, Francisco Larata and Juan López.[106] It soon emerged that Maracen had dealt with heresy independently of the Spanish Inquisition before.[107] The Iberian inquisitors

---

101 ARSI, *Franc. 1*, f.241r.

102 See a record of accusations given to Didacus Hernandez, a professed Jesuit at the college in Monterey, by one of the penitents in question in 1583: BAV, *Ottob. Lat. 495*, f.50r-v, f.63r and f.66r-v. On this case, see also, Astraín, *Historia de la Compañía de Jesús en la asistencia de España*, vol. 3, pp.368–410; Pastore, 'A proposito di Matteo' and Il *Vangelo e la Spada*, pp.439–451.

103 Prosperi, *Tribunali della coscienza*, p.511. On *sollicitatio ad turpia* see Stephen Haliczer, *Sexuality in the Confessional. A Sacrament Profaned* (Oxford: Oxford University Press, 1996); Prosperi, *Tribunali della coscienza*, pp.508–19.

104 BAV, *Ottob. Lat. 495*, f.62r and 66r.

105 The record merely states that 'aliquo tempore praedicta facinora ad notitiam S[anct]i Officii pevenirente... ' Ibid., f.62r.

106 Pastore, *Il Vangelo e la Spada*, pp.440–1.

107 Henry Charles Lea, *A History of the Inquisition of Spain* (Macmillan: New York, 1906–22), 4 vols, vol.2, pp.34–6.

BARGAINING FOR AUTONOMY

convicted the Jesuits involved, but when the Society appealed to Rome Sixtus V revoked the matter to his own jurisdiction.[108] The pope's intervention saved the Jesuits from the clutches of the Spanish Inquisition. Nonetheless, their privilege to absolve heresy would not survive the ensuing debate.

During the Spanish controversy of 1585–7, the Jesuits stood accused of absolving fellow Jesuits of crimes that fell under inquisitorial jurisdiction in Spain and Italy. During this period, complaints about obedience, the centralisation of the Society and privileges converged. This is evident in a duplicate of a Spanish document written by the Jesuits about 'matters necessary for remedy' in the Society, which was sent to the Holy Office during Sixtus V's pontificate.[109] Defending their system of internal discipline, the Jesuits mounted a pragmatic case in this document, saying that Superiors knew how to punish and reform their own subjects better than external authorities. It also stressed that they could do this without causing scandal to the Society or the Church.[110] The Jesuits also referred to privileges enjoyed by the Franciscans and Dominicans to defend their right to discipline their own men.[111] Compendia of privileges for both of these mendicant orders show that they had been given the authority to absolve their own members of heresy and to lift the censures that heresy incurred.[112] When Pius V had made the Society a mendicant order in 1571, he had ordered that Jesuits were to enjoy all the same privileges as other mendicant orders, both at that time and in the future.[113] By absolving members of their own order, the Jesuits argued that they resolved internal problems effectively using an authority that they held legitimately, just like other mendicant orders.

But it was the private absolution of heretics outside the Society that most concerned authorities. In these external cases the Jesuits could not argue that their actions were on a par with other mendicants for no other order claimed to be allowed to absolve heretics outside of their own ranks. The Iberian authorities had already curbed the use of the privilege in Spain after noticing

---

108   Ibid., p.35. An undated document addressed to Sixtus V bound together with letters and memorials of spring 1587 states that Sixtus had 'favoured' the Society in the quarrel. Another letter to in the same cache, dated to 13 April 1587, mentions that Sixtus revoked the matter to Rome because the Jesuits suggested that the Spanish were trying to change the Institute of the Society. See ARSI, *Institutum 185-I*, f.233r.

109   BAV, *Ottob. Lat. 495*, ff.1–10v.

110   ACDF, *Stanza Storica I-5-b*, f.3r.

111   Ibid., ff.2r-3v.

112   Hieronymus Asorbo, *Compendium Privilegiorum Fratrum Minorum et aliorum Mendicantium, and non Mendicantium, ab Alphonso de Casarubios Hispano* (Venice: Haeredes Petri Ricciardi, 1609), p.269.

113   Tomassetti (ed.), *Bullarum diplomatum et privilegiorum*, vol.7, p.923.

that it disturbed the ordinary ecclesiastical hierarchy.[114] A Jesuit record that appears to have been produced in the late 1580s notes that this limitation was reasserted on 8 March 1583, during Gregory XIII's papacy, when the Jesuits were told that they could not absolve those outside of the Society in Spain.[115] Defending the privilege after the Spanish controversy, the Jesuits admitted that they did 'not have it for Spain, nor demand it, if not for those who are of the Society'.[116] As we shall see in the final section of this chapter, the privilege suffered the same fate in Italy when Sixtus realised that the Society's traditional modus operandi disturbed his own ideals of ecclesiastical government.

The narrative of steadily increasing papal power established by scholars such as Paolo Prodi has been disrupted by research highlighting the resistance of curial congregations in the face of papal intervention.[117] However, Sixtus V's revocation of the Jesuit privilege despite the Jesuits' bold defence demonstrated his clear determination to seize control over key areas of papal policy. Moreover, as we shall see in the final chapter, continued papal support for the revocation after Sixtus's death suggests that his efforts were largely successful, even if some Jesuits rebelled against the revocation. Sixtus's transferral of the Spanish and French cases to his own jurisdiction were also effective attempts to assert the papacy as the ultimate arbiter in matters of the faith on a global scale and despite Habsburg political dominance, Gallicanism and increasing local control of religion in both Catholic and Protestant states.[118] Sixtus V's revocation of the privilege would not mark a dramatic watershed in the Society's actions but it would regularise the process that Pius V had begun, permanently

---

114   Nadal, *Epistolae P. Hieronymi Nadal*, vol.4, p.519.
115   ARSI, *Institutum 185-I*, f. 313v.
116   Ibid., f.314r.
117   A critique of the narrative of increasingly centralised power within the Catholic Church, exemplified in works like Prodi's *Il Sovrano Pontefice*, is offered by Ditchfield in his 'In Search of Local Knowledge'. See also Ditchfield, 'In Sarpi's Shadow: coping with Trent the Italian way' in *Studi in memoria di Cesare Mozzarelli* (Milan: VandP, 2008), 2 vols, vol. 1, pp.585–606, especially pp.596–9. See also Pattenden, *Electing the Pope in Early Modern Italy*, pp.185–6.
118   William J. Bouwsma cites Sixtus V's excommunication of Henri of Navarre as a successful attempt to prevent him from receiving the French crown, at least for the duration of his pontificate. See Bouwsma, *Venice and the Defense of Republican Liberty. Renaissance Values in the Age of the Counter Reformation* (Berkeley: University of California Press, 1968), pp.328–9. On the Navarre case see N.M. Sutherland, *Henry IV of France and the politics of religion, 1572–1596*, vol.2, pp.291–335. On Gallicanism see also Nancy Lyman Roelker, 'The Two Faces of Rome: The Fate of Protestantism in France' in Malcolm R. Thorp and Arthur J. Slavin (eds) *Politics, Religion, and diplomacy in early modern Europe: essays in honor of De Lamar Jensen* (Kirksville: Sixteenth Century Journal Publishers, 1994), pp.95–111.

BARGAINING FOR AUTONOMY

eliminating autonomy from the Jesuits' anti-heretical activities and fitting the Society into the centralised ecclesiastical infrastructure that was desired, if not fully realised, by Sixtus V.

3 Defending the Privilege in the Late 1580s

The Jesuits did not relinquish the privilege readily. When Sixtus V's inquisition asked for an explanation of the Society's power the Jesuits mounted a strong defence. Ultimately, their efforts were unsuccessful. Rather than convincing the pope and his inquisition, the Jesuits' defence revealed a chasm between their priorities and those of the Holy See. While the Society remained focused on reconciling heretics on the ground, Sixtus was determined to take full control of the Church's anti-heretical activities. In their defence of the privilege in 1586–7, the Jesuits presented many of the same arguments that they had proposed at the solicitation of the power in the late 40s and early 50s. But whilst popes like Paul III and Julius III had been happy to empower the Jesuits to supplement the inquisitorial system in the aftermath of the Protestant Reformation, the privilege had no place in the late sixteenth-century Church of Sixtus V.

The Jesuits did not anticipate the revocation of the privilege. As we have already seen, their letter to Santoro concerning Bishop Gondi assumed papal support. They wrote to Santoro to ask that he remind the pope that he had promised a new brief when they met at the Congregation of the Holy Office.[119] Less than a year before Sixtus V would revoke the Society's privilege, and in the face of serious criticism from abroad, Acquaviva still felt confident enough of papal support to ask for written evidence of the power.

The Jesuits' confidence at this stage was understandable. An instruction given to members of the Society by Acquaviva in 1585 indicates that, at the beginning of Sixtus's papacy, the privilege was limited but still valid. This 'Instruction for those to whom the faculty of absolving from heresy is conceded in Europe' reinstated Paul IV's rule that heretics who had publicly voiced their heresy must visit the Holy Office before receiving absolution, 'to be provided for in the external forum', that is, to have any judicial censures lifted.[120] This instruction reflected a new state of affairs under Sixtus. This is clear as the 'method of use' outlined in the document differs from the Society's activities during

---

119   ARSI, *Institutum 185-I*, f.309r.
120   Ibid.

146   CHAPTER 4

the pontificate of Sixtus's predecessor, Gregory XIII, when the Jesuits used the
privilege with no caveats. Moreover, the letter of March 1586 indicated that the
discussion of the privilege was far from over, stating that the pope wanted to
talk about how this faculty was used.[121]

A bundle of documents held at the ARSI suggests that these discussions became more serious after the Spanish and French controversies of 1585–6.[122]
This diverse cache reflects the importance of the privilege for the Jesuits and
underlines the variety of factors that led to its demise. The collection comprises three treatises defending the nature and impact of the privilege in Europe
(one in Italian and two in Latin), the letter about Gondi from March 1586, Tucci's 'Response to the questions from France', a list of five points about privileges and their use and a list of concessions of the privilege by various popes.
The Italian treatise states that it was written for cardinal-inquisitor Santoro 'to
satisfy the order that he had given in the name of the Holy Office, beyond the
other written [in] Latin, that was given regarding the faculty to absolve from
heresy'.[123] This note indicates that at least two of the treatises – the Italian document and one of the Latin documents – responded to an inquisitorial order
that the Jesuits explain their privilege. Moreover, all three of the treatises are
addressed to the 'Lord Cardinal Inquisitors of Heretical Depravity'.[124] Although
Santoro was second in command at the Holy Office he was its first point of
contact with Sixtus V.[125] Santoro's personal management of the affair and the
arguments proposed in these documents suggest that it was Sixtus who had
instigated scrutiny of the privilege and its impact, not only in France, Spain
and northern Europe but also in the Italian territories under the jurisdiction of
his Roman Inquisition.

Although all of the documents except the letter about Gondi are undated,
analysis of their content suggests that they were produced during the discussions about the privilege in 1586–7. We know that Tucci's response was an answer to Gondi's criticisms. The Italian treatise also refers to Gondi, mentioning
writings about the privilege that had come lately from Paris and a bishop from
Paris who had recently spoken to the cardinal-inquisitors about the privilege.[126]
The Italian treatise also seems to refer to one of the Latin treatises, stating that

---

121   Ibid.
122   ARSI, *Institutum 185 I*, ff. 309–338.
123   Ibid., f.314r.
124   Ibid., f.313v.
125   Fosi, 'Santoro, Giulio Antonio (Santori, Santorio)' in Lavenia, Prosperi, Tedeschi (eds),
        Dizionario Storico dell'Inquisizione, vol.3, p.1385.
126   ARSI, *Institutum 185-I*, f.314r.

BARGAINING FOR AUTONOMY

it was written because it was necessary to have another document about the privilege in addition to one that had already been written in Latin.[127] Although it is not clear which of the two Latin treatises this refers to the content of both Latin documents has parallels with the Italian text, suggesting that they were produced for the same purpose. The list of concessions of the privilege also seems to date to Sixtus's pontificate, terminating with the concessions of his predecessor, Gregory XIII, and omitting the faculties to absolve northern European heretics from Sixtus's successor, Clement VIII.[128] Whilst there are no explicit references to connect the document on the use of papal privileges to the discussions of 1586–7, its common theme and the links between the other documents in this cache suggest it was produced in the same context.

The three treatises highlight institutional reasons for the necessity of the privilege in northern Europe, underlining how far the Catholic ecclesiastical infrastructure had been ravaged by Protestantism on the continent. The treatises claim that the privilege was absolutely vital for England, Scotland and parts of Ireland because there were simply no Catholic bishops and in places where the scarcity of bishops or size of the diocese made it difficult for penitents to find a bishop to absolve them.[129] Fear of ecclesiastical authorities was also highlighted as a major impediment to securing reconciliations in northern regions. Where there were prelates, the Jesuits claimed that some rustics, women, children and old and infirm people whom they absolved would 'tremble in front of the Bishop'.[130] In many areas, the treatises argue, parish priests could not help with this problem because they themselves were ignorant and depraved.[131] According to the Jesuits, this was the reason that so many penitents came to them instead of to their own clergy, and the reason that bishops referred cases to the Society rather than delegating them to local priests.[132]

The Jesuits' defence of the privilege in Italy was focused on fear. The treatises claimed that northern European Ultramontanes in Italy feared that inquisitors would refuse to reconcile them. Therefore, the Jesuits needed the privilege to reconcile them themselves.[133] Often, the Jesuits stated, penitents feared revealing their heresy in front of several people instead of an individual confessor

---

127   Ibid.
128   Clement VIII clarified Sixtus V's revocation and limited it to Spain and Italy, freeing fathers in other parts of Europe to absolve heretics. See ACDF, *Stanza Storica D-4-a*, f.10r.
129   ARSI, *Institutum 185-I*, f.314r and f.330r.
130   Ibid., f.330v.
131   Ibid., f.314r and f.330r.
132   Ibid.
133   Ibid., f.314r and f.316v.

148   CHAPTER 4

sworn to secrecy. As many of these people refused to renounce their heresy in front of a confessor and two witnesses, the Jesuits found it unsurprising that so many translapine converts never approached the inquisitors to officially join the Church.[134] Fear was such a great impediment to reconciliation that the Society argued that if the pope took the Jesuits' privilege away, the cardinal-inquisitors would have to find another way of offering reconciliation secretly in confession without the obligation to visit a tribunal.[135] For the Jesuits, fear of the inquisitors was so powerful in Italy that a solely judicial system for converting and reconciling heretics was simply inconceivable.

In fact, the Jesuits argued that the private absolution of heretics in Italy complemented rather than undermined the judicial system. The Italian treatise claimed that Jesuit confessors helped the inquisition to find heretics, stating that few heretics handed themselves in to the inquisitors without the encouragement of their confessor.[136] Moreover, the author of this treatise claimed that the privilege allowed the Jesuits to convey valuable information to the inquisitors.[137] Far from impeding the ecclesiastical hierarchy, the Society claimed that the privilege supported it, allowing the Jesuits to work respectfully to promote the agenda of bishops and the Holy See.[138]

These claims are contradictory. On the one hand, the Jesuits suggested that they could convince penitents to reveal themselves to the inquisition. On the other, the Jesuits argued that an entirely extra-judicial means of reconciling heretics was vital because fear of the inquisitors was so great that souls perished avoiding the tribunal. If it was necessary to have a route to reconcile some heretics that totally avoided the inquisitors, the Jesuits could not argue that this route could also serve the inquisition. The presentation of such contrasting arguments in defence of the privilege underlines the Society's concern about losing the power and their willingness to use every possible argument in its defence.

The Jesuits also appealed to the long papal support for the privilege in Italy. According to the Italian treatise, no pope had conceded the privilege without considering the evidence for its necessity.[139] The effects of the privilege were also evident in the concessions themselves, as earlier popes would not have given the Society such a power without an important reason.[140] According

---

134   Ibid., f.317v.
135   Ibid., f.314r.
136   Ibid., f.317r.
137   Ibid., f.314r.
138   Ibid., f.330r-v.
139   Ibid., f.314r.
140   Ibid., f.330r.

BARGAINING FOR AUTONOMY

to the Jesuits, successive popes had seen the great need for an extra-judicial route to deal with heresy, judging that the privilege to absolve heretics should be granted for the salvation of souls, so that 'the lost sheep may not perish for eternity, nor the smoking flax' of conversion 'be extinguished'.[141] The documents claim that the Jesuits had not used the faculty lightly either. When dealing with Italian heretics, cases that the Jesuits claim were much rarer than those of Ultramontanes, the Jesuits were cautious, only conceding the privilege to Provincials who could only grant it to suitable priests for specific cases.[142] In Italy, the Jesuits claimed their privilege was a harmonious and vital complement to the ecclesiastical hierarchy.

The Society did not persuade the pope. In February 1587, Sixtus V promulgated a brief revoking the Society's jurisdiction over heresy and overturning all previous concessions of the privilege. With this brief Sixtus V banned Jesuit confessors from absolving manifest heretics and from claiming to have the privilege to do so.[143] Instead, the Jesuits were ordered to send penitent-heretics to the tribunals of the Roman Inquisition.[144] After 36 years of near continuous use of the privilege, this brief revoked the Jesuits' ability to absolve heretics autonomously across Europe. On the Italian peninsula, the pope would now effectively oversee each and every reconciliation.

The revocation of the privilege suited Sixtus V's broader inquisitorial agenda. For Sixtus, the Holy Office was supreme amongst the administrative congregations of the Holy See as defending the faith was the 'foundation of the entire spiritual edifice'.[145] In the first year of his pontificate, Sixtus had extended the remit of the Roman Inquisition, putting crimes of magic and superstition under its jurisdiction.[146] Sixtus also guaranteed the inquisitors' impunity, promulgating a brief that ordered that their bulls be heeded around the world with no restrictions or caveats.[147] The Jesuits' privilege had represented a dangerous anomaly to Sixtus's ideal centralised anti-heretical system and risked undermining the work of his Holy Office. The Jesuits' defence did nothing to convince the pope that their help warranted an exception to his broader agenda. If the reign of Pius V saw the triumph of the

---

141   Ibid., f.316r.
142   Ibid., f.314r.
143   ACDF, *Stanza Stanza D-4-A*, f.5r.
144   Ibid.
145   Giordano, 'Sisto V', p.207.
146   Tomassetti (ed.), *Bullarum diplomatum*, vol. 8, pp.646–650. See also, Black, *The Italian Inquisition*, pp.131–57.
147   ACDF, *Stanza Storica D-4-a*, f.50r.

150 CHAPTER 4

Roman Inquisition, that of Sixtus V heralded the annulment of all rival jurisdictions.

The revocation of the privilege to absolve heresy was just one aspect of the reforms that Sixtus sought to impose on the Society during his pontificate. Sixtus's desire to change the government of the Society and to limit its jurisdiction over heresy were motivated by common concerns, centred on the belief that the Society had become dangerously autonomous and self-referential. Although it occurred after the privilege had been revoked, the complaint of Vincent Julien highlights the links between obedience, hierarchy and heresy in the Society that so concerned Sixtus.[148] The case began when, in early 1588, Julien sent Loyola's famous letter on blind obedience to the Roman Inquisition and asked that it be censured for heresy. Julien claimed that Loyola's principle of obedience made the theological and doctrinal views of each Superior General law in the Society. In a document held with defenses of the privilege, the Jesuits defended their practice of obedience stating that Julien's claims were 'false, and, nay more, ridiculous'.[149]

Despite these protestations, Sixtus ordered an examination of the *Constitutions* to find any errors that might have contributed to an excessively self-referential way of proceeding.[150] The pope's concerns are highlighted in a list of suggestions from the cardinal-inquisitors about the numerous complaints regarding the Jesuits' form of government. The document, dated 11 January 1590, advises that the Society adopt principles and systems of older religious orders, shorten the term of the Superior General, undergo regular visitations and localise power.[151] This advice reflected the pope's desire to balance and democratise authority in the Society and, in so doing, to transform the Jesuit Generalate into a role that was similar to the leaders of the traditional religious orders. Overall, Sixtus sought to bring the Jesuits into the ecclesiastical hierarchy, working, as other religious, under firmer papal control.

Sixtus V died in August 1590, before his reforms to the *Constitutions* could be implemented. But his revocation of the privilege to absolve heresy endured. A letter written by Cardinal Camillo Borghese after Sixtus's death but before his own pontificate as Clement VIII made the transformation of the Society's autonomy clear. As Sixtus V had revoked the Jesuits' privilege to absolve heretics in the forum of the conscience, Borghese warned them not to use it. Instead, he ordered that they ask the cardinal-inquisitors for permission to

---

148 Mostaccio, *Early modern Jesuits between obedience and conscience*, pp. 86–94.
149 ARSI, *Institutum 185-I*, f.302r.
150 Mostaccio, *Early modern Jesuits between obedience and conscience*, p.96.
151 ACDF, *Stanza Storica N-3-g*, ff.362r-363v.

absolve penitent-heretics on a case-by-case basis, just like bishops and members of other religious orders.[152] From 1587 onwards, the Jesuits could absolve heretics, but only when the papal inquisitors decided it was fit, just like members of the other religious orders.

4   Conclusion

On 11 November 1592, two years after Sixtus V's demise, cardinal-inquisitor Giulio Antonio Santoro summoned Acquaviva's secretary, Diego Ximenez, to the Holy Office. In his account of their meeting, Ximenez stated that Clement VIII had ordered the inquisition to discuss the solicitation of women in confession.[153] In preparation, Santoro had been looking for a decree on the subject made during Sixtus's pontificate. This decree ordered that religious could investigate and absolve cases of solicitation within their order.[154] Santoro could not find it. He had, however, found a decree on the absolution of heretics.[155] Confronting Ximenez with cardinal-inquisitor Sarnano, who had been a confidant of Sixtus V, Santoro told him that he knew that the privilege had been disputed but had now learnt that it had been totally revoked.[156] Reading the decree, Santoro declared that Sixtus V had ordered that Jesuits hold no privileges to absolve manifest heretics.[157] Santoro then told Ximenez that 'this was, up until now, ordered to you'.[158] In response, Ximenez claimed absolute ignorance. In 1592, Ximenez made a remarkable declaration on behalf of the Society, stating that 'such a thing, until today, was not told to us'.[159]

Ximenez claimed that the Jesuits were unaware of the revocation of the privilege because the period in which it had taken place was so turbulent. He wrote that the privilege to absolve heresy had been discussed at length but that the Society and the inquisition had also discussed more troubling matters regarding the Society's foundational documents: the *Institute* and the *Constitutions*.[160] Embroiled in these discussions, they had not resolved the question of the privilege to absolve heretics. Moreover, if anything, Ximenez claimed,

---

152   ARSI, *Stanza Storica D-4-a*, f.6r.
153   ARSI, *Institutum 185-I*, f.319r.
154   Ibid.
155   Ibid.
156   Ibid.
157   Ibid.
158   Ibid.
159   Ibid.
160   Ibid., f.320r.

152 CHAPTER 4

the Jesuits had expected a confirmation of their jurisdiction not its revocation. Indeed, Ximenez had noted the resolution of their discussion on the verso of a document about the privilege sent to the cardinal-inquisitors in 1586. It read: 'These reasons seen by the Most Illustrious Lords, nothing other was said to us than that a draft of a brief in which faculties were conceded to us would be made ... the draft of which was not made'.[161] The reasons seen by the cardinal-inquisitors were, most likely, the defenses of the privilege examined in this chapter. According to Ximenez's account, he had expected the inquisitors to respond to these documents with a brief confirming the Society's privilege. In the end, however, they do not appear to have responded at all.

Although the Society faced many controversies during the pontificate of Sixtus V, it seems unlikely that Ximenez was completely ignorant of the revocation. Acquaviva, who was Ximenez's boss, knew of the revocation, as is clear from the letter discussed at the very beginning of this chapter. What is more, in 1588 Acquaviva sent a letter to the entire Society telling members that they should not involve themselves in inquisitorial matters.[162] Furthermore, the sheer effort with which the Society defended the privilege suggests that it was a key concern in broader debates not a mere side issue that would be forgotten about because of other matters. Indeed, as we have seen, the privilege was an important part of the discussions that shaped the future of the Society during this period. It encapsulated the tension between the agenda of Jesuit authorities and the plans of the ecclesiastical and temporal powers leading the post-Reformation Church. Whilst Ximenez's account of the confused manner in which the question was concluded may be true, his claim of total ignorance was not. So why would he lie? Santoro's revelation of the brief and swift summoning of Ximenez implies that Jesuits were openly using the privilege and he felt the need to warn them not to. This suggests that Ximenez claimed ignorance to underplay the Jesuits' actions and, as he said, to give himself time to tell other Jesuits what Santoro had declared.[163]

Sixtus V did not have a problem with the private absolution of heretics *per se*. However, the Jesuits' unsupervised use of the mechanism did not fit his institutional ideals. As Borghese's letter indicated, the pope's revocation allowed Jesuits to secure powers to reconcile heretics in confession but only when the inquisitors deemed it necessary, not when the Superior General decided that they could. When used within the Jesuits' centralised hierarchy of obedience, the privilege to absolve heretics had transformed the Superior General into the

---

161 Ibid., f.319v.
162 ARSI, *Epistolae Generalium Rom. 1*, f.101r.
163 ARSI, *Institutum 185-I*, f.319v.

BARGAINING FOR AUTONOMY

Jesuits' ultimate authority in matters of heresy, entirely precluding ecclesiastical and temporal authorities affected by his decisions. This was a problem for Sixtus and for men like Bishop Gondi in Paris and Philip II in Spain. In 1586–7 the Jesuits offered a reasoned argument for the pastoral necessity of the privilege, arguing that they provided a vital supplement to judicial systems that was comprehensive on paper but not always in practice. Nonetheless, the Society's plea on the part of fearful penitents did not diminish the broader institutional concerns of Sixtus V. It was for this reason that the pope revoked the privilege.

The disagreement between the papacy and the Jesuits regarding the role of the privilege reflects a contrast that had existed during the Society's first 50 years. The Jesuits had requested the privilege for pragmatic reasons when they encountered flaws in existing systems for reconciling heretics. Sometimes these problems were related to the specific concerns of the Reformation period, such as a lack of resident bishops or a penitent's fear of being stigmatised. More often, however, the problems encountered by Jesuits were caused by human weaknesses and institutional failures that would always exist in one form or another. For the Jesuits, the privilege to absolve heresy was a crucial mechanism for their ongoing mission to ensure that the souls of harmless men who could be saved would not needlessly perish. In contrast, popes from Julius III to Sixtus V saw the Jesuits' privilege as an emergency measure to supplement permanent systems for reconciling heretics during a religious crisis. In the eyes of supportive popes like Julius III and Gregory XIII, it echoed the effects of temporary edicts of grace, expanding the channels through which the fallen could return to the Church. For more reluctant pontiffs, such as Paul IV and Pius V, the private absolution of heretics was a second-rate option to plug the gaps in an inquisitorial system that had not yet reached full efficiency.

On paper, the revocation of the privilege signalled the triumph of Sixtus V's institutional aims over the Jesuits' pastoral ideals. Nonetheless, Ximenez's denial of the revocation five years later suggests that the pope's efforts to centralise power in matters of heresy were not wholly successful. The immediate failure of Sixtus's revocation corroborates scholarship that highlights the contrast between legislative orders and their actual effects.[164] Yet Sixtus V's efforts to centralise jurisdiction over heresy did have a lasting impact. Providing the next step in the process of centralisation and normalisation begun by Pius V, Sixtus eradicated some previously legitimate routes back into the Church and established clear, centralised norms for the reconciliation of heretics. Even if these changes were not consistently observed during Sixtus's pontificate, they

---

164   Ditchfield, 'In Search of Local Knowledge', pp.266–70.

lasted. Sixtus's successor, Clement VIII, reasserted the revocation of the privilege. Moreover, he established further papal institutions for the conversion of heretics, directing all penitents to places and people under his control. Clement's own successor, Paul V, also confirmed papal dominance over the inquisition and the supremacy of the Holy Office over religious orders.[165] By the pontificate of Urban VIII, the pope had more power over the inquisition than ever before.[166] None of these popes would reinstate the Jesuit privilege. Sixtus's reforms, including the revocation of the privilege, were not radical innovations nor did they have full effect immediately. Nonetheless, they were significant steps in the development of an anti-heretical system that functioned solely through papal channels.

Whilst scholars have discussed 'negotiated obedience' between members of the Society and their superiors, Acquaviva's acceptance of the revocation demonstrates that the Society, as an institution, made similar compromises with the pope. 'Negotiated obedience' was the means through which the Jesuits reconciled their ideals and policies with the often conflicting demands of the religious, ecclesiastical, social and political contexts in which they worked.[167] This included the various contexts that came with different papacies. Acquaviva accepted the revocation of the privilege – and with it the notion that the Society was like any other mendicant order – because the Superior General too had to reconcile his pastoral ideals with the institutional aims of the pope, and ultimately with the Society's need to survive as an organisation within the Catholic Church.

---

165   G. Brunelli, 'Paolo V, papa (Camillo Borghese)' in Lavenia, Prosperi, Tedeschi (eds), *Dizionario storico dell'inquisizione*, vol. 3, p.1167 and Mayer, *The Roman Inquisition: A Papal Bureaucracy*, p.12.

166   Mayer, *The Roman Inquisition: A Papal Bureaucracy*, p.7 and pp.76–109. For specific actions of Urban VIII regarding the Holy Office see G.Brunelli, 'Urbano VIII, papa (Maffeo Barberini)' in Lavenia, Prosperi, Tedeschi (eds), *Dizionario storico dell'inquisizione*, vol. 3, pp.1616–7.

167   Alfieri and Ferlan (eds), *Avventure dell'obbedienza nella Compagnia di Gesu*, p.10; Pavone, 'Dissentire per sopravvivere', p.197 and Mostaccio, *Early modern Jesuits between obedience and conscience* and "Perinde ac si cadaver essent".

CHAPTER 5

All Roads Lead to Rome: Jesuit Agents and Rebels at the Close of the Sixteenth Century (1587–1605)

After the revocation of their privilege to absolve heresy worldwide, Jesuits in Italy became papal agents in the fight against heresy. Rather than enjoying autonomous jurisdiction over heresy as they had in the past, the Jesuits could now only absolve heretics privately in cases approved by the pope and his inquisition. Sixtus V and his successor, Clement VIII (pope 1592–1605), granted Jesuits powers to absolve heresy on an ad hoc basis when they thought it desirable. These powers were for specific groups or individuals and were often limited both temporally and geographically. Moreover, they usually required the penitent to visit the Roman Inquisition. A faculty that Sixtus granted on 23 March 1589 was typical. This power allowed Jesuit confessors at the papal penitentiary at the Basilica of St Peter to reconcile heretics who visited them there – but only if these heretics were German and visited the Holy Office to reveal their accomplices.[1] After the revocation of 1587, Jesuits could only reconcile those whom the popes thought deserving, often through institutions that the popes supported and never in direct competition with a Catholic inquisition.

Considering the after-life of the privilege from 1587 onwards, this chapter will show, first, that from the papacies of Sixtus V to Clement VIII the Jesuits could only secure faculties to absolve heretics in limited circumstances dictated by papal aims. Considering the case of the conversion of the household of the French ambassador to Venice, Philippe de Canaye, we will see that, in Italy, the Jesuits' faculties were focused on the reconciliation of foreigners whose conversion served the popes' pastoral and political aims. Secondly, the chapter will illustrate that, for the Jesuits, autonomy remained the crucial characteristic of extra-judicial reconciliations for heresy, showing how after the revocation of the privilege members of the Society continued to absolve heretics as and when they thought it necessary, even when they had no papal faculties to do so. Overall, this chapter will demonstrate that the limitation of the Jesuits' powers of absolution exposed the long-standing gulf between the Society's view of extra-judicial reconciliations and that of the papacy. Popes restricted

---

1 BAV, *Barb. Lat. 5195*, f.106v.

© KONINKLIJKE BRILL NV, LEIDEN, 2020 | DOI:10.1163/9789004413832_007

156   CHAPTER 5

the Jesuits' powers of absolution to suit their newly limited needs. But Jesuits pushed against and violated papal laws to use, as far as they possibly could, the flexible modus operandi that had been exemplified and facilitated by the privilege to absolve heresy.

The limitation of the Jesuits' powers of absolution reflected Sixtus v's desire to centralise ecclesiastical government. It also illustrates the lasting impact of his reforms. Through limited faculties of absolution, Sixtus and Clement offered flexibility to some heretics who sought reconciliation with the Church. However, the Jesuits who used those faculties had none of the flexibility that they had previously enjoyed through their privilege to absolve heresy, which had allowed them to decide whom to absolve independently. Moreover, as such faculties usually required that heretics reveal themselves to the Roman Inquisition, the Jesuits' absolutions were no longer a distinct, autonomous route of reconciliation. It appears that it was only in Savoy-Piedmont, one of the few Italian states where the Roman Inquisition faced continued obstacles, that Jesuits were given faculties that had no requirement for penitent-heretics to denounce themselves to inquisitors.[2] But even there the papal nuncio carefully supervised the delegation and use of such powers. By deciding exactly who could have an extra-judicial absolution and from whom, Sixtus and his successors micro-managed pastoral routes of reconciliation to the Church as well as the judicial means provided by the inquisition.

These faculties of absolution also reflected the Holy See's particular agenda for the conversion of heretics: an increasing focus on converting foreigners in Italy. On the Italian peninsula, Sixtus v and Clement VIII granted faculties almost exclusively for *Oltramontani* or Ultramontanes: English, French, Flemish and German heretics.[3] No such amnesties were granted for native dissenters. From the late sixteenth century, popes sought to neutralise the threat posed by the ever-growing number of people travelling from northern Europe to Italy and especially to Rome, which became a hub for those seeking work, refuge and, sometimes, conversion to Catholicism.[4] Because these foreigners often

---

2   See, for example, this faculty granted to Jesuit Father Rosetti in ACDF, *Stanza Storica D-4-a*, f.422r. On persistent problems in Savoy-Piedmont see Lavenia, 'L'Inquisizione negli stati sabaudi', pp.114–5.

3   On the *Ultramontani* see Fosi, 'Roma e gli Ultramontani. Viaggi, conversioni, identità, in *Quellen und Forschungen aus Italienischen Archiven und Bibliotheken*, 81 (2001), pp.351–396.

4   On early modern Rome as a centre of conversion for foreigners see Fosi, '<<Con cuore sincero e con fede non finta>>: conversioni a Roma in età moderna fra controllo e accoglienza' in Maria-Cristina Pitassi and Daniella Solfaroli Camillocci (eds), *Les Modes de la conversion confessionnelle à l'Époque moderne. Autobiographie, altérité et construction des identités religieuses* (Florence: Leo Olschki, 2010), pp.215–233; 'Conversions de voyageurs protestants dans la Rome baroque' in Rainer Babel and Werner Paravicini, *Grand Tour. Adeliges reisen und*

ALL ROADS LEAD TO ROME

came from regions where Catholicism was no longer the dominant Christian confession the Church identified them as potential dissenters and enemies. When legalistic methods failed to identify and genuinely convert such foreigners the papacy adopted softer, persuasive methods.[5] Successive popes encouraged foreign converts by supporting and running colleges, hospitals, congregations and penitentiaries where religious and cultural groups, often united by nationality, offered foreigners catechesis in their native language, material and moral support, and, often, private absolution.[6] Jesuits worked within these institutions and even ran some of them, like the papal penitentiaries and the English College in Rome. During this period, the Jesuits' faculties of absolution were usually limited to serving the pope in such contexts.

The contrast between the Society's view of their powers of absolution and the practical position of the popes is further underscored by the actions of rebellious Jesuits in this period. For, many Jesuits violated the revocation of the privilege and continued to absolve whomever they thought deserving. In their defence of the privilege in 1585–6, the Society had claimed that, in Italy, they mainly needed the power to absolve heresy for foreigners but also, occasionally, for Italians.[7] Successive popes were unwilling to grant such powers for Italian heretics. Yet despite receiving no faculties permitting it, Jesuits continued to absolve natives on the peninsula. Others sought faculties to absolve heretics autonomously without denouncing them to the inquisition. Sixtus V and Clement VIII denied such requests. That some Jesuits rebelled against the Holy See and that, ostensibly, some Jesuit authorities such as Diego Ximenez overlooked this rebellion expands the conclusions of recent research that has underlined the prevalence of disobedience within the early Society. Current scholarship predominantly focuses on internal conflicts in the Society over

---

Europäische kultur vom 14. bis zum 18. jahrhundert. Akten der internationalen kolloquien in der Villa Vigoni 1999 und im Deutschen Historischen Institut Paris 2000 (Ostfildern: Jan Thorbecke Verlag, 2005), pp.569–78; 'Preparare le strade, accogliere, convertire nella Roma barocca. Percorsi di salvezza'. in Stefano Andretta, Claudio Strinati, Alessandro Zuccari, and Gloria Fossi, *La storia dei giubilei: volume terzo 1600–1775* (Florence: BNL Edizioni, 2000), pp.43–83 and 'Roma e gli Ultramontani'.

5   The motivations and methods of this approach are explored extensively by Fosi in her *Convertire lo straniero*.

6   On national churches, hospitals, and colleges as places of conversion see Fosi, 'Conversion and Autobiography', pp.452–6; *Convertire lo straniero*, pp.37–51; 'The Hospital as a Space of Conversion: Roman Examples from the Seventeenth Century' in Giuseppe Marcocci, Wietse de Boer, Aliocha Maldavsku and Ilaria Pavan (eds), *Space and Conversion in Global Perspective* (Leiden: Brill, 2014), pp.154–74 and Mazur, *Conversion to Catholicism*, pp.43–65.

7   ARSI, *Institutum 185-I*, f.314r.

external institutional matters.[8] Cases in which Jesuits violated the revocation of the privilege to absolve heresy show that some members of the Society not only defied their superiors but resisted papal control and even contravened papal law.[9]

These conclusions disturb previous accounts of the concession of the privilege to absolve heretics and the Jesuits' role in the fight against heresy more generally. Traditionally, histories of the Society have emphasised the importance of the Jesuits' relationship with the pope and the Church, from Polanco in the sixteenth century to Firpo and Prosperi in the twentieth and twenty-first.[10] In these explanations of the privilege, the Society's ongoing fidelity or even servility to the papacy is key. Scholars discuss the Jesuits' role and powers in direct relation to the aims and strategies of the institutional Church, its pope and his inquisition. But a study of how the Jesuits used their powers of absolution, up to and beyond the revocation of their privilege, challenges these interpretations. So far, this book has shown that the Jesuits used the privilege not only in the service of the pope and the Roman Inquisition but also to work autonomously and to help secular authorities. This chapter will demonstrate that it was only after the revocation of the privilege in 1587 that the aims of the institutional Church dominated the Jesuits' use of powers to reconcile heretics privately and that even then Jesuits sometimes defied papal orders. Neither Firpo nor Prosperi explicitly argue that the Jesuits had only used their privilege to serve the aims of the pope and inquisition. Nonetheless, their interpretations are limited as they define the Jesuits' role according to the objectives of the Holy See rather than the ways in which the Jesuits actually used the privilege. In doing so they only tell us how the privilege served the papacy and inquisitors and do not describe how the Jesuits' extra-judicial reconciliations changed over time.

The chapter will also trace the roots of a papal policy that is usually attributed to the last years of the sixteenth century in the Jesuits' faculties of absolution. Clement VIII's acceptance of the penitence of Henri de Navarre and support of pastoral institutions to convert heretics were a turning point in the

---

8   Catto, *La Compagnia divisa*; Romano's verbal comments are referred to in Alfieri and Ferlan, *Avventure dell'obbedienza*; Martin, *Henry III and the Jesuit Politicians*, pp.20–2; Mostaccio, *Early modern Jesuits between obedience and conscience*.

9   Mostaccio has pointed out that, in spite of their vow of papal obedience, the Society resisted papal control. Mostaccio, *Early modern Jesuits between obedience and conscience*, p.84.

10   Firpo, *La presa di potere*, p.65; Polanco in Dalmases and Zapico, *Fontes narrativi de S. Ignatio Loyola et de Societatis Iesu initiis*, vol. 1, p.272 and Prosperi, *Tribunali della coscienza*, pp.230–6; p.569 and p.574.

history of Roman interaction with foreign religious dissenters.[11] Nonetheless, the pastoral and political motivations for Navarre's reconciliation already underlay the special faculties of absolution that Sixtus V granted to the Jesuits after 1587.[12] The history of the Jesuits' faculties in this period shows that the change in papal policy that found its most bold public expression in cases like Navarre's was actually born of a much longer tradition of consolatory approaches to religious dissenters, which the Society had championed and facilitated for many decades before Sixtus's pontificate.

The key contrast between the Jesuits' view of extra-judicial reconciliations and that of the papacy was the role of autonomy. Successive popes allowed the Jesuits to provide extra-judicial reconciliations to penitent-heretics who might otherwise fail to convert. However, once the threat of heresy had waned these popes did not think it necessary to grant those who facilitated these reconciliations the freedom to choose whom they absolved. Despite this, many Jesuits continued to believe that they should have the ability to absolve a penitent-heretic whom they thought worthy without referring to a higher ecclesiastical authority. The strict limitation of the privilege is an example of efforts to centralise ecclesiastical government that are often seen as typical of this period.[13] Despite this restriction, the Jesuits persistently solicited ever greater faculties and, at times, defied the revocation of the privilege outright. Their actions vindicate those scholars who have argued that local resistance often made ecclesiastical centralisation an ideal rather than a reality.[14]

Contrary to traditional (and often persistent) interpretations of the Society as papal agents in the fight against heresy, we can see that the Jesuits had long differed from the papacy in their view of extra-judicial reconciliations. As successive popes took the matter of extra-judicial reconciliations into their own hands this contrast was exposed. Popes from Julius III to Pius IV had not conceded the privilege to absolve heresy to give the Jesuits autonomy *per se* but rather to empower the only religious order able to help them to confront the geographic and human scale of the threat to Catholic orthodoxy in mid-sixteenth-century Italy.[15] When Pius V felt he needed less help from the Jesuits he effectively limited their powers. Gregory XIII wanted Jesuits' support on a

---

11   Fosi, *Convertire lo straniero*, pp.74–85 and Mazur, *Conversion to Catholicism*, p.45.

12   Fosi, *Convertire lo straniero*, pp. 57–60.The fear of foreign heretics coming to Italy existed in the 1550s and Gregory XIII sought to counter negative perceptions of Catholicism amongst northern Europeans in his jubilee of 1575.

13   Del Col, *L'Inquisizione in Italia*, p.509–565.

14   See chapter 4 footnote 77.

15   Romeo, *Ricerche su confessione*, p.52.

160 CHAPTER 5

broader scale and so restored their privilege. Sixtus V and, later, Clement VIII centralised all systems of reconciliation, focusing pastoral means on specific social and cultural groups.[16] For these popes the concession of an autonomous jurisdiction to the Jesuits had none of its previous rewards. On the contrary, it conflicted with the systems of reconciliation that they had established. For the Jesuits, however, the need to absolve heretics privately was an inevitable, permanent requirement of their ministry, which could not be limited to a particular period, need, place or group.

1 The Politics of Conversion at the Turn of the Seventeenth Century

Antonio Possevino's reconciliation of the household of the French ambassador to Venice, Philippe de Canaye, exemplifies the Jesuits' transformed role in the fight against heresy after the revocation of the privilege.[17] When Possevino wanted to convert and reconcile Canaye's household he was bound to solicit the pope for the necessary powers of absolution. In 1602, Possevino successfully secured faculties from Clement VIII, through his inquisition, to absolve Canaye and his wife and daughter.[18] Later, in November 1605 and January 1606, Possevino was also granted faculties to reconcile Anne de Colignon, George Krilgauser and Erhard Perolt, members of Canaye's household and former adherents to the teachings of Calvin and Luther.[19] The Canayes and their household were granted extra-judicial reconciliations, in part, because they were foreigners. But this was not the only reason. The converts of the Canaye household were foreigners who could bolster the Catholic cause,

---

16   Fosi has underlined how even initiatives begun by religious orders like the Oratorians were taken over by the Holy See. Fosi, 'Roma e gli "Ultramontani" ', pp.364–5.

17   For a detailed discussion of the conversion of Canaye and his family in the political context of the Venetian Interdict crisis and early seventeenth-century Europe generally, see Jessica M. Dalton, 'The Politics of Conversion: Antonio Possevino SJ, Rome and the conversion of the family of the French ambassador to Venice (1601–1607)', *Archivum Historicum Societatis Iesu*, vol. 88, fasc. 175 (2019), pp.3–48.

18   Possevino's account of Renée Canaye's conversion and a copy of her abjuration in Italian can be found in ARSI, *Opera Nostrorum 324 – II*, ff.342–3r, with a copy in French on ff. 347r-8v. Possevino's account of the conversion of their daughter on 4 October 1602 is held in the same folder on f.349r. The biography of Canaye in his edited letters incorrectly implies that Renée Canaye and her daughter converted in 1600, the same year as Canaye. See, Canaye, *Lettres et ambassade de messire Philippe Canaye Seigneur de Fresne, Conseiller du Roy en son Conseil d'Estat* (Paris: E. Richer, 1635–6), 3 vols, vol.1, p.8.

19   The abjurations of Colignon, Krilgauser and Perholt can be found in the same cache of letters referenced above: ARSI, *Opera Nostrorum 324 – II*, f.377r and f.379r.

ALL ROADS LEAD TO ROME

pastorally and politically, where it needed it most. This had as much to do with nationality as prestige. The protagonists in the Canaye case were politically powerful. Nonetheless, the pope's motivations for granting them private absolutions and Possevino's role as a papal agent in the conversions were typical of most extra-judicial reconciliations for heresy after the revocation of the privilege. From 1587, popes would micromanage extra-judicial reconciliations without granting any autonomy to the Jesuits. Their concessions would focus on foreigners whose conversion to Catholicism benefitted Rome both pastorally and politically.

Sixtus's successors never reconceded the privilege. Broadly, they were more supportive of the Society than he was but they still retained control over the reconciliation of heretics, whether judicial or extra-judicial. Of the three short pontificates that succeeded Sixtus's that of Gregory XIV (December 1590-October 1591) presented the best opportunity for the Jesuits to regain the privilege. Gregory restored much of the support and independence that Sixtus had withdrawn from the Society, defending the *Constitutions* when they were attacked by the Spanish ambassador, funding Jesuit colleges and restoring the Superior General's power to elect novices personally.[20] But Gregory did not restore the Jesuits' privilege to absolve heresy. Like Sixtus, he stated that the Society should not dictate its own government independently of the pope.[21] Clement VIII showed more promise in this area. When a group of Italian Jesuits demanded the democratisation of authority in the Society, Clement did not intervene as Sixtus had but ordered the Jesuits to resolve the matter autonomously.[22] Nonetheless, Clement steered a similar course to Gregory XIV and Sixtus V in the question of autonomy in cases of heresy. When the Jesuits questioned the revocation of the privilege in 1592, Clement clarified and confirmed its annulment. He also reasserted the revocation in subsequent legislation, for Spain in 1593 and Italy in 1599.[23] Clement did this in spite of protests from Superior General Acquaviva, who told him that the revocation was problematic not only north of the Alps but also in 'other places where His Holiness knows, even through experience, the precise necessity that there was for such

---

20   On the complaint of the Spanish Crown see Astráin, *Historia de la Compañía de Jesús en la Asistencia de España*, vol. 3, pp.473–5. On Gregory's measures see *Bullarium diplomatum*, vol.9, pp.414–5 and 436–442 and Pastor, *History of the Popes*, vol. 22, p.399.

21   *Bullarium diplomatum*, vol. 9, pp.440–1.

22   Catto, *La Compagnia Divisa*, pp.101–44.

23   See ACDF, *Stanza Storica D-4-A*, f.16v; ARSI, *Epistolae Generalium Rom. 1*, f.149r and Louis Delplace, *Synopsis actorum S. Sedis in causa Societatis Iesu: 1540–1605* (Florence: Ex typographia, 1887), p.179.

a faculty'.[24] Despite efforts to regain the privilege by the end of the sixteenth century it was patent that the Jesuits would never again secure autonomous jurisdiction over heresy in lands with Catholic inquisitions.

All of this meant that the Jesuits had to solicit the pope through his inquisition each and every time that they wanted to absolve a penitent-heretic. The process followed by Antonio Possevino in the absolution of the Canaye household in Venice was typical. To secure the necessary faculties for these cases, Possevino negotiated with the pope through cardinal-inquisitor Giulio Antonio Santoro and, after Santoro's death in 1602, cardinal-inquisitor Camillo Borghese, who would become Pope Paul V in 1605. It is known that Clement conflicted with some members of the Holy Office but the pope and the inquisitors collaborated on these concessions.[25] Santoro and Borghese took each of Possevino's solicitations to the pope and then relayed the response, intervening later only with notes about the form that documentation should take. The powers that Possevino secured were extensive, allowing him to absolve his converts in both fora.[26] This power was even broader than the authority that Possevino had enjoyed under the Jesuits' papal privilege, which allowed them to absolve heretics who were unknown to the Holy Office but not to lift censures that the inquisitors had already imposed. Nonetheless, Possevino's faculties could only be used precisely as the papal inquisition had ordered. Possevino solicited the Canayes' abjurations and wrote the sentences using a template written out for him by the papal inquisition. He declared the absolutions as valid 'with the authority given to [him] by Our Most Holy Father Clement VIII, Pope of the Universal Church'.[27] The reconciliations of the Canaye household may have been performed by Possevino but they were the result of a direct, broader collaboration between Possevino and the Holy Office and the Holy See, which established the process and parameters of Possevino's powers.

Possevino's pastoral ambitions extended far beyond the limitations of the faculties granted to him. He did not just want to absolve the Canaye household, he wanted the freedom to absolve all French heretics in Venice. For more than

---

24   ARSI, *Epistolae Generalium Rom. 1*, f.149r.

25   Clement and the inquisition clashed over the distribution of an index and the concession of licenses to read vernacular Bibles. See, Fragnito, *La Bibbia al rogo*, pp.173–198 and Fausto Parente, 'The Index, the Holy Office, the condemnation of the Talmud and publication of Clement VIII's Index', p.190.

26   See Santoro's letter to Possevino in ARSI, *Opera Nostrorum 324 – II*, f.289r.

27   See his statement in ibid., f.346r. The template or 'modo di abiuratione' sent to Possevino by Santoro is held with the correspondence at ff.332r-3v and is an example of the *schede di assoluzione* discussed by Fosi in 'Con cuore sincero', pp.6–8.

ALL ROADS LEAD TO ROME

163

a decade Possevino had been engaged in the battle against heresy in the Kingdom of France, as a preacher, confessor, Jesuit rector and writer of polemic.[28] In Venice, Possevino sought the continuation of this mission to the French. Clement VIII would not hear of it. Responding to Possevino's request, cardinal-inquisitor Santoro stated that the pope would not grant the faculty to absolve French heretics generally, which Possevino had requested in a letter.[29] Instead, Santoro advised Possevino to ask the inquisitors for faculties on a case-by-case basis, like all other Jesuits.[30] Possevino made individual requests for each of his converts in Canaye's household and, in the requests recorded by Possevino, the pope granted them through his inquisition. Conceding these faculties, cardinal-inquisitor Santoro made it clear that Clement VIII intended them for the specified cases only and not for other Frenchmen and Ultramontanes in Venice.[31]

The Canaye household could support the Catholic cause in ways that other foreigners in Venice could not. Clement VIII knew and encouraged this. In the second half of the sixteenth century there was an increasing assumption amongst ecclesiastical and political powers that the religious confession of the ruling classes could dictate the orthodoxy of a whole state, a notion had been made official in some parts of Europe by the Peace of Augsburg of 1555. It was assumed that the Canaye household could solicit further conversions amongst prominent Frenchmen. After granting his family private absolution, Clement VIII encouraged the Canayes to use their position and personal experience of the pope's benevolence to convert others amongst their class in France and in Venice. This is clear from Clement's correspondence with the family. After Possevino had absolved Canaye's wife and daughter, both husband and wife wrote to the pope to thank him for his mercy towards them and Clement responded exhorting them to spread the faith.[32] Clement told Renée Canaye of his delight that she had inspired her daughter to convert too.[33] In his letter to Philippe, the pope lauded the ambassador for converting his Calvinist wife and called him to convert more vigorous men for the Church.[34] Clement's encouragement paid off. In correspondence from Venice, Canaye sought the conversion of eminent

---

28   Mostaccio, *Early modern Jesuits between obedience and conscience*, p.40.
29   ARSI, *Opera Nostrorum 324 – II*, f.292r.
30   Ibid.
31   Ibid.
32   Ibid., f.358v.
33   Ibid., f.360r-v.
34   Ibid., f.360v.

164   CHAPTER 5

friends such as Isaac Casaubon and fellow ambassadors of the French king.[35] Canaye also encouraged others to convert prominent Frenchmen, writing to Cardinal du Perron to urge him to convert two lost sheep who were particularly urgent cases because of their influence in France.[36]

Possevino also urged Canaye to support the Catholic agenda on a much broader scale by promoting Catholic texts and the Society of Jesus in France. Possevino solicited Canaye for printing privileges for Catholic texts in the kingdom, particularly his own. In response Canaye wrote to Nicolas de Neufville, the French secretary of state, to supplicate the chancellor for a privilege that would allow Possevino to print his works there.[37] Possevino also urged Canaye to rehabilitate the Jesuits in the kingdom. Suspicions of pro-Spanish treachery had led King Henri IV to expel the Jesuits in 1595. Attempting to repair the situation on behalf of Possevino and the pope, Canaye wrote to Philippe de Bethune, Henri IV's ambassador to Rome, imploring him to urge the king to welcome the Society back and substantiating his case with Possevino's arguments and good repute.[38] As a former papal diplomat in Sweden, Poland and Russia and a direct participant in the negotiations over the absolution of King Henri IV of France, Possevino had significant experience using religious conversion to build confessional and political alliances.[39] As a prominent convert and French statesman, Canaye was well-placed to use his position to further the pastoral and political aims of the Catholic Church.

---

35   The original copy of his most insistent letter, British Library (hereafter, BL), *MS Burney 364*, ff. 309r-310r, is edited in John Russell (ed.), *Ephemerides Isaaci Casauboni cum praefatione et notis* (Oxford: Oxford University Press, 1850), vol.1, pp.82–5. Canaye suggested that Casaubon come to Venice to meet Paolo Sarpi, possibly desirous to introduce the scholar to a milieu in which he could convert. On the interactions between Sarpi, Canaye and Casaubon see, Gaetano Cozzi, *Paolo Sarpi tra Venezia e l'Europa* (Turin: Einaudi, 1979), pp.33–135, especially pp.60–5.

36   Philippe Canaye, *Lettres et ambassade*, vol.1, book 2, pp.26–7.

37   Ibid., vol. 1, book 1, p.414. See also Luigi Balsamo, *Antonio Possevino S.I. bibliografo della controriforma e diffusione della sua opera in area anglicana* (Leo Olshki: 2006), p.16.

38   In a letter to the ambassador, Nicolas de Neufville, Canaye mentions the English Jesuit Robert Persons, who is suspected of pro-Spanish and anti-French sympathies, urging de Neufville to encourage the king not to punish the entire Society for one man's errors. See, Canaye, *Lettres et ambassade*, vol. 1, book 2, pp.67–8.

39   Sutherland, *King Henry IV of France and the Politics of Religion*, vol. 2, pp.507–8. On Possevino's diplomatic missions see John Patrick Donnelly, 'Antonio Possevino, S.J., as Papal Mediator between Emperor Rudolf II and King Stephan Báthory', *Archivum Historicum Societatis Iesu*, 69 (2000), pp.3–56 and Stéphane Mund, 'La mission diplomatique du père Antonio Possevino (S.J.) chez Ivan le Terrible en 1581–1582 et les premiers écrits jésuites sur la Russie moscovite à la fin du xvie siècle', *Cahiers du monde russe*, 45 (2004), pp.407–440.

ALL ROADS LEAD TO ROME

The notion that confessional affinity translated to political alliances was well-established. Some Frenchmen claimed that Canaye himself had exploited the advantages of being Catholic to further his diplomatic career. When Canaye publicly renounced his Calvinism in 1600, some of his colleagues had suggested that his conversion to Catholicism was merely an attempt to facilitate French diplomacy in Italy and to secure the ambassadorial post in Catholic Venice.[40] Such a move would not have been unusual. Clement VIII himself had shown similar political shrewdness in his absolution of the king, the formerly Protestant Henri of Navarre. We must presume that Clement's motivations in absolving Navarre were, principally, religious. Nonetheless, his decision allowed Henri to become king and so secure France's position as a Catholic state that was large and powerful enough to rival Spain. This was crucial for the pope as Spain had become so powerful that it could threaten him with the establishment of its own national church, as well as with significant influence on the Italian peninsula.[41] In late sixteenth-century Europe, religious conversion could prove to be a powerful political instrument.

Both Clement VIII and his successor Paul V exploited the link between religious affinity and political alliance in the Canaye conversions. Canaye's potential influence on the pope's political standing came to a peak when the Holy See came to blows with the Venetian Republic in 1605. In that year, Paul V placed an interdict on Venice for claiming that the state should control ecclesiastical matters rather than the pope.[42] Retaliating, Venice expelled the Jesuits from their Republic as the order, and particularly Possevino, were vehement supporters of the papal side and refused to celebrate Mass in the Republic after the pope's ban.[43] France soon became a crucial power-broker in the controversy.

---

40   Canaye alluded to such accusations in his letter to another ambassador in ARSI, *Opera Nostrorum 324-II*, f.367v.

41   Clement VIII had been reluctant to lift the papal excommunication of the king, which barred him from the French monarchy, as he had promised the Spanish that he would never do so. He eventually reneged. On Clement VIII's involvement in the papal absolution of Henri IV, see Sutherland, *Henry IV and the Politics of Religion*, vol.2, pp.528–591.

42   On the Venetian Interdict see Bouwsma, *Venice and the Defense of Republican Liberty*, especially pp.293–483.

43   Pietro Pirri, *L'interdetto di Venezia del 1606 e i Gesuiti: silloge di documenti con introduzione* (Rome: 1959). Possevino and Bellarmino became embroiled in a heated debate, through letters and pamphlets supporting the papal cause. Their key opponent was the Venetian Servite Paolo Sarpi, who wrote his *Trattato dell'interdetto di Paolo V nel quale si dimostra che non è legittimamente pubblicato* in 1606. On Sarpi and the interdict see Cozzi, *Paolo Sarpi tra Venezia e l'Europa*; Jaska Kainulainen, *Paolo Sarpi: A Servant of God and State* (Leiden: Brill, 2014) and David Wootton, *Paolo Sarpi: between Renaissance and Enlightenment* (Cambridge: Cambridge University Press, 1983).

Working on Paul v's behalf, Possevino called upon their ally Canaye to argue for the pope's cause. But on this occasion Possevino and Paul were unsuccessful. Canaye's ambitions for France and growing Gallicanism had led him to sympathise with the Venetian argument.[44] Although unsuccessful, these attempts to make such use of a relationship that had been facilitated through private absolutions for heresy indicates that the motivations for helping the Canaye household were political as well as pastoral. Paul v would demonstrate a similar approach in attempts to court the favour of the English ambassador to Venice, Henry Wootton. When the pope became concerned that Wootton and his acolytes were spreading heresy in the Veneto he asked Possevino to befriend Wootton so that they could debate religious controversies and Possevino could solicit support for the Catholic cause in Venice and England.[45] Yes, Possevino and the pope sought the salvation of Wootton's soul. But they also wanted converts who would help them restore and defend the Catholic Church around the world, so that it might also save the souls of many others.

Possevino knew well that the pope's willingness to grant faculties of absolution was motivated by his broader ecclesiastical and political agenda for the Church. For this reason, Possevino ensured that Clement VIII knew that Canaye had granted him favours in return for the private absolution of his household. Possevino and Canaye translated Canaye's entreaties to 'another ambassador of the king' into Italian and wrote to the inquisition of Canaye's efforts to convert Isaac Casaubon so that the pope heard about Canaye's efforts to convert other influential Frenchmen.[46] Possevino's request for faculties to absolve Anne de Colignon, a member of Canaye's household, makes it clear that he thought the pope more likely to grant a private absolution to a convert who could support his agenda to re-Catholicise Europe. In his request, Possevino encouraged Pope Paul v by promising further conversions, stressing that, if reconciled, de Colignon would influence the conversion of others.[47] Later Possevino explicitly assured the pope that his favours to the Canaye household had bought him the ambassador's political favour, writing that, because of the private absolutions, de Colignon and Canaye were indebted to the pope, 'incessantly and on every occasion showing it with most grateful memory to whatsoever French lord and others who pass through there'.[48]

---

44   Bouwsma, 'Gallicanism and the Nature of Christendom' in Bouwsma (ed.), *A Usable Past. Essays in European Cultural History* (Berkeley: University of California Press, 1990), p.320.

45   Giovanni Soranzo, 'Il P. Antonio Possevino e l'ambasciatore inglese a Venezia (1604–1605)', *Aevum*, 7 (October-December 1933), p.390.

46   See, ARSI, *Opera Nostrorum 324-II*, f.366r. There is a French version at ff.335–338v.

47   Ibid., f.372v.

48   Ibid., f.341r.

ALL ROADS LEAD TO ROME

The Canaye case stands out because of the prominence of its protagonists and the richness of the documentation but in all other ways it resembles the numerous episodes in which Jesuits absolved heretics in Italy after the revocation of their privilege. In Venice, Possevino could only play the part prescribed to him by the pope: to serve the pope's ambitions to protect and promote Catholic orthodoxy, principally through the conversion of foreigners. Finally, the pope's inquisition presided over all of his actions. This was true of all reconciliations, judicial and extra-judicial, across the board in Italy.

This broader papal strategy emerged as the sixteenth century neared its close. From this time, systems of reconciliation in Italy were focused increasingly on the conversion of foreigners. As the threat of native heresy decreased, popes from Pius V onwards aimed to ensure that Italian Catholics were not infected with heresies from non-Catholic countries. Italians were banned from visiting heretical states and bound to ostracise and denounce non-Catholic foreigners when they were discovered on their peninsula.[49] Many foreign visitors appeared before the Roman Inquisition spontaneously to renounce their heresy and so avoid persecution. When the Holy See recognised that many foreigners were not converted using repressive methods, which encouraged dissimulation (false conversions out of fear), they offered foreign heretics more appealing, extra-judicial means for reconciling with the Church.[50] To do this, Sixtus V and his successors transformed extra-judicial institutions like penitentiaries, churches and colleges into places of Catholic catechesis, conversion and absolution for foreigners. Working alongside independent Catholic institutions such as national churches and hospices, the papacy supported initiatives to offer moral and material support to foreign converts in Italy as well as instituting its own.[51]

The Jesuits were given powers of absolution to facilitate these initiatives. The faculty that Sixtus V granted to Jesuit confessors at the papal penitentiary at St Peter's basilica in 1589 was typical. As penitentiaries, these fathers were already in the direct employ of the pope, working on his behalf to absolve serious sins over which only he had jurisdiction.[52] In the past, heresy had been counted amongst them but Pius V had limited the penitentiaries' powers to the

---

49   Fosi, 'Conversion and Autobiography', p.440. These regulations were set out in Pius V's *In Coena Domini* of 1568. See Canepa, *La bolla in Coena Domini.*

50   Fosi, 'Con cuore sincero', pp.219–24 and 'Conversion and Autobiography', pp.439–442.

51   On these institutions see Mazur, *Conversion to Catholicism*, p.43–65 and Fosi, *Convertire lo straniero*, which focuses on initiatives and institutions supported by the papacy.

52   Kirsi Salonen, 'The Curia: The Apostolic Penitentiary' in Atria Larson and Keith Sisson, *A Companion to the Medieval Papacy. Growth of an Ideology and Institution* (Leiden: Brill, 2016), p.259. Matthäus Meyer, *Die Pönitentiarie Formularsammlung des Walter Murner von Strassburg. Beitrag zur Geschichte und Diplomatik der päpstlichen Pönitentiarie im*

internal forum and declared that he did not want Jesuit penitentiaries in Rome or at the Holy House of Loreto to reconcile heretics.[53] At first, it might seem that Sixtus v's concession of 1589 was an attempt to restore some independent authority over heresy to Jesuit penitentiaries. Nonetheless, the faculty only applied to Germans who had not yet been discovered by the inquisition and who were willing to visit the inquisition to reveal their accomplices.[54] Rather than empowering the Jesuit penitentiaries to provide an alternative route for reconciling foreign heretics, Sixtus v gave the penitentiaries a limited faculty so that they attracted foreign heretics whom the papacy sought to convert before convincing them to hand themselves in to the Holy Office. Using this faculty, Jesuits acted as papal agents, attracting, converting and absolving the foreign targets that so suited the pope's pastoral and political aims, just like Possevino did in Venice.

Sixtus v granted individual Jesuits faculties with these same characteristics, limiting them for use on foreigners who were willing to co-operate with the Roman Inquisition. In 1590, Sixtus gave Possevino a faculty for absolving Ultramontanes of heresy sacramentally in confession.[55] Like the faculty for the Jesuit penitentiaries, Sixtus limited Possevino's power to heretics from northern Europe, clearly stating that Possevino must not absolve any Portuguese and Spanish in Italy.[56] Possevino's faculty also complemented the work of the Catholic inquisition, requiring that penitent-heretics had first satisfied the Church by denouncing 'any accomplices, if they have any, who are in Italy, or in other Catholic countries and places, so that such delinquents can be proceeded

---

14 Jahrhundert, vol. 25 of *Spicilegium Friburgense* (Freiburg: Universitätsverlag Freiburg Schweiz, 1979), p.8.

[53]   Brambilla, *Alle origini del Sant'Uffizio*, p.475. In 1567 the rector of the Jesuit college at the shrine expressed shock when he was warned that he could no longer delegate the privilege to other fathers at the shrine, indicating that, previously, such absolutions were deemed normal. This episode is discussed in chapter 3. On the Holy House of Loreto and the Jesuit college there see, Lavenia, 'Miracoli e memoria. I gesuiti a Loreto nelle storie della Compagnia (sec. XVI-XVII)', in Massimo Bonafin (ed.) *Figure della memoria culturale. Tipologie, identità, personaggi, testi e segni*, (a special edition of *L'Immagine Riflessa. Testi, Società, Culture*), 22, (2013), pp. 331–348 and Paul V. Murphy :"Your Indies": The Jesuit Mission at the Santa Casa di Loreto in the Sixteenth Century" in Konrad Eisenbichler and Nicholas Terpstra (eds), *The Renaissance in the Streets, Schools and Studies: Essays in Honour of Paul F. Grendler* (Toronto: Centre for Reformation and Renaissance Studies, 2008), pp.210–31. On the college's foundation see, ARSI, *Rom. 122-I*, f.6r and Archivio della Penitenzieria Apostolica (hereafter, APA), *Penitenzieri minori 3*, ff.4r-5v. For the privileges granted to the Jesuits at Loreto by Julius III see ARSI, *Fond. Lauret. 1*, ff. 221–228v.

[54]   See footnote 1 in this chapter.

[55]   BAV, *Barb. Lat. 1370*, ff.266–7r.

[56]   Ibid.

ALL ROADS LEAD TO ROME

against' by the inquisitors.[57] Even powerful Jesuit cardinal Roberto Bellarmino could not secure autonomous jurisdiction over heresy. In 1605, Clement VIII allowed Bellarmino to absolve an English nobleman who had confessed heresy in Rome but only after the man was persuaded to reveal himself to the Holy Office.[58] Bellarmino was a representative of the papacy's pastoral and judicial means of reconciling heretics. He was both an inquisitor and the first cardinal appointed for the conversion of heretics at the head of the new papal 'Congregation for those who come to the faith spontaneously'.[59] This congregation sought to resolve the practical problems faced by foreigners who came to Rome and renounced the faith of their homeland.[60] The congregation's pastoral image also aimed to remedy the Church's reputation for repression, despite the fact that its members collaborated with the Roman Inquisition.[61] Acting as the twin pastoral and judicial face of the pope's anti-heretical strategies, Bellarmino played a role that typified the papal approach to heresy in the late sixteenth and early seventeenth century, facilitating carefully controlled judicial and extra-judicial methods of reconciliation to target those whom the pope wanted to convert. Bellarmino also fulfilled this role when he solicited faculties to absolve individual heretics.

Sometimes the Jesuits were not even agents but merely acted as a direct conduit to the Holy Office without enjoying any faculties of their own. We have proof of this in faculties of absolution granted to some individual inquisitors following the revocation of the Jesuits' privilege in 1587. In that year, for example, Sixtus V gave cardinal-inquisitor Santoro permission to go to the Jesuits' English and German colleges in Rome absolving and reconciling anybody who had expressed an interest in renouncing their heresy without employing the usual inquisitorial processes.[62] Like many national institutions in late

---

57   Ibid., f.267r.

58   Archiginnasio, B1887, f.426r.

59   On Bellarmino's role in the inquisition see Peter Godman, *The Saint as Censor. Robert Bellarmine between Inquisition and Index* (Leiden: Brill, 2000), pp.xii-xiii and Ingrid Rowland, *Giordano Bruno. Philosopher / Heretic*, p.255.

60   Bellarmino's election to the role is noted in Archivio Storico del Vicariato di Roma (hereafter, ASVR), *Atti della segreteria del cardinal vicario*, t.77, f.3v, a letter by Cardinal Francesco Pignatelli, of 25 February 1699, 'circa li scandali et altre materie alle quali si deve provedere nell'anno santo'. On the congregation, see Fosi, 'Fasto e decadenza degli anni santi' in Luigi Fiorani and Adriano Prosperi (eds), *Roma, la città del papa: vita civile e religiosa dal giubileo di Bonifacio VIII al giubileo di papa Wojtyla* (Turin: Einaudi, 2000) (Turin: Einaudi, 2000), p.815; 'Preparare le strade, accogliere, convertire', p.76 and Fosi, 'Roma e gli "ultramontani" ', p.364.

61   Fosi, 'Roma e gli "ultramontani" ', p.364–5.

62   BAV, *Barb. Lat. 5195*, f.106r.

sixteenth and seventeenth-century Rome, the Jesuits' colleges provided a hub for foreigners seeking conversion as well as places of education and moral support.[63] Sometimes churches and hospitals sent foreigners to the Jesuits' colleges when they had expressed a desire to convert.[64] At the colleges, converts could be catechised and potentially abjured by a Jesuit who spoke their native tongue.[65] Still absolutions and reconciliations were usually concluded by the Holy Office or cardinal-inquisitors offering softer options, such as the extrajudicial route offered by Santoro at the German College.

Sixtus V and his successor Clement VIII, sought to control extra-judicial means of reconciliation, including the Jesuits' absolutions. In contrast to their privilege to absolve heresy, the Jesuits' later faculties were bound by the limitations of the popes' mercy and could only be used to fulfil papal ends. The more merciful attitude towards foreign heretics evident in these faculties motivated the Canaye conversions, institutions for conversion, major reconciliations such as that of Henri of Navarre and, later, the initiatives of seventeenth-century popes like Alexander VII.[66] Within their new, limited powers of absolution, the Jesuits had very little room for autonomy or agency. For the first time ever, the Jesuits effectively became papal agents.

2　Jesuit Disobedience

After the revocation of the privilege many Jesuits continued to act as they had in the past, completely ignoring the popes' orders. Remarkably, some of them defied the revocation of the privilege to absolve heretics autonomously as and when they thought it necessary. Inquisitorial decrees record the reprimands of cardinal-inquisitors who had discovered Jesuits absolving heretics autonomously without denouncing them to the tribunal. Despite Diego Ximenez's claim that the Jesuits were unaware of the revocation of their privilege, as seen at the close of chapter 4, declarations from Superior General Acquaviva indicate that it was highly unlikely that the authorities of the order did not know. In this final section of this chapter we shall see that Jesuits actively disobeyed

---

63　On the English College as a place of conversion see Fosi, 'Conversion and Autobiography', pp.452–5. On ways that the inquisition used native preachers to win and secure conversions in national churches see, Fosi, 'Roma e gli "ultramontani"', p.389.

64　Fosi, 'The Hospital as a Space of Conversion', p.157.

65　Fosi, 'Conversion and Autobiography', p.453.

66　Fosi, *Convertire lo straniero*, pp.177–82; Mazur, *Conversion to Catholicism*, pp.43–5 and Sutherland, *Henry IV and the Politics of Religion*.

ALL ROADS LEAD TO ROME

the pope by violating the revocation of the privilege and, therefore, papal law. These cases expand the conclusions of recent historiography, suggesting that the Jesuits were willing to ignore not only the orders of their own leaders but also those of the leader of the entire Catholic Church. And even cases in which Jesuits violated the revocation unknowingly underline the fundamental contrast between the limits of papal policy and the character and ambition of the Jesuits' ministry. This conclusion too weakens the traditional interpretation of the Society as a papal militia.

By violating the limitations placed on their activity, Jesuits demonstrated that autonomy remained key to their use of private absolutions for heresy even if, for the Holy See, jurisdictional independence was prohibited as an obstacle to centralised systems of reconciliation.

The discussion of the privilege to absolve heresy between cardinal-inquisitor Santoro and Diego Ximenez described in the conclusion of chapter 4 is extremely revealing. For it indicates that the Jesuits had continued to absolve heretics five years after the revocation of their privilege to do so. Santoro's need to reveal Sixtus's brief, which he had found whilst looking for another document, suggests that he was surprised at the notion that the Jesuits were banned from absolving heretics privately – perhaps because some Jesuits had continued to do so.[67] Ximenez's claim to be ignorant of the brief corroborates this notion, implying that he thought the Jesuits still had the power to absolve heretics.[68]

Despite Ximenez's denials, we know that the Jesuit authorities were well aware of the revocation of the privilege. In 1588, Acquaviva had used a circular letter to advise Jesuit confessors of the ban. Such letters were one of the means through which Acquaviva sought to unify the activity of Jesuits across Italy, Europe and the rest of the world. In his letter of 1588, Acquaviva ordered all priests of the Society 'not to involve themselves in those [things] which regard the inquisition during confessions'.[69] His letter acknowledged that some Jesuits might think that they could use their faculties to deal with inquisitorial matters but warned them that they should not even absolve a non-heretic who knew of heretics but had not denounced these heretics to the inquisition.[70] In this letter, the authorities responsible for running the Society affirmed Sixtus

---

67   ARSI, *Institutum 185-I*, f.319v.
68   Ibid.
69   ARSI, *Epistolae Generalium Rom. 1*, f.101r.
70   ARSI, *Epistolae Generalium Rom. 1*, f.101r. It seems from this letter that the Superior General's warning was prompted by a case in which a Jesuit sought to absolve from necromancy or witchcraft, which Sixtus V had put under inquisitorial jurisdiction.

172 CHAPTER 5

v's vision for the Jesuits' new limited role in the ecclesiastical hierarchy. As the leaders of a Catholic religious order, Jesuit authorities had little choice but to comply.

Numerous inquisitorial decrees indicate that Jesuits defied Clement VIII's reassertion of Sixtus's revocation of the privilege and continued to reconcile heretics without notifying the tribunal. Sometimes the inquisitors pre-empted a violation of the rules, driven, perhaps, by the Jesuits' past transgressions. In 1599, for example, Clement's inquisitors reminded Jesuit confessors of their obligation to urge the heretics whom they absolved to visit the inquisition, particularly during jubilees when they would have large numbers of penitents.[71] In May 1614, Pope Paul v's inquisitors notified Superior General Acquaviva similarly, warning him that Jesuits could not absolve heretics who had not first satisfied the inquisitors.[72] Similar cases appear in inquisitorial decrees from the next decade. In the spring of 1624, during the pontificate of Gregory xv (pope 1621–3), a certain cardinal-inquisitor Mullino wrote to the inquisitor in Bologna to tell him that a German soldier who had been imprisoned for 'formal' (that is deliberate) heresy in nearby Rimini had claimed that he had been absolved and reconciled by a Jesuit priest who had claimed to have a special faculty for the purpose.[73] In the months that followed, the Holy Office attempted to resolve the case by reasserting Sixtus v's revocation of the privilege, reminding the Jesuits that they did 'not have the faculty of absolving from heresy in Italy' and 'warning them to abstain from it' again.[74]

Inquisitorial correspondence from the 1630s suggests that the Jesuits violated the revocation of the privilege in response to demand from penitents, who still desired a completely distinct route to reconciliation and looked to the Jesuits to administer it. In 1635, the Dominican inquisitor of Ancona, Paolo Egidio Tamergnini da Como, complained that there were very few trials at his tribunal.[75] According to Tamergnini, people went to abjure their heresy and receive absolution with the Jesuit confessors at the penitentiary at Loreto rather than visiting him.[76] Tamergnini claimed that penitents secured an absolution at the penitentiary and were thus 'liberated from the obligation to tell the Holy Office'.[77] Whilst this was just the opinion of one inquisitor, it echoes

---

71   Archiginnasio, *B1887*, 630, f.421r.

72   Ibid., f.908r.

73   The case is recorded in a letter in Archiginnasio, *B1866*, f.143r. On foreign soldiers in Italy see Mazur, *Conversion to Catholicism*, pp.98–115.

74   These orders are recorded in Archiginnasio, *B1887*, 630, f.908r.

75   His letter is in ACDF, SO, *DD-2-d*, f.413r.

76   Ibid.

77   Ibid.

ALL ROADS LEAD TO ROME

the arguments made by Jesuits themselves when they defended the privilege in 1585–6. In their own documents Jesuits stated that they needed to absolve some heretics privately as they simply refused to go to the inquisition, fearing that it would 'deny [them] absolution'.[78]

Tarmegnini's complaint underlines the conflict between the activities of some Jesuits and other systems of absolution at the time. It is difficult to pinpoint which faculties the Jesuit penitentiaries at Loreto had in 1635 but records suggest that it is unlikely that they had received the power to absolve heretics.[79] Whether the Jesuits there acted legitimately or not, Tarmegnini felt that their work was incompatible with the successful functioning of the inquisitorial system. The irritation that prompted Tarmegnini to write to the Holy Office indicates that, nearly fifty years after the revocation of the privilege, some inquisitors believed that Jesuits continued to undermine the ecclesiastical hierarchy within which they were now supposed to operate obediently.

For the Jesuits, a route to reconciliation that was private and autonomous remained vital. Early members of the Society had solicited the privilege after a decade of ministry because the private absolution of heretics was the logical conclusion of both their missionary praxis and the spirituality that informed it. At the close of the sixteenth century, the Jesuits had changed neither their approach nor their activities. Loyola had described the general confession used by the Society as a 'complete conversion by undertaking a devout life'.[80] At the end of the sixteenth century, Acquaviva reiterated this view, urging Jesuits to seek out the most serious sinners so that they worked for those who were most needy rather than faithful Catholics who required less help.[81] For Acquaviva, using confession to support and console the most errant, rather than the most devoted, was fundamental to the formation of every Jesuit.[82] Acquaviva also reiterated Loyola's view that the confessor should be merciful rather than judgmental, stating that the souls of penitents should be considered with their 'defects, passions, propensities [and] temptations' 'not as in front of a judge

---

78   ARSI, *Institutum 185-I*, f.314r.

79   During the pontificate of Sixtus V, jurisdiction over heresy at the penitentiaries seems only to have been delegated through special limited faculties, such as the faculty to absolve Germans in 1589. A list of faculties for the penitentiary at Loreto published in 1636, suggests that the penitentiaries' powers were similarly limited in the period of Tamergnini's letter. See ARSI, *Rom. 222*, p.2.

80   Quoted in Moshe Sluhovsky, 'General Confession and Self-Knowledge in Early Modern Catholicism' in Asaph Ben-Tov, Yaacov Deutsch and Tamar Herzig (eds), *Knowledge and Religion in Early Modern Europe* (Leiden: Brill, 2013), p.39.

81   ARSI, *Institutum 217*, f.34r.

82   Ibid., f.39v.

174   CHAPTER 5

... but as a father'.[83] Such an approach demanded flexibility and the ability to work without referring the penitent to an external judge. These requirements clashed with the increasingly centralised and still mostly judicial approach to heresy supported by the papacy.

Because of this clash in aims, knowingly and unknowingly, legitimately and illegitimately, Jesuits continued to absolve heretics in a manner that conflicted with the orders of popes, cardinal-inquisitors and the administrators of local inquisitorial tribunals. The violation of the revocation of the privilege shows not only that some Jesuits saw a conflict between the pastoral demands of their own ministry and papal policy but that, for many, the demands of ministry were more important than papal law. As we saw in chapter 1, Jesuits like Alfonso Salmerón had absolved heretics who sought reconciliation with the Church in the 1540s, long before the concession of the privilege to absolve heresy.[84] These early absolutions, along with later breaches of the revocation, demonstrate that the Jesuits absolved heretics because their ministry and penitents demanded an alternative route to reconciliation, both before they had the privilege and after it was taken away. We can, therefore, conclude that the Jesuits' violation of papal law was not born of any willful rebellion against the Holy See. Like disobedience within the order, it was driven by a desire to pursue the best possible route to fulfil the Society's divine mission to save souls. For the most part, the Jesuits complied with the changes imposed on them. But when the demands of papal policy competed with the aims of the Jesuits' ministry some fathers listened to their own conscience above the orders of the Holy See.

3   Conclusion

The private reconciliation of the Canaye household illustrated the popes' pastoral and political aims when converting foreign heretics in Italy. The leaders of the Church wanted to save souls but also to promote the Catholic cause to potential converts and bolster Roman interests in their converts' countries of origin. The conversion of foreigners in Italy ensured that orthodoxy was preserved at its heart whilst publicly demonstrating the triumph of Catholic truth over Protestant error. It also demonstrated that the Holy See was a paragon of Christian benevolence, forgiving even those who could be deemed its most

---

83   Original document held at Hauptstaatsarchiv München, *Jesuiten* 9, f.57, quoted by Prosperi in *Tribunali della coscienza*, p.496, fns. 26 and 27.

84   Caravale, *Sulle tracce dell'eresia*, p.281.

ALL ROADS LEAD TO ROME

dangerous enemies. Clement VIII, Possevino and Canaye were all well aware of the political implications of such conversions, having played direct roles in the absolution of Henri of Navarre.[85] Indeed, Canaye's own renunciation of Protestantism had followed the very public and dramatic triumph of Cardinal Jacques du Perron over the Calvinist Philippe de Mornay at the religious debates at Fontainebleau.[86] Men like du Perron saw Canaye's return to Catholicism as a great boon and even used the debate to launch a campaign to convert Causubon and key members of the French Royal Household.[87] This was a generation that knew the potency of religious conversion for both politics and propaganda.

The dynamics of the Canaye case were replicated in Italy during the course of the seventeenth century. They would soon be key to even grander conversions, as the papacy harnessed the impact of foreign converts with ever greater drama. This phenomenon would reach its zenith in 1654 when Alexander VII welcomed the formerly Lutheran Queen Christina of Sweden to Rome with great pomp and ceremony, transporting her through the city's Porta del Popolo on a sedan chair designed by Gianlorenzo Bernini.[88] Though on a less grand scale, the very same pastoral and political aims were fulfilled by papal faculties, institutions and incentives targeted at all levels of the social hierarchy. Jesuits were given powers of absolution to facilitate these papal strategies but nothing further. No longer did popes need a roving, autonomous force to plug gaps in the inquisitorial system across Italy. Instead, they gave the Jesuits powers that allowed them to work as papal agents, faculties that were harmonious with the

---

85   Possevino had acted as a papal representative to Henri of Navarre's envoy to the pope, the Duc de Nevers. Clement VIII had, eventually, granted an absolution to Henri. Canaye was present at Henri's court from 1584 and worked closely with him until his death in 1610. Jill Raitt, *The Colloquy of Montbéliard. Religion and Politics in the Sixteenth Century* (Oxford: Oxford University Press), p.63. Sutherland, *Henry IV of France and the Politics of Religion*, p.507.

86   Hugh Trevor-Roper is suspicious of Canaye's motives for conversion, see Trevor-Roper, *Europe's Physician: The Various Life of Sir Theodore de Mayerne* (London: Yale, 2006), p.123.

87   Nicholas Hardy, *Criticism and Confession. The Bible in the seventeenth-century republic of letters* (Oxford: Oxford University Press, 2017), pp. 63–4. On the attempts of du Perron and de Thou to convert the king's sister, Duchesse de Bar and others see Christina L. Griffiths, 'Confessional Conflict and "Turkish" Tolerance? Philippe Canaye, Sieur de Fresnes, Huguenot and Catholic Convert' in Jane McKee and Randolph Vigne (eds.) *The Huguenots: France, Exile and Diaspora* (Brighton: Sussex Academic Press, 2013), pp.39–42.

88   On the conversion of Queen Christina of Sweeden see Susanna Åkerman, *Queen Christina of Sweden and her circle: the transformation of a seventeenth-century philosophical libertine* (Leiden: Brill, 1991) and Oskar Garstein, *Rome and the Counter-reformation in Scandinavia: The Age of Gustavus Adolphus and Queen Christina of Sweden 1622–1656* (Leiden: Brill, 1992).

work of the inquisition and the popes' strategies to reconcile foreigners in both principle and practice.

These limited papal faculties of absolution conflicted with the Jesuits' pastoral aims and activities. For this reason, after the revocation of 1587 some Jesuits performed absolutions that violated the limits of the powers that the popes were willing to grant them. This contrast between the position of the popes and the Jesuits had always existed. The Jesuits had solicited the privilege to absolve heretics autonomously in order to overcome obstacles in a spiritual ministry focused on conversion and mercy. Successive popes had empowered the Jesuits for more practical reasons, supplementing their inquisition when and where necessary with pastors who were orthodox, available and well-placed. As the Holy Office became more efficient and the threat of religious rebellion diminished so did the contexts in which the Jesuits could absolve heretics extra-judicially. The contrast between the Society and the Holy See would be totally exposed when the ambitions of the Society and the needs of the papacy finally diverged.

The difference between how the Jesuits used their privilege of absolution and how they applied their later, limited faculties weakens the notion that the early Jesuits were papal agents in the fight against heresy. A study of the use of the privilege from the 1550s onwards shows us that it gave the Jesuits the freedom to absolve heretics in a variety of circumstances, often without any papal involvement. Earlier popes may have conceded the privilege to fulfil their own ends but its actual impact and significance went far beyond this. It was only after the revocation of the privilege, when the popes limited the Jesuits' powers to serve their reduced needs, that the Society's legitimate activities to absolve heretics can be defined, almost entirely, by papal objectives. The more detailed chronology of the privilege and its after-life provided in this book thus undermines characterisations of the first Jesuits as a Roman taskforce in the fight against heresy which have persisted in scholarly and popular writing for centuries, even as broader conceptions of the Society have been revised.

The Jesuits' violation of the limits placed on their powers of absolution indicates that papal attempts to centralise pastoral processes of reconciliation had limited success. This evidence bolsters criticisms of scholarship that has taken the centralising dictates of Sixtus V and his successors as a reflection of the activities and approach of those whom they sought to command.[89] Whilst popes from Sixtus onwards reorganised and limited extra-judicial routes of

---

89   Ditchfield, 'In Search of Local Knowledge' and 'Decentering the Catholic Reformation' and Laven, 'Encountering the Catholic-Reformation'.

ALL ROADS LEAD TO ROME

reconciliation, this did not change the ministry of Jesuits who had long granted mercy to penitent-heretics. Neither, according to inquisitor Tamergnini, did it change the expectations of the Jesuits' penitents. On rare occasions popes themselves recognised the limits of their influence, granting Jesuits and Capuchins in some areas of Savoy-Piedmont faculties that did not oblige their penitents to visit the Holy Office.[90] Such concessions, along with the Jesuits' continued requests for broader privileges and, in some cases, their violation of papal law, exposed the contrast that had long underlay the Jesuits' view of extra-judicial reconciliations and that of the papacy. They also prove the Society's argument that there would always be men and women who would only convert to Catholicism if offered a private, genuinely non-inquisitorial route back into the Catholic Church.

---

90   See, for example, the concession in ACDF, Stanza Storica D-4-A, f.422r.

Conclusion

The Society's privilege to absolve heresy allowed a new religious order to occupy a radically broad and flexible role in the fight against heresy in the Catholic heartland of Italy. Using this power, the Jesuits converted religious rebels alone, as papal missionaries and in collaboration with princes, cardinal-inquisitors and bishops. The history of the concession, negation and revocation of the privilege sees the priorities of popes and the central mission of the Jesuits coalesce and then drastically diverge, as the religious emergency of the sixteenth century reached its peak and then subsided. Surprisingly, the irreconcilable difference between the Jesuits and the papacy in negotiations over the privilege was not about the amnesty that the privilege offered to potentially dangerous heretics, but the fact that the privilege allowed the Jesuits to work without supervision. This autonomy was crucial to the effectiveness of Jesuits' anti-heretical activities during the height of the post-Reformation crisis. However, as this emergency waned, the institutional drawbacks of the Jesuits' freedom became greater than its benefits for the pope. The complications introduced by the Society's autonomy in matters of heresy make the popes' initial concession of the privilege to Jesuits in Italy all the more remarkable. The concession of such great autonomy also significantly undermines persistent interpretations of the Jesuits as servile papal or inquisitorial agents. On the contrary, the history presented in this book shows that the relationships between the Jesuits, popes and inquisitors was formed through negotiation and characterised throughout by a shared pragmatism, even when their priorities conflicted. The history of the privilege, therefore, is a vital prism for illuminating how the Jesuit order was shaped as the Society, papacy and Roman Inquisition negotiated their fluctuating pastoral and institutional aims in Italy.

First and foremost, the Jesuits' privilege to absolve heresy must be defined as a mechanism that allowed the Society to fulfil its pastoral mission. Since the foundation of their order, the Jesuits used confession to encourage profound inward conversions and sought to secure the souls of the converted by bringing them back into the institution of the Church. After encountering penitent heretics in their ministry, the Jesuits solicited the privilege to absolve heresy so that they could fulfil this fundamental spiritual and pastoral mission amongst those whom they considered the gravest and most needy sinners, in spite of the barriers ordinarily presented by Canon Law. In fulfilling their salvific mission, the Jesuits also addressed the central challenge facing the Catholic Church in sixteenth-century Italy: the threat of heresy spreading to orthodox believers and damning them to hell. Still, as it was the Jesuits who requested

© KONINKLIJKE BRILL NV, LEIDEN, 2020 | DOI:10.1163/9789004413832_008

CONCLUSION 179

the privilege and not the Church that thrust it upon them, their own motivations, rather than the broader aims of the popes and their congregations, must be the starting point of any account of its nature and impact, at its concession and throughout its history.

Whilst the privilege was borne of the Jesuits' particular mission, it soon become a crucial node of interaction between the Society and the men who ran the major institutions of early modern Italy, namely the popes, the cardinal-inquisitors of Rome and the princes of the Italian states. These figures quickly realised that the Jesuits' effective use of the privilege transformed the Society into a force that could fight religious dissent in areas of Italy where inquisitorial and episcopal systems could not. This was the key reason that successive popes and inquisitors granted and supported the privilege, even though the Jesuits' autonomous jurisdiction could undermine their own judicial means of countering religious dissent. Some popes, such as Julius III, preferred the empowered Jesuits to a Roman Inquisition run by cardinals whom they despised. Nonetheless, the Jesuits' intimate collaborations with the Holy Office from Julius's pontificate onwards make it clear that both he and later popes conceded the privilege principally because it empowered the Jesuits to plug gaps when and where inquisitors faced insurmountable obstacles. As long as such obstacles persisted and the threat of spreading heresy remained high, popes granted the Jesuits the privilege to absolve heretics across Italy, whenever and wherever the occasion arose, without referring to the usual ecclesiastical hierarchy.

Because of the service that it rendered to both the Church and state, the privilege soon allowed the Society to fulfil its institutional as well as pastoral aims. In sixteenth-century Italy, the Jesuits' ability to convert and reconcile heretics where nobody else could transformed them into an invaluable force to both secular and ecclesiastical patrons. Serving such powers, the Society won vital patronage at a time when they needed support to establish their order globally. The Jesuits used ecclesiastical patronage to secure further privileges and favours from the pope. Moreover, they called upon both ecclesiastical and princely supporters to win the funds and permissions necessary to found colleges and houses on the Italian peninsula and beyond. The privilege's role in building the Jesuits' network, and the Jesuits' use of this network to secure the privilege as the decades progressed, demonstrates the inextricable, essential ties between the order's spiritual and institutional objectives and underlines the need to integrate both into any explanation of the Society's actions and development.[1]

---

1 This approach has been vital to recent revisions to Jesuit history. It was pioneered in O'Malley's *The First Jesuits* and has borne fruit in studies on Jesuit obedience such as Mostaccio's

Yet the privilege inevitably caused controversies in the Jesuits' relationship with the papacy and other institutions. In practice, the privilege made the Jesuits an ungovernable force in the grave matter of religious disobedience. Once granted to the Superior General, the privilege put the power to make decisions about orthodoxy and heresy and penitence and obstinance in the Society's hands. This power was delegated within the order through a closed system that excluded any external supervision, even from the pope himself. This genuine autonomy in matters of heresy was essential to the privilege's positive impact on the Church's anti-heretical mission in mid-sixteenth-century Italy. But that very same autonomy also rendered the privilege problematic and controversial. Eventually, it was Jesuit autonomy that would lead popes to revoke the privilege. The willingness of so many popes to delegate such extensive freedom to the Society in the first place, despite its inherent problems, demonstrates the importance of autonomy in the early Jesuits' role and relationship with the papacy, challenging persistent suggestions that they were principally papal agents in the fight to protect and promote Catholic orthodoxy.[2]

The concession of the privilege to absolve heresy represented the willingness of mid-sixteenth-century popes and cardinal-inquisitors to prioritise the salvation of heretics above the desire to rely on an inquisitorial system working under the authority of the pope. Popes from Julius III to Gregory XIII largely overlooked the fact that the Jesuits' privilege could undermine the investigations of their own inquisitors in order to respond effectively to the immediate religious and ecclesiastical crisis that they faced – a truly pragmatic approach. The history of the privilege, therefore, bolsters recent histories of the early modern Church that highlight its reactive, compromising character.[3] However, the popes' pragmatism would not always favour pastoral aims. The revocation of the privilege was also an act of pragmatism, only one that prioritised the

---

  Early modern Jesuits between obedience and conscience and missionary work such as Clossey's *Salvation and Globalization.*

2 This characterisation is seen in explanations such as Prosperi's and Firpo's. Even O'Malley's recent explanation of the Jesuits' relationship with the pope, which emphasises that it was a partnership, states that the addition of the 'defence' of the faith to the Society's mission statement meant defending the papacy, thus tying the Society's anti-heretical activities to service of the pope. O'Malley, *The Jesuits and the popes*, p.22.

3 Such revised interpretations have been proposed by scholars such as Simon Ditchfield, Irene Fosi and Mary Laven in scholarship cited throughout this book. The same approach has been applied directly to the history of the Jesuits by scholars such as Mostaccio, and directly to the Jesuits' role in the fight against heresy in Pierroberto Scaramella's 'I primi gesuiti e l'inquisizione Romana'.

CONCLUSION 181

pope's institutional objectives over his desire to reconcile heretics at any cost. As the threat of spreading heresy subsided in Italy and the Roman Inquisition became more efficient, the benefits of the privilege diminished. At the same time, its negative impact increased. For, in the very same period, popes such as Pius V and Sixtus V focused increasingly on establishing a more centralised ecclesiastical government with which the Jesuits' autonomy in matters of heresy completely clashed. Responding to these religious and ecclesiastical changes, the pragmatism of successive popes led them to prioritise institutional objectives over pastoral aims. As the Society's autonomous jurisdiction clashed with the popes' centralising ambitions pontiffs restricted and then revoked the privilege, transforming the Society's role forever.

The Jesuits' motivations for soliciting the privilege were just as pragmatic as the popes' reasons for conceding it. Nonetheless, the history of the privilege reveals that the priorities of the Society and papacy in early modern Italy were only pushed into alignment briefly by the religious crisis of the mid-sixteenth century. Whilst the popes' priorities shifted, the Jesuits consistently preferred pastoral aims over institutional objectives. The Jesuits requested the privilege in reaction to the religious and ecclesiastical situation that they discovered during their early ministry in Italy. They wanted to be able to absolve and reconcile penitent-heretics, even when those heretics were too frightened to approach an inquisitor or bishop, and even when there was no inquisitor or bishop around to reconcile them. Throughout the privilege's lifespan and even beyond its revocation, the Jesuits remained dedicated to the notion that extra-judicial reconciliations were always essential for some penitent-heretics. When the time came, the Society did not relinquish the privilege because its priorities changed but because its authority as a Catholic religious order relied on the cooperation of the papacy. At that point, the institutional priorities of both the papacy and the Society meant that it was pragmatic for the popes to rescind the privilege and pragmatic for the Jesuits to accept the revocation, even if they did so reluctantly and imperfectly.

The history of the privilege shows that the Society's relationship with the papacy was formed by a constant process of negotiation, not by an abstract concept like papal obedience. The solicitation, concession and revocation of the privilege demonstrate that the precise form of the Society, and the powers that facilitated it, were shaped as the Jesuits applied their ministry to the needs of Catholic powers. As their ministry and order took form, the Jesuits negotiated with popes for the powers and freedoms that they needed in order to work more effectively. The Jesuits' flexible approach to penitents had initially responded to the Church's needs. But when their way of proceeding began to conflict with institutional plans, the popes renegotiated the Jesuits' role. The Jesuits were the inferior party in this partnership but they were not without influence and certainly not servile in their obedience. The persistence of the Jesuits' influence and their ability to negotiate their role is evident in the privilege's afterlife in the limited faculties to absolve heretics extra-judicially granted to the Jesuits and others during the pontificates of Sixtus V and Clement VIII.

The history of the privilege illuminates the nature and influence of the Society's interactions with other institutions and individuals engaged in the fight against heresy. In short, it allows us to apply the *désenclavement* of Jesuit scholarship to the Society's anti-heretical activities in Italy: a central aspect of Jesuit history. The Jesuits' solicitation of the privilege may have arisen from their own particular ministry and spirituality but it affected the crucial work of many authorities, both ecclesiastical and temporal, both locally and centrally. As such, its history traces the development and activities of the early Jesuits as they intersected with and were shaped by their aims and the aims of individuals and institutions outside of the Society. This *désenclavement* of the history of the Society's anti-heretical role corrects not only early Jesuit myths about their activities and aims but also modern interpretations of the privilege that define the authority exclusively according to the objectives of either the papacy or the inquisition, or solely according to the pastoral aims of the Jesuits. This history describes how the Jesuits' own aims interacted with and were affected by the objectives of the individuals and institutions with which they worked. In doing so, it illuminates the Jesuits' relationship with those institutions during an era that was formative for the Society and transformative for the entire Catholic Church.

The conclusions of this history of the use of the privilege in Italy spark further questions about the institutional history of the Church and responses to religious dissent across the early modern world. A sustained, in-depth case study of the Jesuits' use of the privilege in one locale, for example, would allow us to explore its full effects on the local authorities who policed heresy in the various states of sixteenth-century Italy. Such a study could also draw upon emerging scholarship on the changing role of the early modern episcopate, possibly revealing the view of bishops whose status in the fight against heresy changed dramatically over the course of the sixteenth century.[4] More broadly, such a study could be used to analyse changes to the role of territorial

---

4 Local case studies that have focused on the changing role of the episcopate and religious discipline include Al Kalak, *Il riformatore dimenticato*, which discusses some of the Jesuits' work in Modena and Deutsher, *Punishment and Penance: Two Phases in the History of the*

CONCLUSION 183

authorities such as bishops in comparison to that of emerging itinerant, inter-national groups such as the Jesuits.[5]

There is also scope and sources for comparative study between the Jesuits and other religious orders in matters of heresy in Italy. A comparison be-tween the faculties of absolution granted to the Society and the order of the Capuchins in the late sixteenth and early seventeenth century, for example, would respond to those scholars who argue that only comparative work will allow us to assess the originality, peculiarity and contribution of the Jesu-its accurately.[6] In doing so, such a study would also test the argument, pre-sented in this volume, that the popes empowered the Jesuits for pragmatic rather than principled reasons, as the Capuchins had never previously heard lay confessions, let alone developed their own particular approach to the sacrament.[7]

Applying the conclusions of this volume to a broader comparative study is equally promising. I have argued that the popes' approaches to religious dissent were motivated by the desire to save souls and also by their political and governmental objectives. By comparison, the Society remained focused on its salvific mission in Italy, as far as its fundamental reliance on the papacy would allow. A global comparison of the Jesuits' approaches to various forms of religious dissent could test the notion, suggested here and in other recent

---

Bishop's Tribunal of Novara. Fosi has considered the interactions between episcopal courts and inquisitorial tribunals in 'Conflict and Collaboration. The Inquisition in Rome and the Papal Territories (1550–1750)' in Aron-Beller and Black, *The Roman Inquisition*, pp.33–59. The essays in Jennifer DeSilva (ed.) *Episcopal Reform and Politics in Early Modern Europe* (Kirks-ville: Truman State University Press, 2012) considers the changing role of the bishop in this period across the continent. For Italy see particularly the contribution of Celeste McNamara 'Challenges to Episcopal Authority in Seventeenth-Century Padua', pp.173–193 and for con-flict between bishops and inquisitors, that of Jean Pascal Gay 'The Trials that Should Have Been. The Question of Judicial Jurisdiction over French Bishops in the Seventeenth Century and the Self-Narration of the Roman Inquisition' in Jennifer Mara DeSilva (ed.), *Episcopal Reform and Politics in Early Modern Europe* (Kirksville: Truman State University Press, 2012), pp.194–214.

5 This question has been raised in works of legal and theological history such as Brambilla's *Alle origini Sant'Uffizio* but its implications can only be fully explored in case studies.

6 Mostaccio, 'Codificare l'obbedienza' and 'A Conscious Ambiguity', pp.424–5 and 431–2; Fran-co Motta and Sabina Pavone, 'Per una storia comparative degli ordini religiosi' in *Dimensioni e problemi della ricerca storica*, 1 (2005), pp.13–24. Mostaccio states that the benefits of such a comparative approach are seen in Maurizio Sangalli's, 'Le congregazione religiose insegnanti Italia in età moderna: nuove acquisizioni e piste di ricerca' in *Dimensioni e problemi della ricerca storica*, 1 (2005), pp.25–47.

7 Antonio Fregona, *I frati cappuccini nel primo secolo di vita* (Padua: Edizioni messagero, 2006), pp.60–1.

work on global missions, that the Society's mission must be defined in fundamentally soteriological terms, rather than according to the aims of a Counter-Reformation Church based in Italy.[8] Such a study would further the revision of Jesuit histories that consider the order within traditional narratives of the Counter-Reformation by integrating conclusions about the Jesuits' work to counter religious disobedience in Europe into research on their global missions.[9] Additionally, a broader, global comparison of the Jesuits' approach to religious dissent would allow us to integrate the conclusions of recent scholarship on mission, conversion and religious difference, forcing us to consider the effect of local motivations, such as the post-Reformation crisis in Italy, on the ways that religious dissent was defined and approached both inside and outside of early modern Europe.[10]

The Jesuits' privilege to absolve heresy was both typical and exceptional in its time. On the one hand, it was one of a host of papal concessions that allowed the Society to fully and effectively pursue its spiritual mission in its ministry to sinners. Providing flexibility and pragmatism, the privilege reflected both the modus operandi of the Jesuits and the character of the institutional Church at large. At the same time, in the aftermath of the Protestant Reformation, at a time when popes, cardinals, bishops, princes and ordinary laymen feared that heresy could destroy Catholicism at its heart, the stakes of

---

8   For an introduction to such scholarship see Bronwen McShea's introduction to a special edition of the *Journal of Jesuit Studies* on 'Jesuit Missionary Perspectives and Strategies Across the Early Modern Globe', *Journal of Jesuit Studies*, 1 (2014), pp.171–6 and Charles H. Parker's 'The Reformation in Global Perspective', *History Compass*, 12 (2014), pp.1–11. For examples of scholarship that compares the Jesuits' strategies in the Old and New Worlds see, Broggio, *Evangelizzare il mondo*, Clossey, *Salvation and Globalization*, McShea, 'Cultivating Empire Through Print: The Jesuit Strategy for New France and the Parisian "Relations" of 1632 to 1673' (PhD Dissertation, Yale University, 2011) and Jennifer Selwyn, *A Paradise Inhabited by Devils: A Paradise Inhabited by Devils. The Jesuits' Civilizing Mission in Early Modern Naples* (Aldershot: Ashgate, 2004), particularly chapter 3. Parker has applied this approach to Protestant missions in his 'Converting souls across cultural borders: Dutch Calvinism and early modern missionary enterprises', *Journal of Global History*, 8 (2013), pp.50–71. Tadhg Ó'hAnnracháin's *Catholic Europe, 1592–1648. Centre and Peripheries* (Oxford: Oxford University Press, 2015) is also vital for this shift, focusing on early modern Catholicism outside of its heartlands and underlining the varied timescale of and influences on efforts to renew Catholicism across Europe.

9   See, for example, Broggio, *Evangelizzare il mondo*.

10   See Tara Alberts, *Conflict and Conversion: Catholicism in Southeast Asia, 1500–1700* (Oxford: Oxford University Press, 2013) and Stuart B. Schwartz, *All Can Be Saved. Religious Tolerance and Salvation in the Iberian Atlantic World* (New Haven: Yale University Press, 2008). These questions are already being broached in works on Italy such as Biasori, 'Before the Inquisitor: A Thousand Ways of Being Lutheran'.

CONCLUSION   185

the privilege's effects were extraordinary, far exceeding those of other concessions to the Society and other religious and ecclesiastical groups. In effect, the
privilege gave a brand new religious order a power that could even exceed that
of the popes' own men, charged to fight what they saw as a perilous threat to
Christian civilisation. Moreover, whilst the Society enjoyed the privilege to absolve heresy, the Jesuits and their work to battle the most dangerous problem
of the day were almost entirely out of the popes' control.

As popes from Pius v onwards sought to solidify a more centralised ecclesiastical government, the privilege that had been granted to address the greatest
threat to the Church in the immediate aftermath of the Reformation came to
embody the Church's greatest anxieties at the close of sixteenth century. As
the story of a power that responded to both the everyday realities of human
and institutional deficiencies and to one of the greatest crises that the Church
has ever faced, the history of the Jesuits' privilege to absolve heresy is much
broader and more significant than a technical or chronological account of a
single papal concession. The history told here has traced the fluctuating status of the pastoral and institutional concerns that governed the direction of
the Catholic Church and large sections of European society at a time when
the continent was undergoing unprecedented religious, political and social
change. It demonstrates that the negotiation of these aims shaped not only the
Society but also the way that the Church and state responded to the splintering
of Christendom. In doing so, the story of the privilege supports and expands
crucial revisions to the history of the Jesuits and of early modern Catholicism
itself. It challenges previous emphases on obedience, control and hierarchy by
demonstrating that autonomy, flexibility and constant negotiation characterised the Society, the Church and their efforts to protect themselves and souls
across the globe during a period of profound religious change.

Bibliography

Archival Sources

Archivio dell'Archiginnasio, Bologna
B1866
B1887
Archivio della Congregazione per la Dottrina della Fede (ACDF), Rome
Decreta (copia) 1548-58
Decreta 1565-7
Decreta 1592-3
Stanza Storica D-4-a
Stanza Storica I-5-b
Stanza Storica M-3-g
Stanza Storica N-3-g
Stanza Storica R-2-m
Archivio della Penitenzieria Apostolica (APA), Rome
Penitenzieri minori 3
Archivum Romanum Societatis Iesu (ARSI), Rome
Cong. 20B
Epistolae Externorum 1
Epistolae Externorum 7 – I
Epistolae Generalium Italiae 61
Epistolae Generalium Italiae 63
Epistolae Generalium Italiae 66
Epistolae Generalium Italiae 67
Epistolae Generalium Italiae 68
Epistolae Generalium Rom. 1
Epistolae Italiae 107
Epistolae Italiae 122
Epistolae Italiae 134
Epistolae Italiae 135
Epistolae Italiae 136
Epistolae Italiae 139
Epistolae nostrorum 50
Epistolae nostrorum 86
Fond. Lauret.1
Franc. 1 – II,
Gal.92

Institutum 185-I

Institutum 187

Institutum 190

Institutum 194

Institutum 217

Institutum 222

Mediolanensis Historia 79

Mediolanensis Historia 98

Opera Nostorum 324-I and II

Rom. 122-I

Rom. 185

Rom. 222

Archivio Storico del Vicariato di Roma (ASVR), Rome

Atti della segreteria del cardinal vicario, t.77

Archivio di Stato di Genova (ASG), Genoa

Banco di San Giorgio – Cancellieri – Corsica litterarum – Sala 34 – 232

Banco di San Giorgio – Cancellieri – Corsica litterarum – Sala 34 – 593/1382

Banco di San Giorgio – Cancellieri – Corsica litterarum – Sala 34 – 607/2401

Banco di San Giorgio – Cancellieri – Sala 35 – 232

Banco di San Giorgio – Cancellieri – Sala 35 – 233

Archivio di Stato di Modena (ASM), Modena

Inquisizione, Busta 270

Archivio di Stato di Torino (AST), Turin

Lettere di particolari – P, Mazzo 58

Materie ecclesiastiche – Regolari diversi – Torino – Gesuiti

Monteferrato – Feudi per A e B, Mazzo 1

Regolari di qua da Monti, Mazzo 10

Archivio di Stato di Roma, Rome (ASR)

Miscellanea Famiglie Gesuiti, B180

Biblioteca Apostolica Vaticana (BAV), Vatican City

Barb. Lat. 5195

Barb. Lat. 1370

Ottob. Lat. 495

Urb. Lat. 1040

Vat. Lat. 14830

Biblioteca Reale di Torino (BRTO), Turin

Miscellanea patria 101

BIBLIOGRAPHY

189

Printed Primary Sources

Asorbo, Hieronymous, *Compendium Privilegiorum Fratrum Minorum et Aliorum Mendicantium, and Non Mendicantium, Ab Alphonso de Casarubios Hispano* (Venice: Haeredes Petri Ricciardi, 1609).

Bene, Tommasso del, *De officio S. inqvisitionis circa haeresim* (Lyon: sumptibus I.A. Huguetan, 1666).

Catena, Girolamo, and Vincenzo Accolti, *Vita del gloriosissimo Papa Pio quinto* (Rome: Stamperia de Vincenzo Accolti, 1588).

Clement VII, *Bulla Clementis VII in Cena Domini Lecta in Urbe Veteri Anno MDccviii in qua Urbis Direptores Perhorre.do Eterne Maledictio.is Anathemate nunc Primus Da.ati sunt* (Rome, 1528).

Giganti, Girolamo, *Tractatus de crimine laesae maiestatis insignis, et elegans: Cum Summaris, ac Indice materiarum locupletissimo* (Lyon: Giunta, 1557).

Hospinian, Rudolf, *Rodolphi Hospiniani Historia Jesuitica hoc est, de origine, regulis constitutionibus, privilegiis, incrementis, progressu and propagatione Ordinis Jesuitarum. Item de eorum dolis, fraudibus, imposturis, nefariis facinoribus, cruentis consiliis, falsa quoque seditiosa and sanguinolenta doctrina. Cum triplici indice capitum, auctorum, rerum item ac verborum memorabilium* (Zurich: Apud Joannem Rodolphum Wolphium, 1670).

Locati, Umberto, *Cronica dell' origine di Piacenza, gia Latinamente fatta per O. L., ed hora dal medesimo ridotta fedelmente nella volgare nostra favella* (Cremona: Vincenzo Conti, 1564).

Maffei, Giovanni Pietro, *De vita et moribvs Ignatii Loiolae, qvi Societatem Iesv fundauit, libri III. Auctore Ioanne Petro Maffeio, presbytero Societatis eiusdem* (Cologne: Maternum Cholinum, 1585).

Muzio, Girolamo, and Pietro Paolo Vergerio, *Le Vergeriane del Mutio Justinopolitano. Discorso se si convenga ragunar Concilio. Trattato della Comunione de'laici: and delle Mogli de'Cherici* (Venice: G. Giolito, 1550).

Orlandini, Niccolò and Francesco Sacchini, *Historia Societatis Iesu* (Rome; Cologne; Antwerp, 1615-1710), 5 vols.

Pantaleon, Heinricus, *Martyrum Historia: Hoc est, maximarum per Europam persecutionum ac sanctorum dei Martyrum caeterumque rerum insignium, in Ecclesia Christi postremis and periculosis his Temporibus gestorum, atque certo consilio per Regna et Nationes distributarum, Commentarij* (Basel: Nicolaum Brylingerum, 1563).

Paramo, Luiz de, *De Origine et Progressu Officii Sanctae Inquisitionis, eiusque dignitate and utilitate, de Romani Pontificis Potestate and Delegata Inquisitorum: Edicto fidei, and ordine iudiciario Sancti Officij, quaestiones decem. Libri tres* (Madrid: ex Typographia Regia apud Ioannem Flandrum, 1598).

Ribadeneira, Pedro de, *Vita Ignatii Loiolae, Libris Quinque Comprehensa* (Naples: Iosephum Cacchium, 1572).

Rorengo, Marc'Aurelio, *Memorie historiche dell' introduttione dell' heresie nelle valli di Lucerna, marchesato di Saluzzo e altre di Piemonte* (Turin: Gl'heredi di G.D. Tarino, 1649).

Tesauro, Carolo Antonio, *De Poenis Ecclesiasticis, Seu Canonicis. Latae Sententiae à Iure Communi, and Constitutionibus Apostolicis, Decretisq.; Sacrarum Congregationum* (Rome: Hermann Scheus, 1640).

Valero, Juan, *Differentiae inter utrumque forum iudiciale videlicet, et conscientiae; nondum hac nova luce donatae, et magna cum cura, studioque lucubratae, and concinnatae* (Venice: Apud Paulum Baleonium, 1645).

Vignate, Ambrosius de, *Elegans ac vtilis Tractatus de haeresi* (Rome: Ex typographia Georgii Ferrarii, 1581).

Edited Primary Sources

Albèri, Eugenio, *Relazioni degli ambasciatori Veneti al senato* (Florence: Tipografia all'insegna di Clio, 1839–63), 15 vols.

Aldama, Antonio M., *Constitutions of the Society of Jesus: The Formula of the Institute. Notes for a Commentary* (St. Louis: Institute of Jesuit Sources, 1990).

Bernardo Navagero and Daniele Santarelli (ed.), *La corrispondenza di Bernardo Navagero, ambasciatore veneziano a Roma (1555–1558)* (Rome: Aracne, 2011).

Bobadilla, Nicolás A. de, *Bobadillae Monumenta: Nicolai Alphonsi de Bobadilla sacerdotis e Societate Jesu gesta et scripta: ex autograph. aut archetypis potissimum deprompta.* (Rome: Institutum Historicum Societatis Iesu, 1970).

Broët, Pascase, *Epistolae PP. Paschasii Broëti, Claudii Jaji, Joannis Codurii et Simonis Roderici, Societatis Jesu: Ex Autographis Vel Originalibus Exemplis; Potissimum Depromptae* (Madrid: Typis Gabrielis Lopez del Horno, 1903).

Canaye, Philippe de and Robert Regnault (ed.), *Lettres et ambassade de Messire Philippe Canaye, seigneur de Fresne ... avec un sommaire de sa vie, et un récit particulier du procès criminel fait au maréchal de Biron, composé par M. de La Guesle* (Paris: E. Richer, 1647), 3 vols.

Canepa, Mario, 'La Bolla "In Coena Domini" del 1567 in un Memoriale Del Vicerè Spagnolo Di Sardegna', *Archivio Storico Sardo*, 29 (1967), pp.73–137.

Canisius, Peter, *Beati Petri Canisii, Societatis Iesu, Epistulae et Acta. Collegit et Adnotationibus Illustravit Otto Braunsberger* (Freiburg im Breisgau: Herder, 1896), 8 vols.

Dorigny, Jean, *Vita del P. Antonio Possevino. Della medesima Comagnia, ora tradotta nella volgare Italiana, ed illustra con varie note, e più lettere inedite, e parecchi Monumenti aggiunti al fine* (Venice: Remondini, 1759).

BIBLIOGRAPHY 191

Epistolae mixtae ex variis Europae locis ab anno 1537 ad 1556 scriptae nunc primum a patribus Societatis Jesu in lucem editae (Madrid: Monumenta historica Societatis Jesu, 1898–1901), 5 vols.

Firpo, Massimo and Dario Marcatto, *I processi inquisitoriali di Pietro Carnesecchi (1557–1567)* (Vatican City: Archivio Segreto Vaticano, 1998–2000), 2 vols.

Il Processo Inquisitoriale del Cardinal Giovanni Morone : Edizione Critica (Rome: Istituto storico italiano per l'età moderna e contemporanea, 1981–95), 6 vols.

Fontana, Bartolomeo, *Documenti Vaticani contro l'eresia Luterana in Italia* (Roma: R. Societá Romana di storia patria, 1892).

Fonzi, Fausto, *Nunziature di Savoia vol.1. (15 ottobre 1560–29 giugno 1573)* (Rome: Istituto Storico Italiano per l'età moderna e contemporanea, 1960).

Laínez, Diego, *Lainii Monumenta. Epistolae et acta Patris Jacobi Lainii ... ex autographis vel originalibus exemplis potissimum deprompta,* (Madrid: Typis G. Lopez del Horno, 1912–8), 8 vols.

Litterae quadrimestres ex universis praeter Indiam et Brasiliam locis in quibus aliqui de Societate Jesu versabantur Romam missae (Madrid: Rome, 1894–1932), 7 vols.

Loyola, Ignatius, *Monumenta Ignatiana: Ex autographis vel ex antiquioribus exemplis collecta. Series tertia: Sancti Ignatii de Loyola Constitutiones Societatis Jesu* (Rome: Monumenta Historica Soc. Iesu, 1934–8), 3 vols.

Loyola, Ignatius, *Monumenta Ignatiana: Ex autographis vel ex antiquioribus exemplis collecta. Series prima: Sancti Ignatii de Loyola Societatis Jesu Fundatoris Epistolae et Instructiones* (Rome: Institum historicum S. I., 1964–8), 12 vols.

Loyola, Ignatius and Cándido de Dalmases, and Dionysius Fernández Zapico (eds), *Monumenta Ignatiana. Series quarta: Scripta de S. Ignatio. Fontes narrativi de Sancto Ignatio de Loyola et de Societatis Iesu initiis* (Rome: Monumenta Historica Societatis Iesu, 1943–65), 4 vols.

Mutinelli, Fabio, *Storia arcana e aneddotica d'Italia, raccontata dai Veneti Ambasciatori* (Venice: Pietro Naratovich, 1855), 4 vols.

Nadal, Jerónimo, *Epistolae P. Hieronymi Nadal Societatis Jesu ab anno 1546 ad 1577* (Madrid: A. Avrial; Rome: Monumenta Historica Soc[ietatis] Iesu, 1898–1962), 5 vols.

Polanco, Juan Alfonso de, *Breve Directorium ad confessarii ac confitentis munus recte obeundum M. Ioanne Polanco theologo societatis Iesu auctore* (Antwerp: Ioannem Bellerum, 1575).

Polanco, Juan Alfonso de, *Polanci Complementa : Epistolae et Commentaria P. Joannis Alphonsi de Polanco e Societatis Jesu ; Addenda Caeteris Ejusdem Scriptis Dispersis in Monumentis ; Quibus Accedunt Nunnulla Coaeva, Aliorum Auctorum, Illis Conjunctissima.* (Madrid: Typis Gabrielis López de Horno, 1916–7), 2 vols.

Polanco, Juan Alfonso de and John Patrick Donnelly, *Year by Year with the Early Jesuits (1537–1556): Selections from the 'Chronicon' of Juan de Polanco, S.J.* (St. Louis: Institute of Jesuit Sources, 2004).

Ribadeneira, Pedro de, *Patris Petri de Ribadeneira, Societatis Jesu Sacerdotis: Confessiones, epistolae aliaque scripta inedita, ex autographis, antiquissimis apographis et regestis deprompta* (Madrid: Ex officina typographis 'La editorial ibérica', 1920–3), 2 vols.

Salmerón, Alfonso, *Epistolae P. Alphonsi Salmeronis, Societatis Jesu: Ex autographis vel originalibus exemplis potissimum depromptae a patribus ejusdem Societatis nunc primum editae* (Madrid: Typis Gabrielis Lopez del Horno, 1906–7), 2 vols.

Santoro, Giulio Antonio and G. Cugnoni (ed.), 'Vita del Card. Giulio Antonio Santori, detto il Card. di S. Severina, composta e scritta da lui medesimo. Autobiografia di Monsignor G. Antonio Santori, Cardinale di S. Severina', *Archivio della R. Società Romana di storia patria*, 12 (1889), pp.339–52.

Suarez, Francesco, *Opera omnia editio nova, a Carolo Berton, Cathedralis Ecclesiae Ambianensis vicario, iuxta editionem ventiam XXIII tomos in-f.o continentem, accurate recognita, Reverendissimo Ill. Domino Sergent, Episcopo Corsopitensi, ab editore dicata* (Paris: Ludovicum Vives, 1861).

Tomassetti A. (ed.), *Bullarum diplomatum et privilegiorum sanctorum Romanorum pontificum Taurinensis editio locupletior facta* (Turin: Seb. Franco, H. Fory and H. Dalmazzo, 1857–88), 25 vols.

Secondary Sources

Adorni-Braccesi, Simonetta, *'Una città infetta': la repubblica di Lucca nella crisi religiosa del Cinquecento* (Florence: Olschki, 1994).

Aglio, Stefano dall', Donald Weinstein (trans.), *The Duke's Assassin: Exile and Death of Lorenzino De'Medici* (New Haven: Yale University Press, 2015).

Aglio, Stefano dall', 'Voices under Trial. Inquisition, Abjuration, and Preachers' Orality in Sixteenth-Century Italy', *Renaissance Studies*, 31 (February 2017), pp. 25–42.

Åkerman, Susanna, *Queen Christina of Sweden : The Transformation of a Seventeenth-Century Philosophical Libertine* (Leiden: Brill, 1990).

Alfieri, Fernanda, and Claudio Ferlan (eds), *Avventure dell'obbedienza nella Compagnia di Gesù: teorie e prassi fra XVI e XIX secolo* (Bologna: Il Mulino, 2012).

Andretta, Stefano, Claudio Strinati, Alessandro Zuccari, and Gloria Fossi, *La storia dei giubilei: volume terzo 1600–1775* (Florence: BNL Edizioni, 2000).

Aron-Beller, Katherine, and Christopher F. Black. *The Roman Inquisition: Centre versus Peripheries,* (Leiden: Brill, 2018).

Astraín, Antonio, *Historia de La Compañia de Jesús En La Asistencia de España* (Madrid: Administración de Razón y Pe, 1902–1925), 7 vols.

Aubert, Alberto, *Paolo IV: politica, inquisizione e storiografia* (Florence: Le lettere, 1999).

BIBLIOGRAPHY

Bainton, Roland H., *Bernardino Ochino: esule e riformatore senese del cinquecento, 1487–1563* (Florence: G.C. Sansoni, 1980).

Baker-Bates, Piers, and Miles Pattenden (eds), *The Spanish Presence in Sixteenth-Century Italy: Images of Iberia* (Farnham: Ashgate, 2015).

Balsamo, Luigi, *Antonio Possevino S.I.: bibliografo della Controriforma e diffusione della sua opera in area anglicana* (Florence: Olschki, 2006).

Bamji, Alexandra, Geert H. Janssen, and Mary Laven, *The Ashgate Research Companion to the Counter-Reformation* (Farnham: Ashgate, 2013).

Beal, John P, James A Coriden, Thomas J. Green, *New Commentary on the Code of Canon Law* (New York: Paulist Press, 2000).

Benedict, Philip, Silvana Seidel Menchi, and Alain Tallon (eds.), *La Réforme en France et en Italie : Contacts, Comparaisons et Contrastes* (Rome: Ecole française de Rome, 2007).

Bernauer, James William and Robert A. Maryks (eds.), *'The Tragic Couple': Encounters between Jews and Jesuits* (Leiden: Brill, 2014).

Bertomeu Masiá, Ma José, *La Guerra Secreta de Carlos V Contra el Papa : La Cuestión de Parma y Piacenza en la Correspondencia del Cardenal Granvela : Edición, Estudio y Notas.* (Valencia: Universita de València, 2009).

Berton, Charles, and Jacques-Paul Migne. *Dictionnaire Des Cardinaux : Contenant Des Notions Générales Sur Le Cardinalat* (Paris: J.-P. Migne, 1857).

Biagi, Clemente, *Dizionario enciclopedico della teologia, della storia della chiesa, degli autori che hanno scritto intorno alla religione, dei concili, eresie, ordini religiosi ec.* (Florence: Giovanni Pagani, 1820).

Biasori, Lucio, 'Before the Inquisitor: A Thousand Ways of Being Lutheran' in Alberto Melloni (ed.), *Martin Luther: A Christian between Reforms and Modernity* (Berlin: De Gruyter, 2017), pp.509–26.

Black, Christopher F., *The Italian Inquistition* (London: Yale University Press, 2016).

Blouin, Francis X., *Vatican Archives. An Inventory and Guide to Historical Documents of the Holy See. Supplement #1. The Archives of the Congregation for the Doctrine of the Faith. Including the Archives of the Former Congregation for Forbidden Books* (Ann Arbor: Bentley Historical Library, 2003).

Boer, Wietse de, *The Conquest of the Soul : Confession, Discipline and Public Order in Counter-Reformation Milan* (Leiden: Brill, 2001).

Bonafin, Massimo, *Figure della memoria culturale. Tipologie, identità, personaggi testi e segni: atti del convegno (Macerata, 9–11 novembre 2011)* (Alessandria: Edizioni dell'Orso, 2013).

Bonora, Elena, *Giudicare i vescovi: la definizione dei poteri nella Chiesa postridentina* (Rome: Laterza, 2007).

Bonora, Elena, 'I Barnabiti Tra Storia dell'ordine e Storia della Chiesa' in Massimo Firpo (ed.), *Nunc Alia Tempora Alii Mores. Storici e Storia in Età Postridentina. Atti del*

Convegno Ointernazionale, Torino 24–27 Settembre 2003 (Florence: Olshki, 2005), pp.111–40.

Bonora, Elena, *I conflitti della Controriforma: sanità e obbedienza nell'esperienza religiosa dei primi barnabiti* (Florence: Casa Editrice Le Lettere, 1998).

Bonora, Elena, *Roma 1564: la congiura contro il papa* (Rome: Laterza, 2014).

Borromeo, Agostino, 'I Vescovi Italiani e l'applicazione del Concilio di Trento' in *I Tempi Del Concilio: Religione, Cultura e Società nell'Europa Tridentina*, (Rome: Bulzoni, 1997), pp.27–105.

Borromeo, Agostino, (ed.), *L'Inquisizione: atti del simposio internazionale, Città del Vaticano, 29–31 ottobre 1998* (Vatican City: Biblioteca Apostolica Vaticana, 2003).

Bossy, John, *Christianity in the West 1400–1700* (Oxford: Oxford University Press, 1985).

Bossy, John, 'The Social History of Confession in the Age of the Reformation', *Transactions of the Royal Historical Society*, 25 (1975), pp. 21–38.

Bouwsma, William J., *A Usable Past: Essays in European Cultural History* (Berkeley: University of California Press, 1990).

Bouwsma, William J., *Venice and the defense of republican liberty. Renaissance values in the age of the Counter Reformation* (Berkeley: University of California Press, 1968).

Braghi, Gianmarco, *L'Accademia degli Ortolani (1543–1545): eresia, stampa e cultura a Piacenza nel medio Cinquecento* (Piacenza: Edizioni L.I.R, 2011).

Brambilla, Elena, *Alle Origini del Sant'Uffizio : Penitenza, Confessione e Giustizia Spirituale dal Medioevo al 16. Secolo* (Bologna: Il Mulino, 2000).

Brambilla, Elena, 'Il <<foro Della Coscienza>>. La Confessione come Strumento di Delazione', *Società e Storia*, 81 (1998), pp. 591–608.

Broggio, Paolo, *Evangelizzare Il Mondo : Le Missioni della Compagnia di Gesù tra Europa e America (Secoli XVI-XVII)* (Rome: Carocci, 2004).

Broggio, Paolo, 'Le Congregazioni Romane e la Confessione dei Neofiti del Nuovo Mondo tra Facultates e Dubia: Reflessioni e Spunti di Indagine', *Mélanges de l'École Française de Rome – Italie et Méditerranée*, 121 (2009), pp. 173–97.

Broggio, Paolo, Francesca Cantù, Pierre-Antoine Fabre and Antonella Romano (eds), *I gesuiti ai tempi di Claudio Acquavia: Strategie Politiche e Religiose nel Mondo Moderno* (Rome: Aracne, 2004).

Caffiero, Marina, Franco Motta and Sabina Pavone, 'Identità Religiose e Identità Nazionali in Età Moderna'. *In Dimensioni e Problemi della Ricerca Storica*, 1 (2005), pp.7–93.

Calimani, Riccardo, *L'Inquisizione a Venezia: eretici e processi 1548–1674* (Milan: Mondadori, 2014).

Câmara, Luis Gonçalves da, Alexander Eaglestone and Joseph A Munitiz, *Remembering Iñigo: Glimpses of the Life of Saint Ignatius of Loyola ; the Memorials of Luis Gonçalves Da Câmara* (Leominster: Gracewing, 2005).

Cameron, Euan, *The Reformation of the Heretics: The Waldenses of the Alps, 1480–1580* (Oxford: Clarendon Press, 1986).

BIBLIOGRAPHY

Camos, Rosanna Gorris, 'Pia Ricevitrice Di Ogni Cristiano »: Poésie, exil et religion autour de Marguerite de France, Duchesse de Savoie' in Jean Balsamo and Chiara Lastraioli, *Chemins de l'exil Havres de Paix: Migrations d'hommes et d'idées au XVIe siècle; Actes du Colloque de Tours, 8–9 Novembre 2007* (Paris: Champion, 2010), pp.177–228.

Canosa, Romano, *Storia dell'Inquisizione in Italia dalla metà del cinquecento alla fine del settecento. Torino e Genova. Vol. III* (Rome: Sapere, 2002).

Cantimori, Delio, *Eretici italiani del Cinquecento: richerche storiche* (Florence: Sansoni, 1967).

Caponetto, Salvatore, *La riforma protestante nell'Italia del Cinquecento* (Turin: Claudiana, 1997).

Caravale, Giorgio, 'Ambrogio Catarino Politi e i Primi Gesuiti', *Rivista Storica Italiana*, 117 (2005), pp.80–109.

Caravale, Giorgio, *Beyond the Inquisition: Ambrogio Catarino Politi and the Origins of the Counter-Reformation* (Notre Dame: University of Notre Dame Press, 2017).

Caravale, Giorgio, *Sulle tracce dell'eresia: Ambrogio Catarino Politi (1484–1553)* (Florence: Olschki, 2007).

Casanova, Jose, and Thomas F. Banchoff, *The Jesuits and Globalization: Historical Legacies and Contemporary Challenges* (Washington, DC: Georgetown University Press, 2016).

Casaubon, Isaac and John Russell (ed.), *Ephemerides Isaaci Casauboni* (Oxford: Oxford University Press, 1850), 2 vols.

Castignoli, Piero, *Eresia e inquisizione a Piacenza nel Cinquecento* (Piacenza: Tip. Le. Co, 2008).

Catto, Michela, *La Compagnia Divisa : Il Dissenso nell'ordine Gesuitico tra '500 e '600* (Brescia: Morcelliana, 2009).

Catto, Michela, Guido Mongini, and Silvia Mostaccio (eds), *Evangelizzazione e globalizzazione: le missioni gesuitiche nell'età moderna tra storia e storiografia* (Roma: Società editrice Dante Alighieri, 2010).

Cantù, Cesare, *Gli Eretici d'Italia. Discorsi storici* (Turin: Unione Tipografico-Editrice, 1865), 2 vols.

Chabod, Federico, *Lo Stato e la vita religiosa a Milano nell'epoca di Carlo V* (Turin: Einaudi, 1971).

Chabod, Federico, *Per la storia religiosa dello Stato di Milano durante il dominio di Carlo V: note e documenti* (Rome: Istituto storico italiano per l'età moderna e contemporanea, 1962).

Chauvard, Jean-François, Andrea Merlotti and Maria Antonietta Visceglia (eds), *Casa Savoia e Curia romana dal Cinquecento al Risorgimento* (Rome: École Française de Rome, 2015).

Church, Frederic C., *The Italian Reformers, 1534–1564,* (New York: Octagon Books, 1974).

Civale, Gianclaudio, *Guerrieri di Cristo: inquisitori, gesuiti e soldati alla battaglia di Lepanto*. (Milano: Edizioni Unicopli, 2009).

Coffin, David, *Pirro Ligorio: The Renaissance Artist, Architect, and Antiquarian: With a Checklist of Drawings* (University Park: Pennsylvania State University Press, 2004).

Col, Andrea Del and Giovanna Paolin (eds), *L'Inquisizione Romana: Metodologia delle Fonti e Storia Istituzionale* (Trieste: Edizioni Università di Trieste, 2000).

Colombo, Emanuele, 'Gesuitomania. Studi Recenti Sulle Missioni Gesuitiche (1540–1773)' in Michela Catto, Guido Mongini and Silvia Mostaccio (eds), *Evangelizzazione e Globalizzazione. Le missioni gesuitiche nell'età moderna tra storia e storiografia* (Rome: Dante Alighieri, 2010), pp.31–59.

Colombo, Emanuele, 'The Watershed of Conversion: Antonio Possevino, New Christians and Jews' in James Bernauer and Robert A. Maryks (eds.), *The Tragic Couple. Encounters Between Jews and Jesuits* (Leiden: Brill, 2013), pp.25–42.

Comerford, Kathleen M. *Jesuit Foundations and Medici Power, 1532–1621* (Leiden: Brill, 2017).

Comerford, Kathleen M, and Hilmar Pabel, *Early Modern Catholicism Essays in Honour of John W* (Toronto: University of Toronto Press, 2016).

Corsi, Elisabetta, *Órdenes religiosas entre América y Asia: ideas para una historia misionera de los espacios coloniales* (México: El Colegio de México, 2008).

Cozzi, Gaetano, *Paolo Sarpi tra Venezia e l'Europa* (Turin: Einaudi, 1979).

Creagh, Thomas. 'The Promulgation of Pontifical Law', *The Catholic University Bulletin*, 15 (1909), pp.23–41.

Creasman, Allyson F., *Censorship and Civic Order in Reformation Germany, 1517–1648* (Farnham: Ashgate, 2012).

Croce, Benedetto, *Storia della eta barocca in Italia: pensiero, poesia e letteratura, vita morale* (Bari: Laterza, 1929).

Dall'Olio, Guido, *Eretici e inquisitori nella Bologna del Cinquecento* (Bologna: Istituto per la storia di Bologna, 1999).

Dandelet, Thomas James, and John A. Marino, *Spain in Italy : Politics, Society, and Religion 1500–1700* (Leiden: Brill, 2007).

Danieluk, Robert, 'Monumenta Historica Societatis Iesu – Uno Sguardo di Insieme sulla Collana', *Archivum Historicum Societatis Iesu*, 81 (2012), pp.249–89.

Del Col, Andrea, 'Alcune Osservazioni Sui Processi Inquisitoriali Come Fonti Storiche'. *Metodi e Ricerche*, 13 (1994), pp.85–105.

Del Col, Andrea, 'Le Strutture Territoriali e l'attività Dell'Inquisizione Romana' in Agostino Borromeo (ed.), *L'Inquisizione. Atti del Simposio Internazionale*, (Vatican City: Biblioteca Apostolica Vaticana, 2003), pp.345–80.

Del Col, Andrea, *L'inquisizione Nel Patriarcato e Diocesi Di Aquileia 1557–1559* (Trieste: Edizioni Università di Trieste, 1998).

BIBLIOGRAPHY 197

Del Col, Andrea, 'Organizzazione, Composizione e Giurisdizione Dei Tribunali Dell'Inquisizione Romana Nella Repubblica Di Venezia (1500–1550)', *Critica Storica*, 25 (1988), pp.244–94.

Del Col, Andrea, Giuliana Ancona, and Dario Visintin, *Religione, scritture e storiografia* (Montereale Valcellina: Circolo culturale Menocchio, 2013).

Del Col, Andrea, and Giovanna Paolin, *L'Inquisizione Romana in Italia Nell'età Moderna. Archivi, Problemi Di Metodo e Nuove Ricerche. Atti Del Seminario Internazionale Trieste, 18–20 Maggio 1988* (Rome: Ministero per i beni culturali e ambientali ufficio centrale per i beni archivistici, 1991).

Delph, Ronald K., Michelle Fontaine, and John Jeffries Martin, Heresy, *Culture, and Religion in Early Modern Italy: Contexts and Contestations* (Kirksville: Truman State University Press, 2006).

Delplace, Louis, *Synopsis Actorum S. Sedis in causa Societatis Jesu: 1540–1605* (Florence: Ex Typographia a SS. Conceptione, Raphael Ricci, 1887).

Delumeau, Jean, *L'aveu et le Pardon: Les Difficultés de la Confession, 13e-18e siècle* (Paris: Fayard, 1990).

DeSilva, Jennifer, *Episcopal Reform and Politics in Early Modern Europe* (Kirksville: Truman State University Press, 2012).

Deutscher, Thomas Brian, *Punishment and Penance: Two Phases in the History of the Bishop's Tribunal of Novara* (Toronto: University of Toronto Press, 2013).

Ditchfield, Simon, 'Decentering the Catholic Reformation. Papacy and Peoples in the Early Modern World', *Archive for Reformation History*, 101 (2010), pp.186–208.

Ditchfield, Simon, 'In Search of Local Knowledge: Rewriting Early Modern Italian Religious History', *Cristianesimo Nella Storia*, 19 (1998), pp.255–96.

Ditchfield, Simon, 'Innovation and its Limits. The Case of Italy ca.1512-ca.1572' in Philip Benedict, Silvana Seidel Menchi and Alain Tallon (eds), *La Réforme en France et en Italie* (Rome: École Française de Rome, 2007), pp.145–60.

Ditchfield, Simon, *Liturgy, Sanctity and History in Tridentine Italy: Pietro Maria Campi and the Preservation of the Particular* (Cambridge: Cambridge University Press, 2002).

Ditchfield, Simon, 'Of Missions and Models: The Jesuit Enterprise (1540–1773) Reassessed in Recent Literature', *Catholic Historical Review*, 93 (2007), pp.325–43.

Ditchfield, Simon, 'Umberto Locati O.P. (1503–1587): Inquisitore, Vescovo e Storico – Un Profilo Bio-Bibliografico', *Bolletino Storico Piacentino*, 84 (1989), pp.205–21.

Ditchfield, Simon, and Helen Smith (eds), *Conversions: Gender and Religious Change in Early Modern Europe* (Manchester: Manchester University Press, 2017).

Donnelly, John Patrick, 'Antonio Possevino, S.J., as Papal Mediator between Emperor Rudolf II and King Stephan Báthory', *Archivum Historicum Societatis Iesu*, 69 (2000), pp.3–56.

Eisenbichler, Konrad, Paul Frederick Grendler, and Nicholas Terpstra, *The Renaissance in the Streets, Schools, and Studies Essays in Honour of Paul F. Grendler* (Toronto: Centre for Reformation and Renaissance Studies, 2008).

El Alaoui, Youssef, *Jésuites, morisques et indiens: étude comparative des méthodes d'évangélisation de la Compagnie de Jésus d'après les traités de José de Acosta (1588) et d'Ignacio de las Casas (1605–1607)* (Paris: Honoré Champion, 2006).

Elm, Susanna, Éric Rebillard and Antonella Romano, *Orthodoxie, christianisme, histoire* (Rome: École française de Rome, 2000).

Émonet, Pierre, and Thomas M. McCoog, *Ignatius of Loyola: Legend and Reality* (Philadelphia: Saint Joseph's University Press, 2016).

Émonet, Pierre, *Ignatius of Loyola: Legend and Reality* (Philadelphia, PA: Saint Joseph's University Press, 2016).

Erba, Achille, *La chiesa sabauda tra cinque e seicento: ortodossia tridentina, gallicanismo savoiardo e assolutismo ducale (1580–1630)* (Rome: Herder, 1979).

'Eresia, Riforma e Inquisizione nella Repubblica di Venezia del Cinquecento', *Studi Storici Luigi Simeoni*, 57 (2007), pp.73–105.

Fabre, Pierre-Antoine, 'Ignace de Loyola En Procès d'orthodoxie (1525–1622)' in Susanna Elm, Éric Rebillard and Antonella Romano, *Orthodoxie, Christianisme, Histoire* (Rome: Ecole française de Rome, 2000), pp.101–24.

Fabre, Pierre-Antoine, and Antonella Romano, *Les Jésuites dans le monde moderne nouvelles approches*, (Paris: Albin Michel, 1999).

Fagiolo, Marcello and Maria Luisa Madonna (eds), *Sisto V: Vol.1 Roma e il Lazio* (Rome: Istituto Poligrafico e Zecca dello Stato, 1992).

Febvre, Lucien, *The Problem of Unbelief in the Sixteenth Century. The Religion of Rabelais* (London: Harvard University Press, 1982).

Felloni, Giuseppe, *La Casa di San Giorgio: il potere del credito: Atti del Convegno Genova, 11 e 12 novembre 2004* (Genoa: Nella sede della Società Ligure di Storia Patria, 2006).

Fenlon, Dermot, *Heresy and Obedience in Tridentine Italy: Cardinal Pole and the Counter Reformation* (Cambridge: Cambridge University Press, 1972).

Fernández-Santamaría, J. A., *Natural Law, Constitutionalism, Reason of State, and War. Counter-Reformation Spanish Political Thought* (New York: Peter Lang 2005).

Ferraris, Davide, 'I Rapporti della Compagnia di Gesù, <<incarnazione della Riforma>> con il Potere Religioso e Temporale a Genova', *Atti della Società Ligure di Storia Patria Nuova Serie LV*, 129 (2015), pp.75–106.

Fiorani, Luigi, Adriano Prosperi (eds), *Roma, la città del papa: vita civile e religiosa dal giubileo di Bonifacio VIII al giubileo di papa Wojtyla* (Turin: Einaudi, 2000).

Firpo, Massimo, *Inquisizione romana e Controriforma: studi sul cardinal Giovanni Morone (1509–1580) e il suo processo d'eresia* (Bologna: Il Mulino, 1992).

Firpo, Massimo, *Juan de Valdés and the Italian Reformation* (Burlington: Ashgate, 2015).

BIBLIOGRAPHY 199

Firpo, Massimo, *La presa di potere dell'Inquisizione romana 1550–1553* (Rome: Laterza, 2014).

Firpo, Massimo, (ed.) *Nunc Alia Tempora, Alii Mores: Storici e Storia in Età Postridentina ; Atti Del Convegno Internazionale, Torino, 24–27 Settembre 2003* (Florence: Olschki, 2005).

Firpo, Massimo, 'Tribunali Della Coscienza in età Tridentina'. *Studi Storici* 38 (1997), pp.355–82.

Firpo, Massimo, *Vittore Soranzo vescovo ed eretico: riforma della Chiesa e inquisizione nell'Italia del Cinquecento* (Rome: Laterza, 2006).

Firpo, Massimo, Gigliola Fragnito, and Susanna Peyronel Rambaldi (eds), *Atti Del Convegno Olimpia Morata: Cultura Umanistica e Riforma Protestante Tra Ferrara e l'Europa* (Ferrara: Panini, 2007).

Forster, Marc R., *The Counter-Reformation in the Villages: Religion and Reform in the Bishopric of Speyer, 1560–1720* (Ithaca: Cornell University Press, 1992).

Fosi, Irene, '<<Con Cuore Sincero e Con Fede Non Finta>>: Conversioni a Roma in Età Moderna Fra Controllo e Accoglienza' in Maria-Cristina Pitassi and Daniela Solfaroli Camillocci (eds), *Les Modes de la Conversion Confessionnelle à l'Époque Moderne. Autobiographie, Altérité et Construction Des Identités Religieuses* (Florence: Olshki, 2010), pp.215–33.

Fosi, Irene, 'Conversion and Autobiography: Telling Tales before the Roman Inquisition', *Journal of Early Modern History*, 17 (2013), pp.437–56.

Fosi, Irene, 'Conversions de Voyageurs Protestants dans la Rome Baroque' in Rainer Babel and Werner Paravicini (eds), *Grand Tour. Adeliges Reisen Und Europäische Kultur Vom 14. Bis Zum 18. Jahrhundert. Akten Der Internationalen Kolloquien in Der Villa Vigoni 1999 Und Im Deutschen Historischen Institut Paris 2000* (Otfildern: Jan Thorbecke Verlag, 2005), pp.569–78.

Fosi, Irene, *Convertire lo straniero: forestieri e Inquisizione a Roma in età moderna* (Rome: Viella, 2011).

Fosi, Irene ',Fasto e Decadenza Degli Anni Santi' in Luigi Fiorani and Adriano Prosperi (eds), *Roma, la città del papa: vita civile e religiosa dal giubileo di Bonifacio VIII al giubileo di papa Wojtyla* (Turin: Einaudi, 2000), pp.777–821.

Fosi, Irene, *Papal Justice: Subjects and Courts in the Papal State, 1500–1750* (Washington, D.C: Catholic University of America Press, 2011).

Fosi, Irene, 'Preparare Le Strade, Accogliere, Convertire nella Roma Barocca. Percorsi di Salvezza' in Andretta, Stefano, Claudio Strinati, Alessandro Zuccari, and Gloria Fossi, *La storia dei giubilei: volume terzo 1600–1775* (Florence: BNL Edizioni, 2000), pp.43–83.

Fosi, Irene, 'Roma e gli Ultramontani. Viaggi, conversioni, identità', *Quellen Und Forschungen Aus Italienischen Archiven Und Bibliotheken*, 81 (2001), pp.351–96.

Fosi, Irene, 'Roma Patria Comune? Foreigners in Early Modern Rome' in Jill Burke and Michael Bury (eds), *Art and Identity in Early Modern Rome* (Aldershot: Ashgate, 2008), pp.27–43.

Fosi, Irene, 'The Hospital as a Space of Conversion: Roman Examples from the Seventeenth Century' in Giuseppe Marcocci, Wietse de Boer, Aliocha Maldavsky and Ilaria Pavan (eds), *Space and Conversion in Global Perspective*, (Leiden: Brill, 2014), pp.154–74.

Fragnito, Gigliola, *La Bibbia al rogo: la censura ecclesiastica e i volgarizzamenti della Scrittura (1471–1605)* (Bologna: Mulino, 1997).

Fragnito, Gigliola, and Adrian Belton, *Church, Censorship and Culture in Early Modern Italy* (Cambridge: Cambridge University Press, 2011).

Frajese, Vittorio, *La Nascita dell'Indice. La Censura Ecclesiastica dal Rinascimento alla Controriforma* (Brescia: Editrice Morcelliana, 2006).

Francini, Marta Pieroni, 'Itinerari della Pietà negli anni della Controriforma', *Studi Romani*, 35 (1987), pp.296–320.

Fregona, Antonio, *I Frati Cappuccini nel Primo Secolo di Vita, 1525–1619 : Approccio Critico Alle Fonti Storiche, Giuridiche e Letterarie più Importanti* (Padua: Messaggero, 2006).

Friedrich, Markus, 'Circulating and Compiling the Litterae Annuae: Towards a History of the Jesuit System of Communication', *Archivum Historicum Societatis Iesu*, 76 (2008), pp.1–39.

Friedrich, Markus, 'Government and Information Management in Early Modern Europe. The Case of the Society of Jesus (1540–1773)', *Journal of Early Modern History*, 12 (2008), pp. 539–63.

Friedrich, Markus, 'Ignatius's Governing and Administrating the Society of Jesus' in Robert Maryks (ed.), *A Companion to Ignatius of Loyola. Life, Writings, Spirituality, Influence* (Leiden: Brill, 2014), pp.123–40.

Gamberini, Andrea (ed.) *A Companion to Late Medieval and Early Modern Milan: The Distinctive Features of an Italian State* (Leiden: Brill, 2014).

Garcia-Villoslada, Ricardo, *Storia del Collegio Romano dal suo inizio (1551) alla soppressione della Compagnia di Gesú (1773) di Riccardo G. Villoslada* (Rome: Apud Aedes Universitatis Gregorianae, 1954).

Gattoni da Camogli, Maurizio, *Pio V e La Politica Iberica Dello Stato Pontificio (1566–1572)* (Rome: Studium, 2006).

Gay, Jean Pascal, 'The Trials that Should Have Been. The Question of Judicial Jurisdiction over French Bishops in the Seventeenth Century and the Self-Narration of the Roman Inquisition' in Jennifer Mara DeSilva (ed.), *Episcopal Reform and Politics in Early Modern Europe* (Kirksville: Truman State University Press, 2012), pp.194–214.

Giannini, Massimo Carlo, *Papacy, Religious Orders and International Politics in the Sixteenth and Seventeenth Centuries* (Rome: Viella, 2013).

BIBLIOGRAPHY

Giard, Luce, 'Le devoir d'intelligence, ou L'insertion des jésuites dans le monde du savoir' in Giard (ed.), *Jésuites à la Renaissance : système éducatif et production du savoir* (Paris: Press universitaires de France, 1995).

Gleason, Elisabeth G., *Gasparo Contarini: Venice, Rome, and Reform* (Berkeley: University of California Press, 1993).

Gleason, Elisabeth G. 'Who Was the First Counter-Reformation Pope?', *Catholic Historical Review*, 81 (1995), pp.179–84.

Godman, Peter, *The Saint as Censor: Robert Bellarmine between Inquisition and Index* (Leiden: Brill, 2000).

Gorski, Philip S., *Disciplinary Revolution Calvinism and the Rise of the State in Early Modern Europe* (Chicago: University of Chicago Press, 2003).

Graziani, Antoine-Marie, 'Ruptures et Continuites Dans La Politique de Saint-Georges En Corse (1453–1562)' in *La Casa Di San Giorgio: Il Potere Del Credito. Atti Del Convegno, Genova, 11 e 12 Novembre 2004*, (Genoa: Società Ligure di Storia Patria, 2006), pp.75–90.

Greengrass, Mark, *Christendom Destroyed: Europe 1517–1648* (London: Penguin Books, 2015).

Grell, Ole Peter, and Bob Scribner, *Tolerance and Intolerance in the European Reformation* (Cambridge: Cambridge University Press, 1996).

Grendler, Paul F., 'Jesuit Schools in Europe. A Historiographical Essay', *Journal of Jesuit Studies*, 1 (2014), pp.7–25.

Grendler, Paul F. 'Laínez and the Schools in Europe' in *Diego Laínez (1512–1565) and his Generalate. Jesuit with Jewish Roots, Close Confidant of Ignatius Loyola, Preeminent Theologian of the Council of Trent* (Rome: Institutum Historicum Societas Iesu, 2015), pp.649–78.

Grendler, Paul F. *The Jesuits and Italian Universities, 1548–1773* (Washington D.C.: Catholic University of America Press, 2017).

Grendler, Paul F. *The Roman Inquisition and the Venetian Press, 1540–1605 / Paul F. Grendler* (Princeton: Princeton University Press, 1977).

Griffiths, Christina L., 'Confessional Conflict and "Turkish" Tolerance? Philippe Canaye, Sieur de Fresnes, Huguenot and Catholic Convert' in *The Huguenots: France, Exile and Diaspora* (Brighton: Sussex Academic Press, 2013), pp.36–45.

Grosso, M., and M.F. Mellano, *La Controriforma nella Arcidiocesi di Torino (1558–1610)* (Rome: Tipografia Poliglotta Vaticana, 1957), 3 vols.

Guasco, Maurilio, and Angelo Torre, *Pio V nella società e nella politica del suo tempo* (Bologna: Il Mulino, 2005).

Guerra, Alessandro, *Un Generale fra le milizie del papa: La vita di Claudio Acquaviva scritta da Francesco Sacchini della Compagnia di Gesù* (Milan: F. Angeli, 2001).

Guidetti, Armando, 'Silvestro Landini e Paolo Segneri Gesuiti per la pace nella Repubblica di Genova' in *Gesuiti fra impegno religioso e potere politico nella Repubblica di*

Genova. Atti del Convegno Internazionale di Studi sotto l'Alto patronato del Presidente della Repubblica (Genoa: Associazione Amici della Biblioteca Franzoniana, 1992).

Haliczer, Stephen, *Inquisition and Society in Early Modern Europe* (London: Croom Helm, 1987).

Haliczer, Stephen, *Sexuality in the Confessional: A Sacrament Profaned* (Oxford: Oxford University Press, 1996).

Hardy, N. J. S., *Criticism and Confession: The Bible in the Seventeenth Century Republic of Letters* (Oxford: Oxford University Press, 2017).

Helmholz, R. H., *The Spirit of Classical Canon Law* (London: The University of Georgia Press, 2010).

Henningsen, Gustav, John A Tedeschi and Charles Amiel, *The Inquisition in Early Modern Europe: Studies on Sources and Methods* (Dekalb: Northern Illinois University Press, 1986).

Hernán, A. García, 'La Asistencia Religiosa En La Armada de Lepanto', *Anthologica Annua*, 43 (1996), pp.213–63.

Hilmar, John W, M. Pabel, and Kathleen M. Comerford, *Early Modern Catholicism: Essays in Honour of John W. O'Malley, S.J.* (Toronto: University of Toronto Press, 2001).

Hinnebusch, William A., *The History of the Dominican Order* (New York: Alba House, 1973).

Höpfl, Harro, *Jesuit Political Thought: The Society of Jesus and the State, c. 1540–1630* (Cambridge: Cambridge University Press, 2008).

Hsia, R. Po-chia., *A Jesuit in the Forbidden City: Matteo Ricci 1552–1610* (Oxford: Oxford University Press, 2012).

Hsia, R. Po-chia., *Social Discipline in the Reformation: Central Europe 1550–1750* (London: Routledge, 1992).

Hübner, Alexander von, and Filippo Gattari, *Sisto Quinto dietro la scorta delle corrispondenze diplomatiche inedite tratte dagli archivi di stato del Vaticano, di Simancas, di Venezia, di Parigi, di Vienna e di Firenze* (Rome: Tipografia dei Lincei, 1887).

Hudon, William V., *Marcello Cervini and Ecclesiastical Government in Tridentine Italy* (Dekalb: Northern Illinois University Press, 1992).

Hudon, William V., 'The Papacy in the Age of Reform, 1513–1644' in *Early Modern Catholicism, Essays in Honour of John O'Malley* (Toronto: University of Toronto Press, 2001), pp.46–66.

Imbruglia, Girolamo, 'Ideali Di Civilizzazione: La Compagnia Di Gesù e Le Missioni (1550–1600)' in *Il Nuovo Mondo Nella Coscienza Italiana e Tedesca Del Cinquecento* (Bologna: Il Mulino, 1992), pp.287–308.

Longo, Carlo, *Praedicatores, Inquisitores. III. I Domenicani e l'Inquisizione Romana: Atti del III Seminario Internazionale su 'I Domenicani e l'Inquisizione', 15–18 Febbraio 2006, Roma* (Rome: Istituto storico domenicano, 2008).

BIBLIOGRAPHY

Iserloh, Erwin, Joseph Glazik, and Hubert Jedin (eds), *Reformation and Counter Reformation* (New York: Crossroad, 1990).

Jalla, Giovanni, *Storia della riforma in Piemonte. 1* (Turin: Claudiana, 1982).

Jedin, Hubert and Ernest Graf (trans.), *A History of the Council of Trent* (London: T. Nelson and Sons, 1957–61) 2 vols.

Jenkins Blaisdell, Charmarie, 'Politics and Heresy in Ferrara, 1534–1559', *The Sixteenth Century Journal*, 6 (April 1975), pp.67–93.

Jobe, Patricia, 'Inquisitorial Manuscripts in the Biblioteca Apostolica Vaticana: A Preliminary Handlist' in *The Inquisition in Early Modern Europe: Studies on Sources and Methods* (Dekalb: Northern Illinois University Press, 1986), pp.13–32.

Kainulainen, Jaska, *Paolo Sarpi: A Servant of God an State* (Leiden: Brill, 2014).

Kamen, Henry, *The Spanish Inquisition a Historical Revision* (London: Yale University Press, 2014).

Laven, Mary, 'Encountering the Counter-Reformation', *Renaissance Quarterly*, 59 (2006), pp.706–20.

Laven, Mary, *Mission to China : Matteo Ricci and the Jesuit Encounter with the East* (London: Faber, 2012).

Lavenia, Vincenzo, 'Giudici, Eretici, Infedeli. Per Una Storia Dell'inquisizione Nella Marca Nella Prima Età Moderna', *Giornale Di Storia*, 6 (2011), pp.1–38.

Lavenia, Vincenzo, 'Il Tribunale Innominato. Appunti sull'immaginario dell'Inquisizione Romana' in *Religione, Scritture e Storiografia: Omaggio ad Andrea del Col* (Montereale Valcellina: Circolo culturale Menocchio, 2013), pp.289–314.

Lavenia, Vincenzo, *L'infamia e il perdono : Tributi, pene e confessione nella teologia morale della prima età moderna* (Bologna: Il Mulino, 2004).

Lavenia, Vincenzo, 'L'Inquisizione del Duca. I Domenicani e il Sant'Uffizio in Piemonte nella prima età moderna' in *I Domenicani e l'Inquisizione Romana* (Rome: Istituto Storico Domenicano, 2008), pp.415–76.

Lavenia, Vincenzo, 'L'Inqusizione negli stati sabaudi: Roma, Torino e la politica religiosa' in Jean-François Chauvard, Andrea Merlotti and Maria Antonietta (eds), *Casa Savoia e curia romana dal Cinquecento al Risorgimento* (Rome: École française de Rome, 2015), pp.113–28.

Lavenia, Vincenzo, 'Miracoli e Memoria. I Gesuiti a Loreto nelle storie della Compagnia (sec. XVI-XVII)' in *Figure della Memoria culturale. Tipologie, identità, personaggi, Testi e Segni*, 22 (2013), pp.331–48.

Lavenia, Vincenzo, 'Un Inquisitore e i Valdesi Di Calabria. Valerio Malvicini' in *Valdismo Mediterraneo. Tra Centro e Periferia, sulla Storia Moderna dei Valdesi di Calabria* (Salerno: ViValiber, 2013), pp.105–22.

Lea, Henry Charles, *A History of Auricular Confession and Indulgences in the Latin Church* (New York: Greenwood Press, 1968), 3 vols.

Lea, Henry Charles, *A History of the Inquisition of Spain* (New York: Macmillan, 1906), 4 vols.

Lea, Henry Charles, *A History of the Inquisition of the Middle Ages* (New York: Macmillan, 1922), 3 vols.

Lea, Henry Charles, *The Inquisition in the Spanish Dependencies: Sicily, Naples, Sardinia, Milan, the Canaries, Mexico, Peru, New Granada* (Cambridge: Cambridge University Press, 2010).

Lukács, Ladislaus, 'De Origine Collegiorum Externorum Deque Controversiis circa Eorum Paupertatem Obortis 1539–1608', *Archivum Historicum Societatis Iesu*, 29 (1960), pp.189–245.

Luongo, Carlo. *Silvestro Landini e le 'nostre Indie'* (Florence: Atheneum, 2008).

Luria, Keith P., 'Popular Catholicism' in *Early Modern Catholicism. Essays in Honour of John O'Malley* (Toronto: Toronto University Press, 2001), pp.114–30.

Luria, Keith P., *Sacred Boundaries: Religious Coexistence and Conflict in Early-Modern France* (Washington, D.C: Catholic University of America Press, 2005).

Luzzatto, Sergio, Gabriele Pedullà, Amedeo de Vincentiis, Erminia Irace, and Domenico Scarpa, (eds) *Atlante della Letteratura Italiana* (Turin: Einaudi, 2010).

MacCulloch, Diarmaid, *Reformation: Europe's House Divided, 1490–1700* (London: Penguin, 2004).

Mancia, Maria Cristofari, 'Documenti Gesuitici Reperiti nell'archivio di Stato Di Roma 1561–70'. *Archivum Historicum Societatis Iesu*, 35 (1966), pp.79–131.

Marcello del Piazzo, and Candido de Dalmases, 'Il Processo sull'ortodossia di S.Ignazio e dei suoi Compagni svoltosi a Roma nel 1538. Nuovi documenti', *Archivum Historicum Societatis Iesu*, 89 (1966), pp.133–40.

Marchetti, Valerio, *Gruppi ereticali senesi del cinquecento* (Florence: Nuova Italia, 1975).

Marcocci, Giuseppe (ed.), *Space and Conversion in Global Perspective* (Leiden: Brill, 2015).

Marshall, Peter, *1517: Martin Luther and the Invention of the Reformation* (New York: Oxford University Press, 2017).

Martin, A. Lynn, *Henry III and the Jesuit Politicians* (Geneva: Droz, 1973).

Martin, John Jeffries, *Venice's Hidden Enemies: Italian Heretics in a Renaissance City* (Baltimore: Johns Hopkins University Press, 2004).

Maryks, Robert A., *A Companion to Ignatius of Loyola : Life, Writings, Spirituality, Influence* (Leiden: Brill, 2014).

Maryks, Robert A., *Jesuit Order As a Synagogue of Jews : Jesuits of Jewish Ancestry and Purity-of-Blood Laws in the Early Society of Jesus* (Leiden: Brill, 2009).

Maryks, Robert A., *Jesuit Survival and Restoration: A Global History, 1773–1900* (Leiden: Brill, 2015).

Maryks, Robert A., *Exploring Jesuit Distinctiveness: Interdisciplinary Perspectives on Ways of Proceeding within the Society of Jesus* (Leiden: Brill, 2016).

BIBLIOGRAPHY

Maryks, Robert A., *Saint Cicero and the Jesuits: The Influence of the Liberal Arts on the Adoption of Moral Probabalism* (Aldershot: Ashgate, 2008).

Maryks, Robert A., (ed.), *The Boston College Jesuit Bibliography: The New Sommervogel Online (NSO)*, http://bibliographies.brillonline.com/browse/nso.

Mayer, Thomas F., *The Roman Inquisition on the Stage of Italy. 1590–1640*, (Philadelphia.: University of Pennsylvania Press, 2014).

Mayer, Thomas F., *The Roman Inquisition: A Papal Bureaucracy and Its Laws in the Age of Galileo* (Philadelphia: University of Pennsylvania Press, 2012).

Mazur, Peter, *Conversion to Catholicism in early modern Italy* (New York: Routledge, Taylor and Francis Group, 2016).

Mazur, Peter, *The New Christians of Spanish Naples, 1528–1671: A Fragile Elite.* (New York: Palgrave Macmillan, 2013).

Mazzone, Umberto, *Governare lo Stato e curare le anime: La chiesa e Bologna dal quattrocento alla Rivoluzione francese* (Limena: Libreriauniversitaria.it, 2012).

McCoog, Thomas, *The Mercurian Project: Forming Jesuit Culture, 1573–1580* (Rome: Institutum Historicum Societatis Iesu, 2004).

McCoog, Thomas, *The Society of Jesus in Ireland, Scotland, and England, 1589–97: building the faith of Saint Peter upon the King of Spain's monarchy* (Burlington: Ashgate, 2011).

McCoog, Thomas, *The Society of Jesus in Ireland, Scotland, and England, 1598–1606: Lest Our Lamp Be Entirely Extinguished* (Leiden: Brill, 2017).

McShea, Bronwen, 'Cultivating Empire Through Print: The Jesuit Strategy for New France and the Parisian "Relations" of 1632 to 1673' (PhD Dissertation, University of Yale, 2011).

McShea, Bronwen, 'Jesuit Missionary Perspectives and Strategies Across the Early Modern Globe: Introduction', *Journal of Jesuit Studies*, 1 (2014), pp.171–76.

Melloni, Alberto, *Martin Luther: A Christian between Reforms and Modernity* (Berlin: De Gruyter, 2017).

Michelson, Emily, 'Luigi Lippomano, His Vicars, and the Reform of Verona from the Pulpit', *Church History*, 78 (September 2009), pp.584–605.

Michelson, Emily, *The Pulpit and the Press in Reformation Italy* (London: Harvard University Press, 2013).

Milstein, Joanna, *The Gondi Family: Strategy and Survival in Late Sixteenth-Century France* (London: Routledge, 2016).

Mola di Nomaglio, Gustavo, *Feudi e Nobiltà negli Stati dei Savoia: Materiali, Spunti, Spigolature Bibliografiche per una Storia, con la Cronologia Feudale delle Valli di Lanzo* (Turin: Società storica delle Valli di Lanzo, 2006).

Molinari, Franco, *Il cardinale teatino beato Paolo Burali e la riforma tridentina a Piacenza: 1568–1576* (Rome: Apud aedes Universitatis gregorianae, 1957).

Mongini, Guido, <<*Ad Christi Similitudinem*>>: *Ignazio Di Loyola e i Primi Gesuiti tra Eresia e Ortodossia: Studi sulle origini della Compagnia di Gesù* (Alessandria: Edizioni dell'Orso, 2011).

Monti, Alessandro, *La Compagnia di Gesù nel Territorio della Provincia Torinese. Memorie storiche* (Chieri: Stabilimento Tipografico M. Ghirardi, 1914–20), 5 vols.

Mostaccio, Silvia, 'A Conscious Ambiguity: The Jesuits Viewed in Comparative Perspective in Light of Some Recent Italian Literature', *Journal of Early Modern History*, 12 (2008), pp.410–41.

Mostaccio, Silvia, 'Codificare l'obbedienza. Le Fonti Normative di Gesuiti, Oratoriani e Cappuccini a Fine Cinquecento', *Dimensioni e Problemi della Ricerca Storica*, 1 (2005), pp.49–60.

Mostaccio, Silvia, *Early Modern Jesuits between Obedience and Conscience during the Generalate of Claudio Acquaviva (1581–1615)* (Farnham: Ashgate, 2014).

Mostaccio, Silvia, ' "Perinde Ac Si Cadaver Essent". Les Jésuites Dans Une Perspective Comparative: La Tension Constitutive Entre l'obéissance et le "representar" dans Les Sources Normatives des Réguliers'. *Revue d'Histoire Ecclésiastique*, 105 (2010), pp. 44–73.

Motta, Franco (ed.), *Annali di Storia dell'Esegesi*, 19 (2002).

Mozzarelli, Cesare, *Studi in memoria di Cesare Mozzarelli. Storia. Ricerche* (Milan: VandP, 2008).

Mozzarelli, Cesare, and Danilo Zardin (eds.), *I Tempi del Concilio: Religione, Cultura e Società nell'Europa Tridentina* (Rome: Bulzoni, 1997).

Muir, Edward, *Ritual in Early Modern Europe* (Cambridge: Cambridge University Press, 2005).

Mund, Stéphane, 'La Mission Diplomatique du Père Antonio Possevino (S.J.) Chez Ivan le Terrible en 1581–1582 et les Premiers Écrits Jésuites sur la Russie Moscovite à la fin du xvie siècle', *Cahiers Du Monde Russe*, 45 (2004), pp.407–40.

Munitiz, Joseph A., 'Communicating Channels: Letters to Reveal and to Govern', *The Way Supplement*, 70 (1991), pp.64–75.

Murner, Walter and Matthäus Meyer, *Die Pönitentiarie-Formularsammlung Des Walter Murner von Strassburg : Beitrag Zur Geschichte Und Diplomatik Der Päpstlichen Pönitentiarie Im 14. Jahrhundert* (Freiburg: Universitätsverlag, 1979).

Murphy, Paul, ' "Your Indies": The Jesuit Mission at the Santa Casa di Loreto in the Sixteenth Century' in *The Renaissance in the Streets, Schools and Studies: Essays in Honour of Paul F. Grendler*, (Toronto: Centre for Reformation and Renaissance Studies, 2008), pp.210–31.

Myers, W. David. *Poor, Sinning Folk: Confession and Conscience in Counter-Reformation Germany* (London: Cornell University Press, 1996).

Nelson, Eric, *The Jesuits and the Monarchy: Catholic Reform and Political Authority in France (1590–1615)* (Aldershot: Ashgate, 2005).

BIBLIOGRAPHY

Nexon, Daniel H, *The Struggle for Power in Early Modern Europe: Religious Conflict, Dynastic Empires, and International Change* (Princeton: Princeton University Press, 2009).

Noto, Maria Anna, *Viva la Chiesa, mora il tiranno: il sovrano, la legge, la comunità e i ribelli: Benevento 1566* (Naples: Guida, 2010).

O'Banion, Patrick J., *The Sacrament of Penance and Religious Life in Golden Age Spain* (University Park: Pennsylvania State University Press, 2013).

Oberholzer, Paul, *Diego Laínez (1512–1565) and His Generalate: Jesuit with Jewish Roots, Close Confidant of Ignatius of Loyola, Preeminent Theologian of the Council of Trent* (Rome: Institutum Historicum Societas Iesu, 2015).

Ó'hAnnracháin, Tadhg, *Catholic Europe, 1592–1648: Centre and Peripheries* (Oxford: Oxford University Press, 2015).

O'Malley, John W., 'Mission and the Early Jesuits', *The Way Supplement*, 79 (1994), pp.3–10.

O'Malley, John W. *Saints or Devils Incarnate? Studies in Jesuit History* (Leiden: Brill, 2013).

O'Malley, John W. *The First Jesuits* (Cambridge: Harvard University Press, 1993).

O'Malley, John W. 'The Fourth Vow in Its Historical Context: A Historical Study', *Studies in the Spirituality of the Jesuits*, 15 (1983), pp.1–43.

O'Malley, John W. *The Jesuits and the Popes: A Historical Sketch of Their Relationship* (Philadelphia: Saint Josephs University Press, 2016).

O'Malley, John W. *Trent and All That: Renaming Catholicism in the Early Modern Era* (London: Harvard University Press, 2000).

O'Malley, John W. *Trent: What Happened at the Council* (Cambridge: Harvard University Press, 2013).

O'Malley, John W, Gauvin A Bailey, and Giovanni Sale (eds), *The Jesuits and the Arts, 1540–1773* (Philadelphia: Saint Joseph's University Press, 2005).

O'Malley, John W, Gauvin Alexander Bailey, Steven Harris, and Thomas Frank Kennedy (eds), *The Jesuits II: Cultures, Sciences, and the Arts, 1540–1773*, (Toronto: University of Toronto Press, 2006).

Orlandi, Giuseppe, 'La Missione Popolare in Età Moderna' in *Storia dell'Italia Religiosa* (Rome: Laterza, 1994), pp.419–52.

Padberg, John W., Martin D. O'Keefe, and John L. McCarthy, *For Matters of Greater Moment: The First Thirty Jesuit General Congregations: A Brief History and a Translation of the Decrees* (St. Louis: Institute of Jesuit Sources, 1994).

Paolin, Giovanna, 'Gli Ordini Religiosi e l'Inquisizione: Analisi di un Rapporto' in *L'Inquisizione Romana: Metodologia Delle Fonti e Storia Istituzionale: Atti Del Seminario Internazionale, Montereale Valcellina, 23 e 24 Settembre 1999* (Trieste: Edizioni Università di Trieste, 2000), pp.169–85.

Pate, Dennis Edmond, 'Jerónimo Nadal & the Early Development of the Society of Jesus, 1545–1573' (PhD Dissertation, University of California Los Angeles, 1980).

Pattenden, Miles, *Electing the Pope in Early Modern Italy, 1450–1700* (Oxford: Oxford University Press, 2017).

Pattenden, Miles, *Pius V and the Fall of the Carafa: Nepotism and Papal Authority in Counter-Reformation Rome* (Oxford: Oxford University Press, 2013.

Parente, Fausto, 'The Index, the Holy Office, the Condemnation of the Talmud and Publication of Clement VIII's Index' in *Church, Censorship and Culture in Early Modern Italy* (Cambridge: Cambridge University Press, 2001), pp.163–93.

Parente, Ulderico, 'Note sull'attività Missionaria di Nicolás Bobadilla nel Mezzogiorno d'Italia Prima del Concilio di Trento (1540–1541)', *Rivista Storica Italiana*, 117 (2005), pp.64–79.

Parker, Charles H., 'Converting Souls across Cultural Borders: Dutch Calvinism and Early Modern Missionary Enterprises', *Journal of Global History*, 8 (2013), pp.50–71.

Parker, Charles H. 'The Reformation in Global Perspective', *History Compass*, 12 (2014), pp.1–11.

Parker, Geoffrey, *Imprudent King: A New Life of Philip II* (New Haven: Yale University Press, 2014).

Pascal, A., 'La Lotta Contro La Riforma in Piemonte al Tempo di Emanuele Filiberto, Studiata nelle Relazioni Diplomatiche tra la Corte Sabauda e la Santa Sede (1559–1580)', *Bulletin de La Societé d'Histoire Vaudoise*, 53 (1929), pp.5–88.

Pastor, Ludwig von. *History of the Popes: From the Close of the Middle Ages, Drawn from the Secret Archives of the Vatican and Other Original Sources* (London: 1891–53), 40 vols.

Pastore, Stefania, 'A Proposito di Matteo 18.15. Correctio Fraterna e Inquisitione nella Spagna del Cinquecento', *Rivista Storica Italiana*, 113 (2001), pp.352–63.

Pastore, Stefania, *Il Vangelo e La Spada : L'inquisizione di Castiglia e i suoi Critici (1460–1598)* (Roma: Edizioni di storia e letteratura, 2008).

Pate, Dennis Edmond, 'Jerónimo Nadal and the Early Development of the Society of Jesus, 1545–573' (PhD Dissertation, University of California Los Angeles, 1980).

Pattenden, Miles, *Electing the Pope in Early Modern Italy, 1450–1700* (Oxford: Oxford University Press, 2017).

Pattenden, Miles, *Pius IV and the Fall of the Carafa: Nepotism and Papal Authority in Counter-Reformation Rome* (Oxford: Oxford University Press, 2013).

Pavone, Sabina, 'A Saint under Trial. Ignatius of Loyola between Alcalá and Rome' in Robert Maryks (ed.), *A Companion to Ignatius of Loyola: life, writings, spirituality, influence* (Leiden: Brill, 2014), pp.45–65.

Pavone, Sabina, 'Dissentire per Sopravvivere. La Compagnia Di Gesù in Russia Alla Fine Del Settecento' in Fernanda Alfieri and Claudio Ferlan (eds), *Avventure dell'obbedienza nella Compagnia di Gesù: Teorie e Prassi fra XVI e XIX Secolo* (Bologna: Il Mulino, 2012).

Pavone, Sabina, *I Gesuiti: Dalle origini alla soppressione, 1540–1773* (Rome: Laterza, 2004).

BIBLIOGRAPHY 209

Pavone, Sabina, 'I Gesuiti in Italia (1548–1773)' in *Atlante della Letteratura Italiana. Dalla Controriforma alla Restaurazione. Volume 2: Dalla Controriforma alla Ristaurazione* (Turin: Einaudi, 2011), pp.359–73.

Pavone, Sabina, 'Preti Riformati e Riforma della Chiesa: I Gesuiti al Concilio di Trento', *Rivista Storica Italiana*, 117 (2005), pp.110–34.

Pavone, Sabina, *The Wily Jesuits and the Monita Secreta: The Forged Secret Instructions of the Jesuits: Myth and Reality* (Saint Louis: Institute of Jesuit Sources, 2005).

Pavone, Sabina and Franco Motta, 'Per Una Storia Comparative degli Ordini Religiosi', *Dimensioni e Problemi Della Ricerca Storica*, 1 (2005), pp.13–24.

Pennington, Kenneth, 'Ecclesiastical Liberty on the Eve of the Reformation', *Bulletin of Medieval Canon Law*, 185 (2016), pp.185–207.

Pettegree, Andrew, *Brand Luther: 1517, printing and the making of the Reformation* (New York: Penguin Books, 2016).

Pirri, Pietro, *L'Interdetto di Venezia del 1606 e i Gesuiti. Silloge di Documenti con Introduzione.* (Rome: Institutum Historicum Societatis Iesu, 1959).

Pitassi, Maria Cristina and Daniela Solfaroli Camillocci, *Les Modes de la Conversion Confessionnelle à l'époque Moderne: Autobiographie, Altérité et Construction des Identités Religieuses* (Florence: Olschki, 2010).

Pizzorusso, Giovanni, 'La Compagnia di Gesù, gli Ordini Regolari e il Processo di Affermazione della Giurisdizione Pontificia sulle Missioni tra fine XVI e inizio XVII: Tracce di una Ricerca' in Broggio, Paolo, Francesca Cantù, Pierre-Antoine Fabre and Antonella Romano (eds), *Strategie Politiche e Religiose nel Mondo Moderno: La Compagnia di Gesù ai Tempi di Claudio Acquaviva, 1581–1615: Atti delle Giornate di Studi* (Rome: École Française de Rome, 2002), pp.55–85.

Pizzorusso, Giovanni, 'Le Monde et/Ou l'Europe: La Congrégation de Propaganda Fide et la Politique Missionaire du Saint-Siège (XVIIe siècle)', *Institut d'Histoire de la Réformation. Bulletin Annuel*, 35 (April 2013), pp.29–48.

Polanco, Juan Alfonso de, and André Ravier, *La Compagnie de Jésus sous Le Gouvernement d'Ignace de Loyola (1541–1556) d'après les Chroniques de Juan-Alphonso de Polanco* (Paris: Desclée de Brouwer, 1991).

Pomplun, Trent, *Jesuit on the Roof of the World: Ippolito Desideri's Mission to Tibet* (Oxford: Oxford University Press, 2010).

Premoli, Orazio Maria, *La Storia dei Barnabiti nel Tardo Cinquecento* (Rome: Desclée, 1913).

Prodi, Paolo, 'I Concordati tra Savoia e Santa Sede. Linee interpretative generali' in Jean-François Chauvard, Andrea Merlotti and Maria Antonietta (eds), *Casa Savoia e curia romana dal Cinquecento al Risorgimento* (Rome: École française de Rome, 2015), pp.239–99.

Prodi, Paolo, 'Il Sacramento della Penitenza e la Restitutio' in Vincenzo Lavenia and Giovanna Paolin (eds), *Per Adriano Prosperi. Volume 3* (Pisa: Edizioni della Normale, 2011), pp.117–26.

Prodi, Paolo, *Il Sovrano Pontefice: Un Corpo e Due Anime: La monarchia papale nella prima età moderna* (Bologna: Il mulino, 2006).

Prodi, Paolo, *Una Storia della Giustizia: Dal Pluralismo dei fori al moderno dualismo tra coscienza e diritto* (Bologna: Il Mulino, 2000).

Prodi, Paolo and Carla Penuti, *Disciplina dell'anima, disciplina del corpo e disciplina della società tra medioevo ed età moderna. convegno internazionale di studio* (Bologna: Il Mulino, 1993).

Prosperi, Adriano, 'Anime in Trappola. Confessione e Censura Ecclesiastica all'Università di Pisa tra '500 e "600"', *Belfagor*, 54 (May 1999), pp.257–87.

Prosperi, Adriano, *Eresie e Devozioni: La Religione Italiana in Età Moderna* (Rome: Edizioni di storia e letteratura, 2010), 3 vols.

Prosperi, Adriano, *Il Nuovo Mondo nella Coscienza Italiana e Tedesca del Cinquecento* (Bologna: Il Mulino, 1992).

Prosperi, Adriano, 'L'inquisitore come confessore' in Carla Penuti and Paolo Prodi (eds), *Disciplina dell'anima, Disciplina del Corpo e Disciplina della Società tra Medioevo ed Età Moderna* (Bologna: Il Mulino, 1993), pp.187–224.

Prosperi, Adriano, 'L'Inquisizione nella Storia: I Caratteri Originali di una Controversia Secolare' in Prosperi (ed.) *Inquisizione Romana: Letture e Ricerche* (Rome: Storia e Letteratura, 2003), pp. 69–96.

Prosperi, Adriano, (ed.) *L'inquisizone Romana: Letture e Ricerche* (Rome: Edizioni di Storia e letteratura, 2003).

Prosperi, Adriano, 'L'inquisizione: Verso una Nuova Immagine?', *Critica Storica*, 25 (1988), pp.119–45.

Prosperi, Adriano, *Misericordie: Conversioni sotto il Patibolo tra Medioevo ed Età Moderna* (Pisa: Edizioni della Normale, 2008).

Prosperi, Adriano, ' "Otras Indias": Missionari della Controriforma tra Contadini e Selvaggi' in Prosperi (ed.), *America e Apocalipse e Altri Saggi* (Pisa: Istituti Editoriali e Poligrafici Internazionali, 1999), pp.65–87.

Prosperi, Adriano, *La vocazione. Storie di gesuiti tra Cinquecento e Seicento* (Turin: Einaudi, 2016).

Prosperi, Adriano, *Tribunali della Coscienza: Inquisitori, Confessori, Missionari* (Turin: Einaudi, 1996).

Prosperi, Adriano, Guido dall'Olio, Adelisa Malena and Pierroberto Scaramella (eds.) *Per Adriano Prosperi. Vol. I: La fede degli Italiani* (Pisa: Edizioni della Normale, 2011).

Prosperi, Adriano, Vincenzo Lavenia, and John Tedeschi (eds), *Dizionario Storico dell'inquisizione.* (Pisa: Edizioni della Normale, 2010), 4 vols.

Reiffenstuel, Anacleto, *Jus Canonicum Universum, Clara Methodo Juxta Titulos Quinque Librorum Decretalium. In Quaestiones Distributum, Solidisque Responsionibus, and Objectionum Solutionibus Dilucidatum* (Antwerp: Sumptibus Societatis, 1755).

BIBLIOGRAPHY

Ricci, Saverio, *Il Sommo Inquisitore: Giulio Antonio Santori Tra Autobiografia e Storia (1532–1602)* (Rome: Salerno Editrice, 2002).

Rinieri, Ilario, *I Vescovi della Corsica* (Livorno: Giusti, 1934).

Rittgers, Ronald K., *The Reformation of the Keys: Confession, Conscience and Authority in Sixteenth-Century Germany* (London: Harvard University Press, 2004).

Robinson, Adam Patrick, *The Career of Cardinal Giovanni Morone (1509–1580). Between Council and Inquisition* (Farnham: Ashgate, 2012).

Romeo, Giovanni, *L'inquisizione nell'Italia moderna* (Roma: Laterza, 2002).

Romeo, Giovanni, 'Note Sull'Inquisizione Romana Tra Il 1557 e Il 1561', *Rivista Di Storia e Letteratura Religiosa*, 36 (2000), pp.115–41.

Romeo, Giovanni, 'Pio V nelle fonti gesuite: le Epistolae generalium Italiae e le Epistolae Italiae' in Maurilio Guasco and Angelo Torre (eds), *Pio nella società e politica del suo tempo* (Bologna: Il Mulino, 2005).

Romeo, Giovanni, *Ricerche su confessione dei peccati e inquisizione nell'Italia del cinquecento* (Naples: La Città del sole, 1997).

Roper, Lyndal, *Martin Luther: Renegade and Prophet* (London: Vintage, 2017).

Rosso, C., 'Margherita di Valois e lo Stato sabaudo (1559–1574)' in Massimo Firpo, Gigliola Fragnito and Susanna Peyronel Rambaldi (eds), *Atti del convegno Olimpia Morata: cultura umanistica e Riforma protestante tra Ferrara e l'Europa* (Ferrara: Panini, 2007), pp.149–156.

Rothman, E. Natalie, *Brokering Empire: Trans-Imperial Subjects between Venice and Istanbul*, 2016).

Rotondò, Antonio, 'Esuli Italiani in Valtellina Nel Cinquecento', *Rivista Storica Italiana*, 88 (1976), pp.756–91.

Rotondò, Antonio, *Studi e ricerche di storia ereticale italiana del Cinquecento*. Torino: Giappichelli, 1974.

Rowland, Ingrid D., *Giordano Bruno: Philosopher/Heretic* (Chicago: The University of Chicago Press, 2009).

Russell, Camilla, *Giulia Gonzaga and the religious controversies of sixteenth-century Italy* (Turnhout: Brepols, 2006).

Saggioro, Alessandro, 'Storico, Testimonio e Parte. Pietro Tacchi Venturi: Storia, Storiografia e Storia Delle Religioni', *Atti Della Accademia Nazionale dei Lincei, Storiche e Filologiche, Rendiconti*, 13 (2002), pp.451–89.

Salonen, Kirsi, and Christian Krötzl, *The Roman Curia, the Apostolic Penitentiary and the partes in the Later Middle Ages* (Rome: Institutum Romanum Finlandiae, 2003).

Salvatore, Caponetto, *Benedetto da Mantova: Il beneficio di Cristo* (Florence: Sansoni, 1972).

Sangalli, Maurizio, *Per Il Cinquecento Religioso Italiano: Clero, Cultura, Società: Atti Del Convegno Internazionale di Studi, Siena, 27–30 Giugno 2001* (Rome: Edizioni dell'Ateneo, 2003).

Santarelli, Daniele, *Dinamiche interne della Congregazione del Sant'Uffizio dal 1542 al 1572. Il papato di Paolo IV nella crisi politico-religiosa del Cinquecento: le relazioni con la Repubblica di Venezia e l'atteggiamento nei confronti di Carlo V e Filippo II* (Rome: Aracne, 2009).

Santarelli, Daniele, 'Morte di un eretico impenitente. Alcune note e documenti su Pomponio Algeri di Nola', *Medioevo Adriatico*, 1 (2007), pp.117–34.

Saraco, Alessandro, *La Penitenzieria apostolica e il suo archivio: atti della Giornata di studio: Roma, Palazzo della Cancelleria, 18 novembre 2011* (Vatican City: Libreria editrice Vaticana, 2012).

Scaduto, Mario, 'Cristoforo Rodriguez Tra i Valdesi della Capitanata e dell'Irpinia', *Archivum Historicum Societatis Iesu*, 35 (1966), pp.3–77.

Scaduto, Mario, 'Le <<visite>> di Antonio Possevino nei domini dei Gonzaga', *Archivio Storico Lombardo*, 10 (1960), pp.336–410.

Scaduto, Mario, 'Le Missioni di A. Possevino in Piemonte. Propaganda Calvinista e restaurazione Cattolica 1560–1563', *Archivum Historicum Societatis Iesu*, 28 (1959), pp.5–191.

Scaduto, Mario, 'Tra Inquisitori e Riformati. Le Missioni Dei Gesuiti Tra Valdesi Della Calabria e Delle Puglia', *Archivum Historicum Societatis Iesu*, 15 (1946), pp.1–76.

Scaduto, Mario, 'Un Scritto Ignaziano Inedito: Il "Del Offiçio Secretario" del 1547', *Archivum Historicum Societatis Iesu*, 29 (1960), pp.305–28.

Scaglione, Aldo D., *The Liberal Arts and the Jesuit College System* (Amsterdam: J. Benjamins Pub. Co., 1986).

Scaramella, Pierroberto, 'I Primi Gesuiti e l'Inquisizione Romana 1547–62', *Rivista Storica Italiana*, 117 (2005), pp.135–57.

Scaramella, Pierroberto, *Inquisizioni, Eresie, Etnie, Dissenso Religioso e Giustizia Ecclesiastica in Italia (Secc. XVI-XVIII)* (Bari: Cacucci, 2005).

Scaramella, Pierroberto, 'Inquisizione, Eresia e Poteri Feudali nel Viceregno Napoletano alla Metà del Cinquecento' in Maurizio Sangalli (ed.), *Per Il Cinquecento Religioso Italiano. Clero, Cultura, Società* (Rome: Edizioni dell'Ateneo, 2003), vol. 2, pp.513–21.

Scaramella, Pierroberto, *L'inquisizione Romana e i Valdesi di Calabria (1554–1703)* (Naples: Editoriale scientifica, 1999).

Scaramella, Pierroberto, *Le Lettere della Congregazione del Sant'ufficio ai Tribunali di Fede di Napoli 1563–1625* (Trieste: Università di Trieste, 2002).

Schilling, Heinz ','History of Crime' or "History of Sin"? – Some Reflections on the Social History of Early Modern Church Discipline' in E.I. Kouri and Tom Scott (eds), *Politics and Society in Reformation Europe: essays for Sir Geoffrey Elton on his sixty-fifth birthday* (Basingstoke: Macmillan, 1987), pp.289–310.

Schilling, Heinz, and Wolfgang Reinhard, 'Reformation, Counter-Reformation, and the Early Modern State. A Reassessment', *Catholic Historical Review*, 75 (1989), pp.383–494.

BIBLIOGRAPHY

Schutte, Anne Jacobson, *Aspiring Saints: Pretense of Holiness, Inquisition, and Gender in the Republic of Venice 1618–1750* (Baltimore: Johns Hopkins University Press, 2001).

Seckendorff, Veit Ludwig von, *Commentarius historicus et apologeticus de Lutheranismo: sive de reformatione religionis* (Frankfurt: Gleditsch, 1692).

Seidel-Menchi, Silvana, 'The Inquisitor as Mediator' in Ronald K. Delph, Michelle M. Fontaine and John Jeffries Martin, *Heresy, Culture, and Religion in Early Modern Italy: Contexts and Contestations* (Kirksville: Truman State University Press, 2006), pp.173–92.

Selwyn, Jennifer, *A Paradise Inhabited by Devils. The Jesuits' Civilizing Mission in Early Modern Naples* (Aldershot: Ashgate, 2004).

Sibilio, Vincenzo, *I Gesuiti e la Calabria. Attie del Convegno Reggio Calabria, 27–28 Febbraio 1991* (Reggio Calabria: Laruffa Editore, 1992).

Signorotto, Gianvittorio and Maria Antonietta Visceglia, *Court and Politics in Papal Rome, 1492–1700* (Cambridge: Cambridge University Press, 2002).

Simone, Raffaele de, *Tre Anni Decisivi di Storia Valdese. Missioni, Repressione e Tolleranza Nelle Valli Piemontesi dal 1559 al 1561* (Rome: Collegium Romanum Societatis Iesu, 1958).

Sisson, Keith (ed.), *A Companion to the Medieval Papacy: Growth of an Ideology and Institution* (Boston: Brill, 2016).

Sluhovsky, Moshe, 'General Confession and Self-Knowledge in Early Modern Catholicism' in Asaph Ben-Tov, Yaacov Deutsch and Tamar Herzig, *Knowledge and Religion in Early Modern Europe* (Leiden: Brill, 2013), pp.25–48.

Solera, Dennj, 'I Familiares del Sant'Uffizio Romano. Un Profilo Istituzionale e Sociale dei Servitori dell'Inquisizione Papale', *Riforma e Movimenti Religiosi: Rivista Della Società di Studi Valdesi*, 2 (2017), pp.277–86.

Soranzo, Giovanni, 'Il P. Antonio Possevino e l'ambasciatore Inglese a Venezia (1604–1605)', *Aevum*, 7 (December 1933), pp.385–422.

Stella, Aldo, *Dall'anabattismo al socinianesimo nel Cinquecento veneto. Ricerche storiche* (Padua: Liviana, 1967).

Stepan, Alfred and Charles Taylor, *Boundaries of Toleration* (New York: Columbia University Press, 2014).

Sutherland, N.M., *Henry IV of France and the Politics of Religion: 1572–1596. Volume 2: The path to Rome* (Bristol: Elm Bank, 2002).

Tacchi-Venturi, Pietro, 'Della Prima Edizione della vita del N.S.P. Ignazio scritta dal P. Pietro Ribadeneira. Note storiche e bibliographiche del P. Pietro Tacchi Venturi, S.I'., *Lettere Edificanti della Provincia Napoletana*, 9 (1901–2), pp.235–45.

Tacchi Venturi, Pietro and Mario Scaduto, *Storia della Compagnia di Gesù in Italia* (Rome; Milan: Civiltà Cattolica; Società editrice Dante Alighieri, 1950–1992), 5 vols.

Tedeschi, John, *The Prosecution of Heresy: Collected Studies on the Inquisition in Early Modern Italy* (Binghamton: Medieval and Renaissance Texts and Studies, 1991).

Tedesco, Vincenzo, *Storia dei valdesi in Calabria: tra basso Medioevo e prima età moderna* (Soveria Mannelli: Rubbettino, 2015).

Tentler, Thomas N., *Sin and Confession on the Eve of the Reformation* (Princeton: Princeton University Press, 2016).

Thorp, Malcolm R. and Arthur Joseph Slavin, *Politics, Religion and Diplomacy in Early Modern Europe: Essays in Honor of DeLamar Jensen* (Kirksville: Sixteenth Century Journal Publishers, 1994).

Torre, Angelo, *Il consumo di devozioni: religione e comunità nelle compagne dell'Ancien Régime* (Venice: Marsilio, 1995).

Torre, Angelo, 'Politics Cloaked in Worship: State, Church and Local Power in Piedmont 1570–1770', *Past and Present*, 134 (1992), pp.42–92.

Trenti, Giuseppe, *I Processi del Tribunale dell'Inquisizione di Modena. Inventario Generale Analitico 1489–1784* (Modena: Aedes Muratoriana, 2003).

Trevor-Roper, H. R., *Europe's Physician: The Various Life of Sir Theodore de Mayerne* (London: Yale University Press, 2006).

Turrini, Miriam, *La Coscienza e Le Leggi. Morale e Diritto nei Testi per la Confessione della Prima Età Moderna* (Bologna: Il Mulino, 1991).

Tutino, Stefania, *Shadows of Doubt: Language and Truth in Post-Reformation Catholic Culture* (Oxford: Oxford University Press, 2014).

Valente, Michela, *Contro l'Inquisizione: il dibattito europeo sec. 16.-18* (Turin: Claudiana, 2010).

Vanni, Andrea, *<<Fare Diligente Inquisitione>> Gian Pietro Carafa e le Origini dei Chierici Regolari Teatini* (Rome: Viella, 2010).

Venard, Marc, 'Y A-t-Il Une <<stratégie Scolaire>> des Jésuites en France au XVIe siècle?' in *L'Université de Pont-à-Mousson et Les Problèmes de Son Temps* (Nancy: Université de Nancy, 1974), pp.67–85.

Visceglia, Maria Antonietta, *Roma Papale e Spagna: Diplomatici, Nobili e Religiosi tra Due Corti* (Rome: Bulzoni, 2010).

Wickersham, Jane K., *Rituals of Prosecution: The Roman Inquisition and the Prosecution of Philo-Protestants in Sixteenth-Century Italy* (Toronto: University of Toronto Press, 2012).

Wootton, David, *Paolo Sarpi: Between Renaissance and Enlightenment* (Cambridge: Cambridge University Press, 1983).

Zucchini, Giampaolo, *Riforma e società nei Grigioni: G. Zanchi, S. Florillo, S. Lentulo e i conflitti dottrinari e socio-politici a Chiavenna, 1563–1567* (Coira: Archivio di Stato, 1978).

Index

Achille Gagliardi, S.J. 67, 110–113

Adriano Prosperi 17–18, 22–23, 48–49, 158

Aleramo Becutto 120

Alexander VII, Pope 170, 175–176

Alfonso Salmerón S.J. 35, 38–39, 41–46, 51–53, 67–68, 98, 130, 174

Ambrogio Catarino Politi, Archbishop 41, 43–47, 98

André Ravier S.J. 12–13

Andrea Galvanello S.J. 70–71

Annecy 119–120

Antoine Escalin des Aimars 60

Antonio Araoz S.J. 129–133, 136–137

Antonio Maracen S.J. 142–143

Antonio Possevino S.J. 33–34, 111–112, 114–117, 119–120, 160–169

Apostolic Penitentiary 102, 129

Archivio della Congregazione per la Dottrina della Fede (ACDF) 20–21

Archivum Romanum Societatis Iesu (ARSI) 24–25, 27, 46, 67–68, 84–85, 98, 139–140, 146

Barnabites 19–20

Benedetto Palmio S.J. 133–134

Biblioteca Apostolica Vaticana (BAV) 24–25

Black Legend (of the Spanish Inquisition) 81–82

Bologna 27–28, 31, 41–44, 51, 58–59, 80–81

Callisto Fornari 74–77

Capuchins 176–177, 183

Carignano 120

Carlo Borromeo, Archbishop 101–102, 116–117

Carlo Emanuele, Duke of Savoy 113–114

Catholic League 140–141

Cesare Helmi S.J. 1, 3–7, 14, 25–26, 28

Chambery 119–120

Charles V, Emperor 74

Chiavenna 78–79

Christina, Queen of Sweden 175–176

Chronicon 12–13, 56–57

Claude Le Jay S.J. 38–39

Claude Matthieu S.J. 142

Claudio Acquaviva S.J. 16, 26–27, 124–125, 127–128, 130–131, 135, 140–141, 145–146, 154, 161–162, 171–174

Clement VIII, Pope 33–34, 146–147, 150–164, 166, 169–170, 172, 174–175, 181–182

Colleges (Jesuit) 119–120, 135–136, 156–157, 161–162, 167, 169–170, 179

Como 83–84

Compere di San Giorgio 56–58

Confession (sacramental) 3, 5, 18–19, 52, 110, 171–174, 178–179, 183

General confession 173–174

Confessors 19–20, 27–28, 99–100, 107, 147–148, 155, 172–174

Congregation of the Index 20–21, 93–94

Congregation for those who come to the faith spontaneously 168–169

Constitutions (of the Society of Jesus) 17–49, 58, 129–135, 138–142, 150–152, 161–162

Correggio 52–53

Correspondence

Jesuit 25, 85, 95–96

Inquisitorial 26–27, 172–173

Corsica 18–19, 28–29, 31, 52, 54–60, 67–68

Cosimo I de'Medici, Duke of Florence 73

Costanzo de Sarnano, Cardinal 151

Council of Trent 2, 31, 38–39, 46–47, 62, 102, 133–134, 141–142

Cristóbal Rodriguez S.J. 62–63, 65–67, 77–78, 80–81, 83–88, 96, 103–110

Cristóbal de Trugillo S.J. 142–143

Cuneo 120

Decreta (inquisitorial) 26–27

Diego Laínez S.J. 38–39, 69–70, 73, 84–85, 89–90, 111–112, 130–133

Diego Ledesma S.J. 98–99

Diego Ximenez S.J. 151–154, 157–158, 170–172

Dominicans 124, 129–130, 135, 143

Ecclesiastical liberty 120–122

Edicts of Grace 62–63, 80–81

Edmond Auger S.J. 129–130, 132, 140–142

INDEX

Elena Brambilla   23
Elenore de Toledo, Duchess of Florence   37–38, 67, 69
Emanuele Filiberto, Duke of Savoy   32, 73–74, 108–110, 112–120
Emmanuel Gomez S.J.   52, 54–56, 67–68
England   147, 165–166
Ercole d'Este, Duke of Ferrara   37–38, 49, 73–74, 78
Eustache du Bellay, Cardinal   60
Everard Mercurian S.J.   130–131, 133–136
Excommunication   5, 53–54, 56–57, 99–100

Ferrante Gonzaga   74–75
Ferrara   69, 73–74, 88
Florence   69, 73
Foreigners, conversion of in Italy   156–157, 160–163, 167–170, 172, 174–176
Formula of the Institute of the Society of Jesus   35, 60–61, 151–152
Foro conscientiae   3, 5, 26–27, 99–100, 102, 113, 140
Foro externo   99–102
Foro interno   5, 101–102
France   73–74, 78–79, 99–100, 108–113, 125, 127–128, 132, 140–142, 144–145, 162–166
Francesco Bobadilla y Mendoza, Cardinal   76
Francesco Pacheco, Cardinal   93–94
Francesco Papardo   116
Francesco di Ribera S.J.   142–143
Francesco Sacchini S.J.   12–13
Francesco Stefano S.J.   50
Franciscans   129–130, 143
Francisco Borja S.J.   84–85, 93, 97–99, 109–112, 133
Francisco Larata S.J.   142–143
François Bachaud, Bishop   111–112
François, Duke of Guise   78–79

Gallicanism   113–114, 144–145, 165–166
Garcia Manrique   75–79
Gasparo Contarini, Cardinal   37–38
Geneva   111–112, 116, 119–120
Genoa   58–59, 89
German Lands (Germany)   45–46, 99–100, 108–109
Gerolamo Sauli, Archbishop   58–59
Gian Francesco Gambara, Cardinal   93–94

Gianlorenzo Bernini   175–176
Gianpietro Maffei S.J.   12–13
Gigliola Fragnito   20–21
Giorgio Caravale   46–47
Giovanni Battista Scotti   43–44
Giovanni della Casa   44–45
Giovanni Pizzorusso   127
Giovanni Romeo   19–21
Girolamo Massari   82–83
Giulio Antonio Santoro, Cardinal (Santa Severina)   93, 139, 145–146, 151–152, 162–163, 169–171
Giulio Basalù   78–79
Gregory XIII, Pope   7–8, 82–83, 94–95, 123, 126, 133–136, 143–147, 153, 158–159, 180–181
Gregory XIV, Pope   161–162
Gregory XV, Pope   172

Habsburg dynasty   72–74, 77–78, 144–145
Henri, Duke of Guise   140–141
Henri II, King of France   78
Henri III, King of France   140–142
Henri IV, King of France (Henri de Navarre)   158–159, 164–165, 170, 174
Henry Wootton   165

Ignatius Loyola S.J.   3, 12–13, 26–27, 37–39, 48–50, 52–53, 60, 65–66, 69–73, 76–79, 119, 125, 127–133, 135–136, 150, 173–174
In coena domini (papal bull)   100–102, 109–110, 121–122
Index of Prohibited Books   68
Infante Don Enrique, Cardinal   133
Inquisizione del mare   105
Ireland   45, 147
Isaac Causubon   163–164, 166, 174–175
Isabella Bresegna   76–79

Jacques Davy du Perron, Cardinal   163–164, 174–175
Jean Pelletier S.J.   77–79
Jerónimo Manrique, Bishop   138–139
Jerónimo Nadal S.J.   12–13, 98–100, 130–133, 136–137
Jerónimo Rubiols S.J.   67
Jews (in the Society of Jesus)   127–128, 130–131, 133, 136
John Bossy   18
John Calvin   78

INDEX

John III, King of Portugal 69–70, 129–130
John O'Malley S.J. 16
Juan Alfonso Polanco S.J. 12, 39–40, 46, 51, 98, 132–134, 158
Juan Alvarez de Toledo, Cardinal 37–38, 60, 69–71, 76–77
Juan López S.J. 142–143
Julius III, Pope (Cardinal Del Monte) 3, 20–21, 31, 33, 35–41, 44–53, 76–77, 94–95, 98, 135, 145, 153, 159–160, 179–181

Kingdom of Naples 86, 105, 116–117

La Guardia 86
Laesae maiestatis 37
Leão Henriques S.J. 133
Le Marche 62–63, 68, 96, 103–106, 109–110
Lenaert Leys S.J. 138–139
Lombardy 99–100
Loreto 99–100, 141–142, 172–173
Louis XII, King of France 78
Louvain (University of) 138–139
Lucca 69, 73
Luigi Lippomano, Bishop 45
Luis de Santander S.J. 138–139
Luke Clossey 21–22

Macerata 105–106
Marcantonio Amulio, Cardinal 91, 97–98
Marcello Cervini, Cardinal (Santa Croce) 43–45
Marguerite of Valois 116–117
Mario Scaduto S.J. 14–15
Martin Olave S.J. 76–79, 130
Massimo Firpo 36–37, 158
Messina 50
Michele Bonelli, Cardinal 62–63
Miguel de Torres S.J. 132–133
Milan 77–78, 100–101
Modena 28–29
Mondovì 119–120
Monferrat 119–120
Monumenta Societatis Iesu 13–14
Morbegno 70–71

Nicolas de Neufville 164
Niccolò Orlandini S.J. 12–13
Niccolò Orsini 93–94
Nicolás Bobadilla S.J. 49–50, 68, 129–133

Obedience (Jesuit) 48–50, 128–129, 132, 141–142, 154, 157–158, 174, 181–182
Odon Pigenat S.J. 140–141
Otto Truchsess von Walburg, Bishop 38–39

Paolo Broggio 21–22
Papal States 72–74, 100–101, 103–104, 106–108
Paschase Broët S.J. 42–45, 51, 67–68
Paul III, Pope 2, 37–39, 45, 48–49, 73–74, 78, 90–91, 135, 145
Paul IV, Pope (Cardinal Gian Pietro Carafa) 19–20, 32, 67, 69, 73, 80, 82–83, 87, 89–90, 93–95, 97, 131, 153
Paul V, Pope (Cardinal Camillo Borghese) 165–166, 172
Paolo Broggio 127
Paolo Egidio Tamergnini da Como 172–173, 176–177
Paolo Prodi 18–19, 144–145
Peace of Augsburg 112
Pedro de Ribadeneira S.J. 12–13, 89–90, 130–131
Peter Canisius S.J. 38–39, 98–99
Philip II, King of Spain 130–132, 136–137, 142–143, 152–153
Philippe de Bethune 164
Philippe de Canaye 155–156, 160–167, 174–176
Philippe de Mornay 174–175
Piacenza 32, 64, 74–78, 88
Pierluigi Farnese 74
Pierre de Gondi, Bishop 137, 139–142, 146–147, 152–153
Pierroberto Scaramella 22–23, 50–51, 103
Pietro Antonio Marliano 74–75
Pietro Carnesecchi 2, 82, 93
Pietro Ferrero, Bishop 113–114
Pietro Tacchi–Venturi S.J. 14
Pius IV, pope 32, 65–66, 82–83, 89–91, 93–95, 103–104, 107–108, 115–116, 126, 159–160
Pius IV, Pope (Cardinal Michele Ghislieri) 5, 32, 63, 65–66, 80–84, 87–91, 93–112, 115–117, 120–91, 124–126, 134–135, 137, 144–145, 149–150, 153, 159–160, 167–168, 175–176, 180–181, 185
Pomponio Algieri 2, 82–83
Portugal 69–70, 130, 132–134
Prohibited books 53–54

Prohibited marriages   53–54
Protestant Reformation   1–2, 145, 178, 184–185

Renée of France   78
Rimini   172
Roberto Bellarmino S.J.   168–169
Roman Inquisition   2, 6–10, 40–41, 44–45, 54, 63–69, 71–97, 103–104, 108–109, 122–126, 137–139, 145–151, 153–156, 158, 162–163, 167–174, 176, 178–181

Sabina Pavone   21–22
San Ginesio   105–107
San Sisto   86
Savoy–Piedmont   32, 73–74, 96, 108–122, 156, 176–177
Scipione Rebiba, Cardinal   93–94
Scotland   147
Sebastian I, King of Portugal   133
Sebastián de Briviesca S.J.   142–143
Sebastiano Romei   68
Siena   67
Silvestro Landini S.J.   49–50, 52–56, 58–60, 67–69
Silvia Mostaccio   15–16, 21–22, 36–37, 47–48, 127
Simão Rodrigues S.J.   132–133
Sixtus V, Pope   8, 33, 123, 125–126, 131, 136–140, 142–147, 149–162, 167–172, 176–177, 180–182
Sollecitatio ad turpia   142–143, 151
Spain   125, 127–128, 130–131, 136–137, 142–145, 161–162, 165

Spanish Inquisition   100–101, 124, 142–143
Spiritual Exercises (of Ignatius Loyola)   37–38, 41–42, 135
Spontaneous appearances   17–20, 89
Stefania Pastore   22–23
Stefano Tucci S.J.   140, 146–147
Stefano Usodimare   57–58
Superior General (of the Jesuits)   49, 90–91, 125, 127–132, 138–139, 150, 161–162, 180
Switzerland   108–109

Thomas Mayer   20–21
Tomasso de Spinola   58–59
Tübingen   78–79
Turin   27–28, 67, 80–82, 109–111, 113, 119–122

Urban VIII, Pope   153–154

Valero Malvicino   84–85, 87
Venetian Interdict Crisis   165–166
Venice   1, 3–4, 28–29, 33–34, 73, 89–90, 113–114, 155–156, 162–163, 165–167
Vincent Julien S.J.   129–131, 138–139, 150
Vincenzo Lauro   116, 120–121
Vincenzo Lavenia   17–18, 81–82, 106–107
Valtellina   32, 88
Vulturara   28, 32, 64, 84–88

Waldensians   1–2, 28–29, 86–87, 108–109, 116–117

Zürich   78–79

Printed in the United States
By Bookmasters